Bourgs, Talbots, Youngs, Rappolds, Favrets, Landrys, Develles, Jungs, *and* deHebecourts

A Gumbo History of Families Forming a New Orleans Culture

James A. Bourg Jr.

authorHOUSE

AuthorHouse™
1663 Liberty Drive
Bloomington, IN 47403
www.authorhouse.com
Phone: 833-262-8899

Published by AuthorHouse 08/06/2020

ISBN: 978-1-7283-4461-4 (sc)
ISBN: 978-1-7283-4460-7 (hc)
ISBN: 978-1-7283-4459-1 (e)

Library of Congress Control Number: 2020914935

The very name "New Orleans" brings to mind a Mardi Gras pageant moving through the streets at night ... this book is rather like a Mardi Gras parade—a series of impressions. Each chapter is like a decorated float which tells a story. Some of the stories are brave and courageous, others are informative, or musing, or bizarre, or fantastic, or cruel ... but they are all a pageant of a city.

—Lyle Saxon, from his book Fabulous New Orleans *(1928)*

This book is dedicated to my ancestors, who made our family what it is, and to my descendants, who will inherit their culture from these ancestors.

To my beautiful wife, Jeanne, who put up with all the time I spent researching and writing this book.

To the City of New Orleans for its culture and its gift of inspiration.

DISCLOSURE

I, James A. Bourg Jr., do affirm that, to my knowledge, all the information in this book is accurate. Because the research that developed the data and the information is dependent on other researchers, it is possible that some of the information may be incorrect because the sources were incorrect. As best I could, I checked and most of the time double-checked the sources, but it is possible that some information in this narrative may be in error. If that is the case, I apologize in advance for any mistakes you may discover. If you do detect an error, please contact and notify me so corrections can be made to my research data.

Contact Information:
Email: Jim_bourg@att.net
Postal mail: James Bourg
                 4921 James Dr.
                 Metairie, La. 70003

CONTENTS

Introduction xiii

Chapter 1   The Tip of the Arrow 1
Chapter 2   The Descendants of James Anatole Bourg Jr. 21
Chapter 3   The Bourg Family 28
Chapter 4   The Talbot Family 108
Chapter 5   The Young Family and the Rappold Family 134
Chapter 6   The Favret Family 178
Chapter 7   The Landry Family..202
Chapter 8   The Develle Family 241
Chapter 9   A Summary of the People and Culture of New Orleans........... 288

INTRODUCTION

There are no strangers here, only friends you have not met yet.
—William Butler Yeats

I'm not going to lay down in words the lure of this place. Every great writer
in the land, from Faulkner to Twain to Rice to Ford, has tried to do it and
fallen short. It is impossible to capture the essence, tolerance, and spirit of
south Louisiana in words and to try is to roll down a road of clichés, bouncing
over beignets and beads and brass bands and it just is what it is. It is home.
—Chris Rose

We are a continuum. Just as we reach back to our ancestors for our fundamental
values, so we, as guardians of that legacy, must reach ahead to our children
and their children. And we do so with a sense of sacredness in that reaching.
—Paul Tsongas

New Orleans is known, throughout the country and around the world, for its
celebrations and festivals, such as Mardi Gras, New Orleans Jazz and Heritage
Festival, the Irish Channel St. Patrick's Day Parade, Voodoo Fest, and Decadence
Music Festival. It is considered a place to visit because of its party atmosphere,
its excellent food, and its unique and distinct music. Television shows and movies

have never accurately captured the unique accents and style of communicating in this place.

The French Quarter, known for its French and Spanish Creole architecture, is the historic heart of the city. Its nightlife along Bourbon Street is where many tourists visit to "pass a good time." The city has been described by many as the most unique city in the United States. The source of this uniqueness is its location, its people, and its multicultural and multilingual heritage.

Jean-Baptiste Le Moyne de Bienville and his brother, Pierre LeMoyne, Sieur d'Iberville, found New Orleans 1718.[1] It was once the territorial capital of French Louisiana and Spanish Louisiana. New Orleans had been ceded to the Spanish in 1763 following the Seven Years' War in the Treaty of Paris to compensate Spain for the loss of Florida to the British. The British also took the remainder of the French territory east of the Mississippi River. Spain sent no governor to New Orleans to take control for four years until 1766.

French and German settlers tried to restore New Orleans to French in 1768. A year later, Spain reasserted control over New Orleans and formally instituted Spanish law. Although there was a Spanish governor in New Orleans, the city was ruled by the Spanish government in Cuba.

In 1802, King Charles IV of Spain restored New Orleans and Spanish Louisiana to France. In April of 1803, Napoleon sold the territory to the United States in the Louisiana Purchase. By 1840, it was the third most populous US city.

The most significant aspect of New Orleans is its people. Those who grew up in New Orleans have a unique quality that is noted by almost everyone who visits the city. This is often characterized as kindness, friendliness, warmth, being fun-loving, and definitely being carefree. New Orleans is known as "the city that care forgot."

For the most part, these are very religious and spiritual people. The city's colonial history of French and Spanish settlement—along with African American, German, Italian, and Irish immigration—generated a strong Roman Catholic tradition. Influenced by the Bible Belt's prominent Protestant population, New Orleans has a sizable non-Catholic demographic as well: 12.2 percent of the people are Baptist, while another 5.1 percent are from other Christian faiths, including Orthodox Christianity or Oriental Orthodoxy; 3.1 percent are Methodist; 1.8

---

[1] Richard Campanella, "II: Settling the Landscape," in *Bienville's Dilemma: A Historical Geography of New Orleans* (Lafayette, LA: Center for Louisiana Studies, the University of Louisiana at Lafayette, 2008), 113–114 (PDF), retrieved July 12, 2014.

percent are Episcopalian; 0.9 percent are Presbyterian; 0.8 percent are Lutheran; 0.8 percent are Latter-Day Saints; and 0.6 percent are Pentecostal.[2]

This book intertwines the history of an extended family (my family) with the history of the city of New Orleans. It is an attempt to show the culture of the city and how that culture can be explained by the confluence of peoples amalgamated in my family's history. This book is a family history, but in our story, I believe the story of New Orleans culture is seen and documented. This family history is about one extended family that is the culmination of many, many families and people. It is the family history of the Bourg family, the Talbot family, the Young family, the Rappold family, the Favret family, the Landry family, the Develle family, the Jung family, and the d'Hebecourt family.

A Long Time Coming

This book is rooted in genealogy. I have been studying, recording, and archiving the history of my family for over forty-five years. A long time ago, when I was in my late twenties, I learned of a genetic condition involving the teeth of my oldest son, Jason. The medical geneticists we were working with suggested I do a study of the families of my wife and myself. The purpose was to see if we were related. That request started a lifelong investigation into the genealogy of our extended family.

This book is the result of that lifelong study and the need to express what I have learned. It is a narrative that can be used and enjoyed by those not interested in genealogy but more interested in their family's history. I have learned so much about genealogical research during those forty-five years.

Genealogy is a fundamental and useful science and research activity for me. Without it, our family history cannot correctly be conducted, recorded, and preserved. Researching and documenting the family genealogy has always been my burning need and passion. Genealogy triggered my imagination. It encouraged my creativity to know who my family was as well as from where we all came.

One of the fascinations of delving into our family's past is that, for better or worse, I didn't know where that path would lead. Genealogy was my hobby. It created a record of the people and places that came together to create my extended family. The many names in my genealogy tables represent our very extended family. The records tell us their names and locations. However, that does not tell us

---

[2] "New Orleans, Louisiana Religion," www.bestplaces.net, retrieved March 21, 2019.

who these people were and what they did. Understanding those details comprises a real family history.

Genealogy records and family history are entirely different things. A real family history is a story—a narrative about the nature of individuals. The relevance of these stories is easier to understand when we consider connections to people we know. We may have heard about them from those people who are closest to us. We start to understand the nature and the characteristics of these people on a more personal basis: their histories, their personalities, their goals, and their achievements. It is also essential to know where these people were born, lived, and died; what was their nationality, their heritage, and their culture.

A family history comprises personal histories, the stories of the nature of people within a family. It's a close cousin to genealogy but still quite different. While genealogy is a hobby dedicated to creating a family tree, a family history puts leaves on that tree, telling and communicating the stories of the people who populate its branches in a narrative form. Genealogy is the skeleton of the family, but the characteristics, the stories, and the situations make up the muscles, fibers, and organs of the living family. After all, the stories of our ancestors nourish us and give us the sustenance of our family legacies.

This book is a narrative of a single extended family. It tells of a family that was created by the coming together of many families over the years. Although this book will focus on only a few, there are latterly hundreds of family surnames that will be discussed at some level during the telling of the histories. Putting the few in separate chapters allows readers to learn about the entire account or just the chronicles of the family parts in which they are interested.

The Process of Production

Each chapter, although written to stand alone, cannot help but have references and connections to other sections. These references and links come about for two reasons. They overlap in time and, therefore, the historical events of these times, and the family becomes more and more intermingled as it gets closer to my children. Despite these connections, it should be possible for those only interested in one or two of the parts of the family to enjoy the history while only reading the chapters focused on those family components.

For the most part, each chapter follows a specific process and format, discussing the history of the family going continuously backward in time. The most recent members of a particular line of the family—those with the more understood nature and characteristics—will be discussed first. Their progenitors will be addressed in descending chronological order. There are exceptions in some of the chapters, but these do not disrupt the nature of the history.

The process of producing each chapter is also very similar from section to section. A chapter starts with the most recent generation of that family, beginning with the grandparent of my children. It chronicles the history of that ancestor. When completed, it will proceed back down the line of that grandparent's paternal (surname) family history. In the chapter on the Develle family, I include the history of the great-grandparents, since I accumulated a large amount of information on them. They are quite prominent and exciting. Typically, members of that branch of the family had such noteworthy historical characteristics that I thought they deserved inclusion.

When possible, I have included historical information that is part of the time frame of a particular ancestor and not necessarily directly associated with that family member. Those ancestors alive during great wars, plagues, great migrations, or political events, will have those events noted as part of the history of the time in which they lived.

My Difficulties in Writing This Family History

For forty-five years, I enjoyed researching this genealogy-based project. That was the fun part. It made me feel like a television detective, searching for clues to solve a troublesome family history problem. Writing this book, however, just seemed to me for years to be too challenging to be fun. First of all, I am a scientist. Although I can write and have published technical manuscripts, it is not in my comfort zone to do so. In the past, I have relied on a coauthor for the style part of writing a manuscript. But I decided to tackle this writing project alone.

The motivation to tackle this problematic task came from several directions. Firstly, in June of 2016, I was diagnosed with T-cell non-Hodgkin's lymphoma. Having cancer changes one's attitude about longevity. I realized if I was ever going to do this, I had better get started. Secondly, I spoke to my sons about carrying on my genealogical research in case I didn't survive cancer. They suggested that I write a book to make the family history plain and simple for all and anyone who would be interested, including my grandchildren and great-grandchildren. And thirdly, I had to go through two years of chemotherapy and stem cell transplants, which left me with a lot of time on my hands. Because I was prone to infection, I couldn't go out into the world and mingle. I was confined to the house for the most part. Soon I became very bored with reading and watching TV. This available free time was the final straw that made me decide I would write this book.

Sitting down with a blank Microsoft Word page on my computer, I had to make a lot of decisions before I started to write the chapter narratives. I had already written and produced a cookbook with my wife, Jeanne, and my sister-in-law, Mary-Lisa. The cookbook, *Want Some Spit*, was based on the recipes and history of Jeanne Develle Landry. I wanted to do something more substantial than that type of booklet. I decided I would write and publish a hardbound book to serve as a teaching history for all our family members and a reference for other genealogists.

Next, I had to decide on the scope. How much of the family would I include and on which family members would I focus? Would I cover a single line of ancestors or all ancestors? Would I focus on just the grandparents of parts of the family or all of the ancestors? I decided to pick the eight surnames of my sons' great-grandparents, with the addition of the two surnames of their great-great-grandparents. This decision on surnames meant that there were nine family surnames on which I would focus. Each one deserved a chapter or part of a chapter, and their combined names became the title for the book: *Bourgs, Talbots, Youngs, Rappolds, Favrets, Landrys, Develles, Jungs, and d'Hebecourts.*

I had to choose the plots and themes I would follow. Thinking of my ancestors as characters in my family history, what problems and obstacles did these ancestors face? A scheme gave my family history interest and focus. Popular family history plots and themes included the following:

- culture
- immigration and migration patterns
- rags-to-riches storylines
- pioneer or farm life
- surviving ocean travel
- war and battle survival

I wanted my family history, even though nonfiction, to read more like a novel than a dull, dry textbook. I'm not sure I succeeded. It was vital for me to write so that I made the reader feel like an eyewitness to our family's life. Even when an ancestor didn't leave an account of his or her daily life, social histories and US Census records provided information about the experiences of people in a given time and place. Wars, natural disasters, epidemics, occupations, fashion, art, transportation, and common foods of the period and location were all essential components in fleshing out the skeleton of my genealogical history.

Summary

This project, although it was difficult for me, was also a labor of love. While I was writing this book, I visualized the knowledge my ancestors gained and lost over time. It disappeared because it was not communicated and documented adequately. It was lost! I know the body of scientific evidence and work was accumulated throughout history because it was recorded so well in papers, books, and peer reviews. I realized that what I have learned, through a significant amount of work and effort, can only be passed down in this manner as well. This realization gives me a considerable amount of satisfaction, joy, and hope.

I hope that reading this book gives you an understanding and appreciation of the riches this diverse collection of families contributes to each of us and our children, grandchildren, and society. I hope you enjoy this book. And I hope you gain an appreciation for the rich heritage contributed by these families to the culture of the Crescent City.

CHAPTER 1

THE TIP OF THE ARROW
The Confluence of a Diverse Family

America has only three cities: New York, San Francisco,
and New Orleans. Everywhere else is Cleveland.
—Tennessee Williams

Every book is a quotation; and every house is a quotation
out of all forests, and mines, and stone quarries;
and every man is a quotation from all his ancestors.
—Ralph Waldo Emerson

Destiny doesn't always come when it's convenient or when you think
it should. It comes when you're ready, whether you know it or not.
—Kelly Thompson

Having culture means we are the only animal that acquires the
rules of its daily living from the accumulated knowledge of our
ancestors, rather than from the genes they pass to us.
—Mark Pagel

`In genealogy, if you look at an ancestor chart, it's shaped like an arrowhead. The arrowhead represents the geometric progression of ancestors in a family. The tip of the chart represents the first generation of the Bourg family. The author's family history begins with this first generation and moves back in history down each family branch.

The tip of the arrow is the point at which there is a union of two family lines. This narrative is the story of how that union came about.

The Story Begins

This family history starts with the Bourg family: James A. Bourg Jr.; his wife, Jeanne Marie Favret Bourg; and their three children, Jason Pratt (born 1973), Jonathan Ryan (born 1980), and Jameson Lloyd (born 1984). The narrative in this chapter comes from the memories of James and Jeanne. James was born on Saturday, December 21, 1946, as the firstborn son of James Anatole Bourg Sr. (1913–1973) and Agnes Louise Young (1912–1984).

In the spring of 1967, James Jr., also known as Jimmy or Jim, was a student of biology and chemistry at Louisiana State University in New Orleans, which became the University of New Orleans in February 1974. Jim lived at home with his parents. The Bourg family also included Jim's younger siblings, Robert Oliver (1949–2005) and Michael Joseph (1953–). The family lived in a rented house at 932 Phillip Street, near the corner of Phillip and Constance Streets, in the Irish Channel of New Orleans.

James Sr. had lived through the Great Depression and did not believe in buying a house. He always rented, and so the family moved a lot. Although James Sr. kept looking for the best rent situation, they always lived in the Irish Channel, the Redemptorist Parish.

Jim Jr. was not a particularly great student at that time, and struggled to get good grades in college. He was smart enough to have attained a higher GPA, but he was still having fun and not yet focused on learning. He was the first person in his family to attend college, and his parents had no educational experience by which to guide him.

In 1969, something happened that caused him to become more focused on learning: he got married and realized his financial responsibilities. This shift in focus became a significant driver of his personality from that time on and helped him attain his later successes in life. But in 1967, he was not yet there.

2

Jim's intelligence helped him overcome his parents' inability to prepare him for learning or assist him with it. His father provided plenty of parental discipline in the home but little understanding of the relationship between education and future success. Jim had good grades in high school, but after some early academic failures in college, he began to resent his parents for his lack of preparation for learning. Jim wanted to be a doctor or a PhD scientist, but his early lack of academic success had not given him the grades to get into medical school or a doctoral program in science.

This resentment would stay with Jim until his sixties, when he finally learned to forgive his parents both cognitively and emotionally for their inability to give him educational advice and tutoring. With help from his good friend Frank Gullo, a clinical psychologist, Jim finally realized that his parents were simply not capable of giving him learning support because of the way their parents had raised them. His parents' shortcomings became a catalyst for his own approach to raising his children and his love of teaching in general.

In 1967, Jim was in the spring of his junior year, trying to get his act together between school, friends, and family. His grades had stabilized. Increasing maturity left him more focused on school. He had learned to study, although the drive to learn had not yet fully taken hold. He did not have a regular girlfriend, but he was a very social being at school and among his neighborhood friends. Drinking beer was a significant component of his evening activities.

At this time, Jim also became involved in the social justice movement in the United States. He was protesting the Vietnam War, peripherally involved with the civil rights movement, and enamored with the exploding hippie movement. He was somewhat of a hippie himself.

Jim purchased a cheap Silvertone guitar and amplifier from Sears for sixty-nine dollars and started teaching himself to play. Over time, Jim acquired many guitars, mostly acoustic, but one amplified acoustic and one Fender electric. Eventually, he became enough of a guitar player that he played in front of friends and fellow students and at church activities. He was okay as a guitarist but never great.

Put to the Test

Beyond Jimmy's carefree life, the war was looming. As the historian Heber Holbrook noted, "Drafting men into the military in the United States has been employed by the country in five conflicts from the American Revolution through World War II, and the Cold War (including both the Korean War and the Vietnam War)," and the Selective Training and Service Act established a draft that lasted from 1940 to 1973.[3] Men were conscripted to fill vacancies in the US military that could not be filled through voluntary means.

At the outbreak of the Vietnam War, most college students were safe from the draft. Undergraduates were automatically awarded a 2-S deferment for postsecondary education and could not be forced to serve. For those who opposed the war, going to college was a way to avoid the draft. But by 1965, the Vietnam War was escalating, and the US Army found itself in need of more troops. That fall, the Defense Department ordered the highest enlistment quotas since the height of the Korean War. Needing 27,400 men in September and 33,600 in October, the military began to draw from a new pool: college men. The director of the Selective Service System, Lewis B. Hershey, announced the change would affect a small percentage of the 1.8 million male college students.[4]

Students weren't chosen at random. Instead, the Selective Service System put into effect the academic evaluation system. Under this system, local draft boards would defer students based on their abilities as students, as determined by their class ranking and their score on a national aptitude test. The Selective Service College Qualification Test was instituted because so many educationally unqualified young men were in college just to avoid the draft. Undergraduates with a high ranking based on grades or a test score above a specific cutoff were exempt. Everyone else would be eligible for the draft and sent to war.

On December 1, 1969, the Selective Service conducted two lotteries to determine the order of drafting. Everybody was given a draft number. If you had a low number, you had to show up for the draft unless you had a deferment. Jim's draft number was 21.

Jim had registered for the draft when he turned eighteen, as all young men were required to do. As a student at LSU-NO, Jim had a 2-S student deferment. On Saturday, May 14, 1966, he and 400,000 other male students across the country took the first qualification test to determine whether they could keep their deferment. Jim took the test that morning, and that evening his Book of the

---

[3] Heber A. Holbrook, "The Crisis Years: 1940 and 1941," *The Pacific Ship and Shore Historical Review* (July 4, 2001), 2, archived October 19, 2012, at the Wayback Machine.

[4] Laura E. Hatt, "LBJ Wants Your GPA: The Vietnam Exam," *The Harvard* Crimson (May 23, 2016), https://www.thecrimson.com/article/2016/5/23/lbj-wants-your-gpa/.

Month Club selection of *In Cold Blood* came in the mail. He read it all weekend. He never found out whether he had passed the test, but his draft status never changed while he was a student.

Jim was an amiable young man. He liked to party and be with his friends. His beliefs, however, became more antiestablishment and religiously agnostic compared to his parents and neighborhood friends. This change in his belief system came because of his questioning everything, particularly his parents' beliefs. His philosophy as a scientist was to question everything. He was beginning to rebel against his parent's way of life. He loved his mom and dad very much but found it challenging to agree with their belief system.

In the winter of 1967, while Jim and his friends Frank Gullo and Alvin Matthews were playing basketball in the university intramural league, they were introduced to members of the Tau Kappa Epsilon fraternity (TKE). The members, specifically Jimmy Armstrong, invited them to pledge the fraternity, and so they did. TKE was not one of the elite Greek organizations on campus. It had a reputation as being somewhat of a rebel group. However, it was still a mainstream establishment organization. Jim probably pledged because Frank and Alvin did as well.

During this time, Jim started to date Laura Davis. He didn't take their relationship seriously at all; in fact, it was very much one of convenience. But it gave Jim someone he could bring to fraternity parties and someone he could take on a double date with Al Mathews. They had a good time together.

On March 25, 1967, Jim went to a TKE exchange party with the students of the Mercy School of Nursing. He went there with his friends Al and Frank. He also went there drunk. Jim had met up that afternoon with his first cousin Eddie McGinnis, son of his Aunt Dorothy (his mother's sister), who was just back from Vietnam. Jim and Eddie had been close as kids. However, they had drifted apart after Eddie graduated from Redemptorist High School in 1962. They played pool at Tracy's Pool Hall on the corner of Third Street and Magazine streets and drank a lot of beer. The drinking age was eighteen at that time.

Jim was very intoxicated by the time he got to the party. He danced with many of the student nurses and asked for their phone numbers. It seems being drunk gives you the courage you don't typically have; after all, that was the idea of a mixer.

There was one student nurse he was very attracted to, Jeanne Marie "Jeannie" Favret. Al had his 1957 Chevy, so the boys drove some of the girls home after the party. But nothing became of the encounter at that time. Jim was still seeing Laura, and he never used any of the phone numbers he gathered at the party at that time.

On Sunday night, June 18, 1967, Jim was in the Beaconette Lounge on the corner of Claiborne Avenue near Napoleon Ave. He was there with Al Matthews. Laura Davis joined them in the lounge. They were drinking and dancing and having somewhat of a good time listening to the music of the Palace Guards, a garage rock band from Metairie, Louisiana, active in the mid to late 1960s. The British Invasion profoundly influenced their approach; their influence was the Beatles and the Rolling Stones. They also played American folk-rock music. Drummer Frank Bua would later go on to play with the popular funk group the Radiators.

Jeannie Favret walked in with her friend Pam Aucoin. Jim recognized Jeannie and asked her to dance. Jim told Jeannie (whom he called "Shawnee," believing that was her name and that she was Native American) he would call her for a date the following weekend. She didn't stay long that night, as it was Sunday and she had nursing school classes the next morning.

On Monday, Jim retrieved the phone numbers he'd acquired from the fraternity exchange party from his wallet. He realized he had five phone numbers and no names. He called the first number on the list, thinking he had danced with Jeannie first. It was Agnes Frischhertz. He asked her to go on a Wednesday date to grab a beer at Graffanino's bar on the corner of Calhoun and Laurel (uptown near Audubon Park). During their meeting, Jim asked Agnes which phone number was Jeannie's. He called Jeannie later that night and made their first date.

That date took place on June 24, 1967. It was a double date with Al Mathews and Donna Audoin, a nursing student Al met at the exchange party. Jim and Jeannie had follow-up dates on July 1 and again on July 4. Jim knew he was in love by the third date. They dated for a year and a half, became engaged in November of 1968, and got married on May 17, 1969, at St. Lawrence the Martyr church in the Westgate subdivision of Jefferson Parish.

Jim got his driver's license and his first car in August of 1967. He was twenty-one years old. His first car was a used 1960 Nash Rambler that he bought with the help of his dad for three hundred dollars. The Rambler had push-button transmission and a one-barrel carburetor with an overhead straight-six engine. It also had a glass-packed muffler, so it was loud driving down the road.

A significant event in Jim's life was the Beatles release of the *Sgt. Pepper's*

Lonely Hearts Club Band album. It was the Beatles' eighth studio album. Released in the United States on June 2, 1967, it spent fifteen weeks on the US charts at number one. Critics lauded it for its innovations in production, songwriting, and cover design, which bridged the divide between popular music and art. Its cover also provided a musical representation of the generation and the sixties counterculture. *Sgt. Pepper* won four Grammy Awards in 1968, including Album of the Year, the first rock LP to receive this honor. Jim loved this music.

In June of 1967, Jim was doing summer work as a construction helper for Reilly-Benton Insulation. They were insulating a cracking tower at the Tenneco Refinery in Chalmette. That job was hot and dangerous because of the heights at which he was working. It only lasted two weeks.

He worked next in the Brown's Dairy in Central City on Baronne Street. A 1960 newspaper ad touted Brown's new "6-acre, fully air-conditioned plant" as one of the most modern and efficient in the country. He worked in the freezer, loading ice cream trucks.

He purchased *Sgt. Pepper* in June 1967, just before getting pneumonia in both lungs from working in the large walk-in freezer. He was confined to home bedrest for two weeks and listened to the album continuously. It remained his favorite album all his life. In George Martin's opinion, "Without *Pet Sounds*, *Sgt. Pepper* would never have been recorded. *Pepper* was the Beatles attempt to equal *Pet Sounds*." According to the Beatles biographer Hunter Davies, "the serious experimentation" started in April 1966, with the closing track from *Revolver*, "Tomorrow Never Knows."[5] Jim never worked at the Brown's plant again.

Jeannie finished her psychiatric nursing program at DePaul's Hospital in September of 1967. She graduated from Mercy Hospital School of Nursing with her registered nurse certificate in May of 1968. Jim and Jeannie dated continuously from that summer of 1967.

The Vietnam War and the Tet Offensive

The Tet Offensive of 1968 proved that US strategies in the Vietnam War were not proving successful. When the Viet Cong (VC) and People's Army of Vietnam (PAVN) started urban offensives in 1968, the support of the US people for the war began to fade. The Army of Vietnam (ARVN) expanded after Tet

---

[5] Nick Greene, "15 Fascinating Facts About *Pet Sounds*," *Mental Floss* (June 20, 2017), https://www.mentalfloss.com/article/59457/15-facts-about-pet-sounds.cmd.

and was modeled after US doctrine. The VC had heavy casualties during the Tet Offensive, losing over 50,000 men.[6] The CIA's Phoenix Program further degraded the VC's membership and capabilities. By the end of the year, the VC insurgents held almost no territory in South Vietnam, and their recruitment dropped by over 80 percent in 1969. This signifying a drastic reduction in guerrilla operations, necessitating increased use of PAVN regular soldiers from the north.[7]

In 1969, North Vietnam declared a provisional revolutionary government in South Vietnam in an attempt to give the reduced VC a more international stature. Still, the southern guerrillas from then on were sidelined, as PAVN forces begun more conventional combined arms warfare. Operations crossed national borders. Laos was invaded by North Vietnam early on. At the same time, Cambodia was used by North Vietnam as a supply route starting in 1967.

The path through Cambodia began to be bombed by the United States in 1969, while the Laos route had been heavily bombed since 1964. The deposing of the monarch Norodom Sihanouk by the Cambodian National Assembly resulted in a PAVN invasion of the country at the request of the Khmer Rouge. This invasion escalated the Cambodian civil war and resulting in a US–ARVN counterinvasion.[8]

Although many of his friends and family were supportive of the war, Jim was very much against US involvement in Southeast Asia. Jim marched in protest of the war at LSUNO. Jim was also at odds with his father, family, and neighbors over civil rights issues and protested the US policy of segregation.

The Assassination of Martin Luther King

Martin Luther King Jr., the American clergyman and civil rights leader, was fatally shot at the Lorraine Motel in Memphis, Tennessee, on April 4, 1968. King was rushed to a hospital, and he died at 7:05 p.m. King was the primary leader of the civil rights movement and a Nobel Peace Prize laureate. His assassin, James Earl Ray, escaped from the Missouri State Penitentiary. He was finally arrested on June 8 at the London Airport. He was extradited to the United States and charged with the crime.

---

[6] James F. Dunnigan and Albert A. Nofi, *Dirty Little Secrets of the Vietnam War: Military Information You're Not Supposed to Know* (New York: Macmillan, 2000).

[7] Military History Institute of Vietnam, *Victory in Vietnam: The Official History of the People's Army of Vietnam, 1954–1975*, trans. Merle Pribbenow (Lawrence, Kansas: University of Kansas Press, 2002).

[8] "Vietnam War," *Wikipedia*, https://en.wikipedia.org/wiki/Vietnam_War.

On March 10, 1969, Ray pleaded guilty and was sentenced to ninety-nine years in the Tennessee State Penitentiary. He made several attempts to withdraw his guilty plea and be tried by a jury but was unsuccessful. He died at seventy in 1998 while in prison.[9]

Dr. King's supporters in the civil rights movement wanted his followers to respond nonviolently. That was the way to honor his beliefs. James Farmer Jr. said, "Dr. King would be greatly distressed to find that his blood had triggered off bloodshed and disorder." He encouraged the country should stay in a mood of prayer. That would be in accord with King's beliefs. He said, "We should make that kind of dedication and commitment to the goals which his life served." However, the more militant black supporters called for forceful action, saying, "White America killed Dr. King last night."

After Dr. King's assassination, journalists reported words spoken at a white dinner party. One of the women leaned over and said, "I wish you had spit in his face for me." It was wondered for a long time afterward what King could have done to her. But reporters also recounted that King's death immensely saddened many whites. The *New York Times* published an editorial giving King a lot of praise. They called his murder a "national disaster" and his cause "just."[10]

The Assassination of Robert F. Kennedy

The killing of Robert Francis "Bobby" Kennedy took place shortly after midnight on June 5, 1968, in Los Angeles, California. Bobby Kennedy was a United States senator and the brother of assassinated president John Fitzgerald "Jack" Kennedy.

After winning the California and South Dakota 1968 primary elections for the Democratic nomination for president, Bobby was shot by Sirhan Sirhan as he walked through the hotel kitchen. He died in Good Samaritan Hospital twenty-six hours later. Sirhan Sirhan was a twenty-four-year-old Palestinian immigrant. He was convicted of Kennedy's murder and is serving a life sentence for the crime.

Bobby was buried in Arlington National Cemetery near President Kennedy. His death prompted the protection of presidential candidates by the United

---

[9.] William F. Pepper, *An Act of State: The Execution of Martin Luther King* (Brooklyn: Verso Books, 2003), ISBN 978-1859846957.

[10.] "Assassination of Martin Luther King Jr.," *Wikipedia*, https://en.wikipedia.org/wiki/Assassination_of_Martin_Luther_King,_Jr.

States Secret Service. Hubert Humphrey later went on to win the Democratic nomination for the presidency but ultimately lost the election to Republican Richard Nixon. As with his brother John's death, Bobby Kennedy's assassination and the circumstances surrounding it have spawned a variety of conspiracy theories. Kennedy remains one of only two sitting US senators to be assassinated, the other being fellow Democrat Huey Long in 1935.

Jim's Beliefs

The escalation of the Vietnam War caused Jim to question his future as a student and his relationship with Jeannie. He decided he would move forward with a serious relationship with Jeannie, but his military future remained in question. Jim gave Jeannie a Lane cedar chest as a promise of engagement in June of 1968, and he purchased three wedding-related rings: a 0.7 carat diamond engagement ring and two gold wedding rings in preparation for asking Jeanne to marry him. He bought them from Armbruster Jewelers (Mr. Bill Armbruster). The total price for all three rings was three hundred dollars.

Jim proposed to Jeannie on Friday, October 17, 1968, in the kitchen of her father's house at 2425 Michigan Avenue in Metairie. Without a lot of experience and without having asked for advice from his parents, Jim did a terrible job of proposing. Nevertheless, Jeannie said yes.

At the end of the fall semester of 1968, Jim had not completed his graduation requirements for a bachelor of science degree in biology because he was short one field biology course. In January of 1969, he registered for a course on plant physiology to complete his degree. Because this was the only course he took that semester, he was no longer a full-time student at LSUNO, so he lost his 2-S deferment for the draft.

Jim started working for Dr. Clinton Olmsted, his former physiology professor, as a graduate assistant with a salary of three hundred dollars per month in mid-January 1969. Because he'd lost his draft deferment, Jim received his draft notice from the local draft board in February of 1969. Dr. Olmsted filed an appeal for an occupational delay, as Jim was working with Olmsted on a grant with the American Heart Association. Even though Dr. Olmstead believed the draft board would reject the appeal, his action did delay the draft board process for six months.

During this period, Jim tried to enroll in the air force as a flight navigator; a local recruiter had found a position for him in navigator training school. Jim passed the recruitment exam in all phases except hearing. He was rejected because he'd lost most of his ability to hear above 4000 Hz. Jim could not hear the last two keys on a piano (87 and 88, which have a frequency of approximately 4000 Hz.). He probably lost his hearing listening to the music he was playing on his guitar and at the Beaconette Lounge.

Jim applied for a teaching position with the Archdiocese of New Orleans school board even though he did not have a teaching certificate. For two months, he got no takers for a teaching position. He was just about ready to accept a stint in the US Army to study to be a male nurse.

Marriage and Career

Jeannie and Jim were married on in St. Lawrence the Martyr Church on May 17, 1969. Father Woods, an Irish priest, presided. Jeannie wore a beautiful bridal dress hand-sewn by her mother, Jeanne Clair Landry Favret, with appliques of her favorite flower, daisies. Jim wore a white tuxedo coat. Jim's best man was his brother Bob. Jeannie's maid of honor was her cousin Betty Develle. The bridal party included Yvette Everhard (Overby) escorted by Frank Gullo and Mary-Lisa Favret escorted by Mike Bourg.

The reception was at the home of Jeannie's uncle, Pratt Landry, and his wife, Jeanne, on Kent Street. It was a small affair of only approximately a hundred guests, with champagne and punch for beverages and catered finger food. Attending were immediate family, a few relatives, and only a very few close friends. Music was supplied by vinyl LPs. The newlyweds' song was to be "Scotch and Soda" by the Kingston Trio, but Jeannie's mother would not allow the song (because of Lloyd's drinking), so they danced to "More" by Al Martino.

Pictures, receiving line, and dancing were completed by eight in the evening. The happy couple left for their honeymoon at eight thirty. Before they left, Uncle Pratt gave Jimmy fifty dollars and an ice chest with ten bottles of champagne, to be used for each night of the honeymoon. He also gave Jim some solid and much-appreciated advice: "This family can be crazy and may drive you nuts! Don't let them get to you."

He was correct. Pratt's words were advice Jim would use throughout his life. George Pratt Landry II, along with Jim's father-in-law, Lloyd Francis Favret, would be as much of a "father figure" to Jim as his biological father. This relationship changed dramatically in 1973 with the death of Jim's father.

The Early Days

The wedding night was spent in the Broadwater Beach Hotel in Biloxi, Mississippi. The rest of their honeymoon was spent in Gatlinburg, Tennessee. After the honeymoon, Jim graduated from Louisiana State University in New Orleans with a BS in biology, on May 31, 1969.

After returning from the honeymoon and college graduation, Jim and Jeannie settled into a quiet life of really getting to know each other. Jim completed his work with Dr. Olmstead through July. He prepared to start his teaching assignment at Holy Redeemer College Prep in August. His first car, the Nash Rambler, finally conked out, and with the assistance of Uncle Pratt, Jim purchased a brand-new yellow Ford Pinto. He only paid $2,100 for the car, and it got high gas mileage, 32 mpg. During the school year of 1969–1970, Jim commuted both ways each day, and the fuel economy of the Pinto and the thirty-two-cents-per-gallon for gas made this affordable on their budget. Jim was only making three hundred dollars a month.

Jim's Years at Holy Redeemer

Holy Redeemer was a secondary seminary school for Redemptorist Priest candidates. It occupied the site of the former Bayou Gardens, which were created in the 1940s by former Louisiana Governor Richard Leche on the grounds surrounding his home on Bayou Lacombe. By 1950, the gardens were operated as a tourist attraction and as a plant nursery. The gardens were later purchased and maintained by the Redemptorist Priests, a Catholic religious order, which established the Holy Redeemer seminary school on the site in 1960.

There were only seventy-two students in the entire school and nine faculty members when Jim taught there. Teachers had to teach many subjects, and each had many preparations. Jim was teaching chemistry and trig to juniors, algebra to first-year students, and geometry to sophomores. There were no seniors at the school his first year, all having quit in protest after their junior year the term before. Jim enjoyed his teaching activities at Holy Redeemer. He was an excellent teacher, and the boys responded to his method of motivation.

Jim's most challenging class to teach was Algebra I. There were twenty-three freshmen in the school, and all took algebra. The level ranged from one genius student to several students who struggled in math. The diversity made the pace of the course challenging. Jim solved the problem by getting the genius student to help with the slower students, while Jim focused on the middle group. This worked very well.

While at Holy Redeemer, Jim was mentored by Father Gerald Bass, the principal, and the other science teacher on the faculty. Father Bass enjoyed photography, and Jim taught him how to develop and print his pictures. They built a darkroom together.

During Jim's second year at Holy Redeemer, Jim would drive to Lacombe on Monday morning and sleep in one of the unoccupied rooms on campus on Monday night. He would drive home after school on Tuesday. Driving back to school on Wednesday morning, Jim would again sleep there Wednesday evening and drive home after school on Thursday. On Friday, he would drive both ways. This schedule allowed twelve extra hours a week of lesson-planning and reduced his gasoline costs. Jim would eat with the fathers two nights a week. Since Jeannie did not want to move to the north shore, this was an accommodating schedule and s compromise for both of them. Jeannie and Jim would eat each Sunday at Jeannie's mom's house.

Teaching at this school provided Jim with excellent experience on how to teach. It taught him how to manage his time better and how to lead people who were close to his age and experience. After all, at twenty-three, he was only five years older than some of his students.

Teaching at Redemptorist High School

In the late spring of 1971, Jim was contacted by a former Redemptorist High School student and classmate of his, Pat Leonard, with a teaching opportunity at his old high school. During this period, RHS had one of the best and most progressive faculties and staff in the metropolitan area of New Orleans. The idea and the opportunity were to team-teach biology to all sophomores and freshmen students in the school. This schedule would require fifteen periods of phased students and, therefore, three biology teachers.

Pat Leonard was already a biology teacher. He would teach anatomy and organ systems. Frank Gullo, who was a social psychologist, would teach human biology (with a social twist) and sex, reproduction, etc. Jim, if he accepted the opportunity, would teach taxonomy and evolutionary aspects of biology. Each teacher would get five sections for three months and repeat their part three times during the year.

The principal, Sister Marie Thomas, was interested in Jim because the head of the science department, Sister Mary Aiden, was getting ready to retire in a year or two. She taught chemistry and physics. The principal wanted to hire someone who could take over for Sister Aiden. Jim met all those qualifications.

After much reflection, because Jim loved Holy Redeemer, he decided to move to RHS. The decision was made mostly because of the reduced commuting and because Jim got to teach all science classes and no math classes. He was now home every night. With this arrangement, Jim had only one lesson plan to prepare each night. He began teaching at RHS in August of 1971 and taught biology that first year. He also was the moderator of the photography club.

During the school year of 1972, he team-taught physical science to the same two grades. Jim taught the chemistry aspects of physical science. Frank Gullo was not qualified to teach physical science, so he left the school for another assignment. Pat Cox and Louis Garcia replaced him. Throughout the first two and a half years at Redemptorist, Jim attended UNO to become certified as a teacher. He was required to take thirty hours of education courses. He took six hours a semester at night for five straight semesters until he received his teaching certificate. His in-service teaching at Holy Redeemer counted for his student teaching. During his second year at RHS, his first child, Jason, was conceived.

In August of 1973, Sister Aiden retired. Jim became the chemistry and physics teacher, teaching two sections of chemistry and one section of physics. He also taught one part of advanced biology. Sister Marie Thomas asked him to take on the role of department chairman as well. Feedback from his students, then and now, was that he was an excellent teacher.

Mosquito Control Years and Papers

While Jim was teaching at Holy Redeemer and Redemptorist, he took his salary on a ten-month basis. He did this so that his monthly cash flow was better able to meet the family's needs. But this also meant that Jim had to find a summer job. He needed something that would produce the necessary income for the two and a half months of the summer. He began with a summer internship at the New Orleans Mosquito Control.

Jim started in the summer of 1970. That first summer, he performed a lot of manual labor for the department, including digging ditches, collecting mosquitos from light traps, and loading spray trucks. He received an hourly wage, but the opportunity for overtime offered a way to supplement the pay and allowed for a living wage.

Jim worked as much overtime as he could get. From summer to summer, he was given more research responsibilities. These research activities resulted in papers by Dr. Mike Carrol and Jim published in the *Journal of American Mosquito Control*.

By the summer of 1974, Jim had become quite valuable to the department. In the fall of 1974, Mr. George Carmichael, the director of the New Orleans Mosquito Control program, offered Jim a full-time job as an entomologist with the district. Jim did not want to leave teaching, as he loved education and his role at Redemptorist. Still, the position offered a significant increase in salary. That meant a substantial reduction in the amount of overtime he had to work.

Jim accepted Mr. Carmichael's offer and told Sister Marie Thomas he was leaving. She was not too happy with Jim's resigning midyear, but Jim eased the burden by helping her find his replacement.

In January of 1975, Jim started his full-time employment at New Orleans Mosquito Control. His role was to supervise the collection of mosquito detection and population data. He would then analyze the pattern of mosquito activity in Orleans Parish with this information and assign larvicide and adult spraying activities based on this activity. His job also involved measurement of the effectiveness of these activities on the target mosquito and non-target animal populations (including humans). This last component of his responsibilities required extensive research on the efficacy of spraying.

Another specific component of the job was the surveillance and monitoring of encephalitis antibodies in the local and migratory bird populations. Encephalitis is a disease transmitted by mosquitos. This surveillance included the trapping and banding of local birds with mist nets and the shooting of migratory waterfowl. Blood samples were taken and sent to the state lab for analysis of encephalitis antibodies. If the antibody titer became too high, the mosquito population in that area would have to be significantly reduced to prevent an encephalitis outbreak in the city.

In 1975, a large number of cases of St. Louis encephalitis occurred in the country. It killed ninety-five people. The following year, infection rates were down, and they had stayed down in the decades that followed.[11] Some southern cities had encephalitis outbreaks, but not New Orleans. Its encephalitis surveillance program kept the town free of encephalitis.

Jim worked at Mosquito Control for over five years. He coauthored many research papers and reports during this time. He would deliver one of his research reports each year at the annual meeting of the American Mosquito Control Association.

Hewlett Packard

Jim loved his job at Mosquito Control. It allowed him a lot of freedom to research and write about things that were important to that industry. He was dissatisfied, however, because he didn't feel necessary. The Louisiana Mosquito Control community was not perceived by him to be a very prestigious group. The fact that he went to work in very casual clothes was sort of a problem for him. As a teacher, he'd worn a tie every day to work, and now he didn't.

By the late summer of 1979, he had become frustrated with his position in life. He saw an ad in the employment pages of the paper for a customer engineer at Hewlett Packard. Jim applied for the post. The interviewer, Val James, liked Jim very much. But he gave the job to another candidate who was already working for HP. Jim asked Val what he could do to enhance his chances the next time there was an opening. Val suggested more electronics on his résumé. Jim enrolled that September at Delgado Junior College in two classes: AC/DC Electronics and Instrument Control. Jim got an A in both sessions. He sent the grades to Val James.

In March of 1980, he got a call from Val James telling him there was an opening and that he had an interview for the position on April 10 at 1 p.m. The meeting was to be conducted by Sam Payne at the HP office on Williams Boulevard. That morning it rained very hard in Metairie, and most of the significant roads flooded. Jim, dressed in a suit, drove toward the office, taking every back road he could to avoid the flooding. But his car stalled about two blocks from the office and would not restart. Jim took off his shoes, rolled up his pants, and walked there. He arrived dripping wet only to find the office closed. Everyone had been allowed to go home at noon because of the weather.

[11.] Jason Straziuso, "Experts Say West Nile Outbreaks Are Likely to Taper Off," *Topeka Capital Journal* (August 10, 2002), cjonline.com/stories/081102/usw_westnile.shtml.

Jim knocked and knocked, and finally, Sam Payne let him in the door. Sam had been planning to cancel the interview, but because Jim had arrived, he conducted it anyway, saying, "Anyone who wants this job this bad to get to the office in this weather deserves an interview." Jim got the job and started working for Hewlett Packard on May 1, 1980. He went to Palo Alto, California, in early June, expecting to stay there for six months in training. He received top grades in all his classes, and on August 10, was allowed to come home to begin working as a customer service engineer.

He was so good at his job that he became a region specialist in mass spectrometers by 1982. In 1984, he was promoted to a systems engineer and taught both customers and internal employees how to operate the software and chemical methodology of mass spectrometers. He was made region manager for all system engineers in 1989. He was very successful at this job and suggested a unique method to manage systems engineers to reduce their overnight travel.

This new management method, however, put him out of a job. In 1998, Jim was given the position of support quality manager for the entire US support organization. HP split in 2000 into several companies. The chemical analysis group split off as Agilent Technologies Inc. Jim remained a quality manager for Agilent from 1998 until he was forced to retire in 2013. During these fifteen years as quality manager, Jim continued to develop his skills. In 2000, he graduated from Loyola with a master's degree in quality management. In 2008, Jim earned a Six Sigma Black Belt title, and in 2011 he received a Master Black Belt title both from Motorola and Agilent.

Family Matters

Jason Pratt Bourg was born on October 30, 1973. As Jason's teeth developed, it was apparent that there was a problem with them. The surface of his teeth was rough and discolored. Jeanne took him to a periodontist. This doctor accused Jeannie of causing "bottle mouth" in Jason by letting him sleep with his bottle in his mouth.

The problem was that Jason never took a bottle. He went from breastfeeding to a sippy cup. As the problem got worse and potentially more expensive, Jeannie took Jason to LSU Dental School, where she met Dr. Hebert. He identified the problem as a genetic issue and referred Jason to a geneticist.

Jason Bourg and Amelogenesis Imperfecta

Jason was diagnosed with amelogenesis imperfecta, which presents with a rare abnormal formation of the enamel or external layer of the crown of teeth. The coating is composed mostly of mineral that is formed and regulated by the proteins in the tooth. Amelogenesis imperfecta is caused by a protein problem in the enamel. People afflicted with this syndrome have teeth of a yellowish color. The teeth are at a greater risk for cavities. They are hypersensitive to temperature changes as well as excessive calculus deposition and gingival hyperplasia.[12]

Amelogenesis imperfecta has several inheritance patterns. The patterns are dependent on the genes that are affected. They are most commonly inherited in a dominant condition. This condition means both parents must carry the altered gene. Amelogenesis imperfecta is also inherited in an X-linked pattern. In this form, the mutated gene is located on the X chromosome from one of the two parents. Jason had his baby teeth capped in metal crowns when he was two and a half years old.

In most cases, males with an X-linked form have more severe problems. Recent genetic studies suggest that the cause of a significant proportion of amelogenesis imperfecta cases remains to be discovered. It was assumed that Jason's condition was X-linked recessive. However, when his daughter, Elizabeth, showed the trait, it could not have been X-linked recessive unless Maris, her mother, was also a carrier. This relationship is highly unlikely.

Jonathan's Birth

Jim and Jeannie had their son Jason in 1973. They planned to wait four years and before having their second child, hopefully a girl. In 1977, while Jim was working at Mosquito Control and Jeannie was working with Dr. Swan S. Ward as his nurse, they started planning for their second child. They decided to use the Shettles method to improve the odds of having a girl.

The Shettles method had been around since the 1960s and claimed 75 percent success for those wanting to have a girl baby. Dr. Shettles reported that the most important factor for success was timing. The chromosome-carrying sperm determine the baby's sex. Boy sperm migrate faster but do not survive as long as

---

[12.] "Amelogenesis Imperfecta," *Wikipedia*, https://en.wikipedia.org/wiki/Amelogenesis_imperfecta.

their female-producing counterparts. Girl sperm are more durable and resilient, but they swim slower than male sperm. To have a girl baby, Dr. Shettles suggested, you should have sex two to four days before ovulation. Jeanne could tell when she was ovulating, so this method was chosen.

After several months of using this method, Jeanne conceived. However, in her second month, she had a miscarriage on a train returning from Washington, DC, where Jim was delivering a Mosquito Control paper. Jim is Rh-positive and Jeannie is Rh-negative. She had a D&C, and because the baby could have been given Rh-positive antibodies, she was given RhoGAM.

A mother who is Rh-negative may be exposed to Rh-positive blood from the baby during pregnancy. When this exposure happens, it can cause medical problems such as anemia, kidney failure, and shock. RhoGAM is used to keep this immune response to Rh-positive blood from happening in mothers with Rh-negative blood.

Abandoning the Shettles method, Jeannie got pregnant quickly, but this third pregnancy resulted in another miscarriage. Jim believed that the miscarriages were boys who were carrying amelogenesis imperfecta. Jeannie got pregnant again in May of 1979, and this time she delivered full-term. They were sure this was a girl, and Jeannie went into the delivery room at Lakeside Hospital with a pink button that read, "It's a Girl." Imagine their surprise when Dr. Andonie delivered Jonathan Ryan Bourg on February 7, 1980.

Jameson's Birth

Jeannie and Jim only planned on having two children. In the spring of 1984, however, Jeannie decided she wanted a third child. She convinced Jim to have another baby and soon got pregnant. Jameson Lloyd Bourg, Jim and Jeannie's third son, was born on December 5, 1984. He was their most creative child. He was astute, but he wanted to do things innovatively.

Jim's Retirement and Illness

When Jim was forced to retire after thirty-five years of continuous service, he was contracted to teach Six Sigma Green Belt courses for Agilent and did so in Singapore and China. He was enjoying retirement. He would walk four miles each morning at Lafreniere Park. Then he started to get pain in his left ankle from arthritis. In January of 2016, Dr. Field Ogden performed an arthrodesis on Jim's left ankle, inserting two screws to secure the bones together. He was not able to walk on the foot for over three months.

On June 3, 2016, Jim was diagnosed with T-cell non-Hodgkin's lymphoma by his doctors with the tools of a CT scan and a lymph tumor biopsy. His oncologist, Dr. Robert Veith, started a course of the chemotherapy protocol CHOEP. This protocol required six three-week cycles of chemo. Jim would get the CHOEP mixture for five contiguous days during the first week of the period, followed by two weeks of recovery.

The CHOEP protocol consists of cyclophosphamide, hydroxydaunorubicin, oncovin, etoposide, and prednisone. Chemotherapy was performed from June through October 2016. In June of 2017, Jim had an autologous (self-donated) stem-cell transplant. He was confined to the house for several months because of immunity issues. The good news is that as of September of 2019, Jim was cancer-free.

CHAPTER 2

THE DESCENDANTS OF JAMES ANATOLE BOURG JR.

The first thing you notice about New Orleans are the burying grounds—the cemeteries—and they're a cold proposition, one of the best things there are here. Going by, you try to be as quiet as possible, better to let them sleep. Greek, Roman, sepulchers- palatial mausoleums made to order, phantomesque, signs and symbols of hidden decay—ghosts of women and men who have sinned and who've died and are now living in tombs. The past doesn't pass away so quickly here. You could be dead for a long time.

—Bob Dylan

Gratitude makes sense of our past, brings peace for today, and creates a vision for tomorrow.

—Melody Beattie

This chapter tracks the history of the descendants of James Anatole Bourg Jr. at the time of the printing of this book. All the information and the writing was contributed by the three boys (sons) of James and Jeannie Bourg.

James A. Bourg Jr. (1946–) and Jeanne Marie Favret (1947–) were married on

May 17, 1969. Jim and Jeanne were both twenty-three years old. They had three children together.

Jason Pratt Bourg

Jason Pratt Bourg was born on October 30, 1973, when his father and mother were twenty-six years old. They were all living at their home on 3017 Haring Road in Metairie. Jason attended preschool and kindergarten at Memorial Baptist School. It was there that Jason met his lifelong friend, William Peavey. Jason started grammar school at Phoebe Hearst School on 5208 Wabash Street, in Metairie, Louisiana. He tested into the gifted and talented program at Phoebe Hearst and attended school there from first through sixth grades.

When Jason was eleven years old, the family moved to 4921 James Drive in Metairie. After sixth grade at Phoebe Hearst, Jason attended Holy Cross Middle School for seventh and eighth grades. Holy Cross was a great school, but the commute by bus was long and took up several hours of his day. He asked his parents to allow him to move to a school that was a more comfortable commute.

Jim required Jason to attend all the open-house activities at nearby high schools. Although his mother was leaning toward Jesuit High School, once Jason participated at the open house at Brother Martin High School and heard Brother Ivy speak, he wanted to attend school there. He graduated from Brother Martin High in May of 1991.

Jason decided to attend Louisiana State University, where he majored in Chemical Engineering. In May of 1994, while working on homework on campus, he met Maris Lynn Scott. They shared a few classes, and after spending some time together, they became fast friends. Maris made several trips to Metairie and met Jason's family, and while at a Hootie and the Blowfish concert at the Varsity in Baton Rouge in March 1995, they decided to become romantically involved. In December of 1996, Jason proposed to Maris at one of their favorite local Baton Rouge restaurants, and they were married at Southside Baptist Church on Lee Drive in Baton Rouge on July 11, 1998.

Following a honeymoon trip to Cape Cod, Massachusetts, Jason, and Maris took up residence at an apartment complex on Jefferson Highway in Baton Rouge. They stayed there for eighteen months until finding out there were expecting their first child, at which time they moved Frederick Street in Shenandoah Estates in

Southeast Baton Rouge. Elizabeth Marie Bourg was born on April 3, 2000, at Woman's Hospital in Baton Rouge.

Not long after, Jason and Maris found out they were expecting their second child, and on July 18, 2002, Maris gave birth to Harrison Pratt Bourg. There were several scares during Maris's pregnancy with Harrison, but ultimately he was born completely healthy. Jason and Maris decided to round out their family with a third child, and on May 19, 2004, Thomas Reade Bourg was born.

The family lived on Frederick Drive in Shenandoah until March of 2009. At that time, they moved a short distance to a larger house in Shenandoah on Petersburg Drive. In 2014, Jason's company (Chicago Bridge & Iron) relocated him to the Woodlands, Texas, where they purchased a home on North Greenvine Court in the village of Alden Bridge.

All three kids—Elizabeth, Harrison, and Thomas—attended Shenandoah Elementary School. Elizabeth and Harrison attended Sherwood Elementary while living in Baton Rouge. Once they moved to the Woodlands, all three kids attended McCullough Middle School and the Woodlands High School. Elizabeth participated in many dance classes in both Baton Rouge and the Woodlands. She also was a member of the high school choir and active in volunteer organizations.

Both Harrison and Thomas played soccer for the Baton Rouge Soccer Club, Woodlands Rush, and Woodlands Dynamo. Traveling for games on the weekends all over Texas and Louisiana was a big part of the family's life.

When Elizabeth was young, they discovered she had the same genetic problem with her teeth as her father, amelogenesis imperfecta. Amelogenesis imperfecta is a congenital disorder that presents with a rare abnormal formation of the enamel or external layer of the crown of teeth unrelated to any systemic or generalized conditions. Her dentist treated this condition in the Woodlands, and her teeth are today as beautiful as her father's.

At this publishing, Elizabeth is a sophomore at Louisiana State University studying Kinesiology and Physical Therapy.

Jonathan Ryan Bourg

Jonathan Ryan Bourg was born to Jim and Jeannie Bourg in Metairie, Louisiana, on February 7, 1980. He grew up in Metairie, attending grade school at St. Ann Catholic School and high school at Brother Martin High School. In

1998, he moved to Baton Rouge, Louisiana, to attend college at Louisiana State University, where he studied engineering.

While studying in the halls of LSU's engineering building during his junior year, Jonathan met Michelle Ann Pivach, an electrical engineering student. The two hit it off after a spring vacation on the Gulf Coast with friends, and they began dating shortly after that. Michelle graduated in May 2002 with a bachelor of science degree in electrical engineering and began work in New Orleans, Louisiana, for the local electric utility, Entergy. Upon graduation, Jonathan sought to stay close to Michelle and took a job as an engineer at Entergy as well.

From a young age, Jonathan's mother suggested that he had a knack for arguing that would serve him well as an attorney. In August 2004, Jonathan acted on that advice and left Entergy to enroll in law school at Loyola University School of Law in New Orleans. His three years at Loyola proved to be an eventful time in his life. In December 2004, Jonathan proposed to Michelle in New Orleans City Park under the Christmas lights. Their wedding was soon scheduled for May 2006, again in City Park. In August 2005, Hurricane Katrina hit New Orleans, disrupting the lives of Jonathan and Michelle as it did so many. Michelle's job was relocated to Mississippi for over a year, Jonathan had to transfer to LSU law school, and City Park—the place of their engagement and future wedding—was severely damaged by floodwaters.

Just before their wedding in May 2006, the couple received word that the reception venue in City Park had been restored and was ready to host events. Their wedding was one of the first to be held after Hurricane Katrina. The couple honeymooned in Hawaii and returned to their new home in Metairie, Louisiana, on North Labarre Road. Michelle continued to work for Entergy, and in May 2007, Jonathan began practicing law at a law firm in New Orleans. On February 7, 2010, Jonathan celebrated his thirtieth birthday at home in Metairie with his brothers and friends watching the New Orleans Saints win their first Super Bowl.

On January 11, 2011, Jonathan and Michelle were blessed with their first child, Coleman James Bourg, who was born on January 11, 2011. Later that year, the new family moved to the Lakeview neighborhood of New Orleans, to a house built on property that had flooded during Hurricane Katrina. Jonathan also rejoined Michelle at Entergy, where he began a career focused on utility regulation.

On March 10, 2014, Jonathan and Michelle welcomed their first baby girl, Caroline Jeanne Bourg. She was followed by her sister, Claire Mitchell Bourg, who was born on December 21, 2016. All three kids were named with their loving grandparents in mind: Coleman James got his middle name from Jonathan's father; Claire Mitchell got her middle name from Michelle's father, Mitchell Pivach; and Caroline Jeanne was named after both of her grandmothers: Jonathan's mother, Jeanne, and Michelle's mother, Carol Piediscalzo Pivach.

All three children attended grade school at St. Catherine in Metairie, Louisiana. Coleman enjoyed playing sports and was active in soccer, flag football, and baseball. His sister Caroline enjoyed playing soccer as well, and both girls loved dancing, at home and at dancing class. The family's home in Lakeview was only a long walk away from where Jonathan and Michelle were married in City Park, and they often enjoyed time as a family in the park.

Jameson Lloyd Bourg

Jameson Lloyd Bourg was born at Lakeside Hospital in Metairie, Louisiana, on December 5, 1984. He grew up on James Drive. He received his sacraments of initiation at St. Ann, where he attended elementary school till seventh grade and then attended Brother Martin High School for eighth through twelfth grade. At St. Ann, he participated in both academic clubs and sports. Jameson also participated in Cub Scouts (Pack 261—St. Ann) and Boy Scouts (Troop 491—St. Clement of Rome), eventually earning the rank of Eagle Scout at seventeen years old.

During his early childhood, Jameson would mainly play in the street and front lawns with other kids on James Drive. As he entered middle school, he developed a love for music and the outdoors. He sang in the Brother Martin chorus and learned to play piano and guitar. He would frequently go backpacking with his father as part of the Boy Scouts.

One thing of note during Jameson's childhood was his near-drowning. At the age of two, he fell between a pool cover and the side of the pool while at a backyard party. An older boy saw this from across the yard and pulled him out in time. At the age of seven, Jameson fractured his ankle while playing outside but continued to walk on it two weeks for fear that he would get in trouble. His mother eventually noticed his slight limp and brought him to the doctor. People described him as a funny and quirky child. He frequently played silly characters to make the family laugh.

In August 2003, Jameson began attending Louisiana State University, where he studied mechanical engineering. He would go on to graduate in December

2007. Throughout college, Jameson lived both on- and off-campus with his close friends from high school who also attended LSU. He enjoyed seeing the LSU football team win a national championship both his first and last semester.

After Hurricane Katrina in August 2005, Jameson's grandmother Jeannie asked him to locate her close friend Jocelyn Oswald, who had evacuated during the flood emergency in New Orleans. Jeannie knew Jocelyn had a granddaughter at LSU named Katherine (Katie) Dale Coplen who was about Jameson's age, so she asked him to start there. Jameson searched out Katie on the newly launched LSU Facebook website and asked to exchange information so the grandmothers to communicate.

Following this encounter, Jameson and Katie continued talking, developing friendship through a shared sense of humor. They began dating in May 2006. Katie was a theater major with a minor in dance, and Jameson loved her passion for the arts.

After graduation, Katie lived with her parents, Dale and Sandy Coplen, on Dodge Avenue while Jameson moved back to James Drive. He proposed on December 13, 2009, after a date to see Disney's *Princess and the Frog.* The couple was married at St. Dominic on Harrison Avenue on December 18, 2010. They honeymooned in St. Lucia and immediately moved to their first house in Metairie's Bonnabel neighborhood.

Jameson worked as an engineer/project manager and Katie as a schoolteacher. It was a tradition for all three Bourg brothers (Jason, Jonathan, and Jameson) to ride side by side in the Krewe of Thoth parade. Also, Jameson and Jason spent time performing in a recreational rock band called Sweet Potato Sale.

On May 22, 2013, Ronan Dale Bourg was born at Ochsner Medical Center on Jefferson Highway. Doctors monitored his fetal heart development closely for potential Cor Triatriatum but found his heart to be perfect at birth. His sister, Genevieve (Ginny) Claire Bourg, was born on May 4, 2016—at home, much to everyone's surprise. Though the plan was for her to be born at Ochsner Baptist in New Orleans, Katie's contractions accelerated quickly. By the time they were ready to travel to the hospital, Katie refused to get in the car. As Jameson begged her to, her water broke, and she told him she needed to push. After only one hour of labor, Jameson delivered the baby in the driveway of their home as they waited for paramedics to arrive. Katie and the baby were then taken to the hospital via ambulance.

Both kids attended Trinity Episcopal School for elementary—the same school in which their mom taught third grade and music/drama. The family attended church at St. Catherine of Sienna. As children, Ronan and Ginny enjoyed reading, painting, performance art, and dramatic play. Katie performed in local musical theater, while Jameson played guitar for the church retreats. Jameson's favorite memories were the many holidays celebrated with the larger family. He enjoyed seeing the generations of cousins together.

CHAPTER 3

THE BOURG FAMILY

The Ancestors of James Anatole Bourg Jr.

If you cannot get rid of the family skeleton, you may as well make it dance.
—George Bernard Shaw

There are only two lasting bequests we can give our
children - one is roots, and the other, wings.
—Hodding S. Carter

We are all an accumulation of not only our life
experience, but those who were our ancestors.
—Connie H.

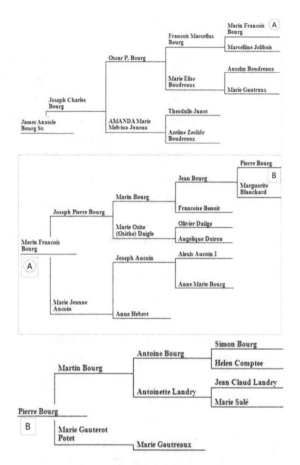

Figure 1 - *The Bourg Family Tree*
Twelve Generations in three graphic steps

This chapter will recount the history of the Bourg family. This family history started in Martaize, France; the family immigrated to Acadia (Nova Scotia) in approximately 1640. They remained in Acadia until they were forcibly returned to France against their will by the British in 1758. They lived in France for twenty-seven years before coming to Louisiana in 1785. There, they resided in Napoleonville, Assumption Parish, Louisiana, until James Anatole Bourg Sr. moved to New Orleans in the 1930s. The family has lived in New Orleans since that time.

This history will drift backward in time from the present day to Simon Bourg, who moved to Acadia in 1640. The sequence will journey through the generations of Bourgs and the history of the times in which they lived.

Generation 1: James Anatole Bourg Sr.

James Anatole Bourg Sr. (Jim) is the father of the author. Jim was born on February 20, 1913, in the rural town of Napoleonville, Louisiana. He was the son of Joseph Charles Bourg (1880–1962) and Lucy Marie Talbot (1888–1972). His parents were both of French Acadian descent, making Jim an authentic Cajun.

When we look at the events in history during the time when Jim was born, the RMS Titanic had sunk just ten months earlier. The Sixteenth Amendment to the United States Constitution was ratified on February 3, 1913, allowing the US government to impose and collect income taxes. Woodrow Wilson was sworn in as the twenty-eighth president of the United States on March 4, 1913. The Ford Motor Company's plant in Highland Park, Michigan, near Detroit, became the first automobile plant in the world to have a moving assembly line. This line started on October 7, 1913. This increased production of the Model T, so it was indeed mass-produced.

In around 1913, Albert Einstein was developing his new theory of gravity that would incorporate his "strong equivalence" principle. By calling on this principle, he realized, he could avoid dealing with gravity as a force altogether. Einstein became a professor of theoretical physics at the Federal Institute of Technology in Zurich. He worked on his universal theory of relativity there. The theory would not be published until 1915.

World War I would start seventeen months after Jim's birth. It was one of the costliest military conflicts in history in terms of lives. France's distrust of Germany caused the war, combined with the tensions between the European powers resulting from the balance of power that divided Europe into two camps: Great Britain, France, and Russia (the Triple Entente) on one side, the German Empire, Austria-Hungary, and Italy (Central Powers) on the other. The Germans wanted to ensure that power was balanced between the two groups.

New Orleans was hit by major hurricanes in 1909 and again in 1915. In 1917, the Storyville District (houses of ill repute) was closed by the federal government. Mayor Martin Behrman objected very much to the ordered closing but could do nothing against the US government. In 1923, the Industrial Canal opened, providing for the first time a direct shipping link between Lake Pontchartrain and the Mississippi River. Locks had to be installed to control the difference in water levels between the river and the lake when their levels differed. In the 1920s, the city removed the old cast-iron balconies from Canal Street to modernize the city's commercial hub. This move came to be regarded as mistakes long after the fact.

Jim's Early Life

Jim grew up as a normal young man in the small agrarian village of Napoleonville, Louisiana. He attended a small grammar school. Jim helped in his father's saddle- and harness-making business. He played football at Assumption High School, the parish public school, as an offensive lineman. He was taller and heavier than most of his classmates. The 1930 team was undefeated.

He attended the *Fais do-dos* (country dances held in southern Louisiana), where he learned to be an excellent dancer. A *Fais do-do* is named for "the gentle command ('go to sleep') young mothers offered bawling infants."[13] To quote early Cajun musician Edwin Duhon of the Hackberry Ramblers: "She'd go to the cry room, give the baby a nipple and sing, 'Fais do-do.' Mom needed to get the baby to sleep fast, 'cause she's worried about her husband dancing with somebody else out there." *Do-do* itself comes from the French verb *dormir* (to sleep) and is used primarily in speaking to small children. The phrase is comparable to the American English *beddy-bye*. It is embodied in an old French lullaby, a song sung to children when putting them down for the night. Its existence in Cajun culture as a source for dances, or bands, comes from the affection for the term itself.[14]

The lullaby in French goes as follows:
Fais do-do, Colas mon p'tit frère,
Fais do-do, t'auras du lolo
Maman est en haut, qui fait des gâteaux
Papa est en bas, qui fait du chocolat
Fait do-do, Colas mon p'tit frère,
Fait do-do, t'auras du lolo

The following is the English translation:

Go to sleep, Colas my little brother,

[13.] Joshua Clegg Caffery, "The Folk Etymology of the Fais Do-Do: A Note," www. louisianafolklife.org/LT/Articles_Essays/lfmfaisdodo.html.
[14.] Notes from the Roots n' Blues CD "Cajun Dance Party—Fais Do-Do," Sony, 1994.

Go to sleep, you will have your milk
Mommy is upstairs, making some cakes
Daddy is downstairs, making hot cocoa,
Go to sleep, Colas, my little brother,
Go to sleep, you will have your milk.[15]

Colas is short for *Nicolas* in French. Jim's mom would sing this lullaby to him when he was a small boy.

Growing up, Jim thought that he would work in the sugarcane industry as a farmer like his great-grandfather. Or he might be a harness and saddle-maker like his father. However, the Great Depression would completely disrupt these expectations.

The Depression

When Jim was sixteen years and eight months old, the stock market crashed in October of 1929. It had been coming on since the early 1920s. America had flourished during that time, with post–World War I industrialization and new technologies fueled an economic and cultural boom. The Dow Jones average soared throughout the Roaring Twenties, and many investors bought a lot of stocks, comforted by the fact that stocks were thought to be extremely safe.

Investors soon bought shares on margin, which is the borrowing of capital to gain leverage. The use of this leverage meant that if a stock went up 1 percent, the investor would make 10 percent. Unfortunately, this leverage also worked the other way. If a stock dropped too much, investors could lose all of their money. They could owe money to the broker as well.

In the 1920s, the Dow Jones rose 340 points. This rise created many new millionaires. Investing in stocks became a favorite pastime of Americans as investors tried to make a quick gain. Some investors mortgaged their homes and invested their life savings into hot stocks, such as Ford and RCA. To the average investor, this was foolproof. Few Americans studied business investments and underlying stocks. Thousands of fly-by-night companies were formed to fool

---

[15] Mama Lisa's World, "Fais dodo, Colas mon p'tit frère," http://www.mamalisa.com/?lang=French&t=es&p=181.

investors. Most people never even thought a crash was possible. In their minds, the stock market never went down.[16]

In 1929, the Federal Reserve tried to cool things by raising interest rates several times. By October, a robust bear market had started. On Thursday, October 24, 1929, panic selling began as investors realized that the stock boom was over. Margin investors tried to sell their shares but could not. Margin investors went bankrupt instantly when the stock market crashed on October 28th and 29th. During November of 1929, the Dow sank.[17]

Many banks had invested in the stock market, causing those banks to fail. When customers tried to withdraw their savings, bank runs occurred. Significant banks and brokerage firms went under, accelerating the stock market crash. The financial system was in chaos. Many bankrupt speculators jumped out of buildings, committing suicide.

The crash of 1929 led to the Great Depression. The Depression lasted from October 1929 to almost 1940. Poverty became the standard for many people, and many workers lost their jobs and were forced to live in shantytowns. Former millionaire investors were reduced to begging and selling apples on street corners. A full third of all Americans lived below the poverty level during the Great Depression. The Dow Jones didn't reach its 1929 high again until 1955.

Depression-Era Louisiana and the Great Flood of 1927

Relying mostly on crops for its economy, Louisiana was very much impacted by the Great Depression. Farm prices reached rock-bottom lows. Cotton dropped to less than five cents a pound. The state's primary economic crop, sugar, fell to less than four cents a pound. The state's other leading commodities—timber, oil, and rice—fell correspondingly. Louisiana's rural population was already living in deep poverty. The Depression pushed these people to even greater deprivation.

To make matters worse, the great 1927 Mississippi River flood and the 1930 and 1931 drought displaced tens of thousands of families. "Louisiana 1927," a song written and recorded by Randy Newman on his *Good Old Boys* album in 1974, recounts the Great Flood that left hundreds of thousands of people homeless in

---

[16]Jesse Colombo, "The Stock Market Crash of 1929," *The Bubble Bubble* (July 17, 2012), http://www.thebubblebubble.com/1929-crash/.

[17]Jesse Colombo, "265 Points in Just Three Days: The Stock Market Crash of 1929," *The Bubble Bubble* (July 17, 2012) http://www.thebubblebubble.com/1929-crash/.

Louisiana and Mississippi. Herbert Hoover described the flood of 1927 as "the greatest peacetime calamity in the history of the country." It inundated over 16.5 million acres (about 26,000 square miles) in 170 counties in seven states. It drove an estimated 1 million people from their homes.

The Mississippi River stayed at flood stage for 153 days. In Louisiana, twenty parishes flooded. The congressional response, the 1928 Flood Control Act, had far-reaching social, political, and physical consequences in Louisiana and throughout the Mississippi River valley.[18]

Hard times were everywhere in the state. The large landowners faced difficulties as well. Farm income fell by 67 percent for more than two years. Many people lost everything to the "Tax Man's sale" or foreclosure by insurance companies and banks.

Though more resilient than agriculture and manufacturing, the oil and natural gas industry had a slowdown in oil production that required layoffs. Still, the oil business proved a stabilizing force in the state's economy throughout the 1930s. This oil stabilization continued, especially after recovery had begun. Baton Rouge, home of Standard Oil, continued to expand during the decade. Shreveport and Monroe also expanded because of considerable petroleum deposits.

New Orleans experienced some of the worst effects of the Depression in the state. It was more like the hurt felt in big northern cities than in the state's rural areas. New Orleans was the South's largest city in 1930, as well as the country's largest port. It felt the crunch of the Depression almost immediately.

As trade declined with other countries, the docks were empty, and there was no activity, as stevedores had no work. By early 1930, one census counted at least 10,000 unemployed workers in the city, and it may have been higher. The city started a welfare program in early 1931. It raised more than a half-million dollars from private sources, all to help those most affected. This money soon ran out, and even a $750,000 bond issue, floated in 1932, proved insufficient to support the high number of unemployed workers and their families.

Louisiana suffered less, however, than other parts of the country. Governor Huey Long committed to infrastructure development when he took office in 1928, and he spent millions of dollars on large construction projects. This buffered the

---

[18] Jim Bradshaw, "Great Flood of 1927," *Knowlouisiana.org Encyclopedia of Louisiana*, ed. David Johnson, Louisiana Endowment for the Humanities, 2010 (May 13, 2011), http://www.knowlouisiana.org/entry/great-flood-of-1927.

full force of the Depression. This program by Huey Long was a preview of the national New Deal started by President Franklin D. Roosevelt two years later.

Long pressed for increased spending in all areas of the state government to stimulate economic growth. He did this on his own without support from and often at odds with financial experts. Huey Long built infrastructure, roads, bridges, and public facilities at a fantastic rate. He also put a lot of federal funds into public education through free schoolbooks, increased teacher salaries, and adult education programs. Between 1928 and 1932, Long spent more than the previous three Louisiana leaders combined.

Public giveaway programs were not something that Huey Long supported. His construction programs put money into infrastructure projects that provided jobs for many laborers around the state. By doing this, he became a national figure, although he concentrated more on Louisiana than on national considerations. Charitable organizations like churches, social clubs, benevolent societies, and other private sources contributed more than 98 percent of all project expenditures in the state. By the time this source of monies faded, Herbert Hoover could see the necessity of a national relief program.[19]

Long moved to representing Louisiana in the US Senate in 1932 after only one term as governor. O. K. Allen was elected governor to take his place. Long, nicknamed "The Kingfish," was assassinated on Sunday, September 8, 1935, at the State Capitol by Dr. Carl Weiss, a Baton Rouge physician. Weiss was the son-in-law of Long's long-time opponent, Judge Benjamin Henry Pavy. After Long's death, an even more significant amount of money cascaded into Louisiana for projects that eventually employed thousands of workers.

The Depression Lifts

Hoover made federal loans to assist all states in August of 1932. In Louisiana, Governor O. K. Allen's government contributed $6.5 million in matching funds while handling over one hundred thousand cases a month on average. When Franklin D. Roosevelt took office in March of 1933, this became part of the Federal Emergency Relief Agency (FERA). Federal dollars started to flow into

---

[19]Matthew Reonas, "Great Depression in Louisiana," *Knowlouisiana.org Encyclopedia of Louisiana*, edited by David Johnson, Louisiana Endowment for the Humanities, 2010 (December 17, 2010), http://www.knowlouisiana.org/entry/great-depression-in-louisiana.

the state at an even higher rate, which made a significant impact on the state's economy.

With the federal recovery programs, known as the New Deal, the Depression in Louisiana started to ease. However, poverty and underemployment continued to impact the lives of many of Louisiana's working-class families until the start of World War II. With economic crisis of the Depression ended, many Louisiana citizens found the latter part of the 1930s to be something of a golden era. In the late 1930s, a time of unified purpose and high-level activity created a significant outpouring of the arts and architecture. In New Orleans, there was a restoration of the French Market. In Shreveport, there was the building of the Louisiana State Exhibit Museum, as well as the creation statewide of public creation of a wide variety of murals. This art celebrated Louisiana's history and culture.

Jim Quits School to Help Support the Family

The Bourg family experienced significant economic hardship for several reasons. The Depression, the decline of Jim's father's harness- and saddle-making business because of the rise of the automobile industry, and Jim's father's health issues were all factors. The Bourgs grew their food, and their wooden water-catching cistern provided water. But there was little money for clothes, electricity, and financial security.

Jim decided to quit school after his junior year and go to work to help support the family. He was only seventeen years old. His younger siblings were ten and eight, so there was little they could do to help.

Jim tried to find work in Napoleonville, but things there were pretty rough. Sometime between 1931–1934, he decided to move to New Orleans. He took a job with New Orleans Public Service (NOPSI) driving a streetcar. Jim didn't earn a lot with this salary, but what he did make was sent back to his mom. Jim's financial contribution helped her with household expenses.

Sometime during this period, Jim met Agnes Louise Young. As we will see in chapter 5, Agnes was born on December 28, 1912, in New Orleans. She worked as a secretary at a wholesale liquor distributor near Canal Street in New Orleans. When Jim would pass in his streetcar, he would ring the bell of the trolley. The other employees in the office would call Jim her "ding dong daddy."

Sometime in the middle 1930s, Jim and Agnes became engaged. Jim may have joined the US Navy as a reservist in 1937, but the only evidence of this is a found picture of him in a navy sailor's uniform.

Before Pearl Harbor, many people in the government and the country believed the United States would be drawn into the war that was being fought in Europe and Asia. Isolationism was still very active in the country. But when France fell to the Nazis in June 1940, Americans grew uneasy about Great Britain's ability to defend itself against Germany. US military preparation was inadequate to fight a world war. Public polls showed an upturn in favor of instituting a draft.

On September 16, 1940, the United States instituted the Selective Training and Service Act of 1940. This act required all men between the ages of twenty-one and forty-five to register for the draft. Jim, who was living at 803 Jackson Avenue, was expected to register. He enrolled with the New Orleans Draft Board on May 15, 1941. This Selective Service activity was the first peacetime draft in US history. Those selected were required to serve at least one year in the armed forces.

The surprise attack on Pearl Harbor was a military strike by the Imperial Japanese Navy against Hawaii on the early morning of December 7, 1941. The attack led to the United States into World War II. The surprise attack shocked the American people. The following day, December 8, the United States declared war on Japan. Several days later, on December 11, it declared war on Germany and Italy, as they declared war on the United States.[20]

On November 21, 1942, Jim was inducted into the army and officially began his service on November 30, 1942. He was very much overweight. He was listed as 5 feet 11 inches and 255 pounds. He had developed Type 2 diabetes like his father. When he was taking his physical for army military service, he saw three doctors. Two rejected Jim for service because of his weight and diabetes, but one passed him for limited duty. During the war, Jim drove a bus at Kilauea Military Camp, a prisoner of war camp in Hawaii.

During the war, Jim would write to Agnes regularly. She was living with her mom and siblings at 1138 St. Andrew Street. During one of his leaves from the military, Jim came home and married Agnes on January 22, 1944. Jim was discharged from the service on January 30, 1946. His rank was army staff sergeant. He arrived home on February 6, 1946[21] and returned to his job with Public Service. This time, he was driving a bus.

[20.] "USS *Arizona* Memorial," *Wikipedia*, https://en.wikipedia.org/wiki/USS_Arizona_Memorial.

[21]"Enlisted Record and Report of Separation—Honorable Discharge."

Agnes and Jim's first home was a rented house at 1230 St. Andrew Street in New Orleans. They moved there in early 1946. Next door, at 1232 St. Andrew, lived the Waldrons. Jimmy Jr. was born eleven months later, on December 21, 1946. Dennis Waldron, Jimmy Jr.'s lifelong friend, was born next door in March of 1947.

By 1948, Jim was making $3,500 per year working as a New Orleans Public Service (NOPSI) transit operator. The family was still living at 1230 St. Andrew. Jim's mom and dad had moved to 927 Third Street in New Orleans during the war so the family could help care for them. They moved to New Orleans because Jim's dad, Joseph Charles Bourg, lost his eye to complications from diabetes.

In 1949, Joseph and Lucy moved back to Napoleonville. Agnes was pregnant with a second child, and she and Jim needed more room. They moved from St. Andrew Street to 927 Third Street, another rented home.

On November 10, 1949, Robert Oliver (Bobby) Bourg, Jim's second son, was born, followed by a third son, Michael Joseph (Mike) Bourg, on November 11, 1953. More will be told about these two brothers later in this chapter.

Jim's Religious Beliefs and Social Agenda

Jim Bourg Sr. was a very spiritual, kind, and generous man. While living in the Irish Channel (which he did all his life), he was a devout parishioner of Redemptorist Parish, its churches, and its organizations. Jim was a member of the Redemptorist Knights of Columbus (the world's largest Catholic fraternal service organization) Council 3330. He served as the council third-degree Grand Knight multiple times. Jim was also a fourth-degree Grand Knight with all of the associated uniform and sword. Besides the Knights of Columbus, Jim was also in the Holy Name Society. A member of the Redemptorist High School Dad's Club, and the Redemptorist Parish church ushers group. He was also active on the Knights of Columbus council bowling team, which usually bowled every Friday evening.

He was so involved with church social organizations that he was rarely home in the evenings. These activities were service motivated, but they were also social activities. Most sessions involved beer-drinking and card-playing afterward.

Jim's Decline and Death

Jim had diabetes most of his adult life. He suffered from it because he didn't understand it and refused to change his dietary habits and lifestyle. Jim smoked a pack of cigaretts per day. Jim lived on a high-carb, high-fat diet. He would go to Knights of Columbus meetings as well as other social club meetings where he would eat all the wrong foods and drink beer. He would then come home and inject himself (or have his son Jimmy inject him) with a hefty dose of insulin.

Diabetes causes the small, medium, and large blood vessels in the body to narrow. Plaque builds up in the vessel walls of small blood vessels, decreasing blood flow. Atherosclerosis develops when the excess fat in the blood builds in the large blood vessel walls. Plaque, the substance that attaches to the walls, narrows blood vessels and decreases blood flow through the arteries. In addition to the narrowing of blood vessels, diabetes increases inflammation within them. People with diabetes have twice the risk of heart attack or stroke from atherosclerosis, the University of Rochester Medical Center website reports.[22]

Peripheral artery plaque often causes decreased blood flow to the legs and feet. Limbs may not receive enough blood flow while a person is walking. Atherosclerosis caused peripheral artery disease in Jim as well as reduced blood flow to his heart and other parts of his body. Symptoms included pain when walking, chest pain (angina) during exertion, high blood pressure, and infections in the feet. People with diabetes have a higher possibility of foot or leg amputation. Smokers with diabetes have the highest risk of amputation because smoking also blocks blood vessels. Jim did nothing to prevent peripheral artery disease.

One day when he was standing too close to a friend's automobile and the car rolled over his foot. This accident required a corrective procedure or he would be in great danger of having one or both of his feet amputated. Jim's doctors suggested lower extremity bypass surgery. The goal was to improve blood flow and prevent amputation.

Lower extremity bypass surgery was a well-established and highly effective, and it was certainly indicated in Jim's case. Like all surgical procedures, however, it carried significant risks, including heart attacks, blood clots, infections, and even death in a high percentage of patients. The use of medications such as aspirin, blood pressure, and cholesterol-lowering drugs is critical before and after the

---

[22] Sharon Perkins, "Why Do Diabetics Have Bad Circulation?" *Healthfully* (November 28, 2018), https://healthfully.com/why-do-diabetics-have-bad-circulation-6112092.html.

operation. Overall, bypass surgery is immediately successful in 90 to 95 percent of cases.[23]

Jim was a perfect candidate for the procedure, and the bypass surgery was performed at Southern Baptist Hospital on the first leg in 1971. It was successful but required a very long period of recovery and rehabilitation. This loss of circulation caused Jim to retire as a transit operator from NOPSI after thirty-five years of service.

Jim and his doctor decided to continue with the second leg. In early January of 1973, Jim entered Baptist Hospital on Napoleon Avenue again for the second bypass. The surgery went very well, and Jim was recovering normally.

On Friday, January 12, 1973, Jimmy Jr. visited his dad in the hospital around four thirty in the afternoon, after the classes he taught at Redemptorist High School. Jimmy was planning an oyster party at his home at 3017 Haring Road that evening for his friends. He stopped off at the seafood store on his way home and bought two sacks of oysters.

While preparing for the party at about seven thirty in the evening, he got a call from the nurse at the hospital. His dad was not doing well and was being moved to the intensive care ward. Jimmy rushed to the hospital, but by the time he got there, his father had already died. A massive heart attack caused by a blood clot dislodging from his surgically repaired leg to his coronary artery killed him.

The wake was held at Donigan's Funeral Home. The funeral Mass was conducted from St. Mary's Assumption Church in the Irish Channel, and he was buried in the Young family tomb in Metairie Cemetery. Father William Grangell, Knights of Columbus chaplain emeritus, delivered a tribute to Jim at the funeral. It was published in the Redemptorist Knight newsletter of March 1973. It read as follows:

At our November memorial service, Jim Bourg had the part of showing us the names of the Knights who died in the past year. Little did he think that he would be the first to die in the New Year! One thing is for sure: he was prepared to meet his God in eternity—give a good account of his life well-lived. Jim was a good man, looking at him from all angles. He was a devout, loyal, practical Catholic, second to none. Jim was the very best of the Knights of Columbus. He loved the order and was a willing, cheerful, tireless worker. Council 3330 will miss him. He was a good loving husband, and through him, we all got to know Agnes and

---

[23] "Lower Extremity Bypass Surgery," UCSF Vascular and Endovascular Surgery, https://vascular.surgery.ucsf.edu/conditions--procedures/lower-extremity-bypass-surgery.aspx.

love her. He will take good care of her from heaven. He was a good father, and his only hope was that his boys would always love God as practical Catholics. He was the kindest of men. His name was Charity. Saying this, we say everything. May Jim Bourg rest in peace with God and His Angles and Saints.[24]

The Siblings of James Anatole Bourg Sr.

Oscar Joseph Bourg (1920–2003)

Oscar Joseph Bourg was born on April 21, 1920, in Napoleonville, Louisiana. When he was born, his father was forty years old, and his mother was thirty-two. His brother Jim was seven or eight years old. Oscar grew up in Napoleonville and was still living home along with his sister Lucille in 1940 when he was twenty.

Oscar, along with his dad and mom, moved to New Orleans by 1942. They were living at 927 Third Street, and Oscar was still unemployed, when World War II broke out. Oscar signed up for the draft. After the war, Oscar married Inez Ann Melancon Marsh.

Inez was born on January 11, 1919, in Plattenville, Louisiana. Her father, Jean Philippe Melancon, was born on June 16, 1883, in Plattenville and died there on January 24, 1919. Her mother, Sydna Elvina Bourg, was born on October 3, 1888, in Louisiana and died in 1967 in Jackson, Mississippi. Inez's first husband, Joseph Beachel Marsh, was born in 1918 and died on December 11, 1947, in Shelby County, Tennessee. Joseph Marsh and Inez had one child together, Joann.

Oscar and Inez were married in August of 1949 in New Orleans. Inez and Oscar had two children together. Peggy Bourg was born on November 11, 1956. She married Robert Michael Dean, who was born on February 7, 1955, in New Orleans. Michael and Peggy had two children together: Shelby Michael, born on January 15, 1988, and Ashley Poimbeuf, born on July 26, 1985.

Oscar and Inez's second child was Richard Shelby (Rickey) Bourg. He was born on April 23, 1955. Rickey was a mail carrier all of his life. Inez died on March 26, 1981, in New Orleans.

---

[24] Brøderbund Family Archive #110, vol. 1, ed. 4, Social Security Death Index: the U.S., Social Security Death Index, Surnames from A through L, Date of Import: September 11th, 1998, Internal Ref. #1.111.4.26249.72.

Lucille Marie Bourg (1922–2003)

Lucille Marie Bourg was born on September 4, 1922, in Napoleonville, Louisiana. She was first married to a man whose name we do not know; she divorced him because we believe he was abusive to her. After her divorce, Lucille married Paul Johnston (1919–2003) in 1952. They had one daughter together, Kitty Johnston, who was born on October 2, 1956.

Kitty went to Redemptorist High School. She married Earl Joseph Primo III. Earl was born on December 15, 1956, in New Orleans. Earl and Kitty had two children together: Britton, born October 31, 1984, and Colin. Earl died on August 20, 2016, in Slidell, Louisiana.

Britton married Patrick Cresson, who was born on April 23, 1984. They had two children together: Rowen, born December 20, 2013, and Grayson, born March 13, 2016.

Lucille Bourg Johnston died on July 10, 2003. Her husband Paul died on November 6, 2003, in Belle Chasse, Louisiana.

The Children of James Anatole Bourg Sr.

Jim and Agnes had three children together: James Anatole Jr., who was discussed in chapter 1 and his descendants in chapter 2; Robert Oliver; and Michael Joseph.

Robert Oliver Bourg (1949–2005)

Robert Oliver (Bobby) Bourg was born on November 10, 1949, in New Orleans. He married Mary Anne Archer (daughter of Thelma Archer); she was also born in New Orleans. They had three children: Mary Anne, who married Keith Spampneto; Heidi, who married Charlie Ford; and Amy.

As a child, Bobby attended St. Alphonsus Grammar School and Redemptorist High School, where he graduated in 1967. He went on to the University of New Orleans, where he received a BA in secondary education. He taught high school at Archbishop Chapell for several years before working at Louisiana Power and Light, which eventually became Entergy.

While working at LP&L, Bobby returned to UNO and received his master's in environmental engineering degree. He worked as an environmental engineer at Entergy until leukemia forced him to stop in 1998. He fought his cancer for almost seven years. His brother Jim donated stem cells for a bone marrow transplant in October of 1999. He went into remission for several years, but his leukemia returned in 2004. He died on March 8, 2005, in Metairie, Louisiana.

Michael Joseph Bourg (1953–)

Jim's third son, Michael Joseph Bourg, was born on November 11, 1953. Jim took his pregnant wife to the hospital in the early morning hours. He called his brother Oscar to come to watch his two boys but had to leave his son Jimmy, age seven, at the house to watch his younger brother Bobby until Oscar came.

Mike was a very healthy infant but later, as an older toddler, he developed a terrible case of bronchitis. There as a brief period when Jim and Agnes did not know if he would survive the bronchial infection.

Mike attended St. Alphonsus grammar school, where he struggled as a student. He went to Redemptorist High School, where he played football. Mike's difficulties with learning convinced him not to attend a university. He went to work as a truck driver and remained in that capacity his entire life.

After his dad's death, Mike and his mom moved from 830 Eighth Street in New Orleans to 8705 Crawford Street in Metairie, Louisiana. Mike lived with his mom until her death in 1984. He never married and suffered from the same health problems as his father. He was always very much overweight and suffered from diabetes. Mike had gastric bypass surgery in 2010 and started to control his diabetes. He is still living alone on Crawford Street.

Generation 2: Joseph Charles Bourg

James Anatole Bourg Sr.'s parents were Joseph Charles Bourg (1880–1962) and Lucy Marie Talbot (1888–1972). Joseph Charles Bourg was born on Thursday, September 30, 1880, the fourth child and the first son of Oscar P. Bourg (1850–1912) and Amanda Marie Melvina Juneau (Junot) (1855–1891).

The 1880s

James A. Garfield, a Republican, was elected the twentieth US president on March 4, 1881. He was shot by an assassin on July 2, 1881, and died seventy-nine days later on September 19, 1881. He opposed the extension of slavery and had become a Republican in 1859.

In 1880, the Civil War had been over for fifteen years, and the building of the Panama Canal had just begun. Henry Draper, an American amateur astronomer, took the first-ever photograph of the Orion Nebula. Thomas Edison patented the electric incandescent bulb on January 27, 1880. Pope Leo XIII published the encyclical *Arcanum* about Christian marriage. This papal encyclical reminded bishops that the meaning of marriage, which is established by God, cannot be changed by human laws. Civil law can only regulate the "civil effects" of marriage.[25]

The US census of 1880 counted 50.1 million people in the country. In that same year, John Philip Sousa became director of the US Marine Corps Band. On New York's Broadway, the city installed electric lights for the first time. The glow on the street earned it the nickname "the Great White Way." The US Congress introduced a women's suffrage amendment in 1878. It was debated for forty years before the amendment finally passed in 1919, with the words unchanged. In 1880, women still didn't have the right to vote.

Joseph Charles: Growing Up and Occupation

Joseph's mother, Amanda, died on July 2, 1891, when he was not quite eleven years old. Joe went to school and could read, write, and speak the English language. The 1890 US Census has him at home, living with his father, mother, and his siblings, except for his sister Marie Antoinette, who at sixteen was already in a Catholic convent. Marie Antoinette would become a catholic num in the order of the Sisters of the Immaculate Conception.

Joseph's occupation at age nineteen was a harness-maker, according to the census. A horse harness-maker's job was to build and repair a wide variety of harnesses, saddles, and other horse-related products. A number of job skills are needed, including the following:

- stitching and cutting heavy leather by hand using a knife, needle, and thread or with a stitching machine
- designing or reading specifications
- having a working understanding of horse anatomy
- fixing or replacing broken leather parts and trim

---

[25] "Marriage: Unique for a Reason," United States Conference of Catholic Bishops, http://www.marriageuniqueforareason.org/tag/pope-leo-xiii/.

- dyeing and burnishing leather edges
- stamping decorative designs into the surface of leather
- dressing leather to produce a glossy finish
- basic carpentry skills
- talking with customers

To become a horse harness-maker, Joseph had to complete school and an apprenticeship of many hours. Harness-makers should have good hand strength to be effective.[26]

The town of Napoleonville is the government seat of Assumption Parish, Louisiana. The population of Napoleonville was probably about six hundred in 1900. As early as 1807, the city that later became Napoleonville was known as Canal. This canal or waterway extended west-southwest from Napoleonville to Lake Verret. Napoleonville was given its name by one of Napoleon Bonaparte's soldiers. The soldier is not buried in Napoleonville but about ten miles away in Plattenville. He lies in the Cemetery of Our Lady of the Assumption Catholic Church.

The French and Spanish settled the first permanent communities in this region of Louisiana by the middle of the eighteenth century along Bayou Lafourche. From 1755 to 1764, the population increased with immigrants from Acadia, by way of France. They entered the area and started to clear the land. The town was officially incorporated on March 11, 1878.[27] Assumption's history is associated with its waterways and its fertile soils, which are ideal for farming.

Louisiana's Economy

Louisiana's economy began to diversify significantly in the late 1800s. When sugar and cotton became profitable in the nineteenth century, planters purchased small holdings to build more extensive plantations. Land in Louisiana consisted of properties ranging from large sugar plantations to small vegetable farms. In between were cotton and some tobacco plantations, livestock ranches, and grain

---

[26] "What Does a Horse Harness Maker (219D) Do?" Apprentice search.com, https://www.apprenticesearch.com/trades/horse-harness-maker-219d.

[27] "Napoleonville, Louisiana," *Wikipedia*, https://en.wikipedia.org/wiki/Napoleonville,_Louisiana.

farms. Many Louisiana people were small subsistence farmers who produced only enough for what they needed.

When we think of the pre-Civil War South, we picture large mansions with slave cabins. Louisiana had many of these self-sufficient plantations, but only a few were as large as in the movies. Slaves produced most of the plantation's needs. Smaller farms usually had no slaves or maybe one who served as a laborer or blacksmith. Most large plantation estates also had one field for growing corn. Corn was the diet for both slaves and farm animals.

Although Louisiana at this time relied on the growing of sugarcane and the production of sugar, the timber industry began to become a factor. Wood products supplemented the state's economy throughout the nineteenth and twentieth centuries. The discovery of abundant oil and gas fields also helped this development. The conservative politicians refused to tax these industries heavily. This protection for business and industry spurred the rise of the left-wing Huey Long, whose slogan was "every man a king."

In New Orleans in the early part of the twentieth century, the French character was still dominant. A 1902 report said that "one-fourth of the population of the city speaks French in ordinary daily intercourse, while another one half can understand the language perfectly."[28] As late as 1945, one still encountered older women who spoke little or no English.[29] The last major French-language newspaper in New Orleans, *L'Abeille de la Nouvelle-Orléans*, ceased publication on December 27, 1923, after ninety-six years.[30]

In 1905, yellow fever spread in the city, which had suffered under repeated epidemics of the disease in the nineteenth century. Understanding that mosquitoes spread the disease, the city embarked on a massive campaign to drain all standing water, the breeding ground for mosquitoes. An effort to educate the public on its vital role in preventing mosquitoes was started. The effort was successful, and the disease subsided without ever reaching epidemic proportions.

President Theodore Roosevelt visited the city to demonstrate that New

---

[28] Scott S. Ellis, *Madame Vieux Carré: the French Quarter in the Twentieth Century* (University of Mississippi, 2010), 8, ISBN 978-1-60473-358-7.

[29] Robert Tallant and Lyle Saxon Gumbo, *Ya-Ya: Folk Tales of Louisiana* (Louisiana Library Commission, 1945), 178.

[30] Carl A. Brasseaux, *French, Cajun, Creole, Houma: A Primer on Francophone Louisiana* (Baton Rouge: Louisiana State University Press, 2005), 32, ISBN 0-8071-3036-2.

Orleans was safe to visit. New Orleans mosquito control came into being in the early 1960s. This activity prevented any new cases of yellow fever since that time.

The harness shop was a thriving business from the turn of the century to about 1920. Joseph C. Bourg was the operator of the one in Napoleonville. Because customers usually had little money, harness-makers catered to the more affluent customers. A custom-made harness could cost a month's wages and take thirty hours to make. However, it would last up to thirty years. Harness-makers made and repaired other leather goods, such as couch cushions, porch awnings, and saddles. Becoming a good harness- or saddle-maker took a long time.

Joseph married Lucy Marie Talbot on April 9, 1912 (more about Lucy in chapter 4). Lucy was twenty-four years old when they married, and Joseph was almost thirty-two. That was a little old to be getting married in 1912 for both a man and a woman. Lucy was a good wife and obedient to her husband. She was, however, the demanding master of the home. Joseph and Lucy had three children: James Anatole, Oscar Joseph, and Lucille Marie (more about them under Generation 1 in this chapter).

Changes in America

Society needed security for the poor and elderly as a result of the Great Depression. The Social Security Act of 1935 was signed into law by President Franklin D. Roosevelt. It created a federal safety net to allow elderly unemployed and disadvantaged Americans a living wage.

The main point of Social Security was to pay financial benefits to retirees over the age of sixty-five based on their lifetime wage contributions. Millions of people have received financial help because of the Social Security Act since its inception. Still, the program had many challenges from its beginning. It has been a political bone of contention for many years, and politics constantly threatens its existence.

Economic security was always an issue in a world where opportunity is unequally distributed and with a growing population. The old and disadvantaged, however, had mostly relied on charity from the wealthy or family and friends. In the early seventeenth century, "poor laws" were used in England to help its less-fortunate people. These were imported to America by the Pilgrims.

Eventually, colonial governments created new systems to care for the poor. Determining who was worthy or eligible for assistance was always the challenge.

By the middle of the nineteenth century, conditions in poorhouses were often deplorable and crowded because of worsening economic conditions. Governments found it difficult to keep up with the costs.

Four changes beginning in the late nineteenth century helped to kill the economic security policies of the time: the Industrial Revolution, America's urbanization, the vanishing extended family, and longer life expectancy. Before the Industrial Revolution, many people were farmers and managed to support themselves during hard times, and the extended family often lived together on family farms or urban compounds. They cared for one another as they got older or struggled.

The Industrial Revolution, however, influenced people to move to cities in large numbers for jobs. Layoffs often threatened these jobs during a recession. Many did not have a way to support themselves and no family to fall back on if they lost their job. The urbanization of America also caused many people to live their lives fending for themselves. As sanitary and living conditions improved, the life expectancy of its citizens grew longer as well. As more people grew older, many were unable to work or became sick, requiring care and support.

The Great Depression caused millions of people to become unemployed. They struggled to feed themselves. It was especially hard on old people. Many states passed laws to protect their elderly citizens. Most of these assistance programs were dismal failures, however. They were underfunded and poorly supported. Those who did receive aid only received about sixty-five cents a day (twenty dollars a day in 2019 currency). As the Depression went on, government officials and private citizens alike tried to find ways to help struggling Americans. Most ideas were federal- or state-financed pension plans.

Most assistance plans in the country required funding from the government, charities, or private citizens. President Roosevelt, however, took a page from Europe's security playbook. He pushed for a program where people contributed to their financial future by taking a portion of their income through payroll tax deductions. The current working generation paid into the program and financed the retired generation's payments.

In June of 1934, President Roosevelt created the Committee on Economic Security (CES). Their task was to develop a bill to provide social security. Frances Perkins, the first woman to hold a cabinet post as Secretary of Labor, led the committee that drafted the Social Security Act. The act was geared toward giving people economic security all through their lives. The bill included an old-age pension program, unemployment insurance funded by employers, health insurance for people in financial distress, and financial assistance for widows with children and disabled individuals. Congress passed the Social Security Act on August 14, 1935, and Roosevelt signed it into law. The act firmly placed the burden of economic security for American citizens on the federal government's shoulders.[31]

Joseph Charles: Later Life

By 1936, Joseph was fifty-six years old, and his health was failing due to his type 2 diabetes. He had one of his eyes surgically removed because of poor circulation caused by the disease. He couldn't do his harness-making job. His health, along with the failing harness business, caused him to take a job at the Godchaux sugar refinery in 1937.

At this time, his older son, Jim, was twenty-four; younger son, Oscar, was sixteen; and daughter, Lucille, was twelve. Jim moved to New Orleans so he could get a job and help support the family. Because Joseph was no longer self-employed, he was required to register for the new Social Security Act. He did this on April 22, 1937.[32]

As of the 1940 census, Joseph was living in Napoleonville, but he moved to New Orleans in 1941.[33] There is uncertainty as to the reason for this move. It could be because of his health and eye operation or because Jim was living in New Orleans. However, Joseph and his wife, Lucy, lived at 927 Third Street until 1949, when they moved back to their home in Napoleonville. At the same time, their son Jim and his family moved to 927 Third Street.

Joseph and Lucy lived in Napoleonville for the next thirteen years. In the tradition of his Cajun ancestors, Joseph started a truck farm garden in the field created by the filled-in canal in front of his house. He grew all sorts of vegetables in the garden: corn, okra, string beans, butter beans, tomatoes, squash, and eggplant. His sons would cut the grass on the weekends during day trips from

---

[31]History.com Editors, "Social Security Act," History.com, https://www.history.com/topics/great-depression/social-security-act

[32]"Social Security Act," *Wikipedia*, https://en.wikipedia.org/wiki/Social_Security_Act.

[33]Draft registration card for Oscar Joseph Bourg has him living at 927 Third Street with his parents.

New Orleans. His grandkids would visit during the summer and spend time with their grandparents.

James A. Bourg Jr. remembers Grandpa waking at four in the morning and listening to the farm report on WWL radio. He would be in the garden at first light, picking the ripe produce. Joe would sell these to the local grocery stores in barter for some of his other grocery needs. He and Lucy would be in bed as soon as it grew dark. Electric lights, although present, were hardly ever used in their house. (There was an implication, however, that Joseph would visit the local taverns in the evening, where he would drink and play cards.)

Joseph died on August 7, 1962, in Napoleonville at the age of 81. His funeral was from Napoleonville's St. Ann Church and burial was in Saint Anne Catholic Cemetery.

The Siblings of Joseph Charles Bourg

Joseph C. Bourg had the following six siblings:

- Marie Antoinette Bourg was born on May 31, 1875, in Napoleonville, Louisiana.[34] She became a Catholic nun, Sister Mary Beatrix.
- Anna Louisa Bourg was born on June 1, 1877, in Napoleonville, and baptized in St. Ann Church.[35] Anna died on May 15, 1966.
- Agnes Seraphine Bourg was born on September 12, 1878, in Labadieville, Louisiana, and baptized in St. Philomena Church.[36] She married Phillip L. Giroir and had one son and two daughters with Phillip; Phillip L. Giroir Jr. (1905-1967), Evy May Giroir (1906-1983), and Maxine Giroir (1909-1998).

---

[34] Church records, St. Ann's, from Diocese of Baton Rouge church Records, vol. 13, 86: Marie Antoinette Bourg (Oscar Bourg and Amanda Junot) bn. 31 May 1875, bt. 6 July 1875 spouse Auguste Boudreaux and Marie Junot (SAN - 1,18).

[35] Baptismal records, Diocese of Baton Rouge church records, vol. 14, 90: Anna Louisa Bourg (Oscar Bourg and Amanda Junot) bn. 1 June 1877 bt. 6 June 1877, spouse Oniere Junot and Celestine Boudreau (SAN, 1 - 45).

[36] Baptismal records, Diocese of Baton Rouge church records, vol 14, 90: Agnes Seraphine Bourg (Oscar Bourg and Amanda Junot) bn. 12 Sept 1878 bt. 27 Dec 1878 sponsor Leonce Junor and Lidia Davis (SPH-9,82).

- Albert Louis Bourg was born on February 15, 1883 (1883-1935), in Labideville, Louisiana.[37] He died on June 3,1935.[38] He married Anna C. Boudreaux. They had four children together; Verna B. Bourg (1905-), Louis A. Bourg (1907-), armen W. Bourg Duffy (1909 – 1993), and Camelia W. Bourg (1910-).
- Julia Bourg was born on May 15, 1885, in Labadieville. She married George Parenton in New Orleans. Their son, Clifford Marks, was married to Mary Young (the author's aunt).
- Oscar P. Bourg Jr. was born on October 12, 1888, in Labadieville, Louisiana. He died on February 16, 1961, in New Orleans.[39]

Generation 3: Oscar P. Bourg

Joseph Charles Bourg's father was Oscar P. Bourg. His mother was Amanda Marie Melvina Juneau (Junot). Oscar was born on Tuesday, April 9, 1850, in Labadieville, Louisiana. He died on September 13, 1912, in Thibodeaux, Louisiana. Amanda was born on September 25, 1855, in Labadieville, Louisiana, and died there on July 2, 1891.

The Siblings of Oscar P. Bourg

Oscar was the third child and son of François Marcellus Bourg (1821–1853) and Marie Elise Boudreaux (1829–1857). Oscar had the following siblings:

- Wilfred François Bourg was born on June 8, 1847. Wilfred married Cecile Hebert on August 20, 1877, in Plattenville in the Assumption of the Blessed Virgin Mary Catholic Church. Cecile was the daughter of Felix Hebert and Zephire Charlet. Wilfred's date of death is unknown.
- Thomasile Alfred Bourg was born on January 25, 1849, in Labadieville. He married Louisiane Hebert, daughter of Valerie Hebert and Aselie Prejean, on July 1, 1871, in St. Philomena Church, Labadieville, Louisiana. Thomasile died on May 26, 1898.
- Marie Philomene Bourg was born on April 18, 1852, in Labadieville.

---

[37] Reference source: gravestone, St. Philomina Cemetary.

[38] Burial: St. Philomena Cemetery, Labadieville, La. gravestone.

[39] *Times-Picayune*, February 17, 1961, C5, 2.

- Twins Azema Philomene Bourg and Marie Pamela Bourg were born on February 5, 1854, in Labadieville, four months after their father's death.

The 1850s

The 1850 census indicates there were only thirty states in the United States at the time. The California Gold Rush of 1849 (actually 1848 to1855) began on January 24, 1848, James W. Marshall found gold at Sutter's Mill, California. The news of finding gold brought 300,000 people to California very quickly. These people came from all over. The rapid influx of immigration and gold into the US money supply reinvigorated the American economy, making California an essential piece of property.

Only a few struck it rich, however, and many returned home disappointed. Many appreciated the other economic opportunities in California, however, especially in agriculture, and brought their families to join them. California became the thirty-first US state in 1850 and played a small role in the American Civil War. Chinese immigrants to California increasingly came under attack from whites, and they were forced into Chinatowns.

California started to become a highly productive agricultural society. The railroads, beginning in 1869, connected its vibrant economy with the rest of the United States. This economic growth attracted a steady stream of migrants. By the late nineteenth century, the population of Southern California, especially Los Angeles, started to snowball.

California was one of the few American states, outside of the thirteen original colonies, to go directly to statehood without first becoming a territory. All this happened as a result of the Compromise of 1850. Although it had only been a part of the United States for less than two years, on September 9, 1850, California became the thirty-first state.

Many great ideas were emerging in the United States in the 1850s. Ice was beginning to be made by refrigeration. The women's rights movement became an issue. The common belief at the time was that women belonged in the home (cooking, cleaning, doing housework, taking care of children, etc.) and did not have the same status as men. The less fortunate women worked in factories. Women could not vote at this time in history. Married women could not own property or write a will.

In many cases, women could not keep the money they earned but had to return it to their husbands or fathers. The Women's Reform Movement was just getting started. There were parades, boycotts, meetings, public talks, petitions, pamphlets, and books. The movement was very, very disorganized.

On August 23, 1850, the first US National Women's Rights Convention convened in Worcester, Massachusetts. New Orleans was a conservative Southern city; the woman's reform movement did not get any traction in New Orleans until the middle of the twentieth century. The social justice and protest movements percolated across the country in the 1960s as feminists sought liberation and equal rights for women in New Orleans and Louisiana.

Slavery

But by far, the biggest issue in the United States in 1850 when Oscar was born was slavery. The writers of the US Constitution avoided dealing with slavery when they drafted the document in 1777. No compromise between the North and the South was forthcoming at that time. The issue threatened to destroy the formation of a constitution and its ratification in 1788.

The founders considered slavery "a necessary evil." White people of that time feared that the emancipation of black slaves would have more harmful social and economic effects than the continuation of slavery. Whites did not want freed slaves living in the same community as them, and there was no place to move emancipated blacks. In 1820, Thomas Jefferson penned in a letter saying, "with slavery, we have the wolf by the ear, and we can neither hold him nor safely let him go. Justice is on one side of the scale, and self-preservation on the other."

By 1850, slavery was a problem that could no longer be avoided. With new states being admitted, the issue of whether slavery would be allowed in these states had to be resolved. On January 29, 1850, Whig senator and orator Henry Clay introduced a compromise bill on slavery to the US Senate. It was drafted by Henry Clay of Kentucky and Democratic Senator Stephen Douglas of Illinois.

The Missouri Compromise of 1850 was a package of five separate bills passed by the United States Congress in September of 1850. The compromise dealt with the confrontation about the status of territories acquired during the Mexican–American War (1846–1848). After the war, the question of whether to allow slavery in those territories obtained from Mexico caused a bitter sectional conflict. Texas attracted interest from both pro-slavery and anti-slavery camps on a national scale because of its size. Texas claimed territory north of the 36°30' demarcation line for slavery. This set up the 1820 Missouri Compromise.

The compromise was greeted with relief, but each side disliked some of its specific provisions. The territorial results were as follows:

- California was admitted as a free state.
- Texas surrendered its claim to New Mexico as well as its claims north of 36°30'. Texas kept the Panhandle, and the federal government took over the state's public debt. Slavery was allowed in the new Texas.
- New Mexico became the New Mexico Territory. The South prevented the adoption of the Wilmot Proviso. That would outlaw slavery in the new territories, and the new Utah Territory and New Mexico Territory were allowed, under popular sovereignty, to decide whether to allow slavery in their borders. In truth, the land was unsuited for extensive plantation agriculture. Because they did not need slaves, the people there were not interested in the concept of slavery.
- The buying of slaves was banned in the District of Columbia, but not slavery altogether. The compromise enacted a more stringent Fugitive Slave Law.

The compromise only became possible after the sudden death of President Zachary Taylor, who, although a slave owner, wanted to exclude slavery from the Southwest. Henry Clay had designed a compromise which failed to pass in early 1850 because of opposition by both pro-slavery Southern Democrats, led by Calhoun, and anti-slavery Northern Whigs. Upon Clay's instruction, Douglas then divided Clay's bill into several smaller pieces. He narrowly won their passage over the opposition of radicals on both sides. It settled some of the issues of slavery, but at this point in history, the Civil War was inevitable.

History of Slavery in Louisiana and New Orleans

The French introduced African slavery to the Louisiana Territory and New Orleans in 1710. They did this by capturing several slaves after the War of the Spanish Succession. Trying to develop the new region, the French transported more than two thousand Africans to New Orleans between 1717 and 1721 on at least eight ships. When Alejandro O'Reilly took over in 1768, he banned the trade of Native American slaves on December 7, 1769, but there was no movement to abolish the slave trade.

Under Spanish control, a new law was introduced called *coartación*. This law allowed slaves to buy their freedom and that of other slaves. The demand for slaves increased in Louisiana after the invention of the cotton gin (1793) and the Louisiana Purchase (1803). Although sugarcane continued to be the predominant crop in southern Louisiana—because of the alluvial soil, sugar was the state's prime export during this time—the cotton gin allowed the processing of short-staple cotton in the upland areas.

The United States banned the importation of slaves for a short time (1807–1808), and a brisk domestic slave trade developed within the country. Slaveholders sold thousands of black slaves in the upper South to buyers in the Deep South. In 1811, a slave revolt occurred about thirty miles outside of New Orleans. Slaves rebelled against the brutal practices of sugar plantations.

There had been a sizable influx of French refugee planters from the former French colony of Saint-Domingue following the Haitian Revolution (1791–1804). These French planters brought slaves with them. Their practices were very harsh and caused the revolt. This uprising was called the German Coast Uprising. It ended with white militias and soldiers hunting down black slaves and publicly executing them.

Slavery was officially abolished by the Louisiana State Constitution of 1864, during the American Civil War. Louisiana's French Code Noir and, later, its Spanish equivalent, the Código Negro, gave slaves rights that were different from those in the rest of the south. Louisiana slaves were protected from cruel punishment or torture. They had the right to marry, and married couples and their children could not be separated. The code required owners to instruct slaves in the Catholic faith, implying that Africans were human beings endowed with a soul. Slaves as humans was an idea that had not been put forth until that time.

The Code Noir was a more permeable historic French system involving free people of color, often born to white fathers. According to the 1830 census, there was a higher percentage of free African Americans in Louisiana than elsewhere (13.2 percent in Louisiana compared to 0.8 percent in Mississippi). The free black people were, on average, exceptionally literate. A significant number of them owned property and even slaves.

When the United States purchased Louisiana, Catholic social norms were deeply rooted in the territory. Catholic social beliefs were in contrast with predominantly Protestant parts of the young nation, where English churches prevailed.

Oscar P. Bourg's Life and Death

Marie Elise Boudreaux Bourg was thirty years old when she had Oscar. She had just turned seventeen when she married François and had been married thirteen years when Oscar was born in Labadieville, Louisiana.

Oscar learned to be a carpenter, carriage-trimmer, and harness-maker and was employed for years as a carriage-trimmer in the establishment of Mr. E. P. Lefort. Lefort operated the livery stable in Thibodeaux. A carriage trimmer worked on all kinds of wagons and carriages, including railroad carriages. The job required upholstery work, leatherwork, and carpentry.

Oscar moved from Labadieville to Thibodeaux when he was quite young. The US Civil War took place when he was only eleven years old. He was too young to be a soldier. His older brothers were probably also too young to be involved in the conflict.

After the war was over, Oscar married Amanda Marie Melvina Juneau (Junot) on June 11, 1874, in Napoleonville, Louisiana, at the age of twenty-four. Amanda was the daughter of Pierre Theodulle Junot. Pierre was born on February 4, 1832, and died on February 28, 1921. Her mother was Antionette Azelina Boudreaux (1837–1916). Amanda Marie was born on September 25, 1855, in Labadieville and died there on July 2, 1891.

Oscar and Amanda had seven children together. They are listed as the siblings of Joseph Charles Bourg above. Oscar lived a quiet life. He passed away in the late summer of 1912 when he was sixty-two years old. His obituary read as follows:

Mr. Oscar Bourg—A sad and untimely death Sunday night was that of Mr. Oscar Bourg, a quiet and unpretentious citizen of this town (Thibodeaux). Death was rendered all the sadder and reminded all that even in life, we are in the midst of death, for the reason that it occurred at the fair given in this town for the benefit of the Thibodeaux College. Mr. Bourg was mingling with the crowd, and it is reported that he had just left the restaurant, where he enjoyed a repast and was walking on the grounds when he was overcome with faintness and asked for a chair. Being seated near one of the booths, medical aid was summoned and Dr. Seigle, being the closest physician on the grounds to relieve him, while Father

Hubert gave absolution. He was unconscious, beyond medical aid, and passed away like a flash of lightning.

The death necessarily caused a stir and cast a gloom over the fair. Rev. Father Barbier ordered the music discontinued, and the festival practically ended for the evening. Death was thought to be caused by heart trouble or acute indigestion. The deceased was immediately taken to his home, a short distance away. His remains were conveyed to Labadieville Monday afternoon, where internment was conducted at the Catholic Cemetery after services at the St. Philomena Catholic Church.

Seven children survive the deceased, four daughters Mrs. William Weber of New Orleans, Mrs. Phillip Giroir of Labadieville, Antoinette Bourg, a nun in the convent at Labidieville, Julia (Mrs. Julia Parenton, and three sons, Messers Joseph Bourg of Napoleonville, Albert and Sidney Bourg of this town, besides several grandchildren and other relatives. He had been employed for years as a carriage trimmer in the establishment of Mr. E. P. Lefort, operated in connection with the livery stable.

Bourg Generation 4: François Marcellus Bourg

The parents of Oscar P. Bourg were François Marcellus Bourg (1821–1853) and Marie Elise Boudreaux (1829–1857). François was born on August 3, 1821 in Thibodaux, Lafourche Parish, Louisiana. There is not too much information about him and little gleaned from the genealogical records. We know he married Marie Elise Boudreaux in a Thibodeaux church on June 29, 1846. Marie was born on September 8, 1829, in Thibodaux.

François was the son of Marin François Bourg (1792–1835) and Elisabeth Marcelline Jolibois (?–1876). Marie Elise Boudreaux was the daughter of Anselm Boudreaux and Marie Gautreaux. François and Marie had six children together before his death on October 8, 1853, in Labadieville. The children were listed above as the siblings of Oscar P. Bourg. François died on October 8, 1853, in Labadieville. His wife, Marie Elise Boudreaux, died on May 25, 1857.

The First Quarter of the Nineteenth Century

When François was born on a warm midsummer Friday, the United States had just twenty-three states, and James Monroe was the president. The states of

Alabama, Mississippi, Illinois, Indiana, Louisiana, and Maine had only recently been added. The country also had the following territories: the Arkansas Territory, the Michigan Territory, and the Missouri Territory. According to the 1820 US Census, the total population of the country was determined to be approximately 10 million citizens, with 1.6 million (16 percent) being slaves.[40] New Orleans was the biggest city in the South, with a population of 27,176.

President James Monroe

President James Monroe was born on April 28, 1758, and died on July 4, 1831. He was an American statesman and Founding Father who served as the fifth president of the United States. He served two terms, from 1817 to 1825. Monroe's presidency was called an "Era of Good Feelings."

Monroe was born in Virginia, fought in the American Revolutionary War, and was wounded in the Battle of Trenton. After studying law under Jefferson from 1780 to 1783, he served as a delegate to the Continental Congress.[41]

The Federalists argued that the Constitution would create a new federal government that was more powerful than the state governments. As an anti-Federalist, Monroe did not want a strong national government but powerful state governments. Anti-Federalists saw two large holes in the limitation on federal power: the Necessary and Proper Clause and a Supreme Court to interpret the Constitution. Congress could interfere with the rights of the states if it were necessary and proper. The Supreme Court could interpret the Constitution and limit federal power in a comprehensive way. History proved these anti-Federalists were correct in some respects.[42]

Concerned that the Constitution provided for no guarantee of individual rights and liberties, the anti-Federalists pressed for amendments, which became the Bill of Rights. James Madison wrote them in 1791.

The Federalist Party was in such disarray that Monroe was easily elected president in 1816, winning over 80 percent of the electoral vote. As president, he eased partisan tensions and took a tour of the country. With the signing of the

---

[40] Henry Louis Gates Jr., "Slavery, by the Numbers," *The Root* (February 10, 2014), https://www.theroot.com/slavery-by-the-numbers-1790874492.

[41] "The Presidents: James Monroe," Caroll Bryant's blog, https://carrollbryant.blogspot.com/2013/02/the-presidents-james-monroe.html.

[42] "Anti-Federalists," *Conservapedia*, https://www.conservapedia.com/Anti-Federalists.

Treaty of 1818, negotiated by Secretary of State John Quincy Adams, the country now extended from ocean to ocean.

The United States owned the Oregon Territory jointly with Britain. It was America's first attempt at creating an "American empire." As nationalism increased, partisan fighting subsided. This swell of partisan feelings ended when the Panic of 1819 struck, and a fight over the admission of Missouri angered the country in 1820. Nonetheless, Monroe won near-unanimous reelection.[43] In 1823, Monroe announced the Monroe Doctrine, which became a landmark in American foreign policy. This doctrine set the country's opposition to any European intervention into the Western Hemisphere.

Monroe's presidency ended the first period of American history before the beginning of Jacksonian democracy and the Second Party System era. Following his retirement in 1825, financial difficulties plagued Monroe. He died in New York City on July 4, 1831. He is ranked historically as an above-average president.[44]

A Time of Innovation

From 1800 to 1825, the world of science and mathematics was rapidly progressing:

- In 1805, John Dalton proposed the Atomic Theory (chemistry).
- In 1820, Hans Christian Ørsted established a deep relationship between electricity and magnetism (electromagnetism).
- In 1821, Thomas Johann Seebeck was the first to observe a property of semiconductors.
- In 1824 Carnot described the idealized heat engine.
- In 1827, Georg Ohm proposed the electrical relationship known as Ohm's law.
- In1827, Amedeo Avogadro introduced a gas law identified today as Avogadro's law.
- In 1830, Nikolai Lobachevsky created non-Euclidean geometry.
- In 1831, Michael Faraday discovered electromagnetic induction.
- In 1838, Matthias Schleiden proved that all plants consist of cells.

---

[43] "James Monroe, 5th President of the USA," *Geni,* https://www.geni.com/people/James-Monroe 5th president of the USA /4239120304610034677.

[44] "James Monroe," *Wikipedia*, https://en.wikipedia.org/wiki/James_Monroe.

Several inventions led to a second Industrial Revolution (1865–1900). These were useable electricity, steel, and petroleum products. All this stimulated the growth of railways and steamships, faster and broader means of communication, and inventions with names we all know today.

In 1804, a Frenchman, Joseph Marie Jacquard, invented the Jacquard loom. The power loom simplified the process of manufacturing textiles and allowed such intricate patterns as brocade, damask, and matelassé. Also in 1800, Alessandro Giuseppe Antonio Anastasio Volta—an Italian physicist, chemist, and pioneer of electricity and power—invented the electrical battery and discovered methane. He proved the chemical generation of electricity.

In 1804, Freidrich Winzer (Winsor) was the first person to patent gaslights. Richard Trevithick, an English mining engineer, developed the first steam-powered locomotive. Unfortunately, the machine was so heavy that it broke the very rails it was traveling on.

In 1809, Humphry Davy invented the first electric arc lamp. In 1810, a German, Frederick Koenig, invented an improved printing press, and Peter Durand invented the tin can. In 1814, Joseph Nicéphore Niépce took the first photograph. One picture took eight hours.

The Territory of Orleans and the History of Louisiana

In 1803, Louisiana and New Orleans became the property of the United States. The Louisiana Purchase brought in a new wave of English, Irish, and Italian settlers. Acadians adopted some of their customs. They became known as Cajuns. But there were no mass migration into and within the state. The Acadians settled into their new home in Louisiana. Cajuns didn't change very much over the century. The Cajuns, however, did adapt to and assimilate parts of the culture.

The nineteenth century saw the Acadian lifestyle slowly evolve. Some ended the century in much the same way as their grandparents entered it. But some, especially those who established larger farms and ranches and those who lived in cities, changed more rapidly. At the beginning of the nineteenth century, just about every Acadian spoke French, worked with livestock and crops, and was a Catholic. By the end of the century, most Cajuns still maintained those three ways of life. But others became Protestant, would speak English in their business and perhaps in the home, and worked in a variety of occupations.[45]

Their time in Acadia had seen numerous changes of national ownership to the region. Since they came to Louisiana, Spain had governed Louisiana. The Louisiana Purchase marked the last time that the ruling authorities.

Jefferson sent representatives to Napoleon to pursue purchasing Louisiana and the Isle of Orleans. The purchase would allow the United States the unfettered ability to allow ships up and down the Mississippi River. When Napoleon lost control of Santo Domingo, he no longer needed Louisiana. All of Louisiana was offered to the United States for fifteen million dollars. The change was rapid. In a matter of weeks, Louisiana transferred from Spain to France and from France to the United States.

The Louisiana Purchase opened immigration to people of all nationalities. Immigrants moved in and acquired land, and Louisiana became a state in 1812. Gradually, these immigrants migrated across Louisiana. Many of them came for financial reasons. Since the settlers had already taken all of the land fronting the Mississippi River, the new arrivals often had to start on swampy or wooded back property. They soon began buying out neighbors to grow their holdings. Since the Mississippi River offered the most accessibility to transportation and commerce, it was the first area invaded by the new settlers.

At first, the century saw plantation land develop. The decision to move inland away from the river came from the Acadians, who profited from this. By selling their land along the Mississippi, Acadians made a lot of money. The river property was the most fertile and brought a reasonable price. The Acadians hated debt. By selling, they found a way to pay off their creditors and have some left over. They could move to the bayous for less cost or even for free.

In some cases, they sold their land for more than it was worth. Successful small-scale living was not a good example for the slaves to see, and plantation owners were happy to be rid of their Acadian neighbors. H. M. Brackenridge wrote in 1814 in "Views of Louisiana" that the value of land in Louisiana had increased in price. The rise was because of the demand for sugar plantations. Large plantations also brought a dramatic rise in the slave population of Louisiana. In the first quarter-century, the number of slaves increased several times over.

---

[45] "Cajuns in the 19th Century," Acadian-Cajun Genealogy and History, www.acadian-cajun.com/hiscaj3.htm.

Generation 5: Marin François Bourg

Marin François Bourg (1792–1835) was born on a spring day, Monday, April 16, 1792, in Pointe Coupee Parish, northwest of Baton Rouge. His father, Joseph Pierre Bourg (1765–1826), was born on June 27, 1765, in Côtes-du-Nord, Plouër, Saint-Malo, France. His mother, Marie Magdelaine Jeanne Aucoin, was born on August 23, 1774, in Côtes-du-Nord, Nord-Pas-de-Calais, France. Marin was born seven years after Joseph arrived in New Orleans and two years after he married Marie Jeanne in Pointe Coupee, where the Bourg family moved after they came to Louisiana in 1785.

Marin was the oldest of eight siblings: one other boy and six girls. We know very little about his youth, his education, or the work he was trained to do. Being an Acadian, he was probably a farmer, and it is suspected that his father taught him in the way of Acadian life. His father, Joseph Pierre, was of Acadian (Cajun) ancestry but was born after the great Acadian expulsion in 1758. Joseph Pierre came to Louisiana with his family when he was twenty years old in 1785.

The Bourgs Settle in Acadiana

Acadiana (or l'Acadiane) was the official name given to the French Louisiana region that was historically home to the state's Acadian population. Many residents of this region are of Acadian descent and now identified as Cajun.[46] Of the sixty-four parishes in Louisiana, twenty-two named civil parishes with a similar cultural composition make up this intrastate region.[47] In 1971, the state legislature officially recognized twenty-two Louisiana parishes as "other parishes of the similar cultural environment" for their "strong French Acadian cultural aspects" and made "the Heart of Acadiana" the official name of the region. The residents, however, prefers the name Acadiana.[48]

French European Americans organized Pointe Coupee Parish in 1805 as part of the Territory of Orleans. It was one of the original twelve counties of the

---

[46] "What Is Cajun—Explore Lafayette, Louisiana," Lafayette Louisiana, https://www.lafayettetravel.com/explore/what-is-cajun/.

[47] "The Cajun Kingdom of the Bayou," *New York Times* (January 27, 1991).

[48] Shane K. Bernard, *The Cajuns: Americanization of a People* (Jackson: University Press of Mississippi, 2003), 80.

Territory of Orleans. The original Pointe Coupee Parish included parts of present-day Iberville and West Baton Rouge Parishes.

The French Revolution was felt in Louisiana. When Louis XVI was executed, Spain declared war on France. Rumors of rebellion started up in Louisiana, so the Spanish governor, Carondelet, ruled that citizens couldn't read or discuss the French Revolution. If they did, they were subject to a fine or imprisonment. He forced seventy people to leave Louisiana and sent six leaders to prison. He built boats to patrol the river. Carondelet encouraged French citizens to come to Louisiana, hoping the horror stories they brought would discourage sympathizers in the colony.[49]

The Acadians, at this point, were staying out of the French Revolution. Although their heritage was French, that country hadn't supported them during the exile period. Spain had given them a place to make a New Acadia. The evidence shows that the Acadians did not take part in any French Revolutionary activities.[50]

In the 1780s, people moved farther down the bayous. The government had restricted most movement since the 1760s, but they were running out of room. Once a father died, his male descendants divided his land between them. After two generations, the property for a descendant's family became a narrow strip. The descendants looked for available land along the more remote bayous of Louisiana. This land migration increased throughout the 1790s. Settlement communities were becoming more common in lower Lafourche and along smaller bayous of the area. Four families, including the Bourgs, settled along the Attakapas Canal between 1793 and 1803.[51]

The Bourg family settled above Baton Rouge at Bayou des Ecores. In August of 1794, when Marin François was just over two years old, a hurricane destroyed the crops, animals, and fences of this settlement. The family moved down to Bayou Lafourche to live, joining family and friends. Land was still available in central and lower Lafourche Parish.[52]

In 1795, Jean Étienne Boré developed a process of refining sugar by boiling cane juice until it reached the saturation point. Up to this time, cotton was the

---

[49] Sue Eakin and Manie Culbertson, *Louisiana: The Land and Its People*, 159-160.

[50] "Cajuns in the 18th Century," Acadian-Cajun Genealogy and History, http://www.acadian-cajun.com/hiscaj2d.htm.

[51] "Cajuns in the 18th Century."

[52] PPC, 209:356, Anselme Blanchard to Carondelet.

major crop in the territory. The final years of the 1700s resulted in sugar becoming the main crop.

Although Marin François was born in Pointe Coupee and lived there until he was two, his family was now residing along Bayou Lafourche near Thibodaux. He started to court a girl from Plattenville, Elisabeth Marcelline Jolibois. She and Marin were married on June 29, 1846.

Elisabeth's father, Phillipe Jolibois, was born in Montréal, Quebec, in 1768. After immigrating to Louisiana, he married Marie Louise Charpentier on January 14, 1793, in St James, Louisiana, and moved to Plattenville. They had the following children:

- Marie Françoise Jolibois was born on April 1, 1793, in Plattenville, Assumption, Louisiana, and died in 1853.
- Philippe Gregoire Jolibois was born on May 27, 1795, in Assumption, and died in 1816.
- Elisabeth Marcelline Jolibois was born in 1799 in Plattenville, and died on May 10, 1833 in Plattenville.[53]
- Barthelmy Jolibois was born on July 28, 1799, in Assumption, and died in 1844.
- Joseph Jolibois was born on June 13, 1801, in New Orleans.
- Cyprien Joseph Jolibois was born on October 21, 1803, in Plattenville, and died in 1808.

The Children of Marin François Bourg

Marin François Bourg and Elisabeth Marcelline Jolibois had four male children together:

- François Marcellus Bourg was born on August 3, 1821, and died on October 8, 1853, in Labadieville, Louisiana. His life is discussed in Generation 4 above.
- Ursin Bourg was born on August 12, 1824, in Plattenville, Louisiana, and died in 1894.
- Didier Bourg was born on May 22, 1830, in Plattenville.
- Joseph Silvere Bourg was born in May 1833 in Plattenville.

---

[53] Catholic Church Records, Baton Rouge, vol 13, 86.

Marin François died on April 28, 1835. Elisabeth Marcelline died on May 10, 1833, in Plattenville, probably in childbirth (or complications from childbirth) with her son Joseph Silvere.

The Louisiana Purchase

The United States acquired Louisiana from France in 1803. The United States paid $15 million to acquire 828,000 square miles (530,000,000 acres) of territory. French Treasury Minister François Barbé-Marbois negotiated the treaty with James Monroe and Robert R. Livingston on behalf of President Thomas Jefferson.[54]

France had owned the Louisiana Territory from 1699 until 1762, when it ceded the land to Spain. In 1800, Napoleon regained ownership of Louisiana in an attempt to reestablish a French empire in the New World. However, France suffered a revolt in Santo Domingo. This revolt, along with the probability of war with the British, caused Napoleon to move forward with the sale of territory to the United States.

Acquiring Louisiana was a major goal for Jefferson, who wanted to gain control of the port of New Orleans. Jefferson gave Monroe and Livingston the responsibility of buying New Orleans, but the American representatives quickly agreed to negotiate for the purchase of the entire territory of Louisiana after Napoleon offered to sell it. Jefferson and Secretary of State Madison convinced Congress to ratify and fund the Louisiana Purchase.[55]

The Louisiana Purchase expanded United States ownership across the Mississippi River, nearly doubling the size of the country. The purchase included land associated with fifteen future US states and two Canadian provinces. The western borders of the purchase were disputed with Spain, but these disputes were settled by the 1819 Adams–Onís Treaty. The Treaty of 1818 with Britain adjusted the northern limits of the acquisition.

Louisiana became a state on April 30, 1812, nine years after the Louisiana Purchase. The debate over Louisiana's admission into the Union lasted from early

---

[54.] "1803 Newspaper the Louisiana Purchase Made by the US frm France Thomas Jefferson," *WorthPoint*, https://www.worthpoint.com/worthopedia/1803-newspaper-louisiana-purchase-2009483783.

[55.] "Louisiana Purchase," *Wikipedia*, https://en.wikipedia.org/wiki/The_Louisiana_Purchase.

1811 through ratification, with issues of boundaries and the voting rights of the state being raised in both houses of the federal legislature.[56]

1787: Drafting a US Constitution

On May 14, 1787, five years before Marin François was born, the Constitutional Convention was called.[57] With a quorum of seven states reached on May 25th, 1787, deliberations began. Eventually, twelve states were represented in the convention.[58] The delegates generally agreed that a central government with many enforceable powers should replace the government of the Articles of Confederation.

From the beginning, there were two plans for the structure of the federal government.

1. The Virginia Plan wanted a legislature with two chambers, both elected on population. This plan favored the most highly populated states. It used the philosophy of John Locke to rely on the consent of the governed.[59]
2. The New Jersey Plan proposed that the legislature be a single body with one vote per state. This greatly favored the less-populous states and reflected the belief that the states were independent entities and, as they entered the United States of America freely and individually, remained so.[60]

The convention tried to work out a compromise on representation in the legislature. For the legislature, two issues had to be decided: allocation of votes by states in Congress and how representatives were to be elected. With great compromise, the committee settled on proportional representation for seats in the House of Representatives based on population (with the people voting for representatives) and equal representation for each state in the Senate (with each

---

[56.] "When Did Louisiana Become a State?" Reference.com, https://www.reference.com/article/did-louisiana-become-state-f0fd88c9c28f0fd1?aq=when+did+louisiana+become+a+state&qo=cdpArticles.

[57.] Pauline Maier, *Ratification: The People Debate the Constitution, 1787–1788* (New York: Simon & Schuster, 2010), 27.

[58.] "America's Founding Fathers—Delegates to the Constitutional Convention," The US National Archives and Records Administration, retrieved April 16, 2016.

[59.] "Constitution of the United States," *Wikipedia*, https://en.wikipedia.org/wiki/Constitution_of_United_States.

[60.] "Constitution of the United States."

state's legislators generally choosing their respective senators), and that all money bills would originate in the House.[61]

On July 24, a committee including John Rutledge of South Carolina, Edmund Randolph of Virginia, Nathaniel Gorham of Massachusetts, Oliver Ellsworth of Connecticut, and James Wilson of Pennsylvania was elected to draft a detailed constitution. This detailed draft was to reflect the resolutions passed by the convention up to that point.[62] The committee presented a twenty-three-article (plus preamble) constitution. From early August until late September, the convention deliberated on committee's submission.[63] The final draft presented on September 12 contained seven articles, a preamble, and a closing endorsement.[64]

Generations 6, 7, and 8

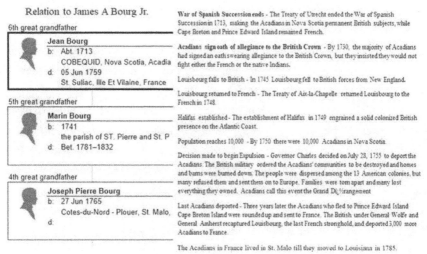

Figure 2 – The Bourg Ancestors of Acadia

The three generations of Bourgs that follow were part of the history of the Acadian experience and the Great Expulsion of the Acadians (*Le Grand Dérangement*). They were part of the Acadian people forcibly removed by the

---

[61.] "Madison Debates July 16," Avalon Project at Yale Law School, retrieved March 31, 2014.
[62.] "Committees at the Constitutional Convention," *US Constitution Online*, Retrieved April 16, 2016.
[63.] "Madison Debates August 6," Avalon Project at Yale Law School, retrieved April 16, 2016.
[64.] "America's Founding Fathers—Delegates to the Constitutional Convention," US National Archives and Records Administration, retrieved April 16, 2016.

British from the present-day Canadian Maritime provinces and the area known as Acadia. They were also part of the tremendous elective ship transportation of these Acadians from Saint-Malo, France, to Louisiana in 1785. With these generations, we will work forward from eldest to youngest.

Generation 8: Jean Bourg

Jean Bourg (1713–June 5, 1759) was the great-grandfather of Marin François Bourg. He was the son of Pierre Bourg (1681–1722) and Marguerite Blanchard (1689–1714). Jean was the husband of Françoise Benoit (1724–1759). Françoise was the daughter of Martin Blanchard and Marguerite Guilbaut.

Both Jean and Francoise were born and lived in Acadia. Jean Bourg was born in Cobequid, Acadia, and Françoise Benoit was born nearby in Point à La Jeunesse on Isle Royal Acadia. Jean was eleven years older than his wife.

Jean and Françoise were married in 1740 in Cobequid. They both died in June of 1759 within a month of each other. They died in Saint-Suliac, Ille-et-Vilaine, France, after their perilous voyage and forced expulsion from Acadia in the fall of 1758. He was forty-six, and she was thirty-five.

Ille-et-Vilaine is a department of France located in the region of Brittany in the northwest of the country. A department is a governmental division of France. It is the same as a county in the United States. This one is named after the two main rivers within it, the Ille and the Vilaine. Their confluence is in Rennes, the capital of the department and the region. Saint-Malo is in this department.

Jean Bourg was a highly skilled Acadian farmer, fisherman, and trapper. Together with the members of his immediate and extended family, he kept the family surviving by providing the necessary capital of life, including food, such as meat (from farm animals, fish, and wild game) and vegetables and grain from the garden and fields (plowing, seeding, weeding, and harvesting); shelter (working to ensure a stable house, barn, and fences); repairs; and clothing materials (wool from sheep and cotton from the fields). In the family, the wife and children would take care of the daily chores of cooking, cleaning, weaving, washing, sewing, and fire-tending.

Although there was a conflict with the British who wanted to control all the territory of North America, life was pretty stable, and the Bourgs were content. Largely ignored by the French monarchy, the Acadians quickly grew independent-minded. With their friends and allies, the Native American Mi'kmaq, they felt secure, even when sovereignty over their land passed from France to Britain after the Treaty of Utrecht in 1713, which ended the War of the Spanish Succession (1701–14).

The treaty confirmed the definitive defeat of New France by England after several wars and its conquest in 1710 over France. By the treaty with Britain, signed on April 11, 1714, France recognized Queen Anne as the British sovereign and undertook to cease supporting James Edward, the son of the deposed King James II. France ceded Newfoundland, Acadia (Nova Scotia), and all the Hudson Bay territory.[65]

Although Acadia had initially been a French colony, it was now owned by the British after the Treaty of Utrecht. The Acadians were allowed to stay in their homeland with some provisions. In 1730, the British required the Acadians to swear allegiance or at least neutrality in any activities between France and England. And over Jean and Françoise's lifetime, the situation with the Acadians became more and more precarious.

The Children of Jean Bourg

Jean and Françoise were married in 1740 at Cobequid, Acadia. They had eight children. All were born in Acadia. Because of the Great Expulsion, which was about to take place in 1758, not all of them died there. Their children were as follows:

- Marin Bourg was born in 1741 in the parish of St. Pierre and St. Paul of Cobequid and died in 1769 in France. He married Marie Ozite (Osithe) Daigle (Daigre), daughter of Olivier Daigle and Angelique Doiron, on January 18, 1763, in Côtes-du-Nord, Plouër, France. Marie was born in 1745 in the parish of l'Annunciation in Acadie. She died in July of 1810 in Assumption Parish, Louisiana.
- Luce-Perpetue Bourg was born in 1744. She married Jean-Baptiste Hebert on April 29, 1766, in Saint-Suliac, Ille-et-Vilaine, France. She died on January 13, 1812, in Plattenville, Louisiana.
- Gertrude Bourg was born in 1748 in Cobequid. She married Marin Gauterot, son of Honore Gauterot and Marguerite Robichaux, on May 5, 1768, in Saint-Suliac. She died on January 31, 1849, in Plattenville.

---

[65] "Peace of Utrecht," *Wikipedia*, https://en.wikipedia.org/wiki/Peace_of_Utrecht.

- Anne-Marie Bourg was born in 1750 in Cobequid, Acadia, and died in 1759 at sea during the crossing to France at age nine.
- Joseph Barthelemy Bourg was born on August 7, 1750, in Cobequid.
- Jean Baptiste Bourg was born in July 1752 in Pointe la Jeunesse, Isle Royale, Acadia, and died in 1759 in Saint-Suliac exile camp, France.
- Theodore Bourg was born in 1754 and died in 1759 at sea during the crossing to France.
- Elizabeth Bourg was born in 1756 in Isle Saint-Jean, New Brunswick, Canada

Activities That Led to the Great Expulsion

As previously discussed, the War of the Spanish Succession was triggered by the death of Charles II of Spain in November of 1700. Charles was childless. With no heir to take the throne, the balance of power in Europe became unbalanced. Resolution of the balance hinged upon the stability of the monarchs of each country.

Charles' closest heirs were members of the Austrian Habsburg and French Bourbon families. The acquisition of an undivided Spanish Empire by either monarchy threatened the European balance of power. The situation eventually evolved into a global conflict due to overseas colonies and allies. Much of the fighting was in North America. In 1713, the Treaty of Utrecht, which ended the conflict, gave Acadia to Great Britain while allowing the Acadians to keep their lands.

The Acadians refused to sign an unconditional oath of loyalty to Great Britain, which would have made them British subjects. Instead, they negotiated a conditional promise that agreed to neutrality in any conflicts. The problem was partly religion. The British were Protestant, Church of England, and the Acadians were Catholic. Signing the oath might commit Acadian men to fight against France in a conflict. Their Mi'kmaq neighbors also might think they acknowledged the British claim to Acadia.[66] Other Acadians did not sign an oath because they were anti-British. Some were labeled *neutral* when they were not.[67]

When the Acadians were expelled, there was already a long history of

---

[66] John G. Reid, *Nova Scotia: A Pocket History* (Fernwood, 2009), 49.

[67] "Expulsion of the Acadians," *Wikipedia*, https://en.wikipedia.org/wiki/Expulsion_of_the_Acadians.

resistance by Acadians to the British occupation of Acadia.[68], [69] The Mi'kmaq resisted the British occupation and were joined on numerous occasions by Acadians. These efforts were supported and led by French priests in the region.[70]

The French and Indian War broke out between the Acadians and the British colonies in America. Each side was backed by military units from the parent countries and by their American Indian allies. When the Acadian conflicts began, the British colonies had a population of 2 million people, while the French colonies had only 60,000 settlers.[71] The French were outnumbered 30:1 and depended on their Native American allies, the Wabanaki.

The *Last of the Mohicans*, a book about the French and Indian War, was written in 1826 by James Fenimore Cooper. The novel tells the story of the two daughters of British Colonel Munro: Alice and Cora. They are journeying to their father and safety at Fort William Henry, a British fort in upper New York. They are escorted and guarded by frontiersman Natty Bumppo (Hawkeye), British Major Duncan Heyward, and the Native Americans Chingachgook and Uncas. Hawkeye is a white frontiersman who was raised by the Indians. These characters are a microcosm of the evolving American society, particularly their racial composition.[72] The novel has been one of the most popular English-language books since its publication and is frequently assigned reading in American literature courses.[73] It was adapted numerous times and in many languages.

The name *French and Indian War* is used mainly in the United States, referring to the two enemies of the British colonists. European historians use the term *Seven Years' War*, as do English-speaking Canadians.[74]

In 1755, while Françoise was pregnant with her last child, Elizabeth (who

---

[68] "Expulsion of the Acadians."

[69] "Siege of Port Royal (1710)," *Wikipedia*, https://en.wikipedia.org/wiki/Siege_of_Port_Royal_ (1710).

[70] "Expulsion of the Acadians."

[71] "French and Indian War," *Wikipedia*, https://en.wikipedia.org/?title=French_and_Indian_War; Gary Walton, *History of the American Economy*, 27.

[72] "New Ideas of Race: *The Last of the Mohicans*," in Fiona J. Stafford, *The Last of the Race: The Growth of a Myth from Milton to Darwin* (Oxford Scholarship: 1994).

[73] "*Last of the Mohicans*," in Martin J. Manning (ed.), Clarence R. Wyatt (ed.), *Encyclopedia of Media and Propaganda in Wartime America*, https://www.abc-clio.com/ABC-CLIOCorporate/ product.aspx?pc=A1855C.

[74] M. Brook Taylor, *Canadian History: a Reader's Guide: Volume 1: Beginnings to Confederation* (1994), 39–48, 72–74.

would be born in 1756), six colonial governors met with General Edward Braddock, the newly arrived British Army commander. In the meeting, they planned an attack on the French. It did not succeed. The main attack by Braddock's forces was a loss at the Battle of the Monongahela on July 9, 1755. The general was injured and died a few days later.

British activity failed in the Province of Pennsylvania and New York from 1755 to 1757. The failure was due to poor management and active Acadian scouts, French regular forces, and Native American warrior allies.[75]

Le Grand Dérangement

The forced exportation of the Acadians by the British[76] began in 1755, after Fort Beauséjour on the border separating the Canadian mainland from Acadia (near Beaubassin) was captured by the British. The victors decided it was time they ordered the expulsion of the Acadians from what they were calling New Scottland (Nova Scotia). Commander-in-Chief William Shirley gave orders for the deportation without direction from Great Britain. He wanted all the Acadians removed—not only armed combatants but those colonists who had sworn the loyalty oath to the king. Their Native American allies were likewise driven off the land to make way for settlers from New England.

The expulsion of the Acadians began on August 10, 1755, with the Bay of Fundy (the southwestern end of the island).[77] Most Acadians in this first wave were sent to rural areas in Massachusetts, Connecticut, New York, Pennsylvania, Maryland, and South Carolina. In general, however, they refused to stay where they were put.

After the Fort William Henry loss, French-allied Native Americans tortured and massacred their British colonial victims. This battle was depicted in *The Last*

---

[75] "The Seven Years' War: 1754-1763," Boundless US History, https://courses.lumenlearning. com/boundless-ushistory/chapter/the-seven-years-war-1754-1763/; "French and Indian War," *Wikipedia*, https://en.wikipedia.org/wiki/French_and_Indian_War.

[76] "Expulsion of the Acadians," *Wikipedia*, https://en.wikipedia.org/wiki/Expulsion_of_the_ Acadians; "10th of February," Today in Naval History, https://shipsofscale.com/sosforums/ threads/10th-of-february-today-in-naval-history-naval-maritime-events-in-history.2104/ page-74.

[77] The British ordered all Acadians in that area to be removed after the Battle of Beauséjour in 1755. The removal started at Chignecto and then quickly moved to Grand-Pré and Annapolis Royal.

of the Mohicans. Outraged by this French activity, William Pitt ramped up British troops in North America. France was not willing to spend the money to aid the smaller forces they had in New France. They concentrated their efforts against the Prussian alliance, which they were fighting in the Seven Years' War in Europe.[78]

Some Acadians fought in military activities against the British and maintained contact with the French fortresses of Louisbourg and Beauséjour.[79] The British sought to eliminate any future military threat by removing them from the area. The Fortress of Louisbourg is an eighteenth-century French fortress at Louisbourg on Cape Breton Island, Nova Scotia. Its two sieges, especially that of 1758, were both turning points in the Anglo-French struggle for what today is Canada.

When Fort Beauséjour fell to the English forces in June 1755, the British found 270 Acadian militia fighters inside. Helping the French army was not in accord with their promise of staying neutral. The British met with the Acadians in July 1755 in Halifax and insisted they take an oath of allegiance to Britain with no qualifications. The Acadians refused, because they feared the oath would make them British subjects. When they did, they were imprisoned, and their deportation was ordered.

Lawrence had strong support for his council from New England immigrants, who wanted the Acadians' land. Boston traders frequently asked why the French Acadians were allowed to stay and own such beautiful land in a colony that was now British. Colonel John Winslow ordered on September 5, 1755, that all males ages ten years and older gather in the church in Grand-Pré for an important message. The message read, "Your Land and homes, your cattle, your livestock, are forfeited to the Crown with all other of your effects; savings your money and Household Goods. You will be removed from this island."

It was Charles Morris who suggested that British soldiers surround Acadian churches on Sunday morning. They captured as many men as possible, breached their dikes, and burnt the houses and crops. The men refused to go, but soldiers threatened family members with bayonets. They all went reluctantly while praying, singing, and crying. Some 1,100 Acadians had been put aboard ships headed for South Carolina, Georgia, and Pennsylvania by the fall of 1755. No Acadians went to France during this first wave of expulsion in 1755.

Lawrence told his officers to pay no attention to any remorse from any of the

---

[78.] "French and Indian War," *Wikipedia*, https://en.wikipedia.org/wiki/French_and_Indian_War.
[79.] John Grenier, *The Far Reaches of Empire: War in Nova Scotia 1710–1760* (Oklahoma University Press: 2008).

inhabitants. When the soldiers read the deportation order, although it was their duty, it was very upsetting for them. One soldier said, "It is not my business to protest, but to obey such orders as I receive."

Some Acadians resisted. Joseph Beausoleil Brossard launched several retaliatory raids against the British troops. In 1755, 6,950 Acadians were exported from the Port-Royal area to various destinations in New England: 2,000 were sent to Massachusetts, 1,100 to Virginia, 1,000 to Maryland, 700 to Connecticut, 500 to Pennsylvania, North Carolina, and South Carolina, 400 to Georgia, and 250 to New York.

In 1755, Jean Bourg and the Bourg clan in Cobiquid were in a group of 1,500 who fled north. The exact destination is not known, but Jean Bourg and his family made their way to Prince Edward Island. The British sort of left them alone at first. After a bitter fight with French soldiers and citizen militia, the British finally defeated the French with the Siege of Fort Louisbourg in1758. At this point, the attitude of the British changed. They wanted all French Acadians out of what they called Nova Scotia (New Scottland).

The second wave of expulsion began in the fall of 1758. Thousands of Acadians, including the Bourg clan, were deported from Isle Saint-Jean (Prince Edward Island) and Isle Royale (Cape Breton Island). This time, the British decided to deport the Acadians directly to France rather than to other British colonies. Over three thousand Acadians were exiled to France because, unlike the Acadians previously deported, the British claimed they were subjects of the king of France. They boarded ships and were transported directly to France. The boats, which held an average of 215 people each, were the *Brition*, the *Duke William*, the *John and Samuel*, the *Mathias*, the *Neptune*, the *Parnassus*, the *Patience*, the *Restoration*, the *Ruby*, the *du Supply*, the *Tamerlane*, the *Three Sisters*, the *Violet*, and the *Yarmouth*.

The trip across the Atlantic was much longer and more dangerous than those of the vessels sent along the American coast in 1755. A voyage over the Atlantic Ocean in winter is a hazardous activity. Three of the fourteen ships sank, with the loss of about 850 Acadian lives. The Bourg clan was transported on several boats, but the ancestors described in this chapter were on the *du Supply*. The 850 Acadians who died were on the transport ships *Duke William*, *Violet*, and *Ruby*.

The *Duke William* sank in the ocean on December 13, 1758; all 360 lives aboard were lost.[80] The ship had set sail from France from Isle Saint-Jean on October 20 with her compliment of Acadians on board. The ship sailed in convoy with nine other vessels, two of which were the *Violet* (with 280 Acadians) and the *Ruby* (with approximately 310 Acadians).

On the third day at sea, there was a storm, and the *Duke William* became separated from the other two ships. The *Ruby* ran aground and sank in a storm on Pico Island in the Azores, and 213 Acadians died. Almost two weeks after the ships were separated, late in the day on December 10, the *Duke William* reencountered the *Violet*, which was sinking. The *Duke William* sprung a leak, and the Acadians assisted at the pumps. On the morning of December 11, after a brief storm, the *Violet* sank with all the Acadians on board. On the *Violet* were some 360 Acadian souls.

For three days, everyone aboard the *Duke William* tried to pump the water out. Captain Nichols wrote: "We continued in this dismal situation for three days. The ship disregarded our efforts. We are expected to sink every minute." Nichols gave up and announced to the Acadians and crew, "We must be content with our fate; and as we sure certain we have done our duty, we should submit to Providence, and the Almighty's will, with pious resignation."[81]

Despite this resignation, Captain Nichols dispatched the longboats on board to try to reach any passing vessels. On the morning of December 13, two English ships were within sight of the *Duke William*. Captain Nichols records: "I went and acquainted the priest [Girrard] and the old gentleman [Noël Doiron] with the good news. The old man took me in his aged arms and cried for joy." The ships did not stop, however. When the longboat returned, a Danish ship was spotted. Again, those aboard thought they were saved, but the Danish ship just sailed away.

Boats in the eighteenth century were designed for work, not lifesaving.[82] Captain Nichols recorded in his logbook the following decision of Noël Doiron: "About half an hour after ... Noël Doiron, came to me, crying; he took me in his arms and said he came with the voice of the whole people, to desire that my men and I would endeavor to save some lives, in our boats but we could not carry them

---

[80]S. Scott and T. Scott, "Noel Doiron and the East Hants Acadians," *Journal of the Royal Nova Scotia Historical Society* (2008), 45–60.

[81] Journal of William Nichols, "The Naval Chronicle," 180.

[82] Tony Horwitz, *Blue Latitudes* (New York: Picador Publishing, 2002), 168.

all. They were convinced that God Almighty had ordained them to drown, and they hoped that we should be able to get safely ashore."[83]

The boats on board were lowered into the English Channel, carrying only the captain, his crew, and the parish priest Girrard. Upon lowering the lifeboats, Noël Doiron sharply reprimanded Jean-Pierre LeBlanc, an Acadian, for trying to board a boat while abandoning his wife and children. As Priest Girrard got in the raft, he saluted Noel Doiron. After Captain Nichols could no longer see the ship, four Acadians got into another boat and arrived safely in Falmouth, England.[84]

The *Duke William* sank about seventy miles from the French coast shortly after four o'clock in the afternoon on December 13, 1758. Noël Doiron; his wife, Marie; five of their children with their spouses; and over thirty grandchildren died—120 family members in total.[85]

Because of the challenging conditions for passengers on the eleven ships that did not sink traveling over the long distances on a winter sea, the death rate, especially among children, was very high. No manifest of the Acadians was found for any of the ships. However, we know Jean Bourg and his family traveled on board the vessel *du Supply*, where Ann Marie and Theodore Bourg died at sea because of the deplorable conditions on the ship. On December 20, 1758, the *du Supply* arrived in Bideford, England, with 160 deportees from Isle Saint-Jean on board. A few of these deportees went on to Bristol, but the majority, 140, reach Saint-Malo on March 9, 1759.[86]

The *du Supply* was the last ship to arrive in France from the 1758 exile, on March 9, 1759. Of the 191 Acadians who had boarded the boat, 24 died at sea and 19 more died soon after arriving. Because the winter deportation across the Atlantic was so stressful, Jean and Francoise Bourg both died three months after they arrived in France. Jean died on June 5 (possibly 15), 1759, and Françoise died on June 30, 1759. He was forty-six years old, and she was thirty-five. They were both buried in Saint-Suliac, Ille-et-Vilaine, France, just eight miles from where they landed in Saint-Malo. Jean Bourg's family settled in France for about twenty-six years.

---

[83] "Duke William (ship)," *Wikipedia*, https://en.wikipedia.org/wiki/Duke_William_(ship).

[84] "Noël Doiron," *Wikipedia*, https://en.wikipedia.org/wiki/Noël_Doiron.

[85] "Duke William (ship)," https://en.wikipedia.org/wiki/Duke_William_(ship).

[86] Paul Delaney, "The Chronology of the Deportation and Migrations of the Acadians 1755-1816," Acadian & French Canadian Ancestral Home, www.acadian-home.org/Paul-Delaney-Chronology.html.

The Acadians from the Isle Saint-Jean expulsion had the most significant percentage of deaths of all the deported Acadians. By the time the second wave of the deportation started, the British had discarded sending the Acadians to the thirteen colonies. They began deporting them directly to France.[87] Acadians who had been in England since 1756 joined the Acadians in France in 1763.

The sinking of the ships *Violet* (with about 280 persons aboard) and *Duke William* (with over 360 persons aboard) caused the highest numbers of fatalities during the expulsion.[88] Stephen White is compiling a reconstructed list of ship passengers for the *Violet* and *Duke William*. His list is being compiled based on the census of Isle Saint-Jean and Isle Royale before the exile and the census after 1758. The expulsion proved unnecessary for military reasons and was later judged inhumane. Lawrence's actions were driven by greed, confusion, misunderstanding, and fear.[89]

The Acadians settled in small towns around the Saint-Malo area. But some Acadians went to Cherbourg, Boulogne-sur-Mer, La Havre, Brest (the Britannia debarked Acadians on Oct. 26, 1758), Rochefort, and other coastal cities.[90]

The government thought that the Acadians would meld into the French population, but that didn't happen. They went on government welfare at six sols a day. The Acadians became a pawn in internal French bureaucracy. All government plans called for settling the Acadians on poor land or in terrible climates. They struggled in France because they were no longer Frenchmen; they were Acadians.

Generation 7: Marin Bourg

Marin Bourg (1741–March 27, 1797) was Jean Bourg's oldest son. Although he was born in Acadia in 1741, he was deported with his family to France in 1758 when he was seventeen years old. He met his future wife, Marie Ozite (Osithe) Daigle (Daigre), in Plouër, Saint-Malo, and married her in Plouër on January 18, 1763, just four years after they both arrived in France at the age of twenty-two.

Marin's siblings, the children of Jean Bourg, are listed at the start of the

---

[87.] Geoffrey Plank, *An Unsettled Conquest: The British Campaign Against the Peoples of Acadia* (University of Pennsylvania Press, 2001).

[88.] Earle Lockerby, *Deportation of the Prince Edward Island Acadians* (Nimbus, 2008).

[89.] "Exile Destination: France," Acadian-Cajun Genealogy and History, http://www.acadian-cajun.com/exfr.htm.

[90.] "Acadians," *Wikipedia*, https://en.wikipedia.org/wiki/Acadians.

previous section. All were born in Acadia but lived in France before the revolution. France was still a kingdom. There would have been a great divide between the rich and the poor at this time. Nobles lived in castles or at court and had servants. Bourgeois lived in towns and were educated as lawyers and doctors or wealthier shopkeepers. They could afford to hire labor. Then there were many poor people in cities doing simple tasks like working for others and selling cakes or flowers in the streets; there were carriers, laborers, beggars, thieves. In the country, most peasants would eke out a living by farming and raising chickens and farm animals, paying taxes to the lord of the manor.

Getting around would have been simple: horses, donkeys, or mules and carts. Most people smelled and were very dirty. They only had well water and streams to drink. They didn't have many extra clothes. The French Revolution seemed inevitable, with trees waiting to convert to guillotines and the spirit of rebellion silently infecting the countryside. Similar disturbances were common across England, with highway robberies on the increase and thievery reaching into high society. Executions were frequent for both minor and major offenses.[91]

The government had varying viewpoints on what to do with the Acadian refugees. The French considered them ungrateful peasants who should just blend in. By 1772, the Acadians appealed to the king. Louis XVI ordered that a place be found for them in France.[92]

The head of the French navy, LeMoyne, ordered a census of the Acadians living in France. The census was conducted in 1772 and found there were 2,566 Acadians in France. The distribution was as follows:

- 1,727 in the Saint-Malo area
- 228 in Cherbourg
- 179 in Morlaix
- 166 in Le Havre
- 103 in Belle-Île-en-Mer
- 79 in Rochefort
- 42 in La Rochelle
- 27 in Lorient
- 10 in Bordeaux

[91.] "What Was France Like in 1775?" Yahoo! Answers, https://answers.yahoo.com/question/index?qid=20101219125311AA1y3Db.

[92.] "Acadians," *Wikipedia*, https://en.wikipedia.org/wiki/Acadians.

- 3 in Paris
- 2 in Boulogne

Most of the Acadians moved to Nantes. Only 160 were still in the area the following year.

The Children of Marin Bourg

Marin Bourg and his wife, Marie Ozite (Osithe) Daigle, stayed in the Plouër/ Saint-Malo area after their marriage. They concentrated on making a living the best they could as they had in Acadia. They also started a family. Marin and Marie had the following nine children:

- Marie-Luce Bourg was born on January 23, 1764, in Plouër, Côtes-du-Nord, France, and died in 1814 in Plattenville, Louisiana. She married Simon Landry, son of Prosper Landry and Ysabel Petre, on July 5, 1795, in Assumption Church of Plattenville.[93] Simon died in 1815 in Plattenville. They had three children during their marriage. Marie-Luce passed away on December 24, 1814, in Plattenville at the age of fifty.
- Joseph (Jean) Pierre Bourg was born on January 27, 1764, in Plouër. He married Marie Jeanne Aucoin, daughter of Joseph Aucoin and Anne Hebert, on May 20, 1790, in Pointe Coupee, Louisiana.[94]
- Marguerite Josephine Bourg was born in 1768.
- Marin Joseph Bourg was born on July 10, 1769, in Plouër. He married Marie Madeleine Aucoin (1774-1819) on May 20, 1790, in Pointe Coupee. He died on April 28, 1835, in Thibodaux, Louisiana.
- Rose-Magdelaine Bourg was born in 1772.
- Pierre Jean-Baptiste Bourg was born on August 4, 1770, in Saint-Suliac, Ille-et-Vilaine, Bretagne, France. He married Marie Madeleine Rose Pitre (1780–1844) on June 10, 1798, in Plattenville. He died on July 20, 1836, in Thibodaux.
- Marie Françoise Magdelaine Josephe Bourg was born in 1775.

---

[93] ASM 2-13.
[94] PCP-19,33.

- Françoise Georges Bourg was born in 1778 in Saint-Malo. He married Adelaida Bertrand, daughter of Pedro Bertrand and Catharine Bourg, on March 27, 1797.[95] She was born in Nantes, France.
- Guillaume Jean Bourg was born in 1781.

Life After Expulsion

The most significant concentration of Acadians in France would be at Nantes. Gerard Braud wrote the books *From Nantes to Louisiana* and *Les Acadiens en France: Nantes et Paimboeuf, 1775-1785*, which lists thousands of people in hundreds of family groups. It is printed in French and English.

For the Acadians, there were many hardships and sufferings during the period of the expulsion. This exile, which for some Acadians extended for over thirty years, did not end when they arrived in their native France. Too soon, they realized that, in reality, they were Acadians and not Frenchmen. They would never be reabsorbed easily into French society. The moment was right to act on another opportunity—to settle in Louisiana.

Spain placed the responsibility for organizing and removing the Acadians to Louisiana upon her ambassador in Paris, Don Pedro Pablo Abarca de Bolea, Count de Aranda. However, it was the Spanish counsel of Saint-Malo, Don Manuel d'Aspres, who drew the contracts, organized the expeditions, and dispatched the Acadians to Louisiana. By this time in history, the successful settlement of Acadians in Louisiana was old news. Talk began to migrate to the French Acadians as well. But the primary concern of the Acadians for the next decade was providing for themselves.[96]

Acadians got the okay from Spain to sail to Louisiana in October 1777. In 1783, a Frenchman, Henri Peyroux de la Coudreniere, with the help of the Acadian cobbler Olivier Theriot, worked on moving Acadians to Louisiana. France wouldn't cooperate at first because Louisiana was now a Spanish colony. They finalized a deal in late 1784, and in 1785, about 1,600 Acadians sailed for Louisiana in seven ships. Six of the boats left from the Nantes/Paimboeuf area. Another, *La Ville d'Archangel*, departed from Saint-Malo.

---

[95] ASM–2,25.

[96] Steven A. Cormier, "Acadians Who Found Refuge in Louisiana, February 1764–early 1800s," *Acadians in Gray*, www.acadiansingray.com/Appendices-ATLAL-LANOUX.htm.

The Seven Ships and Their Passenger Lists

In 1785, Spain paid for seven ships to transport Acadians to settle in the then Spanish colony of Louisiana. Spain wanted settlers to buffer the zone between Spanish land to the west and the British territories to the east. For the Acadians, this was a chance to join their fellow Acadians and to regain some of what they lost during the exile. The ships and their departures were as follows:[97]

- *Le Bon Papa* was the first of the seven ships to sail with Acadians to Louisiana. It sailed from Nantes, on May 10, 1785, and arrived in Louisiana on July 29, 1785. It spent eighty days on the ocean.
- The second vessel was *La Bergere*. It left France just four days after *Le Bon Papa* on May 14, 1785. After ninety-three days at sea, it arrived in Louisiana on August 15, 1785.
- The third ship sailed from Nantes after almost a month on June 11, 1785. After sixty-nine days on the ocean, it arrived in Louisiana on August 19, 1785.
- The fourth ship, *Le Beaumont*, left Nantes on June 11, 1785, and arrived in Louisiana sixty-nine days later on August 19, 1785.
- *Le Saint-Remi*, the fifth boat, left Nantes on June 27, 1785. Seventy-five days later, it reached Louisiana on September 10, 1785.
- The sixth ship, *L'Amitie*, departed from Nantes on August 20, 1785. It arrived in Louisiana on November 8, 1785, after eighty days at sea.
- The seventh ship, *La Ville d'Archangel*, was the only vessel to leave France but not from Nantes. It departed from Saint-Malo on August 12, 1785. It arrived in Louisiana 113 days later on December 3, 1785.
- *La Caroline* left Nantes on October 19, 1785. It arrived in Louisiana fifty-six days later on December 17, 1785.[98]

The manifest lists for these ships are available in print. The lists of names appeared in *Winzerlings' Acadian Odyssey* in 1955. Milton and Norma Reider's *The Crew and Passenger Registration Lists of the Seven Acadian Expeditions*

---

[97] "Ships Transporting Acadians to Louisiana," Acadian.org, https://www.acadian.org/culture/louisiana/ships-transportation-acadians-louisiana/.

[98] "The 7 Ships Passenger Lists," Acadian-Cajun Genealogy, http://www.acadian-cajun.com/7ships.htm.

of 1785 was the first to transcribe the entire lists. The lists can also be found in Gerard Braud's book *From Nantes to Louisiana*. The Rev. Don Hébert recently published a book called *Acadian Families in Exile, 1785* that contains both the embarkation and debarkation lists. This book is the best work on the subject.[99]

La Ville d'Archangel was a six-hundred-ton ship. It sailed to an outpost at the mouth of the Mississippi River named Balize. It ran aground in the shallows of the Mississippi River sound on November 4. The ship had run out of food days before. More than three dozen people were ill. Food and supplies to continue were obtained from the people in New Orleans. On a high tide, the ship sailed on to New Orleans after 113 days of the voyage. It arrived there on December 3, 1785.

The ship ended up with sixty families of 299 people in all. The trip saw fifteen deaths and two desertions. But there were also seven marriage, eleven adult additions, and two births. This group sent most of its people to the Bayou Lafourche area. The Bourgs were among fifty-three families (271 people) who decided to go to Bayou des Ecores (near Thompson Creek, north of Baton Rouge) in what was then Pointe Coupee. One family (seven people) did not leave New Orleans, while six families (twenty-one people) decided to go to the Bayou Lafourche area.

Part of the transcribed list of passengers aboard the *La Ville d'Archangel* includes the following:

- Marin BOURG – 45
- Marie Osithe DAIGLE – 40
- Marie Luce BOURG, daughter – 22
- Jean (Joseph) Pierre BOURG, son – 20
- Marguerite Joseph BOURG, daughter – 17
- Marin Joseph BOURG, son – 16
- Rose Magdelaine BOURG, daughter – 13
- Pierre Jean Baptiste BOURG, son – 12
- Marie Francoise Magdelaine Joseph BOURG, daughter – 10
- Francois George BOURG, son – 7
- Guillaume Jean BOURG, son – 4

---

[99] Donald J. Hébert, *Acadian Families in Exile, 1785*, Open Library, https://openlibrary.org/works/OL536331W/Acadian_families_in_exile_178.

After a hurricane about a decade later destroyed their settlement, many of the Bayou des Ecores settlers, including the Bourgs, moved south to join the other Acadians along Bayou Lafourche.

Generation 6: Joseph (Jean) Pierre Bourg

Joseph Pierre Bourg (the great-great-great-great-grandfather of the author) was born on Friday, January 27, 1764, in Côtes-du-Nord, Plouër, Saint-Malo, France. He was the son of Marin Bourg and Marie Ozite (Osithe) Daigle. He died on June 10, 1826, in Plattenville, Louisiana. In some references, Joseph is listed as Jean Pierre Bourg.

Joseph married Marie (Magdelaine) Jeanne Aucoin on May 20, 1790, in the Bayou des Ecores settlement in Point Coupee. Marie was also a daughter of Acadian exiles, Joseph Aucoin and Anne Hebert. She was born on August 23, 1774, in Côtes-du-Nord, Nord-Pas-de-Calais, France. She was also on *La Ville d'Archangel* with her family in 1785 for the trip to Louisiana. The manifest of the *La Ville d'Archangel* for her family reads;

- Joseph AUCOIN – 64
- Anne HEBERT, wife – 48
- Francois AUCOIN, son – 15
- Anne AUCOIN, daughter – 21
- Gabriel AUCOIN, son – 13
- Marie Magdelaine AUCOIN, daughter – 11
- Francoise AUCOIN, daughter – 8
- Jacinta AUCOIN, son – infant (b. April 5, 1785)

The Children of Joseph Pierre Bourg

Joseph and Marie had the following nine children together:

- Mathilda Bourg married Barthelemi Jolibois, son of Flibra Jolibois and Marie Louise Charpentier, on August 12, 1822.
- Anriette Bourg married Francisco Marguet de Bordes on July 8, 1830.
- Marin Francois Bourg (on direct ancestor line to the author) was born on April 16, 1792, in Pointe Coupee, and died on April 28, 1835. Marin's life is discussed in Generation 5 above.

- Armand Louis Bourg was born on May 7, 1794, in Assumption Parish Church.
- Rosa Anastasia Bourg was born on April 30, 1797. She was married twice. Her first husband was Louis Luce, son of Claude Romain Luce and Marguerite Locque; they were married on January 26, 1819.[100] She married her second husband, Andrew P. Skinner, on June 14, 1834.[101] He was born in Gothenburg, Sweden.
- Marianna Bourg was born on September 30, 1798.
- Escolastica Juliana Bourg was born on January 25, 1802. She married Kelp Walkings.[102] She died on May 6, 1822, at the age of twenty.[103]
- Pauline Bourg was born on March 15th, 1807. She died on July 28, 1827.[104]
- Rosalina Bourg was born on February 10, 1811.[105]

Marie died in 1819 in Bayou des Ecors, West Feliciana, Louisiana. Joseph passed away on June 10, 1826, in Assumption Parish, Louisiana.

Generations 9, 10, 11, and 12

The Bourg Family Members Born or Immigrated to Acadia

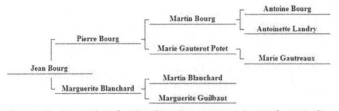

Figure 3 – Bourg Family Members Born or Immigrated to Acadia

Generation 12: Simon Jean Bourg

Simon Jean Bourg was born in Martaize, Vienne, France sometime between 1576 and 1590. He was the son of Niclas Grandjehan Bourg and Margeurite

---

[100] Reference: church records, ASM-7, 41.

[101] In Thib., ch. v.1, 45.

[102] ASM-1, 229.

[103] ASM-1, 229, and Thib., ch. v.1, 3.

[104] ASM-6, 132; Thib. ch. v.1, 30; Thib. ch. v.1, 34.

[105] ASM-6, 231.

François Bourgois. Simon had seven siblings (only two of which we know of: Robert Bourg and Marie Petit Bourg).

Simon married Hélène Comtee in 1600 in Touraine, Indre-et-Loire, France, when she was twenty-one years old. Hélène was born in 1579 in Martaizé, Vienne, France. Her father, François, was born in 1558. He was twenty-one when Hélène was born. Her mother, Georgine, was born in 1560. Georgine was only nineteen years old when Hélène was born.

The Children of Simon Jean Bourg

Hélène and Simon had six children together; Hélène also had one daughter from another relationship. Hélène died on January 24, 1627, in Rennes, Ille-et-Vilaine, France, at the age of forty-eight. Her six children with Simon were as follows:

- René Vincent Breau (Bourg) was born in 1603 in Amberre, Vienne, France. Simon was nineteen and Hélène was twenty-four when he was born. René had one son and one daughter from one relationship. He then married Marye Réyaulme, and they had six children together. He also had one daughter with Marie Renaulme. He died as a young father in 1628 at the age of twenty-five and was buried in La Chaussée, Vienne, France.
- Antoine Bourg was born in 1609 in Martaizé, Vienne, France, when his father, Simon, was twenty-five, and his mother, Hélène, was thirty. He married Antoinette Landry in 1641 in Annapolis Royal, Nova Scotia. Antoinette was the daughter of Jean Claud Landry (whom we will visit in chapter 7) and Marie Salé. Antoine and Antoinette had twelve children together in thirty-seven years. Antoine died on October 5, 1687, having lived a long life of seventy-eight years. He was buried in Annapolis Royal, Nova Scotia, Canada.
- Perrine Bourg (Riau) was born in 1611 in Martaizé. Her father, Simon, was twenty-seven, and her mother, Hélène, was thirty-two. She died in 1673 in Annapolis Royal, Nova Scotia, at the age of sixty-two.
- Marie Bourg was born in 1612 in Loudun, Vienne, France, when her father, Simon, was twenty-eight, and her mother, Hélène, was thirty-three. She died on September 1, 1681, in Paris at the age of sixty-nine.

- Marie Renne Bourg was born in 1616 in Loudun when her father, Simon, was thirty-two, and her mother, Hélene, was thirty-seven. She died in 1645 in her hometown at the age of twenty-nine.
- Maria Anna Bourg

Reasons for France's Colonization in North America

At this time in history, Spain was the great military power in Europe. The reason for this military might was Spain's deep financial pockets—the wealth obtained from the gold and silver brought from its colonies in South and Central America. Treasures from Mexico and Peru brought great military and political strength but did not stimulate private investment and industrial production. Their colonial exploitation only encouraged men to look for shortcuts to riches and wealth.

As long as Spain maintained, with its navy, control of the crucial Atlantic sea-lanes, it secured its wealth and power. If Spain ever lost this naval control, however, it would quickly lose its wealth. During this Spanish golden age of power, there was no social change. Spain's vast economic resources were going to royalty, the nobility, and the Catholic Church. They were not going to the common man.[106]

Spain and its colonies had inferior commercial links. The middle class was of minimal importance and strictly controlled. The majority of the population was uneducated, superstitious, and poor. Spain was rich and powerful, but it was very vulnerable.

France should have been Europe's most significant power at the start of the seventeenth century. Given its size, large population, fertile soil, and advantageous location in Europe, it should have commanded economic growth and great prosperity. However, in 1600, France had just finished the Wars of Religion (1562–1598). Religious wars in France were the result of much tension between Catholics and Protestants. Three million people died because of the

---

[106.] "The Shaping of Modern Europe: 17th Century Europe Introduction: Europe in the 1600s: Spain in the 1600s," the Open Door Web Site, saburchill.com/history/chapters/chap5119.html.

fighting, starvation, and disease.[107] This vicious conflict severely damaged the country's economy as well as the unity of its people.[108]

The French powers that be at that time realized they needed colonization in the New World (North America).[109] England had begun the colonization of North America by this time. The first attempt made to establish an English colony in North America was underway. A colony at Roanoke was started and failed. The modern state of Virginia is still named after the English queen.[110]

The French explored and colonized the Americas beginning in the sixteenth century. France continued to colonize and create its world power in the New World. France founded settlements in much of North America, on several Caribbean islands, and in South America. Most colonies were founded to send products such as fish, rice, sugar, and furs back to France.

As they explored the New World, the French established forts and settlements. These would eventually become cities like Quebec and Montreal in Canada. The French established the cities of Detroit, Green Bay, St. Louis, Cape Girardeau, Mobile, Biloxi, Baton Rouge and New Orleans in the United States. Port-au-Prince, Cap-Haïtien in Haiti were also colonies that became French cities.[111]

The French first came to the New World as explorers looking for a route to the Pacific Ocean. They also were looking for wealth. In 1524, King Francis sent Italian-born Giovanni da Verrazzano to look for a path to the Pacific Ocean. Verrazzano was promoting French interests between New Spain and English Newfoundland.[112]

In 1534, France sent Jacques Cartier to explore the coast of Newfoundland and the St. Lawrence River. On the first of three voyages, he founded New France by planting a cross on the shore of a peninsula along the banks of the St. Lawrence

---

[107] Robert J. Knecht, *The French Religious Wars 1562–1598* (Oxford: Osprey Publishing, 2002), 91; "French Wars of Religion," *Wikipedia*, https://en.wikipedia.org/wiki/Huguenot_Wars.

[108] "The Shaping of Modern Europe: 17th Century Europe: Introduction: Europe in the 1600s: France in the 1600s," the Open Door Web Site, saburchill.com/history/chapters/chap5119.html.

[109] "French Colonization of the Americas," *Wikipedia*, https://en.wikipedia.org/wiki/French_colonization_of_the_Americas.

[110] "The Shaping of Modern Europe: 17th Century Europe: Introduction: Europe in the 1600s: England in the 1600s," The Open Door Web Site, saburchill.com/history/chapters/chap5119.html.

[111] "French Colonization of the Americas."

[112] "French Colonization of the Americas."

River. The French continued to try to start colonies throughout North America, but they failed, due to weather, disease, or conflict with other European powers.[113]

Cartier attempted to start the first permanent European settlement in North America at Quebec in 1541, with four hundred settlers. The colony was abandoned the next year after bad weather and attacks from Native Americans in the area. The settlement was moved to Port-Royal the following year, located on the western shore of Nova Scotia.

Generation 11: Antoine Abraham Bourg

Antoine Abraham Bourg was born in 1609 in Martaizé, Vienne, France. Simon, his father, was twenty-five at his birth, and his mother, Hélene, was thirty. Antoine emigrated to Acadia in 1640 when he was thirty-one years old.[114] When Antoine arrived in Acadia, the colony still very much belonged to France. However, by 1713, the settlement was governed by the British.

Why did Antoine come to Acadia? By 1627, France had realized that the possibility of wealth that was available was more than fur trading. A commercial company formed called the Company of One Hundred Associates (La Compagnie des Cent-Associés). Its purpose was to promote and establish more agricultural settlements in New France. Encouraging religious missionary activity was also part of its purpose. In return for title to land in Acadia and a right to all commerce except fishing interests, the company agreed to settle the land with four thousand French Catholics between 1627 and 1643.[115] Antoine was probably one of these French Catholic settlers.

The early immigrants included merchants, professional men, landless nobles, skilled workers, soldiers, and of course, religious missionaries. All immigrants were indentured for three years to pay off their passage and lodging costs. However, after these people established communities, settlers who would permanently occupy the land came and became inhabitants, not just immigrants.

Many of the colonists came from Normandy, Île-de-France, Poitou, Aunis, Brittany, and Saintonge. The majority of those who came were single men. This

---

[113.] "French Colonization of the Americas."

[114.] Stephen A. White, *La généalogie des trente-sept familles hôtesses des "Retrouvailles 94,"* Bourque.

[115.] "Canada, French Immigration (New France)," FamilySearch, https://www.familysearch.org/wiki/en/Canada,_French_Immigration_(New_France)_(National_Institute).

large number of unmarried men created an enormous need for marriageable women. There were ten times more men of marriageable age than women in the colony. Many of these men could not find a wife and returned to France after their three-year agreement ended. One solution that was tried was to encourage men to marry native women. A dowry of 150 French livres was promised to any native woman marrying a Frenchman, but this plan was not successful and was eventually dropped.[116]

French authorities persuaded several unmarried young women to emigrate, their passage paid by the Crown. They were promised a place to live when they arrived, and they were encouraged to marry. They were called *filles à marier* (marriageable girls), but they soon became known as *filles du Roi* (the king's daughters).[117] These women came from houses of charity in French cities. Most were orphans, foundlings, or women who were jailed for prostitution and vagrancy. Some of the top-standing women were recruited for officers.[118]

Initial attempts at a settlement between 1627 and 1634 were mostly unsuccessful. Several exploratory efforts failed because of wars with England. Many settlers arrived in 1634. They began colonies farther west along the river to Montréal. Despite these attempts, however, the population of New France was still in the low hundreds by 1641, well short of the promised four thousand.

Antoine married Antoinette Landry in 1641 in Annapolis Royal, Acadia. Antoinette was born about 1618 in La Chausse, Martaize, France. She was the daughter of Jean Claud Landry and Marie Salé, who we will meet and find out more about in chapter 7 on the Landrys. This union is where the Bourg family and the Landry family first intersect.

Antoinette probably came to Acadia with her family. Her father died there in 1671. Her mother died there in 1686.

The Children of Antoine Abraham Bourg

Antoine and Antoinette had the following eleven children together in thirty-seven years:

---

[116] Knowles 1990, 11; Gagné 2001, 17.
[117] Canada, French Immigration (New France).
[118] Knowles 1990, 11; Gagné 2001, 17.

- François Bourg was born in 1644 in Acadia and died in 1684. He married Marguerite Boudrot, daughter of Michel Boudrot and Michelle Aucoin, in 1665. Marguerite was born in 1648 in Port-Royal, Acadia.

- Marie Bourg was born in 1645 in Port-Royal. She married Vincent Brault in 1661. He was born in 1631 in Loudun, France, and moved to Acadia in 1652.

- Jean Bourg was born in 1647 in Port-Royal. He moved himself and his clan to Cobequid, Acadia. He passed away in about 1695 in Cobequid. He married Marguerite Martin about 1667 in Port-Royal. She was born about 1639 in Port-Royal and died there on April 24, 1707.

- Bernard Amand Bourg was born in 1649 and died between 1693–1741. He married Françoise Brun, daughter of Vincent dit Lebrun Brun and Marie Renee Breaux, about 1670. She was born about 1652 in Port-Royal, Acadia. She died between 1692–1747.

- Martin Bourg was born in 1650 in Cobequid and died between 1694 and 1742. He is Generation 10 of this story.

- Marie-Jeanne Bourg was born in 1653 in Port-Royal.

- Renée Bourg was born in 1655 in Port-Royal and died before 1686. She married Charles Boudrot, son of Michel Boudrot and Michelle Aucoin, in 1674. Her husband, Charles, was born about 1649 in Pisquit, Acadia. He died about 1690 in Pisquit.

- Huguette Bourg was born in 1657 in Port-Royal and died between 1693-1752. She married Sebastian Brun about 1675. He was born about 1654 in Port-Royal and died between 1693-1745.

- Jeanne Bourg was born in 1659 in Port-Royal and died between 1709–1754. She married Pierre dit l'Aine dit l'Esturgeion Comeaux, son of Pierre Comeau and Rose Boyol, about 1677 in Port-Royal. He was born about 1653 in France and moved to Port-Royal.

- Abraham Bourg was born in 1662 in Port-Royal and died between 1701–1753. He married Marie Brun, daughter of Vincent dit Lebrun Brun and Marie Renee Breaux, about 1683. She was born about 1659 in Port-Royal and died on April 14, 1736.

- Marguerite Bourg was born in about 1667 in Port-Royal and passed away between 1696 and 1761. She married Louis Allain about 1690 in Port-Royal. Louis, her husband, was born about 1654 in France and died on June 16, 1717 in Port-Royal.

Exploration and Expansion

The French were economically interested in Canada because of fishing off the Grand Banks. However, by 1600, France was more interested in income from the fur trade. A fur trading post was founded at Tadoussac in 1600. Champlain made his first trip to Canada to trade for furs four years later. He sketched a map of the St. Lawrence River, and on his return to France, he filed a report entitled "Savages" relating his stay in a tribe of Montagnais near Tadoussac.[119]

Champlain needed to report his findings to Henry IV. He participated in another expedition to New France in the spring of 1604, conducted by Pierre Du Gua de Monts. It helped the foundation of a settlement on St. Croix Island, the first French settlement in the New World, which was abandoned following winter. The expedition then founded the colony of Port-Royal.[120]

In 1608, Champlain founded a fur post that would become the city of Quebec. This city would become the capital of New France. In Quebec, Champlain forged alliances between France and the Huron and Ottawa against their traditional enemies, the Iroquois. Champlain and other French travelers then continued to explore North America, with canoes made from birchbark, to move quickly through the Great Lakes and their tributaries. In 1634, the Normand explorer Jean Nicolet pushed his exploration to the west up to Wisconsin.[121]

Antoine Abraham Bourg arrived in Acadia in approximately 1640. Following the capitulation of Quebec by David Kieke and the Kirke brothers, the British occupied the city of Quebec and all of Canada from 1629 to 1632. Samuel de Champlain was taken prisoner, and there followed the bankruptcy of the Company of the Hundred Associates.

Following the Treaty of Saint-Germain-en-Laye, France took possession of the colony in 1632. The city of Trois-Rivières started in 1634. In 1642, the Angevin Jérôme le Royer de la Dauversière founded Ville-Marie (later Montreal),

---

[119] *Des sauvages, ou, Voyage de Samuel Champlain, de Brouage, fait en la France Nouuelle, l'an mil six cens trois* (Paris: Chez Claude de Monstr'œil, tenant sa boutique en la Cour du Palais, au nom de Iesus, 1603). OCLC 71251137

[120] "French Colonization of the Americas," Wikipedia, *https*://en.wikipedia.org/wiki/French_colonization_of_the_Americas.

[121] James MacPherson Le Moine, *Quebec, Past and Present: a History of Quebec, 1608-1876* (1876), online.

which was at that time a fort as protection against Iroquois attacks (the first great Iroquois war lasted from 1642 to 1667).[122]

Despite this rapid expansion, the colony of Port-Royal developed very slowly. The Iroquois wars and diseases were the leading causes of death in the French colony. In 1663, when Louis XIV provided the royal government, the population of New France was only 2,500 European inhabitants. That year, to increase the size of the community, Louis XIV sent between eight hundred and nine hundred "king's daughters" to become the wives of French settlers. The people of New France then grew to seven thousand in 1674 and fifteen thousand by 1689.[123]

Life in Acadia

Farming was a significant part of the livelihood of the colony in Acadia. But these were not like the farmers we know and think of today, clearing land to make their fields and planting crops. They created farmland using a system of diking (building levees). They used knowledge and skills that were familiar to them from France.

The high tides and vast marshlands of Port-Royal made this location ideal for applying these techniques. It is likely part of the reason they chose the site in the first place. Upon their arrival, the Acadians knew what to do and began the process of diking immediately.[124]

---

[122] Hubert, et al. Charbonneau, "The population of the St-Lawrence Valley, 1608–1760," in *A Population History of North America* (2000), 99-142.

[123] Francis Parkman, *Count Frontenac, and New France under Louis XIV* (1877).

[124] "Life in Acadia Before the Deportation," Acadian Genealogy, https://www.acadian.org/history/life-acadia-deportation/; "The Acadians and the Creation of the Dykeland 1680–1755," Landscape of le Paysage de Grand Pré, http://www.landscapeofgrandpre.ca/the-acadians-and-the-creation-of-the-dykeland-1680ndash1755.html.

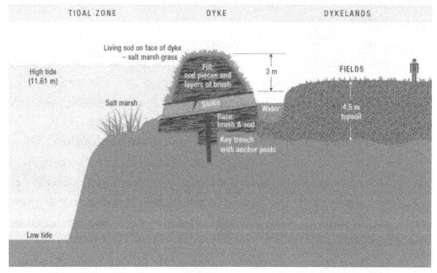

Figure 4 – The System of Farming and Levees in Acadia

The Acadians lived on the banks of rivers, which emptied into the Bay of Fundy. Because of the funnel-like shape of the Bay of Fundy, tides were very high. The high tide also affected all the rivers and streams. At high tide, the rivers would overflow their banks. The flooding covered much of the lowlands or marshes. When the flow went out, these lands were still wet with leftover salt tidewater. The damp swamp built up from layers of fine fertile soil due to the tidal activity over many centuries.

To make use of these fertile lands, the Acadians built dikes or long walls around the perimeter of the areas affected by tidal flooding. The dams were well compacted and so tight that they stopped the river water from flooding as the tide rose. The Acadians dug ditches that drained towards an aboiteau. An aboiteau is a one-way door or gate, which leads back out through the dam to the river. This gate allowed the rain and snow to wash the salt from the land and back out to sea through the aboiteau or sluice. The soil would drain at low tide when there was no saltwater on the seaside of the gate. The salt river water could not come in when the tide was high, because the doors only opened one way. As the tide came in, the sea would push on the sluice. This pressure caused the gate to close and seal even tighter. After two years of this land drainage process, the salty soil on the marshes became desalted and dry, and these marshes thus made excellent fertile soil for farming.[125]

Sometimes the dikes were built by driving five or six rows of logs into the ground, laying other logs from trees on top of each other between these rows, filling all spaces between the logs with well-packed clay, and then covering everything over with sod cut from the marsh itself. Sometimes dikes were built by merely laying sod over mounds of earth.

The Acadians were called lazy by settlers from other communities. They were referred to as *defricheurs d'eau* (clearers of water) because they built dikes and cultivated the natural meadows and marshes, rarely clearing the upland forests for agriculture purposes. For example, it is the complaint of Governor de Broullan in 1701 that "they [the Acadians] retreated to small portions of land, although their concessions are large."

Upon deeper reflection, it was evident that the Acadians used the higher ground just above the marsh for their houses and buildings to guarantee a dry location. Rather than being lazy, they were simply good readers of their landscape, being in harmony with it and knowing well how to harness the natural resources around them. Given the agricultural methods of the period, using the marshlands was more efficient and more productive than clearing the uplands for agrarian purposes.

Sally Ross and Alphonse Deveau are the best source of firsthand description of life in the settlements of Rivière Dauphin (Annapolis River). Dièreville writes the following concerning the Acadians' efficiency and hard work:

It costs a great deal to prepare the lands which they wish to cultivate. To grow wheat, the marshes which are inundated by the Sea at high tide, must be drained; these are called Lowlands, and they are quite good, but what labor is needed to make them for cultivations! The ebb and flow of the Sea cannot easily be stopped, but the Acadians succeed in doing so by employing great dikes, called aboiteaux.

Coarse salt hay (spartina) on the seaside of the dikes, which grew in the marshes in the saltwater ebbing of the tides, was another natural resource that the Acadians quickly harvested. During the low tide, the spartina became exposed. The Acadians cut the salt hay and piled in on *saddles* (platforms) that they built to keep it above the highest seasonal tidemark so that it could stay dry. They later baled the hay and stored it in barns to feed their animals all winter. Thus

---

[125] "Life in Acadia Before the Deportation," Acadian Genalogy, https://www.acadian.org/history/life-acadia-deportation/

it was not necessary for them to slaughter their cattle for lack of winter fodder, as it was in most of the New England colonies. Consequently, unlike the New England colonies, they were not dependent on receiving new cattle from Europe each spring to replace those they had to slaughter the previous fall. This method provided the Acadians at Port-Royal with stability and self-sufficiency.

The Acadians soon had more delicate grasses growing on the dry landside of the dikes replacing the spartina hay, which had always flourished in the tidewaters. However, they continued to harvest it on the seaward side of the levees. Before 1755, the Acadians lived largely self-sufficient lives on their marshland farms. They tilled the soil, and it yielded abundant crops of wheat, oats, barley, rye, peas, corn, flax, and hemp. They also kept gardens in which they grew beets, carrots, parsnips, onions, chives, shallots, herbs, salad greens, cabbages, and turnips. Cabbages and turnips seem to have been particularly influential in their diet.

The Acadians kept cattle and sheep, as seen from the census documents. Pigs roamed freely in the forest behind the houses. They were also fed on kitchen scraps and, in winter especially, on leaves and peelings from the cabbages and turnips stored in the gardens and covered with straw until needed. The Acadians seem to have eaten a lot of pork but relatively little beef, preferring to keep their cattle for milk, as working animals (oxen), and for trade.

The Acadian life was hard but pleasant in many ways. They understood their landscape and made it work for them. In a land where regulations were kept to a bare minimum, the settlers could supplement their needs by hunting and fishing, as well as berry picking and making various liquids. They brewed their beer from branches of fir trees and dried fruit and berries as food.

Those Acadians who devoted their lives to farming were very busy, depending on the season. Their day consisted, for the most part, of dike building, making hay, fencing, house-and-barn-building, cutting firewood, clearing land in wooded areas, gardening, hunting, looking after domestic animals, and making candles, soap, butter, dye, and clothing. Also, they prepared and preserved food, and in their leisure time, they made furniture, tools, and toys.

After living a hard, full life as a frontier farmer, Antoine Abraham Bourg died on October 5, 1687. He lived a long life of seventy-eight years and was buried in Annapolis Royal, Acadia (today Nova Scotia). He was the progenitor of all the Bourgs in Acadia.

Generation 10: Martin Bourg

Martin Bourg was born in 1650 in Cobequid, Acadia. He was the fifth child and fourth son of Antoine Abraham Bourg. His father was forty-one years old when he was born. Like his father, Martin grew up as a farmer, learning the ways of Acadian farming from his family.

When he was twenty-five years old (about 1675), he courted and married Marie Gauterot Potet, a girl from Bourg village in Cobequid. Marie was the daughter of Jehan Potet and Marie Gautreaux in Acadia. She was born about 1657 in Port-Royal. She died on May 5, 1700. Marie is the third cousin of Martin, as Jehan is the son of Perrine Bourg, Antoine's sister.

The Children of Martin Bourg

Martin Bourg and Marie Gauterot Potet had the following twelve children:

- Marie Bourg was born in 1676. She married Pierre Terriot, son of Germain Terriot and André Brun, in 1695. He was born about 1671. He died between 1717 and 1763 in Acadia.
- Abraham Bourg was born in 1679 and died between 1711and 1770. He married Anne Dugas, daughter of Claude Dugas and Françoise Bourgeois, in 1704 in Port-Royal, Acadia. He married Anne Dugas about 1704 in Cobequid. She was born about 1679 in Port-Royal. She died between 1710–1773.
- Pierre Bourg was born in 1681 in Port-Royal and died between 1762–1781. He married Marguerite Blanchard, daughter of Martin Blanchard and Marguerite Guilbaut, about 1706 in Cobequid. She was born about 1689 in Cobequid and died between 1762 and 1787.
- Jeanne Bourg was born in 1684. She married Michel Aucoin, son of Martin Aucoin and Marie Gaudet, in 1700. He was born in Grand-Pre. He died between 1718 and1768.
- Ambroise Bourg was born in 1686 and died between 1718 and 1777. He married Elizabeth Melanson in 1710. She was born in 1691 and died between 1719 and 1785.
- Francois-Louis Bourg was born in 1688. He married Cecile Michel, daughter of François Michel and Marguerite Meunier, in 1715.

- Anne Marie Bourg was born in 1691 and died about 1766 in Boulogne-sur-Mer, Haute Saone, France. She married Alexis Aucoin about 1707 in Cobequid. He was born on March 14, 1684 in Grand Pre. He died on March 14, 1759, in Cobequid.

- Madeleine Bourg was born in 1694. She married René Aucoin, son of Martin Aucoin and Marie Gaudet, in 1713.

- Charles Bourg was born in 1697 and died between 1754 and 1788. He married Marie Anne (Boudrot) Boudreaux about 1726 in Port-Royal. She was born about 1709 in Port-Royal. She died between 1755 and 1804.

- Pierre Bourg was born about 1681 in Port-Royal and died between 1762–1781. He married Marguerite Blanchard, daughter of Martin Blanchard and Marguerite Guilbaut, about 1760 in Cobequid. She was born about 1689 in Cobequid and died between 1762–1787.

- Marie Bourg was born about 1682 and died between 1718 and 1777 in Acadia. She married Pierre Terriot, son of Germain Terriot and André Brun, between 1694 and 1725. He was born about 1671 and died between 1717 and 1763 in Acadie.

- Jeanne Bourg was born about 1684 in Cobequid and died between 1718 and 1779. She married Michel Aucoin, son of Martin Aucoin and Marie Gaudet, about 1700. He was born in Grand-Pre. He died between 1718 and 1768.

Family Life

Acadians had large families. When a son married, he would settle some distance from his father's house and start another little village. Any group of two or three houses was called a village. In the census of 1671, there were 361 souls, and in 1686 almost double that: 622 souls, including thirty soldiers. By 1733, when Mitchell's map was drawn, there were small Acadian villages as far away as Paradise. Acadian communities, as seen from Port-Royal maps of the day, formed little family hamlets. It was a sort of clan or extended family concept that was very common in France.

According to Acadian.org, "The extended family ... gathered at the same hearth and under the same roof, a large social group, based on several generations, with the old parents, the married children and their spouses, the youngsters of the different couples ..." It was a patriarchal family dominated by the male head of the family. He decided the destiny of the group. He directed the management of the farm, allotted the tasks, and chose his successor. These solidly established family communities were generally linked to the possession of the property.[126]

The Woman's Role in the Extended Family

The early settlements in Acadia were almost exclusively male, and the men in these frontier establishments would intermarry with the native population. From 1632 onward, settlements became more permanent, however, and the land was brought under cultivation by entire families recruited to come to the new colony.

Brenda Dunn, in her article "Looking into Acadia," discusses the "Lives of Women in Ancienne Acadie." She explains how French law ensured the respect of women in their own right. She writes:

Legally, men and women were both considered minors until the age of 25, or marriage, whichever came first. Even after marriage, though, women continued to be known by their original family surname, although the name of the married couple, was the husbands. The custom of Paris provided for a marriage contract to be drawn up before a couple wedded, and that marriage established a community of goods, between the couple. Neither husband nor wife could conduct property transactions without the other's written consent.[127]

Dunn continues:

Marriage contracts usually stipulated that, on the death of one spouse, one half of the couple's property was to be inherited by the survivor, and the other half divided among the children, male and female. This stipulation meant that widows and widowers had legal autonomy, at least until remarriage (which was almost inevitable). There appears to have been very few single women in Acadie; perhaps the pressures of survival in the new land, demanded partnership. "The family was the cornerstone of Acadian life in the 17th and 18th centuries. By 1650, some 50 families were living in or near Port Royal and constituted the foundation of the Acadian People.[128]

Brenda Dunn elaborates on women's roles as follows:

[126.] "Life in Acadia Before the Deportation," Acadian.org, https://www.acadian.org/history/life-acadia-deportation/.

[127.] "Life in Acadia Before the Deportation."

[128.] Sally Ross and Alphonse Deveau, *Acadians of Nova Scotia*, https://www.amazon.com/Acadians-Nova-Scotia-Sally-Ross/dp/1551090120.

Women played important roles in a society based on family and kinship networks. There were a few aspects of Acadian life that they were not involved in. There was very little variety in Acadian Christian names. The majority of Acadian women were named Marie, Anne, Madeleine, Cécile, Jeanne, or Françoise. One of the reasons for the repetition was the children often took their godparents' names. Wives kept their maiden names all their lives. Widows in seigneurial families were the exceptions. They were known as "Madame" rather than a widow. This widow's title is seen in the 1707 census, where we find "Mde. le Belleisle widow", "Mde Freneuse", … along with "widow Naquin".[129]

Although Acadian society believed that all people are equal and deserve equal rights and opportunities more than the people of France in the late 17th and 18th centuries, there was some belief in society levels. The upper level consisted of those granted seigneuries. A seigneurial grant gave them status, even if they were not necessarily wealthy.

Acadian women were very busy. They were often married as young as sixteen and had large families. These large families meant that their small villages were full of close relatives who could help care for the children. Women were also responsible for hard work and household chores. They spun, dyed, and wove wool and flax for clothing, tended gardens, cooked and baked, and helped as necessary with other, heavy labor.

Brenda Dunn continues as follows:

The everyday dress of the 18th century Acadian women is believed to have been linen chemise, worn under either a vest or a jacket, with woven wool or linen skirt often striped. An apron, neck scarf, and cap would complete the outfit. No respectable women of the period would have been seen with her head uncovered. Different regions of France had a distinctive style of cap. Knit stockings and wooden shoes were worn for everyday wear. Leather shoes were probably worn on occasions, such as attending Church.[130]

Acadian women were responsible for culling the fish entangled in the weirs at high tide. They had few luxuries and little time for relaxation. Women wore wooden shoes while working, like men.

As discussed above, the building of dikes and houses were two major community events in which Acadians demonstrated their support for each other and their community. They came together as friends, neighbors, and extended

---

[129] "Life in Acadia Before the Deportation."
[130] "Life in Acadia Before the Deportation."

family to complete the task at hand. Big tasks such as the cutting and storing of hay were group activities.

Jean Daigle describes this vital community spirit:

Despite the continual attacks and looting ... Port Royal was attacked once in 1704, twice in 1707, and again in 1710, the Acadians held firm. They had developed an ability to resist and adapt that kept these difficulties from becoming insurmountable. The system of the family organization goes a long way toward explaining how Acadians could cling to a territory coveted by several great powers, for over 150 years.[131]

Limited immigration to Acadia meant that, after three or four generations, all inhabitants of the various settlements were related to one another. These blood ties were created by a kinship that established solidarity and independence. This kinship grew into the Acadian extended family, a traditional society that was able to resist the social upheavals of the period. This kinship continued through their move to Louisiana and is exhibited in the culture of south Louisiana. It's part of the culture the Cajuns donated to New Orleans.

Religion

Religion was an essential part of Acadian life. Sally Ross and Alphonse Deveau quote Father Petit, a priest who, in 1676, who became first Vicar-General of Québec: "One sees no drunkenness or loose living and hears no swearing or blasphemy. Even though they spread out four or five leagues along the shores of the river, they come to church in large numbers every Sunday and on Holy Days."[132]

The Acadians were very friendly with the Mi'kmaq, who helped them in many ways to survive this new land. They traded with the Indians and other French settlements. As power shifted back and forth between France and Britain, the Acadians and the Mi'kmaq became closer and closer. Together they developed character and way of life.

The following information on trade comes from the Nova Scotia Museum publication, *The Acadians: Settlement*:

Although the Acadians were remarkably self-sufficient, there were some things they could not make or grow themselves, and for these needs, they

---

[131] "Life in Acadia Before the Deportation."
[132] "Life in Acadia Before the Deportation."

established trading links with New England and with other French settlement. Molasses, cooking pots, broad axes, clay pipes, gunpowder, fabrics, and rum, came from New England. Through Louisburg, they obtained cotton, thread, lace, firearms, and religious items, from France.[133]

Acadians were fond of smoking (both men and women smoked). Their clay pipes came mostly from England, although at times they did fashion their own using local red clay. In return for these items, the Acadians traded grain from their fertile reclaimed marshlands, their cattle which were healthy and well-fed on salt-marsh hay, and furs they had obtained from trapping and trade with the Micmac Indians.

Martin Bourg died sometime in August of 1717 in Annapolis County, Acadia.

Generation 9: Pierre Bourg

Pierre Bourg was born in 1681 in Port-Royal, Nova Scotia, Acadia. Like his ancestors before him, he grew up as an Acadian farmer and fisherman. From 1689 to 1713, French settlers were faced with almost constant battle during the French and Indian Wars. From 1689 to 1697, they fought the British in the Nine Years' War. In 1690 and 1711, Quebec City successfully resisted the attacks of the British army and navy.

The British took advantage of the second war. With the signing of the Treaty of Utrecht in 1713, France ceded Acadia (with a population of 1,700 people) to Britain. Under the Sovereign Council, the number of people in the colony grew more quickly. However, the population growth was far inferior to that of the thirteen British colonies in the south.

In the middle of the eighteenth century, New France accounted for 60,000 people, while the British colonies had more than a million. This unequal number placed Acadia at a tremendous military disadvantage against the British. The war between the colonies resumed in 1744, lasting until 1748. A final and decisive battle began in 1754. Numerous alliances, especially with Native Americans, helped the Canadians and the French. They were usually outnumbered on the battlefield.[134]

Pierre Bourg married Marguerite Blanchard, daughter of Martin Blanchard

---

[133] "Life in Acadia Before the Deportation."
[134] R. Cole Harris, *Historical Atlas of Canada: Volume I: From the Beginning to 1800* (University of Toronto Press, 2016).

and Marguerite Guilbaut, about 1706 in Cobequid, Acadia. She was born in Cobequid. When Marguerite Blanchard was born in 1689, her father, Martin, was forty-two, and her mother, Marguerite, was twenty. Marguerite died as a young mother in 1714 in Cobequid at the age of twenty-five.

The Children of Pierre Bourg

Pierre Bourg and Marguerite Blanchard had the following children:

- Pierre Bourg Jr. was born on February 2, 1708, in Cobequid and died between 1709 and 1798.
- François Bourg was born about 1709 in Cobequid and died on February 23,1759 in Saint-Malo, Ille-et-Vilaine, France. He was married twice. He married his first wife, Emelienne Thibodaux, about 1747 in Cobequid. She was born about 1716 in Pisiquit, Acadia. She died on February 14, 1759 in Saint-Malo. François married his second wife, Marguerite Hebert, about 1736 in Cobequid. She was born about 1709 in Cobequid. She died between 1747 and 1804.
- Joseph Bourg was born in 1711 in Cobequid and died between 1755 and 1803. He married Françoise Dugas in 1735 in Cobequid. She was born about 1713 in Acadia. She died between 1754 and 1808.
- Jean Bourg was born about 1713 in Cobequid and died on June 5, 1759 in Saint-Suliac, Ille-et-Vilaine, France. Jean was discussed earlier in this chapter in Generation 8.
- Madeleine Bourg was born in 1714 in Cobequid. It is probable that her mother, Marguerite, died as a result of this childbirth. Madeleine died in 1758 at sea during the crossing to France at the age of forty-four years. She was married to Ambroise Hebert about 1735 in Cobequid. He was born about 1712 in Cobequid. He died on January 10, 1778, in Nantes, France. He died between 1762 and 1781.

Daily Life in Acadia

The survival of the Acadian home required constant effort. Yet their days were not highly stressful. The Acadians' way of life followed the advice of Matthew 6:34: "Take therefore no thought for the morrow: for the morrow shall take thought for the things of itself." To stay alive, they did the seasonal chores when needed and recurring chores day after day.[135]

Daily duties included, for the mother, minding the fire, getting the water, cooking, and cleaning; for the father, clean the stable and barn, feeding the animals, doing emergency repairs, tending the fields, and producing food from animals or the sea; and for the children, milking the cows and gathering eggs. Sons would be responsible for helping the father with his chores. Daughters were responsible for assisting the mother by cooking, cleaning, sewing, and taking care of the younger children.

The Yearly Cycles

Though the routine of an Acadian home remained similar from one day to the next, the year was punctuated by duties and special occasions involving the family as a whole, sometimes the entire community. Religious and agricultural calendars were tightly linked. These rest periods were more numerous during the winter.

In this traditional society, where existence mainly depended upon the seasonal activities of summer, the active year started with snowmelt in the spring. It ended in late fall. In early spring came the preparation of seeding and land for cultivation. This preparation was followed by the hunting, harvesting, and slaughtering of animals. It might be said that those chores, along with the collection and preservation of food, marked the coming of the cold season. For example, a good part of the crop of berries (strawberries, raspberries, currant, blueberries, choke-cherries, etc.) of the summer was well appreciated in winter in the form of jams and preserves.

This break does not mean that Acadians were idle throughout the winter. They had to do the chores overlooked during the summer. Animals, of course, still had to be tended. When fall came, the family spent more time indoors. At this time, the mother could then give special care, as she did in the spring, to the cleanliness of the home with a thorough, top-to-bottom housecleaning. This preparation left her with "leisure time" in the winter, when she would create and mend clothes and handmade pieces with the wool and flax from the summer season.

[135.] "Lifestyles in the Days of Our Ancestors," Exposition-Acadia, http://www.virtualmuseum. ca/Exhibitions/Acadie/exposition_e.html.

The Role of Marriage

Marriage played a prominent role in the life of all Acadians. The survival of their community depended on it. It alone allowed family life and children. Indeed, this was considered its primary function. Very little time went by until the young bride became pregnant and gave birth to the first of many children to come.

Marriage was crucial to the survival of the individual. As soon as adolescents made their solemn Communion, about age fourteen for girls and sixteen for boys, marriage was considered. Marriage marked the passage into adulthood. If the matter was not quite so pressing for the Acadian man, who first had to settle down, the Acadian woman worried about her fate early. She did not wish to reach her twenty-fifth birthday unmarried.

If a wedding marked first and foremost the creation of a new family, it also established, in the Acadian view, an alliance between two family groups. A vital ritual surrounded it. The *grande demande*, or official marriage proposal, occurred when the suitor expressed his wish to the parents of the young girl and tried to demonstrate that he was capable of taking good care of her as his wife.

Very often in the Acadia of old, marriage was the result of respect more than of true love. On both sides, a favorable match was sought, someone likely to help establish a home. For their part, parents also wished to set up links with a family able to bring support and help in case of need. In such circumstances, parental approval of the marriage was crucial. Therefore, an official proposal was critical, allowing the young man a chance to speak about his assets and the girl's parents to clearly express their opinion.

To meet regularly, both of the young people had to respect certain traditions. They were together in public, in plain sight of everyone, and probably met on a few occasions. After some time, the young man would pay an occasional visit to the home of the young girl. Then, after approximately six months, he would pop the question to her, although this was not necessarily to get her consent, for she likely would have let her lack of interest be known sooner if such was the case. What he wanted to know was how her parents saw their relationship: "Do you think your parents would agree?" If the answer was yes, he would then proceed with an official request.

Even if the result was practically a foregone conclusion—the girl's parents would doubtless have long before expressed their disagreement—the marriage proposal nonetheless remained a mandatory ritual. This formality over, the marriage banner was published, announcing the wedding to be held in about three weeks.

The Acadian Diet

The daily diet of Acadians depended, for a good part, upon their occupation and their environment. Products from the farm or fishing and hunting constituted the major part of their food supply. Their recipes were generally simple and typically quite salty due to food conservation methods, which relied heavily on the use of sea salt. This salting was true for meat as well as fish.

In fact, for many Acadian families, the diet was more varied in the winter. Reserves set aside during the warm season were then used. Those were the fruits from the foodstuffs produced at the time: from every product of the harvesting, fishing, hunting, or gathering, only a portion was consumed fresh, the rest being processed and stored for the cold season. For instance, at the fall slaughtering of animals, only part of the pork (sometimes beef) meat was served fresh; the rest was salted and saved for the winter months.

Since the Acadians' lands yielded in many cases a mediocre crop, salted herring and potatoes (boiled, roasted, or grated) were often featured on the menu. To these staples, of course, several vegetables from the garden were added (onion, peas, beans, corn, etc.), and generally served boiled.

From their fields, Acadians harvested oats, buckwheat (especially popular in Madawaska), and barley, which often replaced wheat in the preparation of flour used in the making of bread, pancakes, and biscuits. Bread, a food essential to existence, was fashioned from a hops-based yeast and baked in the embers of the fireplace, in a double-decker stove, or an ordinary clay oven. Of course, bread was particularly favored with molasses and tea procured from storekeepers in exchange for meat, butter, or fresh eggs from the farm.

Continuing French and British Conflict

As France and England continued to fight for control of North America, most Acadians wanted to stay neutral. Unfortunately, neither the French nor the British would allow them to do so. Both powers wanted the Acadians to support their cause and, hopefully, fight for it.

The Acadians were considered neutral by the French. After all, they spoke

French, they were from French ancestors, and they were Roman Catholics. However, since the Treaty of Utrecht in 1713, signed by the French government, the British viewed the Acadians as British subjects. Only a few Acadians were loyal to France. While only a very few allied with the British, most Acadians were caught in the middle. After the Treaty of Utrecht, the Acadians at first refused to sign an oath of loyalty to England. They did pledge to remain neutral between the two superpowers.

In 1729, most Acadians agreed to a modified conditional agreement put forth by the British. The British governor assured them they would not have to fight against the French and their Native American friends if they promised to remain neutral. By 1750, though, activities by the Acadians caused the British to violate their assurance of neutrality. The British were also troubled with the situation with the Mi'kmaq. The British signed treaties with the Native American peoples of those regions, but by 1744 they had a problem with these treaties. Great Britain found itself at war with France after decades of peace. This conflict was because of the War of the Austrian Succession.

In the summer of 1744, a French advancement came through the Acadian villages asking Acadian men to join the initiative against the British. Few men joined the cause. Acadians wanted to remain neutral. The Acadian response in 1744 disappointed the French and worried the British, who had hoped the Acadians would turn against the French.

The following year, in 1745, the French started an unsuccessful attack on the British fort at Annapolis Royal. At around the same time, a vast army of provincial soldiers from New England, supported by British warships, captured the French fort at Louisburg. In 1746, France sent a large expedition to cross the ocean on a mission to regain Louisburg and retake Annapolis Royal. The French wanted to force the Acadians to commit to the French cause. The expedition ended in disaster because of storms and illness.

Both the French and the British reinforced their positions in Acadia in the late 1740s. By the autumn of 1746, because of earlier French actions in the area, the British sent five hundred New England soldiers to establish a stronghold in the village of Grand-Pré. The British-American troops took over several houses. A group of 250 French soldiers and 50 Native-American warriors heard reports of the New Englanders' occupation of Grand-Pré. Despite being outnumbered two to one and the difficult winter travel, they went to Grand-Pré in January 1747, assisted by a few Acadians who were sympathetic to the French cause.

Some pro-British Acadians gave the New England soldiers a warning about the attack. The New Englanders ignored the warnings. They thought the severe winter conditions made an attack unlikely.

On the morning of February 11, 1747, in the middle of a blinding snowstorm, the French, the Maliseet, and the Mi'kmaq forces caught the New Englanders by surprise and defeated them. It was known as the Attack at Grand-Pré. The fight left eighty New England men dead, including their commander.

The attack was a big part of the thinking of some British leaders in 1755 when they decided to remove all of the Acadians. Not long after, both France and Britain increased their military numbers in Canada. France's significant move was to send an expedition of several thousand colonists to re-occupy Louisburg in 1749. From 1749 to 1751, the French built two forts in the Chignecto region at Beauséjour and Gaspareaux. The British, meanwhile, sent a massive expedition to establish Halifax in 1749 as a counterbalance to Louisburg. The British also established several new posts, forts, and settlements beyond Halifax. They included Fort Edward within the Acadian community at Pisiquid, a small fort at Vieux Logis (Horton Landing) near Grand-Pré, Fort Lawrence in the Chignecto region (opposite Fort Beauséjour), and a sizeable new town of "foreign Protestants," mostly of German and Swiss origin, at Lunenburg, on Nova Scotia's southeastern shore.

The deportation of the rest of the Acadians from Ile-Saint-Jean and Ile-Royale took place in 1758. Because these Acadians were now considered loyal subjects of the French king, they were sent directly to France. The route of these ships across the Atlantic was much longer and, therefore, much more dangerous than for those exiled in 1755. Three of the 1758 ships sank, with the loss of about 850 Acadian lives. Because of challenging conditions for passengers traveling over long distances on a winter sea, the death rate, especially among children, had been very high when the boats arrived at their ports of destination in France.

Pierre Bourg and Marguerite Blanchard were put on the ship *du Supply* in 1758. They were all deported to Saint-Malo together with their entire family (all their children).

CHAPTER 4

THE TALBOT FAMILY

Ancestors of Lucy Marie Talbot

When a society or a civilization perishes, one condition can always be found. They forgot where they came from.

—Carle Sandburg

Every man is a quotation from all his ancestors.

— Ralph Waldo Emerson

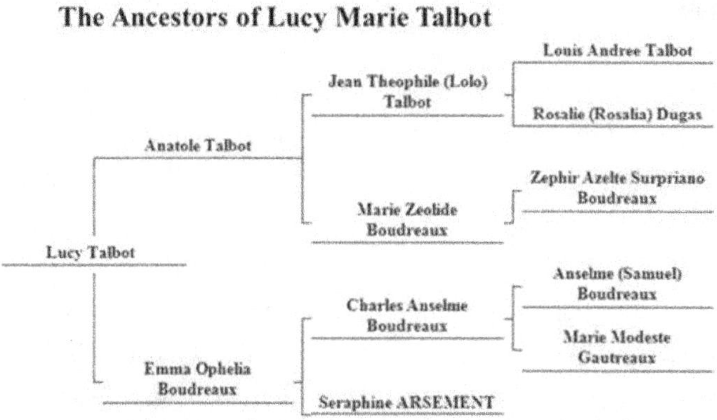

The Ancestors of Lucy Marie Talbot

Figure 5 – The Ancestors of Lucy Marie Talbot

Generation 1: Lucy Marie Talbot

Lucy Marie Talbot (the paternal grandmother of James Anatole Bourg Jr.) was born on Friday, September 14, 1888, in Napoleonville, LA. In 1800, women were pregnant an average of seven times during their lives. Women often had as many as ten births during this time; possibly as many as one-third had that many children. Getting pregnant was an expected life event, but it could also be hazardous for both baby and mother.[136] Lucy's mother, Emma, died on May 9, 1897, just days after the birth of Lucy's sister Agnes, when Lucy was only nine years old. Emma's death was probably a complication of childbirth.

Lucy was the daughter of Pierre Anatole Talbot. Pierre was born on November 21, 1857, and died on February 6, 1925. He had two wives during his lifetime. His first wife was Emma Ophelia Boudreaux [Lucy's mother] (1858–1897), who was born on December 29, 1858. Emma's mother and father were Charles Anselme Boudreaux (1832–1908) and Seraphine Arsement (1839–1853). Charles and Seraphine were married on June 16, 1855, in Assumption Parish, Louisiana.

Pierre Anatole and Emma were married on October 10, 1882, and had six children together. So Lucy had five siblings from her biological mother: Annie Seraphine (1885-1949), George C. "Cook" (1886-1970), Theophile Joseph (1890-1959), Shelby E. (1891-1930), and Agnes (1897-1972).

The presidential election of 1888 was significant. It was also very

---

[136.] Amy Wilde, "Pregnancy in the 1800s," *Classroom,* https://classroom.synonym.com/pregnancy-1800s-9138.html

controversial. The Republican candidate was Benjamin Harrison from Indiana. Grover Cleveland, the incumbent, was the Democratic candidate for president. Harrison had the advantage over Cleveland because Harrison was a Civil War soldier with a good record. He was very popular with Union soldiers. Cleveland had made numerous enemies during his presidency while trying to end a lot of corrupt practices.

The election marked the third time in American history that a presidential nominee won more popular votes but lost the election. This way of becoming president would be repeated by the election of President George W. Bush in 2000 and Donald Trump in 2016. The 1876 election had a lot of dispute and controversy behind-the-scenes. The election of 1824 was lost by Andrew Jackson in the House of Representatives, even though Andrew Jackson had won more electoral votes and more popular votes because Jackson had not won an absolute majority.[137]

This election was odd because Jackson won more popular votes but did not win the Presidency. The same thing happened in the elections of 2000 and 2016.

Lucy's Father Remarries

After Emma's death in May of 1897, Lucy's father, Anatole, was in a bind. He had six children under the age of thirteen, one a very young toddler. He needed help. A year and a half after Emma's death, he met and married Lucina Josephine Templet. The wedding was on January 12, 1899, at the Attakapas Canal Church. Pierre Anatole was 41 years old and Lucina was only 24 years old.

When Pierre married Lucina, his new young wife wanted children of her own. She couldn't raise Pierre's existing kids and grow a new family, so Pierre asked his brother Myrtle to help raise his older children. According to the 1910 census, Lucy was living with her Uncle Myrtle at the age of twenty-one, along with her brother George and her sister Agnes.

Pierre and Lucina had seven children together, making thirteen children overall for Pierre. The children of this second family were Irene, Leonide Gertrude (Bourg), Louis Anatole, Richard Augustine, Bessie Valerie (Bergeron), Stephen Talbot, and Anatole (Gabriel) Pierre Jr. The 1910 US Census shows that Anatole and Lucina (listed as Lucie in the census) were living with just six of their children. Pierre's children from Emma were not living with them.

---

[137] "Election of 1888," Laws, https://constitution.laws.com/election-of-1888

Lucy Marries

Lucy married Joseph Charles Bourg on April 9, 1912, at St. Anne Catholic Church in Napoleonville, Louisiana. The church was built in 1909. It was located about four blocks inland from Bayou Lafourche at 417 St. Joseph Street. Lucy was only twenty-three when she got married. Joseph was thirty-two years of age. Just five days later, on April 14, the *Titanic* struck an iceberg on its maiden voyage to the United States and sunk in the early morning hours of April 15, 1912.

The Louisiana governor election of 1912 was held days after the sinking on April 16, 1912. At this time, the Republican Party of Louisiana had little electoral support and was virtually nonexistent. The Democratic Party primary, held on January 23, 1912, decided who would be governor because of this lack of Republican presence. Democrat Luther E. Hall won the election as governor of Louisiana.

The 1912 US presidential election took place in Louisiana on November 5, 1912. In this election, Louisiana was won by Princeton University President Woodrow Wilson (D–Virginia), running with the governor of Indiana, Thomas R. Marshall. Wilson won with 76.81 percent of the popular vote against the incumbent Republican President, William Howard Taft, the twenty-sixth president of the United States former Republican Theodore Roosevelt (P–New York), who was running as an independent of the "Bull Moose" party with the governor of California, Hiram Johnson and got 11.71 percent of the popular vote. The five-time candidate of the Socialist Party, Eugene V. Debs (S–Indiana), had the first socialist mayor in the United States as his running mate.

In 1912, after dropping out of the Fisk School at age eleven, Louis Armstrong sang with a quartet of boys on the streets of New Orleans for money. But Louis began to get into trouble at this age. Bunk Johnson, another horn player, said he taught eleven-year-old Armstrong to play the horn by ear. He did this tutoring at Dago Tony's Tonk in New Orleans. Armstrong drew inspiration from his misguided youth. Armstrong once said, "Every time I close my eyes blowing that trumpet of mine, I look right in the heart of good old New Orleans … It has given me something to live for."[138]

On January 6, 1912, New Mexico was the forty-seventh state admitted to the Union. On February 14, 1912, Arizona became the forty-eighth. The Boston Red

---

[138] "Why is Louie Armstrong important to history?" Yahoo Answers, https://answers.yahoo.com/question/index?qid=20080305082522AA4ATEd

Sox defeated the New York Giants in the 1912 World Series. Boston won four games to three (with one tie). This dramatic series showcased pitching from Giant great Christy Mathewson and Boston fireballer Smoky Joe Wood. Smoky Joe won two of his three starts. In the final game, he pitched in relief. In this deciding game, Boston got two runs in the tenth inning to rally thanks to two costly fielding errors by the Giants. Mathewson started three games and completed all three. He compiled a 0.94 earned-run average for the series. For his efforts, he got two losses and a no-decision.[139]

On February 20, 1913, James A. Bourg, Sr., was born. Joseph and Lucy went on to have Oscar Joseph Bourg and Lucille Bourg. The family lived in New Orleans between 1940 and 1949 because of the loss of Joseph's eye due to diabetes. They moved back to Napoleonville in 1949 and lived there until Joseph died in 1962. Lucy became senile in the late 1960s and was moved to New Orleans to live in St. Margaret's Daughters Home, where she died on July 1, 1972. She is buried in St. Anne Catholic Cemetery in Napoleonville. Her Find A Grave Memorial # is 124503884.

Lucy's obituary reads as follows:

Lucy Talbot Bourg, on Saturday, July 1st, 1972 at 3:05 p.m.; beloved wife of the late Joseph C. Bourg; mother of James A. and Oscar J. Bourg and Mrs. Lucille Johnston; sister of Mrs. Dave Bergeron, Mrs. Leonide Bourg, Mrs. Bessie Bergeron, Sam, Richard, and Anatole Talbot; also survived by six grandchildren; a native of Napoleonville, La. and a resident of this city (New Orleans) for three years. Relatives and friends of the family, also employees of the National American Bank, New Orleans Public Service, Pan American Oil Co., and Naval Support Activity, are invited to attend the funeral. Services from the P. J. Donegan Funeral Home, 839 Jackson Ave. at Laurel, on Monday, July 3rd, 1972, at 9:15 a.m., followed by Requiem Mass at St. Alphonsus Catholic Church. Internment St. Anne's cemetery, Napoleonville, La. Visitation hours from 3 p.m. until 11 p.m.

Generation 2: Pierre Anatole Talbot

Pierre Anatole Talbot was born on Saturday, November 21, 1857, in the town of Attakapas Canal, Assumption Parish, Louisiana. He was the father of Lucy

---

[139.] Lot Detail: 1912 Giants vs. Red Sox "Opening Game of the World Series" Panoramic Postcard, 2018 Fall Classic Auction, http://auction.steinersports.com/1912_giants_vs__red_sox__opening_game_of_world_ser-lot119713.aspx.

Marie Talbot and the son of Jean Theophile (Lolo) Talbot (1826–1913) and Marie Zeolide Boudreaux (1835–1877). Marie Zeolide was born on November 16, 1835. She was the daughter of Zephir Azelte Surpriano Boudreaux (1807–?) and Louise A. (marriage name Boudreaux).

In 1857, Elisha Otis installed his first elevator at 488 Broadway in New York City. Herman Melville published *Moby Dick*. The Panic of 1857 began, setting off one of the most severe economic crises in US history short of the Great Depression of 1929. The Civil War had not yet started.

The Supreme Court made its decision on the Dred Scott case in March of 1857. Dred Scott was a slave in Virginia in the 1790s. His original owners sold him to John Emerson, a doctor serving in the US army, and Scott traveled about with him. In 1836, he married Harriet Robinson, a fellow slave. Her ownership transferred to Emerson so they could be together. Following Emerson's death in 1843, Scott sought to buy freedom for him and his family. Emerson's wife refused.

Scott filed a case in 1846 in a local St. Louis court. The case was tried in 1847 and then tried again in 1850. The court ruled the Scotts should be freed due to living in states where slavery was illegal. Their owner appealed, and the case went to the Supreme Court, which ruled, in 1857, that those of African descent did not have the right to be citizens and be free.

By this stage, Scott was the most famous slave in America. Scott and his family were finally freed three months after the court ruling. Scott died less than two years later. Dred Scott's case contributed to the tensions of the Civil War, which influenced Lincoln's Emancipation Proclamation and the thirteenth, fourteenth, and fifteenth amendments to the constitution.

The Siblings of Pierre Anatole Talbot

Pierre Anatole is the third son of Jean Theophile (Lolo) Talbot and Marie Zeolide Boudreaux. They had eight other children: Claiborne Theophile (1853–?), Valmont Adam (1855–1932), Myrtle Leandre (1860–1948), Philomene Sidonie (1862–1952), Etienne Clarife (1866–1921), Ondine Louise (1870–1956), Marie Madora (1860–?), and Jules J. Talbot (1875–1905).

The 1860 US Census shows Jean Theophile (Lolo) Talbot's family with the first three children. Pierre Anatole is listed only as Anatole Talbot (two years old). Jean Theophile (Lolo) was a sugarcane farmer. Pierre was too young to fight in the Civil War, as he was only eight years old when the war ended.

The Children of Pierre Anatole Talbot

On October 10, 1882, just before his twenty-fifth birthday, Pierre Anatole married Emma Ophelia Boudreaux. She was two months short of twenty-five years old. Pierre's best man was Ernest Talbot, and Emma's maid of honor was Donatille Boudreaux.[140] Emma was the daughter of Charles Anselme Boudreaux (1832–1908) and Seraphine Arsement (1839–1853) from Thibodaux, Lafourche Parish, Louisiana. Pierre and Emma had the following children:

* Annie Seraphine Talbot was born on May 13, 1885, in Napoleonville, Assumption Parish, Louisiana, and died on May 28, 1949, in Plattenville, Assumption Parish, Louisiana. She married Dave Bergeron. He was born in Lafayette, Louisiana.
* Lucy Marie Talbot was born on September 14, 1888, in Napoleonville and died on July 1, 1972, in New Orleans. She is the subject of Chapter 2 - Generation 1 above.
* Theophile Joseph Talbot was born on December 19, 1890, in Napoleonville.
* Shelby E. Talbot was born on August 18, 1891, and died on September 16, 1930, in Camp Beauregard, Alexandria, Rapides Parish, Louisiana, with burial at St. Anne Catholic Church Cemetery in Napoleonville.
* George C. "Cook" Talbot was born in 1887.
* Sara Talbot was born in 1897.

Emma Ophelia Boudreaux Talbot died on May 9, 1897, probably as a complication in the birth of Sara Talbot. She was only thirty-eight years old. Just twenty months after Emma's death, Pierre married a new wife, Lucina Josephine Templet, on January 12, 1899. Pierre Anatole was forty-one years old and Lucina was twenty-three. Lucina was the daughter of Narcisse (1832–1923) and Evelina Templet. As mentioned above in Generation 1, Pierre and Lucina had seven children together: Irene, Leonide Gertrude (Bourg), Louis Anatole, Richard Augustine, Bessie Valerie (Bergeron), Stephen, and Anatole (Gabriel) Pierre Jr.

Pierre died on February 6, 1925, in Attakapas Canal, having lived there all his life. He was sixty-seven years old. His obituary read as follows:

On Friday at 9 a.m., Mr. Anatole Talbot, aged 67 years, died at his home at

---

[140.] Archdiocese of Baton Rouge Church records, IMC-Canal-1,1.

Attakapas Canal after an illness of several weeks. Deceased was a native a lifelong resident of this parish; he was a prominent citizen of his community, being a son of the late Theophile Talbot, a leading citizen of this parish. He was married twice; his first wife was Emma Boudreaux, who died several years ago, and from which union the following children were born: Theophile P, Mrs. A. M. Guillot, George C. of Donaldsonville, Mrs. Joseph

Marie Zeolide Boudreaux Mother: Jean Theophile (Lolo) Talbot Father: Male Pierre-Anatole Talbot Individual Summary: Notes: Theophile P, Mrs. A. M. Guillot, George C. of Donaldsonville, Mrs. Joseph C. Bourg, Shelby E. of Tucson, Ariz., and Mrs. Dave Bergeron of Lafayette. He was married a second time to Lucina Templet, who survived him. From this marriage, the following children were born: Louis, Irene, Sam, Richard, Stephens, Anatole, Bessie, and Mrs. Aubert Bourg. Funeral services will be held at the Canal Church this morning at 9' o'clock. To the bereaved family, we offer our deepest sympathy.

The death of his 2nd wife, Lucenia Templet Talbot, occurred on March 28th, 1949. Her obituary was in the New Orleans newspaper: Talbot – At Marrero, La on Monday, March 28, 1949, at 7:45 p.m., Lucenia Templet Talbot, beloved wife of the late Anatole Talbot Sr., mother of Louis Talbot of New Orleans, La.; Samuel Talbot of Gretna, La.; Richard Talbot of Harvey, La.; and Anatole Talbot Jr. of Westwego, La.; Mrs. Louis Blanchard of Napoleonville, La.; Mrs. Aubin Bourg of Marrero, La.; Mrs. Wilbert Bergeron of Baton Rouge, La. and the late Stephen and Albert Talbot.; Stepmother of Mrs. Sarah Guillot of Plattenville, La.; Mrs. Joe Bourg of New Orleans, La. Mrs. Dave Bergeron of Lafayette, La. and the late Theophile and Shelby Talbot of Napoleonville, La.; also survived by 18 grandchildren and six great-grandchildren; age 75 years; a native of Plattenville, La.

Relatives and friends of the family are respectfully invited to attend the funeral, which will take place on Wednesday, March 30th, a949 at 9 a.m. Religious services at Immaculate Conception Catholic Church, Canal Route, Napoleonville, La. Internment in Assumption cemetery, Plattenville, La. Chauvin, and Thibodaux funeral home, Thibodaux, La. in charge. [141]

Generation 3: Jean Theophile (Lolo) Talbot

Jean Theophile (Lolo) Talbot was the son of Louis Andree Talbot (1796–1872) and Rosalie (Rosalia) Dugas (1800–1872). Jean was born on Sunday, January

---

[141.] Archdiocese of Baton Rouge Church Records, 547.

1, 1826, in Labadieville, Louisiana. That winter, an influenza epidemic hit the South, New York, and New England. Despite being an epidemic, it did not kill many people.

John Quincy Adams (1767–1848) served as the sixth President of the United States from 1825 to 1829. He was the son of John Adams, the second president of the U.S. John Quincy's political career included the following positions:

- US Minister to the United Kingdom from June 8, 1815, to May 14, 1817
- US Minister to Russia from November 5, 1809, to April 28, 1814
- US Minister to Prussia from December 5, 1797, to May 5, 1801
- US Minister to the Netherlands from November 6, 1794, to June 20, 1797.
- US Secretary of State from September 22, 1817, to March 4, 1825, in the cabinet of President James Monroe
- US Senator from Massachusetts from March 4, 1803, to June 8, 1808
- US House of Representatives from Massachusetts from March 4, 1831, to February 23, 1848

John Quincy Adams was a Federalist. The Federalist Party believed in a national bank, taxes, and good relations with Great Britain.

The Federalists' political opponents, the Democratic-Republicans led by Thomas Jefferson, denounced most of these policies. Jefferson believed the Jay Treaty with the British was a sell-out of US values to the British. The Federalists held a strong base in the nation's cities and New England. After the Democratic-Republicans, whose support was in the rural South, won the presidential election of 1800, the Federalists never returned to power.[142] The Federalist Party left a lasting legacy in the country in the form of a strong Federal government with a sound financial base. After losing executive power, they decisively shaped Supreme Court policy for another three decades through Chief Justice John Marshall.[143]

Thomas Jefferson wanted to sell some of his property through a lottery. Before the Revolution, this was common, but in 1826 it required legislative approval. In 1823, Jefferson's debts totaled over $40,000. His farm business brought in a mere $10,000 annually. Besides having a large extended family,

---

[142] Gordon S. Wood, *Empire of Liberty: A History of the Early Repu*blic, *1789–1815* (Oxford University Press: 2009).

[143] "Federalist Party," *Wikipedia*, https://en.wikipedia.org/wiki/Federalist_Party.

Jefferson always entertained at Monticello, and the cost of maintaining a country gentleman's lifestyle was becoming a lot more than he could afford.

By that time, word of Jefferson's financial problems had spread throughout the country, and people began sending gifts of money to their former president. The people raised well over $16,000 in funds. Jefferson called this an unsolicited offering of love. He added, "I have spent three times as much money and given my whole life to my country, and now they nobly come forward, in the only way they can, to repay me and save an old servant from being turned out like a dog."

In April, Henry Clay and John Randolph fought a duel in Virginia. Neither was injured. Randolph had accused Clay of being corrupt. On July 4, the 50th anniversary of the signing of the Declaration of Independence, Thomas Jefferson died. Hours later, another signer, former President John Adams, died at his home in Quincy, Massachusetts. At this time in history, only one of the document's signers, Charles Carroll, remained alive.

In 1849, Jean Theophile (Lolo) Talbot met Marie Zeolide Boudreaux (1835–1877) from Thibodaux, Louisiana. Marie was the daughter of Zephir Azelte Surpriano Boudreaux and Celia Azelie Dugas. Marie Zeolide was only fifteen years old, having been born on November 16, 1835. Jean Theophile was nine years older, at twenty-four years of age. They were married in 1853 in Thibodaux.

Jean Theophile was a very successful sugarcane planter in Assumption Parish. He had a small plantation, Cyprus Grove Plantation, on the Attakapas Canal. The sugarcane planter requires for his cane a warm, moist climate, with intervals of hot, dry weather and little danger from frost. The plantation also requires a soil not too fertile, containing lime and magnesium, and good drainage. These conditions are found in the Lower Mississippi Valley. The cuttings are planted in holes about two feet apart. As the canes grow, they are weeded, and all the dead leaves are removed.

Sugarcane begins to grow in Louisiana in February, and harvest takes place in the fall. It sends up another growth of cane, called *ratoons*, which get smaller with each new cutting. The cane yields sweeter juice and more refined sugar.

One planting will last many years, but Louisiana sugarcane growers plan on only three years' worth of product. They plant a third of the entire plantation (sugar ground) with new plants each year. Rats, ants, lice, and some minute animals produce parasites which hurt the growing plants. Wind and frost are also deterrents to good sugar production. At cutting time, the canes are bundled up and carried to the mill, often, on the large plantations, on narrow donkey railways.

Louisiana plantations, when the crop is full, are indeed a beautiful sight, with their broad expanse of green cane. In 1883, over 172,000 acres of cane produced a total yield of 128,000 tons of sugar. This yield was one of the best harvests in the state. But in the next year, floods spoiled so much of the crop that only 118,650 acres produced only 94,000 tons of sugar. It takes about 20,000 men in Louisiana to keep sugar production on track based on statistics and scientific study.[144]

The Children of Jean Theophile (Lolo) Talbot

Jean Theophile and Marie Zeolide Boudreaux had the following ten children together:

- Claiborne Theophile Talbot was born on October 7,1853.[145] Godparents were Claiborne Boudreaux and Alsida Talbot.[146]
- Valmont Adam Talbot was born on January 7, 1855, in Napoleonville, Louisiana, and died on December 8, 1932, in Morgan City, Louisiana. He married Marie Corinne Adolphe on July 25, 1878, in Napoleonville. She was born on November 7, 1854, in Plattenville, Louisiana. She died on August 19, 1921, in Napoleonville.[147]
- Pierre Anatole Talbot was born on November 21, 1857, in Attakapas Canal, Assumption, Louisiana, and died on February 6, 1925, in Attakapas Canal. Pierre Anatole's life is discussed in Generation 2 above.
- Medora Talbot was born in 1860 in Napoleonville.
- Myrtle Leandre Talbot was born on February 26, 1860, in Napoleonville and died on January 19, 1948, in Napoleonville. He married Nycee

---

[144] *Harpers Monthly*, vol. 73, 1886.

[145] Notes for Claiborne Theophile Talbot: Archdiocese of Baton Rouge Church Records vol?, 547, Claiborne Theophile, son of Theophile Talbot and Zeolide Boudreaux, born October 7th, 1853, and baptized October 9, 1853 (ASM-13, 5).

[146] ASM-13,5

[147] Notes for Valmont Adam Talbot: Archdiocese of Baton Rouge Church Records, vol ?, 547, Valmont Adam (Theophile Talbot and Zeolide Boudreaux) bn. January 7th, 1855, bt. January 16th, 1855 sponsors - Etienne Talbot and Zouleme Boudreaux (ASM-13,31).

Augustine Boudreaux in 1881. She was born on April 26, 1863, in Attakapas Canal and died on January 31, 1921, in Louisiana.[148]

- Philomène Sidonie Talbot was born on September 12, 1862, in Napoleonville and died on September 25, 1952, in Napoleonville. She married Henry Joseph Talbot on May 15, 1883, in Napoleonville. He was born on July 15, 1860, in Thibodaux, Louisiana. He died on June 16, 1942, in Napoleonville.

- Etienne Clarife Talbot was born on August 3, 1866, in Napoleonville and died on January 16, 1921, in Louisiana. He married Aliciennee Canc on December 31, 1889. She was born on February 5, 1869, in Christian County, Illinois.[149]

- Ondine Louise Talbot was born on February 13, 1870, in Attakapas Canal and died in 1956 in Napoleonville. She married Willie Talbot on April 10, 1888, in Napoleonville. He was born in 1865 in Thibodaux, Louisiana.[150]

- Marie Madora Talbot was born on March 15, 1872, in Napoleonville. She married Liscome Gros Daumond. He was born in 1862.[151]

- Jules J. Talbot was born in 1875 in IMC Canal, Louisiana and died in 1905 in Louisiana.

- Marie Zeolide Boudreaux Talbot died on August 31, 1877, at the age of forty-one.

On September 22, 1877, Lolo married Katherine Birdsal in Attakapas Canal, just twenty-two days after Zeolide's death. His oldest son was twenty-four years old, but he still had young children who needed a mother. He was fifty-one years

---

[148.] Notes for Myrtle Leandre Talbot, Archdiocese of Baton Rouge Church Records, vol?, 510, Mirtyl Leandre (Theophile Talbot and Zeolide Boudreau) bn February 26th, 1860 bt. March 15th, 1860 sponsors - Henry Clement and Cecilia Marie (IMC-Canal-1, 12).

[149.] Notes for Etienne Clarife Talbot, Archdiocese of Baton Rouge Church Records, vol?, 547, Etienne Cleofa (Theophile Talbot and Zeolide Boudreau) bn. August 3rd, 1866, bt. August 29th, 1866 sponsors Emile Talbot and Felicie Boudreau (IMC-Canal-1,36).

[150.] Notes for Ondine Louise Talbot: Arch of Baton Rouge Church Records, vol?, 496, Ondine Louise (Theophile Talbot and Zeolide Boudreau) bn. February 13th,1870, bt. March 15th, 1870 sponsors Valmont Talbot and Catherine Bardsell (IMCC-1,41).

[151.] Notes for Marie Madora Talbot: Archdiocese of Baton Rouge Church Records, vol?, 559, Marie Medora (Theophile Talbot and Zeolide Boudreau) bn March 15th, 1872 bt. March 23rd, 1872 sponsors Adrian Callet and Mary Isley, represented by Catherine Birdsall (IMCC-1,48),

old when Marie died. He had no children with Katherine Birdsal. Katherine died in 1905, and on August 28, 1905, Lolo married Marie Estelle LeBlanc, a sixty-two-year-old woman.

Jean Theophile (Lolo) Talbot passed away on May 27th, 1913, on Cyprus Grove Plantation at Attakapas Canal, Assumption Parish. His obituary follows:

Napoleonville La. May 28th - Theophile P. Talbot, age 89, a prominent planter of Assumption Parish, passed away yesterday at his home on Cyprus Grove Plantation on the Attakapas Canal after an illness lasting over six months. Decedent was born near Labadieville and moved to his plantation in 1829, where he resided until his death. Funeral services and internment took place this evening at the Attakapas Canal Chapel and Cemetery. He was married twice and left a wife and the following children: Valmont, Anatole, Myrtle, Clerfait, Mrs. Henry Talbot, and Mrs. Licomb Dodmon, besides 44 grandchildren and 17 great-grandchildren.

Another obituary, from the *Napoleonville Pioneer*, reads as follows:

Valiant Citizen called to his reward. Pioneer Cane Planter and venerable gentleman. In the death of Jean Theophile Talbot, which occurred Tuesday evening at 5 o'clock, the parish of Assumption and the Attakapas Canal mourn one of its foremost citizens, one who's life was woven with the history of this parish. Born in the parish near Labadieville in the year 1824, the deceased spent all of his useful life here. He was engaged in the cane planting business, in which he was successful despite the several overflows of the late seventies and early eighties, which visited this section of the parish. He was the son of Andre Louis Talbot and Rosalie Dugas. Pioneer Cane Planter and Venerable Gentleman. In the death of Jean Theophile Talbot, which occurred Tuesday evening at 5 o'clock, the parish of Assumption and the Attakapas Canal, mourn one of its foremost citizens: one whose life was woven with the history of this parish. Born in the church near Labadieville in the year 1824, the deceased spent all of his useful life here engaged in the cane planting business, in which he was successful despite the several overflows of the late seventies and the early eighties, which visited his section of the parish.

He was the son of Andre Louis Talbot and Rosalie Dugas, and out of a family of eleven, he is survived by a brother, Mr. Ernest Talbot, of the Canal. He has been a resident of the Attakapas Canal since the year 1829 and had been on Cypress Grove Plantation, his home, for 43 years. When 15 years of age, he carried U. S. Mail from Morgan City to Donaldsonville for eight years. He took up the trade of a cooper, which he followed for several years, and from that business, he worked in the swamps a while, after which he entered the cane planting business, which he followed all of his life.

He was loved and respected for his sterling qualities. The people of his community looked upon him as a kind of father whose advice was always sought whenever anything important was considered. His deeds of charity which he modestly performed were many, and like the genuinely Christian man he was, he considered it a pleasure to help anyone in need.

He was married three times. His first wife was Zeolid Boudreaux; his second wife, Katherine Birdsal, and his third wife, who survives him, Sicilian LeBlanc. The following children survive him: Valmont, Anatole, Myrtle, and Clerfee Talbot, and Mrs. Willie Talbot, Mrs. Henry Talbot, and Mrs. Liscomb Daudmon. He leaves forty-four grandchildren and seventeen great-grandchildren.

Funeral services were held Wednesday evening at 5 o'clock at the Canal Chapel, and hundreds of people from every section of the parish were present. The funeral was the largest ever seen in the Canal. Father L'Anglais, who conducted the funeral, spoke feelingly on the life of the deceased. To the family, the Pioneer extends its sincere sympathy.

Generation 4: Louis Andree Talbot

At this point, the Talbot family history gets a little unclear and very weird. I will try to report the best information I can about the Talbots at this point in their heritage, but this part of history is the most mysterious, with two competing narratives.

We will start with what we know with some certainty. Louis Andree Talbot Sr. (for he had a son, Louis Andree Talbot Jr.) was born about 1796 in the Bordeaux, France, parish of St. Luis. Some data suggests he was born in Rhode Island.[152] He died in 1872 in Labadieville, Louisiana, at the age of seventy-six. When he was twenty years old, he married Rosalie (Rosalia) Dugas, daughter of Pedro Marino Dugas and Francoise Arsener, on November 25, 1816, in the Assumption Parish

---

[152.] 1850 US Census has Louis A. Talbot (age fifty-three) born in Rhode Island.

Church of Plattenville.[153] Rosalia was born on February 16, 1800, in Plattenville. She died sometime after 1872 in Assumption Parish, probably Plattenville.[154]

The Children of Louis Andree Talbot

Louis and Rosalie had the following children together:

- Marie Mathilde Talbot was born on January 25,1818, in Napoleonville, Louisiana. There is no record of her ever marrying. She died in 1889 in Napoleonville.
- Louise Blatilde Talbot was born on January 26, 1818, in Plattenville (apparently a twin). She married her first husband, Ambrose Arsene Naquin, on May 21, 1836, in Plattenville. She married her second husband, Edmond Blanchard, on January 20, 1847.
- Louis Basile Talbot was born on March 18, 1819, in Labadieville, Louisiana, and died on December 9, 1880, in Napoleonville. He married his first wife, Marie Josephine Blanchard, on January 11, 1847, in Assumption Parish Catholic Church (ASM). She was born on May 13, 1831, in Napoleonville. He married his second wife, Marie Josephine Henry, on November 5, 1838, in Labadieville. She was born on December 26, 1817, in Assumption Parish. She died on September 12, 1845, in Thibodaux, Louisiana.
- Caroline Adeline Talbot was born on October 30, 1821, in Labadieville, and died there on September 4, 1824.[155]

[153.] ASM 2-272.

[154.] Notes for Louis Andree Talbot, Church Records of the Archdiocese of Baton Rouge, vol. 3, 806, Luis of Bordeaux, parish of St. Luis (parents - Guillermo and Luisa Lafitte) married November 25th, 1816 - married Rosalia Dugat (daughter of Pedro Marino and Francisca Arsement) wit.: Pedro Francisco Pelletier, Juan Pedro Legrange; Alexandro deLaunne (ASM 2-,272) Notes for Rosalie (Rosalia) Dugas: Church Records of Baton Rouge - 1816 Rosalia Dugas (Pedro Marino and Francisca Arsement) m. November 25th, 1816 Luis Talbot of Bordeaux, Parish of St. Luis (Guillermo and Luisa Lafitte) wit: Pedro Francisco Pelletier; Juan Pedro Lagrange; Alexander deLaunne (ASM-2, 272).

[155.] Notes for Caroline Adeline Talbot, Archdiocese of Baton Rouge Church Records, vol?, 547, Arvilla (L.A. Talbot and Rosalie Dugas) m. January 14th, 1856 Luc Silvanie Landry (Simon Landry, decd. and Rosalie Giroir) wit. Marie Landry; Theodule Landry, Clairville Landry; L.A. Talbot (ASM-14,14).

- Louis Andree Talbot Jr. was born on October 3, 1821, in Labadieville and died there on September 4, 1824. He married Josephine (Dauphine).

- Henri Theophile Talbot was born in December of 1823 in Plattenville and died on March 20, 1825, in Labadieville.

- Clovis Amede Talbot (son) was born on October 18, 1825, in Labadieville and died on January 1, 1863, in the battle of Vicksburg, Mississippi. He married Azelie Henri.[156]

- Jean Theophile (Lolo) Talbot was born on January 1, 1826, in Labadieville. His story is told in Generation 3 above.

- Marie Bathilde Talbot (either the second child with this name or the information was wrong for the first child) was born on September 28, 1830, in Labadieville and died on November 5, 1898, in Attakapas Canal, Louisiana. She married Pierre Edmond Blanchard on January 20, 1847, in the Assumption Parish Church. Pierre was born on October 26, 1816, in Assumption Parish and died in 1898 in Napoleonville.

- Jules Andre Talbot was born on January 26, 1833, in Labadieville and died on January 7, 1863, in the battle of Vicksburg. He married Celestine Bourg, daughter of Urbain Bourg and his wife, Marie, on October 4, 1858, in Attakapas Canal.[157]

- Etienne Valmont Talbot was born on April 8, 1836, in Labadieville and died on January 23, 1901, in Napoleonville.

- Louis Talbot was born on August 27, 1837, in Labadieville. He died on August 27, 1837 in Assumption Parish.[158]

- Antoinette (Annie) Arville Talbot was born on August 3, 1839, in Attakapas Canal and died on December 28, 1901, in Jeanerette, Louisiana.[159]

- Louis Ernest Talbot was born on April 21, 1841, in Assumption Parish[160] and died on September 3, 1913, in Napoleonville. He married his first wife, Elmire Barbier, daughter of Hubert Barbier and Rosalie Melancon,

---

[156] SPH-2,40.

[157] IMC-Canal-1,384.

[158] ASM 3,266.

[159] Notes for Antoinette (Annie) Arville Talbot, Archdiocese of Baton Rouge Catholic Church Records, vol?, 604, Antoinette, age two years (Pepe Pepin and omit, adopted by Louis Talbot) bur. July 30th, 1842 (ASM-10,31).

[160] ASM-9,160.

on December 26, 1865, in Assumption Parish.[161] She was born in 1844 in Assumption Parish. He married his second wife, Elodie Philomine Braud, on October 8, 1872, in Attakapas Canal. She was born on April 12, 1846, in Assumption Parish.[162]

- Louis Emile Talbot was born on August 20, 1843, in Attakapas Canal[163] and died on November 30, 1878, in Napoleonville. He married Cecilia Richard, daughter of Louis Richard and Marie Thibodeaux, on January 26, 1867.[164] She was born on December 20, 1844, in Thibodaux. She died on November 30, 1878, in Labadieville.

- Eulalie Adolphine Talbot was born on May 23, 1844[165] and died on May 29, 1922, in Napoleonville. Nothing more is known about her.

Coming to America

The 1790s were a time of far-reaching social and political upheaval in France. The French Revolution (1789–1799) increased French emigration to America. The Revolution resulted in the religious persecution of the Catholics in France. It is estimated that over 10,000 religious and political refugees and aristocrats left France for America during the French Revolution.

Louis Andree and his family emigrated from France to Louisiana sometime between 1798 and 1815—probably closer to 1800. They sailed from France to New Orleans and then onto the Acadiana France parishes west of New Orleans.

During this time, French Americans, especially those who came to the United States as refugees from the French Revolution, were thought of as a potential threat to US security. In 1798, the Alien and Sedition Acts were passed; they were intended to monitor and limit the power of immigrant groups. The Federalists

---

[161] ASM-14,56.

[162] Notes for Louis Ernest Talbot, Catholic Church Records, Archdiosces of Baton Rouge, vol?, 604, Louis Ernes (Louis Andre Talbot and Rosalie Dugas) bn. April 21st, 1841, bt. September 3rd, 1841, sponsors - Louis Talbot and Marie Talbot (ASM-9,160). Arch of Baton Rouge Church Records - vol? P 547 - Ernest (Louis Talbot and Rosalie Dugas) m. December 26th, 1865 Elmire Barbier (Hubert Barbier and Rosalie Melancon) wit. Evela Blanchard, Elosie Naquin, Joseph Barbier, Francois Faletman; Helen Melancon (ASM-14,56) 9.

[163] ASM-9,218.

[164] SPH-4, 212 and SPH-7,21.

[165] ASM-9,218.

passed the acts, and they were signed into law by President John Adams in 1798.[166] They made naturalization harder and allowed the president to imprison and deport non-citizens who were deemed dangerous[167] [168] [169]

The acts lengthened the residency requirement from five to fourteen years before immigrants were allowed to vote. They required ships to have a file on each immigrant passenger. They granted the government the power to deport anyone considered "dangerous." The acts became the subject of considerable public outrage and were allowed to expire two years later.

Two Narratives

Louis Andree Talbot died about 1872 in Labadieville at the age of seventy-six. His wife, Rosalie (Rosalia) Dugas, died in 1872 at the age of seventy-two. We know about Louis Andree's descendants. His ancestors are a lot more mysterious. Although we do believe, because of the best genealogy evidence, that Louis's father was Guillaume (William) Talbot and his grandfather was Charles Louis Talbot, there is a second narrative that suggests otherwise. Because of the link between Guillaume and Charles Louis, the second narrative has some plausibility. Let me put forward both narratives.

Narrative #1

Louis Andree Talbot was born in 1796, the son of Guillaume (William) Talbot and Luisa Lafitte. Guillaume was an Acadian by heritage. According to this narrative, he was born on February 18, 1759, in France. Guillaume's father (in this narrative) was Charles Louis Talbot, who was born in French Acadia on May 3, 1743. Guillaume and his family were deported from Ille St. Jean in 1758 by the British as part of the Great Upheaval, the Great Expulsion, the Great Deportation, and Le Grand Dérangement. They were sent to France.

Guillaume's parents died very shortly after their ship arrived in France. Charles Louis died on March 20, 1759. Guillaume's mother, Marie Francoise

---

[166.] "The Alien and Sedition Acts: Defining American Freedom," Constitutional Rights Foundation, 2003, retrieved October 14, 2015.

[167.] "An Act Concerning Aliens," sess II, chap. 58; 5th Congress; June 25, 1798.

[168.] "An Act Respecting Alien Enemies," sess II, chap. 58; 1 Stat. 577, 5th Congress; ch. 66, June 25, 1798, library.uwb.edu.

[169.] Sess II, chap. 74; 5th Congress; July 14, 1798.

Douville, died a few days later on March 25, 1759, in Saint-Malo, France. We do not know the exact cause of the death of this family. However, it can be assumed that the long winter voyage from Nova Scotia to Saint-Malo on a small crowded ship must have contributed to the cause either by childbirth, disease, or dysentery.

Charles was fifteen years old when he died (which seems odd, although their situation was bizarre and complex). His wife, Francoise Laqueille, must have been relatively young as well. At fifteen and with no record of a marriage, it seems odd that they had Guillaume. They were both Catholic, and there should have been some evidence of their marriage in Acadia. Since they were both very young, this may have been a union of opportunity, given the fact that they were being deported from their home.

Guillaume was born shortly before his parents' death on February 18, 1759. It is listed that he was born in France, but it is possible that he was born on the ship bound for France with all the Acadian refugees. Guillaume met and married Luisa Lafitte sometime in early 1790, and together they had Louis Andree Talbot in France sometime before 1796.

Narrative #2

The following information on Louis comes from Ancestry.com member Aliceannaal. I'm not sure of her sources.

Louis Andre Talbot, it is believed, at some point in history, was the Sheriff of Lafourche Parish. He gave power of attorney to Andree Lafitte in a document that I got at the Terrill Historical Library. I also have records of his wife's father's will listing him and Rosalie Dugas. I have a sale of land document to a Constance Dugas and where Louis was sued. Wedding record: Witness: Pedro Francisco Pelletier: Juan Pedro LaGrange, Alexandro deLaunne (ASM-2, 272) DBRCCR V3.

It is unclear where he grew up, but he was a literate man and had beautiful penmanship. He was the son of Andre Lafitte and Marie Louisa Talbot. There are records in Rhode Island where his mother had booked two passages into Rhode Island in December of 1798.

He (Louis) married Rosalie Dugas on November 25th, 1816, in Assumption Parish, Louisiana. Witnesses at the wedding were Pierre Francois (Pedro Francisco) Pelletier and Jean Pierre (Juan Pedro) LaGrange and Alexandre (Alexandro) deLaunne. They were married in Assumption Parish, Louisiana. (ASM-2, 272) DBRCCR V3. Rosalie Dugas was born on February 15th, 1800, in Assumption,

Louisiana. She was the daughter of Pierre Marin Jean Dugas and Francoise Rose Arsement. She was baptized on October 9th, 1800. Her godparents were Jean Pelletier and her mother's sister Perrine Madeleine Arsement.

Louis and Rosalie lived for a short time with her parents after their wedding, and they eventually settled on Bayou Lafourche and had 14 children over 25 years. Their first child was Louise Bathilde, born 14 months after they were married and three weeks short of Rosalie's 18th birthday. A son, Louis Basile, followed on March 18th, 1819. The third daughter, Caroline Adeline, was born on October 30th, 1830. Little Caroline died just short of her fourth birthday on September 4th, 1824. A son, Louis Talbot, was stillborn on August 22nd, 1837. Rosalie had her last child, Louis Emile, on August 20th, 1843. She was 43½ years old.

Several legal documents trace Louis and Rosalie and give a glimpse into their lives. Louis sold a tract of land on March 26th, 1824, that was one arpent, five toises and four feet fronting and forty arpents deep to Rosalie's widowed sister, Constance Dugas Maillet, widow of Cyprian. On February 8th, 1825. Charles Maurin petitioned the court for a judgment against Louis for $43.75 that was owed to him that Louis had refused to pay. The decision was against Louis, and he paid to the court the sum of $43.75 on April 11th, 1825. On June 1st, 1826, Louis took Gregoire Aucoin to court for the amount of $90. Mr. Aucoin had signed a promissory note dated April 20th, 1824, for value received to his satisfaction and that he had neglected and refused to pay. Judgment for in favor of Louis with interest till paid.

On August 15th, 1826, Louis Andre Talbot became the Sheriff of the Interior parish of Lafourche. He, as principal, and Joseph Robichaux and Bastien Landry, as securities, put up a penal sum of four thousand dollars of lawful money. Louise was now responsible to "faithfully execute and make a true return as according to the law" "and truly pay overall sums of money that shall come into his hands as sheriff." Our esteemed ancestor was now indeed a Louisiana politician! On May 15th, 1827, Head & Lyons of the City of Natchez in Mississippi sued Louis for the sums of $150 and $52 & $10.87. Louis had received documents giving him authority as Sheriff to seize the property of a Mr. William Tabor. Mr. Tabor had a female slave, and Louis was directed to take the slave. According to the legal papers, Louis seized the slave but noted on the records that no property was found. Louis had to pay the sum of $8112. It is not indicated what happened to the slave.

Rosalie's parents died within a short time of each other. Her father died on October 30th, 1832, and her mother died on May 16th, 1833. Rosalie inherited two slaves, Thomas 38 years old and Charles, nine years old. They were valued at $1,025.00. She also inherited property. On April 7th, 1838, Joseph Robichaux (who had put up part of the security bond for Louis) filed for the recovery of $281.92 that he had to pay out due to Louis being sued by the following:

⦙ $73.97½ paid to George Bisset on February 11th, 1829
⦙ $56.95 paid to Head and Lyons of City of Natchez, Mississippi,
⦙ $151 paid to M. Tilghman

The judge ruled in favor of Joseph Robichaux for $200 with interest and the cost of the suit.

On April 14th, 1838, Louis filed a Conveyance of Property to his wife, Rosalie Dugas. He "sold" to her a tract of land containing six arpents front by twenty arpents deep, bounded above by land of Pierre Lefre and below by Constance Dugas Maillet, her widowed sister. It came with all the buildings and improvements, horses, mules, oxen, cows, calves, and other animals, household and kitchen furniture, and the instruments of husbandry. There were two slaves, Charles, 14 years old, and a negress, Eugenie, aged about eighteen. He "sold" her inheritance from her parents to her for the sum of $2,880 The documents state that it is a "sum he is bound to answer for, replace & restore to the said wife, this act is done under Article 2421 C. Code."

On April 1st, 1850, A. F. Hickman, Sheriff of the Parish of Assumption, received a suit filed by Edouard Pellitier, commanding him to seize and sell the property, movables and immovables, rights, and credits belonging to Louis A. Talbot so satisfy the sum of $151.40.

Louis and Rosalie Talbot are listed in the 1850 census. Louis is listed as a Laborer, and his age is recorded as 58. Rosalie is listed as 45. Rosalie was 50 in 1850, as she was born in 1800. They are registered with their children, Jules, 19, Valmont, 14, Arvila, 12, Ernest, 10, and Emile, 8. Their son, Louis, was 26 and living with his wife Dauphine and their children Delphine, Adolphe, and Philomene. In the 1860 Census, Louis Talbot, Jr. (Louis Joseph Talbot) is listed as 38 yrs old and a Laborer living with his wife Dauphine and their children, Josephine, Adolphe, Philomene, Oscar, Marie, Clovis, Anatole, and Ozeme. In the same census, Louis Emile is listed as living with his godfather, Louis Parenton. Louis Andre Talbot is listed as 68 years old and living with his son Clovis and his wife, Cesaire. They are living with their two children Emile, five years old,

Jules, two years old and four others, Marie Arsement 16 yrs, Dolphine Arsement, 15 yrs, Zoe Arsement 12 yrs, and Victorine Arsement, 10yrs. Rosalie's mother was an Arsement, so these are possibly orphaned children. Jules Talbot is now 25 years old and is listed as a cooper. He is living with his wife Celestine and their daughter, Arvilla, who is nine months old.

He married Rosalie Dugas on November 25th, 1816, in Assumption Parish, Louisiana. Witnesses at the wedding were Pierre Francois (Pedro Francisco) Pelletier and Jean Pierre (Juan Pedro) LaGrange and Alexandre (Alexandro) deLaunne. They were married in Assumption Parish, Louisiana. (ASM-2, 272) DBRCCR V3 17. Rosalie Dugas, was born on February 15th, 1800, in Assumption, Louisiana. She was the daughter of 34. Pierre Marin Jean Dugas and 35. Francoise Rose Arsement. She was baptized on October 9th, 1800. Her godparents were Jean Pelletier & her mother's sister Perrine Madeleine Arsement.

Louis and Rosalie lived for a short time with her parents after their wedding, and they eventually settled on Bayou Lafourche and had 14 children over 25 years. Their first child was Louise Bathilde, born 14 months after they were married and three weeks short of Rosalie's 18th birthday. A son, Louis Basile, followed on March 18th, 1819. The third daughter, Caroline Adeline, was born on October 30th, 1830. Little Caroline died just short of her fourth birthday on September 4th, 1824. A son, Louis Talbot, was stillborn on August 22nd, 1837. Rosalie had her last child, Louis Emile, on August 20th, 1843. She was 43 ½ years old.

Several legal documents trace Louis and Rosalie and give a glimpse into their lives. Louis sold a tract of land on March 26th, 1824, that was one arpent, five toises and four feet fronting and forty arpents deep to Rosalie's widowed sister, Constance Dugas Maillet, widow of Cyprian. On February 8th, 1825, Charles Maurin petitioned the court for a judgment against Louis for $43.75 that was owed to him that Louis had refused to pay. The decision was against Louis, and he paid to the court the sum of $43.75 on April 11th, 1825. On June 1st, 1826, Louis took Gregoire Aucoin to court for the amount of $90. Mr. Aucoin had signed a promissory note dated April 20th, 1824, for value received to his satisfaction and that he had neglected and refused to pay Judgement for in favor of Louis with interest till paid.

On August 15th, 1826, Louis Andre Talbot became the Sheriff of the Interior parish of Lafourche. He, as principal, and Joseph Robichaux and Bastien Landry, as securities, put up a penal sum of four thousand dollars of lawful money. Louise was now responsible to "faithfully execute and make a true return as according to the law" "and truly pay overall sums of money that shall come into his hands as sheriff." Our esteemed ancestor was now indeed a Louisiana politician! On May 15th, 1827, Head & Lyons of the City of Natchez in Mississippi sued Louis for the sums of $150 and $52 & $10.87. Louis had received documents giving him authority as Sheriff to seize the property of a Mr. William Tabor. Mr. Tabor had a female slave, and Louis was directed to take the slave. According to the legal papers, Louis seized the slave but noted on the records that no property was found. Louis had to pay the sum of $81.12. It is not indicated what happened to the slave.

Rosalie's parents died within a short time of each other. Her father died on October 30th, 1832, and her mother died on May 16th, 1833. Rosalie inherited two slaves, Thomas 38 years old and Charles, nine years old. They were valued at $1,025.00. She also inherited property.

On April 7th, 1838, Joseph Robichaux (who had put up part of the security bond for Louis) filed for the recovery of $281.92 that he had had to pay out due to Louis being sued by the following:

╎ $73.97½ paid to George Bisset on February 11th, 1829
╎ $56.95 paid to Head and Lyons of City of Natchez, Mississippi
╎ $151 paid to M. Tilghman

The judge ruled in favor of Joseph Robichaux for $200 with interest and cost of suit.

On April 14th, 1838, Louis filed a Conveyance of Property to his wife, Rosalie Dugas. He "sold" to her a tract of land containing six arpents front by twenty arpents deep, bounded above by land of Pierre Lefre and below by Constance Dugas Maillet, her widowed sister. It came with all the buildings and improvements, horses, mules, oxen, cows, calves, and other animals, household and kitchen furniture, and the instruments of husbandry. There were two slaves, Charles, 14 years old, and a negress Eugenie aged about eighteen. He "sold" her inheritance from her parents to her for the sum of $2,880. The documents state that it is a "sum he is bound to answer for, replace & restore to the said wife, this act is done under Article 2421 C. Code."

On April 1st, 1850, A. F. Hickman, Sheriff of the Parish of Assumption, received a suit filed by Edouard Pellitier commanding him to seize and sell the property, movables and immovables, rights and credits belonging to Louis A. Talbot so satisfy the sum of $151.40

Louis and Rosalie Talbot are listed in the 1850 census. Louis is listed as a Laborer, and his age is recorded as 58. Rosalie is listed as 45. Rosalie was 50 in 1850, as she was born in 1800. They are listed with their children, Jules, 19, Valmont, 14, Arvila, 12, Ernest, 10, and Emile, 8. Their son, Louis, was 26 and living with his wife Dauphine and their children Delphine, Adolphe, and Philomene.

In the 1860 Census, Louis Talbot, Jr. (Louis Joseph Talbot) is listed as 38 yrs old and a Laborer living with his wife Dauphine and their children, Josephine, Adolphe, Philomene, Oscar, Marie, Clovis, Anatole, and Ozeme. In the same census, Louis Emile is listed as living with his godfather, Louis Parenton. Louis Andre Talbot is listed as 68 years old and living with his son Clovis and his wife, Cesaire. They are living with their two children Emile, five years old, Jules, two years old and four others, Marie Arsement 16 yrs, Dolphine Arsement, 15 yrs, Zoe Arsement 12 yrs, and Victorine Arsement, 10 yrs. Rosalie's mother was an Arsement, so these are possibly orphaned children. Jules Talbot is now 25 years old and is listed as a cooper. He is living with his wife Celestine and their daughter, Arvilla, who is nine months old.

The World of Young Louis Andree Talbot

Louis Andree grew up in the era at the end of the French Revolution in Bordeaux, France. Globally, the French Revolution facilitated the rise of democracies around the world. It led to the development of many modern political ideologies, including liberalism, radicalism, nationalism, and secularism. The revolution also produced the evolution of large-scale war.[170],[171]The Declaration of the Rights of Man continued to inspire movements such as abolitionism and universal suffrage in the next century.[172]

Both the American Revolution (June 1775–November 1782) and the French Revolution (1789–1799) were the products of Enlightenment ideals. The French Revolution lasted for ten years. Demands for change were put forth in terms of Enlightenment ideals and contributed to the convocation of the French Estates-General in May 1789.

After the French Revolution, not as many aristocrats remained. Those who did found their wealth and power curtailed, along with the wealth and power of

---

[170.] "French Revolution," *Wikipedia*, https://en.wikipedia.org/wiki/The_French_Revolution.

[171.] Suzanne Desan, et al., eds., *The French Revolution in Global Perspective* (2013), 3, 8, 10.

[172.] Thomas H. Marshall, *Citizenship and Social Class*, vol. 11 (Cambridge, 1950).

the Church. Life improved for ordinary people. The positive aspects of the French Revolution are clearer to see with the benefit of hindsight. It established the trend of representational, democratic government, now the model of governance in much of the world. It also established liberal social principles of equality among all citizens, fundamental property rights, and the separation of church and state, as did the American Revolution.

As stated earlier, Louis Andree Talbot was born about 1796 in Bordeaux, France, in the church parish of St. Luis. After the Revolution, France was a difficult place to live for poor Catholics. Louis Andree and his family emigrated to Louisiana sometime between 1812 and 1816. It is assumed they landed in New Orleans but very quickly moved to Assumption Parish so they could live with people who also spoke French.

Louis married Rosalie (Rosalia) Dugas, the daughter of Pedro Marino Dugas and Francoise Arsener, on November 25, 1816, in Assumption Church of Plattenville, Louisiana.[173] Louis was twenty years old, and Rosalie, who was born on February 16, 1800, in Plattenville, was only sixteen. She died after 1872 in Assumption Parish, Louisiana. Louis died in 1872 in Labadieville, Assumption, Louisiana.[174]

Generation 5: Guillaume (William) Talbot

Of all the people documented in this family history book, Guillaume (William) Talbot is the most mysterious and the one I am least sure about the facts of his history. I know that he was born on May 3, 1743, in Canada (either in Acadia or Quebec). He is probably the son of Charles Louis Talbot (1743 in Canada–1759 in France) and Luisa Lafitte (?–1798). Charles married Luisa Lafitte, daughter of Bernard Lafitte or Antoine Lafitte, before 1797 in France. She died on August 3, 1798, in Opelousas, Louisiana.

France was already slipping toward its Revolution because the monarchy was

---

[173] ASM 2-272.

[174] Notes for Louis Andree Talbot: Church Records of the Archdiocese of Baton Rouge, vol. 3, 806, Luis of Bordeaux, par of St. Luis (Guillermo and Luisa Lafitte) m. November 25th, 1816 Rosalia Dugat (Pedro Marino and Francisca Arsement) wit.: Pedro Francisco Pelletier, Juan Pedro Legrange; Alexandro deLaunne (ASM 2-,272). Notes for Rosalie (Rosalia) Dugas: Church Records of Baton Rouge - 1816 Rosalia Dugas (Pedro Marino and Francisca Arsement) m. November 25th, 1816 Luis Talbot of Bordeaux, Parish of St. Luis (Guillermo and Luisa Lafitte) wit: Pedro Francisco Pelletier; Juan Pedro Lagrange; Alexander deLaunne (ASM-2, 272).

spending money on many of its global projects and wars. The expense associated with all this spending was being heaped on the backs of the landed gentry and the peasants of the country. When King Louis XV died in 1774, his grandson, Louis XVI, came to power. He inherited a substantial legacy of ruined finances, unhappy subjects, and a faulty and incompetent government. Regardless, the people still had confidence in royalty, and the accession of Louis XVI was welcomed with enthusiasm.[175]

A decade later, the Seven Years' War (1756–1763) and the American Revolutionary War (1775–1783), in which France supported the American Colonies as an ally, bankrupted France. The taxation system was highly inefficient. Several years of bad harvests and an inferior transportation system had caused rising food prices, hunger, and malnutrition; the country was further destabilized by the lower classes' increased feeling that the royal court was indifferent to their hardships.

---

[175] William J Roberts, *France: A Reference Guide from the Renaissance to the Present* (2004), 34.

CHAPTER 5

THE YOUNG FAMILY AND THE RAPPOLD FAMILY
The Ancestors of Agnes Louise Young

It's important to teach our children their heritage. Who are your ancestors? What were their traditions? Each of us has a story to tell. If these stories are unwritten, then how are your children going to know of their parentage?
—Linda Weaver Clarke

My charge, then, in putting down my pen, and giving over this work to posterity, is this: Take the time. Take the time to preserve the stories, the photographs, and the small mementos that mean so much. This is your legacy to future generations. Give it the attention it deserves. Your children and your grandchildren will thank you for it.
—Laurence Overmire, *One Immigrant's Legacy*

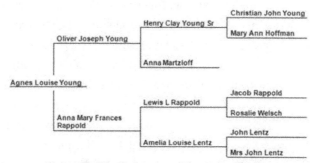

Figure 6 – The Ancestors of Agnes Louise Young

It's time to turn my family history away from the French and French Acadian side of the family and toward the German side. We will document the family history of the Youngs and the Rappolds. Those of German ancestry contributed much to the culture of New Orleans.

I have less historical information on the Youngs and Rappolds because my history research does not go back more than five generations. The format of this chapter will be a little different than the previous ones. After starting with my mother, I'll jump back to the oldest generations and move forward. This chapter will cover Young generations 4, 3, 2, and 1, and then Rappold generations 2 and 3.

The Young Family

Generation 1: Agnes Louise Young

On Saturday, December 28, 1912, Agnes Louise Young was born in New Orleans, Louisiana. She was the third child and daughter of Oliver Joseph Young (1878–1928) and Anna Mary Frances Rappold (1884–1954). We will discuss the lives of her siblings later in this chapter.

Agnes grew up at her family's home on St. Andrew Street and Camp Street. She attended Redemptorist High School, where besides her general education, she learned secretarial skills. Agnes was a fantastic typist and was able to type faster than 120 words per minute on a manual typewriter. After graduation in 1930, she went to work as a secretary for a liquor distributor in the downtown New Orleans area.

Her future husband, Jim Bourg, was living at 830 Jackson Avenue. Because he lived in the parish, they probably met at Redemptorist Parish social events.

They started dating, but Jim could not financially afford a family because he was still sending most of his money home to help support his mother and family. All the information regarding Jim and Agnes is written in chapters one through three.

When Agnes was born, the world population was about 1.6 billion people—nearly twice as many as there were a hundred years before. The U.S. population was 95 million. If someone had given Agnes twenty dollars on the day of her birth, that would be like them giving her five hundred dollars today in 2020.

Eight months before her birth, on April 14, 1912, the RMS *Titanic* hit an iceberg at 11:40 p.m. off Newfoundland and sank the next day at 2:27 a.m. Ten months before she was born, in February 1912, Arizona was admitted to the Union as the forty-eighth state. In March, US Army Captain Albert Berry performed the first parachute jump from an airplane, and Isabella Goodwin was appointed the first U.S. woman detective in New York City.

In March of 1912, Roald Amundsen of Norway led the Antarctic expedition of 1910–12, becoming the first to reach the South Pole. He beat Robert Scott's team by thirty-four days. Amundsen is known as the first person to have reached both poles. He is also known as heading the first expedition to traverse the Artic's Northwest Passage (1903–06). Also, in March, pitcher Cy Young retired from baseball with 511 wins.

In the summer, the Chicago Republican National Convention was split between incumbent president William Howard Taft and former president Theodore Roosevelt; after Taft was nominated, Roosevelt and progressive elements of the party formed the Progressive Party, also known as the Bull Moose Party. The 1912 US presidential election was the country's thirty-second. It was, held on Tuesday, November 5, 1912. The Democratic candidate, New Jersey governor Woodrow Wilson, defeated Taft and Roosevelt in a three-way race. Roosevelt remains the only third-party candidate in US history to finish second in the popular and electoral vote.

American athlete Jim Thorpe won four of the five events to win the Pentathlon gold medal at the 1912 Summer Olympics in Stockholm. The medal was stripped from him in 1913 because he played pro baseball. The medal was reinstated in 1982. Also in 1912, Edgar Rice Burroughs published *Tarzan of the Apes*.

The Importance of the German Presence and Heritage in Louisiana and New Orleans

When thinking of Louisiana and New Orleans history, it is common to remember the influence of the French, the Spanish, and even the Italians. I learned of these heritages and cultures studying Louisiana history in grammar school. The culture we did not consider or talk about very much during those days (the 1960s) was the Germans. This was probably because memories of the great world wars were still fresh in our minds. However, it should be remembered that German immigrants to Louisiana contributed significantly to the development of South Louisiana and New Orleans traditions, celebrations, growth, and infrastructure. From 1850 - 1900, the Germans of New Orleans were "still inspired by the determination and loyalty which motivated them to build their communities in Europe."[176]

John Fredrick Nau, in his history of the German people of New Orleans observed this in the building of their churches and schools. He also saw it in their benevolent societies and their businesses and industries. Many are still in operation today. He observed that "the influence of the Germans on the city of New Orleans continues. German-American contributions to New Orleans are visible everywhere," Nau commented in his history of the New Orleans Germans, that he repeatedly found they "helped to make New Orleans a city of commerce, industry, and business. Germans built New Orleans." He concluded, "To correctly see the history of New Orleans, one must consider the part Germans played in molding the culture and life of this city."[177]

The history of the German presence and heritage in Louisiana starts with the French. When Louis XIV's wars had nearly bankrupted the French, he sought a way out of the financial mess without reducing spending. He took up the economic principles of Scottish financier John Law. In 1716, Louis XV gave Law a charter for the Royal Bank (*Banque Royale*). Under this charter, Louis assigned the French national debt to the bank in return for Law receiving privileges.

The key to the agreement was that the national debt would be paid from revenues derived from opening the Mississippi Valley to development and exploration. The bank was tied to the Mississippi Company. This Company had a

---

[176] Ellen C. Merrill, *Germans of Louisiana*, http://www.doyletics.com/arj/germanso.shtml.

[177] John Fredrick Nau, *The German People of New Orleans, 1850-1900* (E.J. Brill, 1958), 13.

monopoly on trade and minerals. The company boomed on paper, and Louis gave Law the title of *duc d'Arkansas*.[178]

Through an effective marketing scheme, Law exaggerated the wealth of Louisiana. This scheme led to speculation on shares of the company in 1719. The popularity of the company's shares sparked a need for more paper banknotes, and when stocks generated profits, investors were paid in paper banknotes. In 1720, the bank and company merged, and Law was granted by Philippe II, Duke of Orleans, the title of Comptroller General of Finances. Law's pioneering note-issuing bank thrived until the government had to admit that the number of paper notes issued by the Banque Royale exceeded the value of its metal coinage.[179]

The scheme collapsed at the end of 1720, when opponents of the financier attempted to convert their notes into cash, forcing the bank to stop payment on its paper notes. Philippe d'Orléans dismissed Law from his positions by the end of 1720. Law then fled France to Brussels and then to Venice. He was buried in the Church San Moisè in Venice.[180]

By 1718, only seven hundred Europeans lived in Louisiana. The Mississippi Company arranged ships to move eight hundred more. They landed in Louisiana in 1718. John Law encouraged Germans, particularly those from the Alsatian region who had recently fallen under French rule, to emigrate. France wanted people to immigrate to New Orleans in the eighteenth century, and Germans were some of the first to heed the call.

According to Judge Barron Burmaster, president of the German-American Cultural Center, "There were published requests in Germany and particularly in the Rhineland for people to come to New Orleans. They promised them a land of milk and honey. It was going to be this great place." These people gave their name to the Côte des Allemands and the Lac des Allemands in Louisiana (Lake of the Germans).[181]

The French answered the call by setting prisoners free in Paris in September 1719. They required that the prisoners marry prostitutes and go with them to Louisiana. The newly married couples were handcuffed together and taken to the

[178] John E. Sandrock, *John Law's Banque Royale and the Mississippi Bubble*, thecurrencycollector. com/pdfs/John_Laws_Banque_Royale.pdf.

[179] Andrew Beattie, "What Burst the Mississippi Bubble?" Investopedia.com, June 17, 2009.

[180] Jon Moen, "John Law and the Mississippi Bubble: 1718–1720," (October 2001).

[181] Mark Deane, "NOLA 300: When Germans Came to New Orleans," WGNO (May 7, 2018), https://wgno.com/2018/05/07/nola-300-when-germans-came-to-new-orleans/.

port. In May of 1720, after complaints about these types of immigrants, the French government prohibited such deportations. There was, however, a third shipment of prisoners in 1721.[182]

A group of German colonists set sail on the *Portefaix*, a French warship converted to transport duties. It landed in Biloxi in 1720, just at the time Law's company and a plan for an economic monopoly in the French colonies collapsed. An ethnic German from Swedish Pomerania (present-day Estonia), Karl d'Arensbourg, assumed the leadership of these Germans. The surviving settlers left the province and traveled to New Orleans, where they intended to sail back to Europe. Once they arrived in New Orleans, however, they were persuaded to follow d'Arensbourg and settle there. They ended up about twenty-five miles upriver from New Orleans.

The "German Coast" survived the hurricanes and the various Indian attacks and went on to prosper as the greengrocer for the city. Sugarcane became the cash crop. D'Arensbourg's group had a commission to sell their surplus harvest to supply New Orleans. As early as 1724, the French superior council recognized the importance of these goods by issuing a decree guaranteeing these crop's protection during transportation to New Orleans from the settlement.

When John Law's bankruptcy caused the company to disintegrate in 1731, the settlers ceased to be obligated to anyone but continued to supply New Orleans. As census records and scholarly works found in THNOC's German Study File illustrate, the contributions made by this community to the health and growth of New Orleans increased consistently throughout the eighteenth century.

The Germans were not only supplying the provincial capital with staples but also sent timber and rice to Cap François, the wealthy capital of the flourishing St. Dominque colony, and to France itself. In 1803, Napoleon's prefect to Louisiana, Pierre Clément de Laussat, even recommended introducing a regular flow of German settlers to the region, as they were the only group that had as yet proven themselves capable of taming the Louisiana wilderness.

Every summer for a century, residents of New Orleans lived in fear of the ever-approaching summer season. Summers in New Orleans brought not only incredible heat and hurricanes but also, most terrifyingly, yellow fever, which is transmitted by mosquitoes.[183] Like other hemorrhagic diseases, it cause blood

---

[182.] John Cuevas, *Cat Island: The History of a Mississippi Gulf Coast Barrier Island.*

[183.] Elizabeth D. Barnett, "Yellow Fever: Epidemiology and Prevention," *Clinical Infectious Diseases*, vol. 44, no. 6 (March 15, 2007), 850–856.

vessels throughout the body to hemorrhage or bleed, and it is, therefore, a severe illness. It started in the United States in the late eighteenth century. The disease spread throughout the young nation from the 1790s to the 1870s. The mode of transmission was unknown until the early 1900s, and so effective treatment of the disease was lacking during the time in the century that it was most destructive.[184]

Yellow fever disappeared for a few years, better drainage caused the city to become plague free, and immigration was reopened immigration to Germans again. The disease proved to be hard on the German immigrants, however.[185] In the summer of 1853, yellow fever broke out worse than before. Eight thousand New Orleans' residents had the plague, almost two-thirds of whom were German. The "fever" was mainly among the foreign-born, who had no natural immunity. Those who worked digging the city's canals were very vulnerable.

During this epidemic, new arrivals were moved up the river to avoid a stopover in New Orleans. To combat the plague, the Howard Association organized to help take care of the victims in the city. The association set up temporary clinics and refuges for orphans, and every known means was used to limit the spread of the yellow fever. But the epidemic defeated all efforts to contain it. Families died or were separated forever. Many orphans didn't know their last names because they were too young.

D'Arensbourg's settlement quickly moved from sustenance farming to a surplus economy, supplying the French colonies downriver with crops and eventually timber and finished goods. The German community continued to grow, and by the 1820s, Germans were migrating from upriver to New Orleans proper. Records show the establishment of the first German-speaking Evangelical congregation in 1826. This church, located initially on Clio Street between St. Charles Avenue and Carondelet Street, is now the First Trinity Evangelical United Church of Christ, located on N. Murat Street.

The Germans continued to migrate from the rural settlements to the city, and the first Catholic community was formed in the 1840s in the Irish Channel. The Germans were the dominant portion of the Irish Channel's Redemptorist Parish throughout the mid-nineteenth century. Their first church, the original St. Mary's Assumption, was constructed in 1844 on the corner of Constance and Josephine. In 1857, they dismantled the original wood-frame church and built the massive

---

[184] Jo-Ann Carrigan, "Yellow Fever in New Orleans, 1853: Abstractions and Realities," *Journal of Southern History* 25.3 (1959), 339–55, JSTOR, Web, February 20, 2013.
[185] Ellen C. Merrill, *Germans of Louisiana*, references, page 64.

church that stands on that corner. That church is St. Mary's Assumption Church in the Irish Channel.

Burmaster reports that another wave of German immigrants arrived in New Orleans in the mid-1850s: "A lot of people estimate that by the middle of the 1850s, one in every five people living in Louisiana spoke German as their primary language." German immigrants started many businesses that New Orleanians will remember.[186] This growing community in the city naturally attracted new German immigrants, as did the groups of German-speaking Jews who made their way to New Orleans. Those who were not already skilled workers, artisans, and craftsmen quickly learned and developed into useful laborers. The German community not only had its religious congregations by the time of the Civil War but social and civil organizations a well, such as Kosmos Lodge #171, Germania Lodge #46, and Free and Accepted Masons, located on Bienville Street in Mid City.[187]

After the Civil War and during Reconstruction, German-owned businesses proliferated in all areas of commerce. The Roosevelt Hotel was originally a German hotel, the Grunewald. Kolb's was probably the last major German restaurant. The Faubachers owned banks and investment houses catering to the German community (Isidore Newman's firm was one of these). Breweries included Jax Brewery (brewed in the French Quarter and named after Andrew Jackson) and the Dixie Brewing Company, founded by Valentine Merz, which began production in 1907. During Prohibition, the latter became the Dixie Beverage Company.[188]

Germans started retail groceries and dry goods businesses (Schwarz, Maison Blanche, Schwegmann's, and many others). Fritz Jahncke began one of the most-visible German-owned companies. Jahncke's company provided the concrete that originally paved many New Orleans streets, and created many of its enduring monuments, such as the former Lee Circle. Another classic mix of New Orleans culture is the Leidenheimer Bakery. This German bakery is one of the leading producers of New Orleans French bread.

As in other parts of the country, the German community in New Orleans experienced some backlash with the outbreak of World War I. Anti-German hysteria swept the nation, and membership in German groups shriveled up.

[186] Mark Deane, "NOLA 300: When Germans Came to New Orleans," WGNO (May 7, 2018), https://wgno.com/2018/05/07/nola-300-when-germans-came-to-new-orleans/.
[187] Courtesy The Lost Word.
[188] NOLABrewHistory.com, 2011, retrieved May 3, 2013.

While this backlash was nowhere near what Japanese-Americans in Hawaii and California experienced thirty years later, many businesses with overtly German names changed them. Thus, the Grunewald Hotel on Canal Street became the Roosevelt. Berlin Street in uptown New Orleans became General Pershing Street, and the Fabachers began selling JAX Beer.

The World Wars were a tough time for Germans in New Orleans, because Americans were fighting a German enemy overseas. The Louisiana legislature passed an act during WWI to prohibit the use of the German language and the teaching of German in schools. The Germans in New Orleans came through both wars okay, as did all Americans. They continued to be a vital part of the city's growth and future. In 1927, two of the city's larger German clubs, the Turn-Verein (Turner's Society, an athletic organization) and the Harugari Mannerchor (a singing society), merged to form Deutsches Haus. German heritage groups united to hosts the city's annual Oktoberfest celebration.

New Orleans was the only free port in the world for the poor. The German Society fought against all prejudices against the Germans. They acknowledged that the members of the German Society were valuable immigrants. They were mainly farmers with excellent character. They were industrious people.

Around 1850, Michael Hahn became the governor of Louisiana, the "first German-born citizen to become a governor of an American state." He started a community in St. Charles Parish that carries his name. Hahnville is the parish seat of St. Charles Parish, and the courthouse originally contained Hahnville High School. Today, Hahnville High School is located on Highway 90 west of Boutte but retains its original name.[189]

Generation 4: Christian John Young

The Young Family Arrives in New Orleans

Christian John Young (28 Oct 1818 - 08 Jan 1863} was born on October 28, 1818, in Württemberg, Germany. Württemberg is located in the southwest corner of today's Germany, in Bavaria. Christian was the son of Georg Heinrich Jung, who was born on October 9, 1781, and died on February 10, 1826. Georg was also from Wuerttemberg, Germany. Christian's mother was Louisa Christiana Fischer,

---

[189.] Ellen C. Merrill, *Germans of Louisiana*, http://www.doyletics.com/arj/germanso.shtml.

who was born on August 20, 1786, and died on September 14, 1829. George Heinrich and Louisa Christina were married on May 15, 1810, in Evangelisch, Aichelberg, Donaukreis Church in Württemberg. Notice the last name change from his father (Jung) to Christian (Young). This change probably occurred during the emigration from Germany to the United States, as noted below.

Württemberg developed as a political entity in southwest Germany, with the core established around Stuttgart. Württemberg survived Germany's religious wars, changes in imperial policy, and invasions from France. It was recognized as a kingdom in 1806, and its territory now forms part of the modern German state of Baden-Württemberg, one of the sixteen states of Germany.

German emigration to the United States happened in three significant waves. The first wave occurred mainly from southwestern Germany in the years 1845–1855. It consisted of 939,149 men, women, and children, 97 percent of whom came from the Bavarian region: the states of Nassau, Hesse, the Rhineland, Pfalz, Baden, and Wurttemberg.

The second wave did not start until ten years later, when a million people reached the United States between 1865 and 1873. Most came from northwestern Germany, specifically from the states of Schleswig-Holstein, Ost Fnesland, Hanover, Oldenburg, and Westphaha, an area of prosperous middle-sized grain farms. The third wave began in 1880. This wave coincided with the beginning of the great influx of southern and eastern Europeans. Of the 1.8 million people who came in this migration, the vast majority came from northeastern Germany, an area dominated by Prussia, Pornerania, Upper Silesia, and Mecklenburg. This area was the domain of the Prussian aristocracy, which led to the industrialization of the region.

Christian came to the United States in about 1828, arriving in New York City. The name change from Jung to Young probably happened on his immigration. When people boarded a ship to travel to America, they had to give their name (papers were probably not used). The vessel would record the name as it sounded to them. *Jung* in German is pronounced *Young* in English. That was more than likely how it was written down on the ship's manifest. When immigrants entered the United States, US Customs used the ship's manifest to record the names of the immigrants. Hence *Jung* became *Young*.

Christian's future wife, Mary Ann Hoffman, was born on May 13, 1827. She was also born in Ruschbach, Rhine, Bayern, Germany. Mary Ann Hoffman was the daughter of Joseph Hoffmann (mother unknown). She probably emigrated to

New Orleans around 1843, as her obituary states that at the time of her death at the age of eighty-one in 1908, she had been a resident for sixty-five years.[190] In New Orleans, the family lived (as many immigrants did) along the river in the Jefferson City and Irish Channel neighborhood.

Jefferson City was an area with a significant component of the German population, as more and more immigrants settled in the area. Incorporated initially, in 1846, as the Borough of Freeport, it was annexed in 1870 by New Orleans as the Sixth District. The boundaries of Jefferson City began at Toledano Street (downriver) and extended upriver to Joseph Street. According to the census of 1860, almost half of the population of this area was German.

A congruent neighborhood of Jefferson City, where they moved, was the Irish Channel. "The Channel" was a sub-district of the Central City–Garden District–Jefferson City area. Its boundaries were First Street to the east, Magazine Street to the north, Toledano Street to the west, and the Mississippi River to the south.[191] This working-class neighborhood was, as the name implies, settled mainly by immigrants from Ireland in the early nineteenth century, even though people of other ethnicities also settled there, including German, Italian, and African Americans. All these ethnic groups lived in very close proximity to each other.

The name *Channel* comes from the Irish "pouring like a channel" into the area.[192] Significant immigration from Ireland, as well as Germany, to the United States occurred during the period of 1810–1850, with an unusually large wave during the decade of the 1830s. With many immigrants penniless, they took up residence in simple cottages, providing the beginnings of today's shotgun houses.[193]

Irish and German immigrants arrived primarily to dig the New Basin Canal and were regarded as expendable labor. New Orleans subsequently had the most significant Irish population in the south. These Irish immigrants were Roman Catholic, in contrast to the Protestant Scotch-Irish who were more common in the rest of the Southeastern United States. Many Irish immigrants settled as well

---

[190] Passenger and Immigration Lists Index, the 1500s-1900s - Source Publication Code 503.10.91 - Source Bibliography - Bentley, Elizabeth P. Passenger Arrivals at the Port of New York, 1820-1829. Baltimore: Genealogical Publishing Co., 1999, pp. 655-1373 (Ju-Z).

[191] "Irish Channel, New Orleans," *Wikipedia*, https://en.wikipedia.org/wiki/Irish_Channel,_New_Orleans.

[192] J. Martin, as interviewed by A .N. McGrath in *Irish Eyes*, vol. 2, no. 2 (July/August 1995), 7.

[193] Irish Channel Neighborhood, accessed June 10, 2012.

at Irish Bayou in present-day Eastern New Orleans. St. Mary's Assumption, the German church, was built in 1844 across the street from the future St. Alphonsus Church, the Irish church, constructed in 1855. Both were supervised and served in their religious and cultural needs by the Redemptorist Fathers.[194]

A painting of Our Lady of Perpetual Help came to St. Alphonsus Church in 1874. A National Shrine was established there. For generations, Irish schoolchildren, as well as parishioners and visitors, would participate in novenas to Mary at the church. So many Catholics attended that the city placed additional streetcars and buses into service to carry a large number of attendees.[195] In these early years, the community built churches to serve various other ethnic groups. In addition to the German and Irish churches previously discussed, Notre Dame de Bon Secours Church served the French.

The Irish Channel developed a reputation for ruffian gangs early in its history.[196] Much of this reputation centered on conflicts between ethnic groups, such as the St. Mary's Market Gang, the Shot Tower Gang, the Pine Knot Gang, the Ripsaw Gang, and the Crowbar Gang.[197] The riverfront housed most of the thieves and prostitutes, although much of the gang activity of the time was on the corner of St. Mary Street and Religious Street.[198] Through the early twentieth century, many worked in the port of New Orleans before modern shipping innovations significantly reduced the need for stevedores and similar jobs. The local breweries had a significant role in easing the poverty that existed in the area.[199]

Parades and parties held on and around St. Patrick's Day were enjoyed by many locals, whether of Irish ancestry or not. An example of organizations that paraded on St. Patrick's Day and promoted other civic activities were the Irish Channel Corner Club. Parasol's Bar and Tracey's Bar, a block apart on Third Street, were a focal point for St. Patrick's Day parades in the Irish Channel. The area is known today for the surviving working-class and middle-class nineteenth-century residential architecture, including many shotgun houses.

---

[194] History of the St. Alphonsus Art and Cultural Center, accessed June 16, 2012.

[195] Margaret Varnell Clark, *The Irish in Louisiana* (Bijoux Press: 2013), 48.

[196] *Daily Delta*, July 10, 1861.

[197] L. Saxon, E. Dreyer, R. Tallant, *Gumbo Ya-Ya*, Pelican Publishing Co., 1998, pp. 50 - 74, ISBN 0882896458.

[198] Irish Channel Neighborhood, accessed June 10th, 2012.

[199] Change in the Irish Channel, accessed June 10th, 2012.

Growth

The history of the first half of the nineteenth century in New Orleans was one of uninterrupted growth. By the 1850 US Census, New Orleans ranked as the sixth largest city in the country, with a population reported at 168,675.[200] New Orleans was the only city in the South with a population of over 100,000.

By 1840, New Orleans also had the most extensive slave market in the nation. This market contributed significantly to its wealth. During the pre-Civil War years, 700,000 slaves moved from the Upper South in forced migration to the Deep South. Estimates are that the slaves generated 13.5 per cent of the revenue per person, making tens of billions of dollars through the years.[201]

New Orleans was the business heart of the south. Cotton comprised half of the estimated $156 million in 1857 dollars. Tobacco and sugar followed. Half of all cotton in the US passed through the port of New Orleans each year (1.4 million bales). That was fully three times more than at the second-leading port of Mobile. The city also boasted several federal buildings, including the US Mint and the US Customs House.[202]

The Children of Christian John Young

Christian and Mary Ann Hoffmann Young met while living in these neighborhoods in New Orleans during this historical time. They were married in St. Patrick's Church in October of 1846. Christian and Mary Ann had the following five children together:

- George Washington Young was born on October 18, 1848. He married Claire Elizabeth Mcginn (1904–1991) in September of 1928 in New Orleans.[203] He was listed as a bookkeeper in 1870. He was living in 1880 on 447 Chippewa Street and is listed as a banker in 1900. He married Mary S. (Young), and they had two known daughters together: Mary Young, born about 1871, and Carrie Young, born about 1874. George

[200]https://en.wikipedia.org/wiki/New_Orleans_in_the_American_Civil_War
[201]Walter Johnson, *Soul by Soul: Life Inside the Antebellum Slave Market*, pp.2 and 6
[202]Harper's Weekly, February 16th, 1861
[203] Alphabetical Birth Indexes for Orleans Parish 1796-1900, "Y."

died in New Orleans on January 22, 1911, at the age of sixty-two. He is also listed as George Christian Young.[204],[205]

- Henry Clay Young (an ancestor of Agnes Young, the mother of the author)[206] was born on January 16, 1851. He is the great-great-grandfather of Jason, Jonathan, and Jameson Bourg. He married Annie (Anna) Martzloff on August 24, 1878. He died on July 20, 1898. (More about him later in this chapter.)

- Christian John Young II was born on February (or April) 4, 1853, and died just six days later on February 10, 1853. The cause of death is unknown.

- Mary Elizabeth "Lizzie" Young was born in 1855 and died on April 19, 1892, at only thirty-seven years of age.[207] She married Joseph Oliver Morainville Dallimore on November 27, 1879, in New Orleans. Her children were Sidney J. (1909–1997), George Urban (1884–1891), Joseph Oliver Morainville (1886–?), and Mary Cecilia (1888–1905). Her obituary reads as follows:

After a painful illness of two weeks, Mrs. Mary Elizabeth Young, wife of Joseph O. Dallimore, yesterday evening departed this life at the age of 37 years. Her sweet and lovely nature spread her fragrance wherever she went. Ever faithful to her noble nature, her life was like a beautiful star- the darker the hour, the severer the trial, the brighter and purer she appeared. Faithful, constant devoted her pure spirit guided her steps with unerring certainty. The lady was the sister of Messers Henry C. Wm. F. and George W. Young. To them and her husband and children, heartfelt expressions of sympathy are extended. The funeral will take place from her late residence on 376 Chippewa street, opposite Clay Square, at 3:30 this afternoon.

- William Frederick Young was born on January 23, 1860. He married Josephine Shaefers.[208] In 1910, they were renting a house at 922 Phillip Street which, ironically, was just a few houses down the block from 932

---

[204] www.ancestry.com, Family Lines, ID 103706, Reference Number 3706.

[205] *New Orleans, Louisiana Birth Records Index, 1790-1899*, vol. 11, 345.

[206] Alphabetical Birth Indexes for Orleans Parish 1796-1900, New Orleans, Louisiana.

[207] "New Orleans, Louisiana, Death Records Index, 1804-1949," Ancestry.com online database (Provo, UT: Ancestry.com Operations Inc, 2002).

[208] "New Orleans, Louisiana, Birth Records Index, 1790-1915," Ancestry.com online database (Provo, UT: Ancestry.com Operations, Inc., 2002).

Phillip Street, the home of James A. Bourg Sr. (and his family, including Jim Bourg Jr.) from 1963 to 1967. According to the 1910 US Census, William was a solicitor working for a coffee company. He lived there with his wife, Josephine Frances Schaefers—who was born in New Orleans on April 8, 1858, and died there in January 1937—and their children George J. Young (age twenty), Altie M. Young (nineteen), Mary R. Young (seventeen), Agnes M. Young (sixteen), and Gerrad B. Young (fifteen).[209] William died in New Orleans on November 15, 1923.

Louisiana seceded from the Union on January 22, 1861. New Orleans soon became a primary source of troops, armament, and supplies to the Confederate States Army. Several area residents rapidly became prominent in this army, including Beauregard, Bragg, Blanchard, and Harry T. Hays, who led the famed Louisiana Tigers infantry brigade, which had a large contingent of Irish American New Orleanians. Several German regiments fought in the Confederate army. Two thousand Germans served voluntarily, with another three thousand serving against their will.

The city was the site of a Confederate navy depot. New Orleans ship-fitters produced very innovative warships. The Confederate Navy defended the Mississippi River during the War. Early in the Civil War, New Orleans was a prime target for the Union Navy, which planned an attack to capture the city and its vital port. The commercial importance of New Orleans, and its strategic position, marked it as necessary for the Union. The government selected Captain David Farragut for the command of the Union Squadron in January 1862.

The primary defense of the river consisted of two forts, Fort Jackson and Fort St. Philip. These two forts, armed with heavy guns, were of masonry and brick construction. They were located on either riverbank to command long stretches of the river. Also, the Confederates had some improvised ironclads and gunboats, large and small, but these were outnumbered and outgunned by the Union Navy fleet.

On April 16, the Union's fleet steamed into position below the forts and prepared for battle. On April 18, they opened fire. Their guns were very accurate, and Fort Jackson was severely damaged. After a second bombardment on April 19, the Union ships broached a boom between the forts designed to detain vessels.

---

[209] "1910 United States Federal Census," Ancestry.com online database (Lehi, UT: Ancestry.com Operations Inc, 2006).

At night, their gunboats were repeatedly sent to destroy the barrier, but they had little success.

They finally broke through, and at noon on April 25, Farragut anchored in front of the city. Forts Jackson and St. Philip surrendered on April 28. Soon afterward, the infantry marched into New Orleans and occupied the city without further resistance.

New Orleans was captured with no battle in the city. The city was spared the destruction of other cities in the South. It retained its history and its charm. It kept its nineteenth-century structures, including the French Quarter. New Orleans was in Confederate hands for only 455 days.

Christian Young was listed as a city policeman. He became a Confederate soldier in Company I of the 2nd regiment, 2nd brigade, 1st division of the Louisiana Confederate militia.[210] It is not known the circumstances of his belonging to this militia unit. As was stated earlier, there were several German regiments in the Confederate army, some serving voluntarily and some against their will. Christian passed away on January 8, 1863—just eight days short of his forty-fifth birthday. The cause of his death is not known. There was Yellow Fever in 1863, but not in January (there is little mosquito activity in winter). His death could have been Civil War–related, but this is not certain. This would be a good research project for his descendants.

After the death of Christian, Mary Ann Hoffman Young lived with her children Henry Clay, Merry, and William (George having moved out and Christian John having died in a house at 316 Tchoupitoulas Street in New Orleans). Mary Ann is listed as a dressmaker. The four were sharing the residence with Alice Swain (sixteen years old and born in Pennsylvania), a seamstress; Maria Swain (fourteen years old), also listed as a seamstress; and Josephine Swain (ten years old). The relationship is not known or understood if there was one.

In 1885, Mary Ann lived at 270 Chippewa Street. In 1890, she lived on 376 Chippewa Street.[211] Mary Ann Hoffman Young died on May 13, 1908, in New Orleans. Her obituary in the *Daily Picayune* of May 14, 1908 read as follows:

Mary A. Hoffman Young, the widow of the late Christian J. Young, a native of Rosebech, Reinish Bavaria, Germany, and a resident of the city for 67 years,

---

[210] "U.S. Civil War Soldiers, 1861-1865," National Park Service online database (Provo, UT: Ancestry.com Operations Inc, 2007). Original data: National Park Service, "Civil War Soldiers and Sailors System," http://www.itd.nps.gov/cwss/, acquired 2007.

[211] New Orleans city directory.

died Wed. May 13th, 1908, at 6:15 p.m. Funeral will take place on Thursday, May 14th, at 4 o'clock at the residence of her son, George Washington Young, 560 Walnut Street.

Her obituary in the *New Orleans Morning Star* read as follows:

She was one of those rare characters who are sought after and loved and whose memory remains a subtle helpful incentive to a higher and nobler purpose. Miss Hoffman was married in October 1846, to Mr. Christian John Young, in St. Patrick's Church in this city. Their Union was an ideal one, founded upon that high and earnest dignity of thought and character, which beget lasting respect and affection. Children came to bless this union founded in God. Today but two survive Mr. George W. Young, the well-known vice president of the Canal Bank & Trust Co., and Mr. William F. Young. Into the home so dear to her, Mrs. Young threw all the grace and strength of her beautiful character and the finest and noblest impulses of her heart. She enveloped it with the dignity and glory of spotless Catholic womanhood, and it became a shrine toward which husband and children turned as the spot next to the altar, which gave them the foretaste of heaven on earth.

For many years, since the death of her good and noble husband, she made her home with her devoted son, Mr. George W. Young, and here the affection and tenderness that were lavished upon her by loving sons and daughter and granddaughter in a measure compensated for the loss of him to whom she had pledged her heart in her bonnie youth. Kind, charitable, forgiving, her life was a benediction to all about her, especially to the poor and suffering who came to her, sure of the aid that was never denied. Her life was centered in God and duty, and to the end she held steadfast and true, dying in the rich years of a harvest of good works, and passing hence as gently as a summer's cloud floats from the land far out upon the sea. To the end, she retained her bright, cheerful interest in books and people and was stricken last Wednesday week, as she sat reading of higher and purer things. She died as she had lived, fortified with all the sacraments of the Church, which she has loved so deeply, and of which she had been such a faithful and consistent member.

The funeral took place on Thursday, May 14th, and was attended by the most prominent people of the city. Beautiful flowers adorned the bier of her, whose life was all fragrance and glory. The funeral services were conducted by Very Rev. Albert Bievor, S.J., and rector of the Church of the Holy Name of Jesus, assisted by Rev. Fathers Ryan and Field, S.J. The pallbearers were Messrs. J.B. Levert, L.E. Cenas, D.B. Haggerty, T.P. Thompson, J.P. Boyle, and P.J. Nevin.

The funeral took place on Thursday, laid in the family tomb in Greenwood Cemetery. And there beside the dear husband, who had been her friend and helper on the pathway to heaven, and the loving children who had clustered around her mother heart, as the vines twine around the parent stem, the remains of this noble Christian and Catholic Lady were left to await the resurrection dawn.

To the family, bereft of her gracious presence, the *Morning Star* extends its deepest sympathy. But for them, there should be no grief, no tears. In the fullness of years and the richness of God's grace, the devoted mother has only been translated to the Heart of her loving Savior. With the apostles, she can say: "I have fought the good fight, I have kept the faith, and for me is laid up the crown of victory."

Generation 3: Henry Clay Young

The second child (and son) of Christian and Mary Ann Hoffmann Young was Henry Clay Young. He was born on January 16, 1851. He is the great-great-grandfather of Jason, Jonathan, and Jameson Bourg.[212] He died on July 20, 1898, in New Orleans, when he was only forty-seven years old. He married Anna M. (Addie) Marzloff on August 24, 1878, in New Orleans, when he was twenty-seven years old. Henry Clay Young was a retail grocer, according to the US Census.

Anna Martzloff was born in September of 1856 in New Orleans.[213] She died in New Orleans on November 3, 1927. She was seventy-one years of age when she died.

The Children of Henry Clay Young

Henry Clay and Anna had the following children together:

* Oliver Joseph Young was born on November 20, 1878, in New Orleans and died there on February 20, 1928. He married Anna Mary Frances Rappold. Anna was born on March 16, 1884, in New Orleans. She died on

---

[212] Alphabetical Birth Indexes for Orleans Parish 1796-1900.

[213] 1900 Census, New Orleans Ward 11, Orleans, Louisiana, Roll T623 574, page 11A, enumeration district 110.

January 23, 1954, at 927 Third Street, New Orleans. This was the great grandfather of Jason, Jonathan and Jameson Bourg.

- William F. Young (Uncle Willie, as my mother called him) was born on August 20, 1882, in New Orleans and died on January 12, 1972 in Shreveport, Caddo Parish, Louisiana.
- George Washington Young was born on December 17, 1886, in New Orleans. The date and place of his death is not known at this time.
- Eva Marie Young was born in November of 1887 in New Orleans. She married a Mr. Lockwood.
- Mathias Henry Young was born on October 28, 1890, in New Orleans and died in 1959.
- Henry Clay Young Jr. was born on November 14, 1893, in New Orleans and died in July of 1981 in Tennessee.

Turbulent Times

Henry Clay Young was born in the year 1851, a year leading up to the Civil War. Unfortunately, at this time in history, the Civil War was inevitable. There were enough irreconcilable differences between the northern population of the country and the southern population to make it inevitable. The causes for the Civil War were many, including the following:

- **Ecconomic Differences between North and South**
  The North and South of the United States developed in different ways. The South's economy was predominantly based on agriculture, while the North's was mostly based on industrialization. These differences resulted in diverging political beliefs as well as types of society. These differences led to disagreements on issues such as taxes, tariffs, internal improvements, and states' rights versus federal rights.[214]
- **Slavery**
  Slavery and the debate over its future, was the primary cause of the Civil War. The agriculture-based South needed slaves to tend to its large plantations. Right before the beginning of the Civil War, there were approximately 4 million Africans slaves in the South. Slavery had, for a long time, been part of the fabric of the South's economy.

[214] "Causes of the Civil War," https://www.historynet.com/causes-of-the-civil-war.

Only a small number of Southerners owned slaves, but ownership of even a handful of slaves brought respect and social position. Slaves were like chattel; they could be traded and sold for any reason. Slaves represented the greatest component of the region's wealth. As the price of cotton and land declined, the cost of slaves increased.

One by one, the Northern states abolished slavery. A continuous flow of immigrants from Germany and Ireland came to supply the North with laborers during the potato famine of the 1840s and 1850s. The Irish were usually hired at very low wages, diminishing the need for the institution of slavery.[215]

- **States' Rights**

    The federal government and individual states fought over political power. This struggle was mostly about slavery in the individual states. Did the federal government have the right to regulate or even abolish it? This debate again was primarily between the North and the South.

- **Abolitionist Movement**

    By the early 1830s, abolitionists, who wished to see slavery abolished within the United States, were becoming more strident and influential. Obedience to a "higher law" over obedience to the Constitution's legal guarantee of slave-owner rights was at heart of this movement. Many smaller issues added to this movement.

- **The Passing of the Fugitive Slave Act**

    On September 18, 1850, with the Compromise of 1850, the United States passed the Fugitive Slave Act.[216] One of the most disputed pieces of the 1850 compromise was this provision, which required that all escaped slaves be returned to their masters upon capture. Abolitionists called it the "Bloodhound Law." Dogs were used to track down runaway slaves.[217]

- **Uncle Tom's Cabin**

    Harriet Beecher Stowe published *Uncle Tom's Cabin* in 1852. It was a nationwide and worldwide bestseller within two years. It depicted the evils of slavery and gave a look into slavery that few in the country

---

[215] "Causes of the Civil War."

[216] James C. Cobb, "One of American History's Worst Laws Was Passed 165 Years Ago," (September 18, 2015).

[217] Allan Nevins, *The Ordeal of the Union: Fruits of Manifest Destiny, 1847–1852* (Collier Books: 1947).

had seen before. The book succeeded in starting a wave of anti-slavery sentiment across the country. When President Lincoln met Stowe, he remarked, "So you're the little woman who wrote the book that started this Great War."[218]

- **The Underground Railroad**

Some abolitionists helped runaway slaves to escape. This was called the Underground Railroad. There were stories in which men sent to retrieve runaway slaves were attacked and beaten by abolitionists. To the slaveholding states, this indicated that abolitionist were choosing which parts of the Constitution they would support, but they expected the South to honor the entire Constitution. The most famous abolitionist in the Railroad was Harriet Tubman, a nurse and a spy in the Civil War. She was called "the Moses of her people."

- **The Missouri Compromise**

The new territories gained as a result of the US–Mexican War of 1846–1848 complicated the slavery issue. Abolitionists wanted to declare slavery illegal in these new territories. The Northwest Ordinance of 1787 had done the same in the region. Advocates of slavery thought that if slavery was prohibited in any states, the slaveholding states' political power would be at risk. The possibility of slavery being outlawed everywhere was at stake.

- **John Brown**

In Kansas, there were violent clashes between the two sides. One abolitionist in particular became infamous for battles that caused the deaths of pro-slavery settlers in Kansas. His name was John Brown. Ultimately, he carried his fight closer to the bosom of slavery. On the night of October 16, 1859, John Brown and his followers took the federal arsenal at Harper's Ferry, Virginia (now West Virginia) in an attempt to arm a slave rebellion. The US Marines overcame the group, with Lieutenant Colonel Robert E. Lee leading the Marines. Brown was put on trial for treason, convicted, and hanged. Northern abolitionists made a martyr of him. Brown's raid thus became a step on the road to conflict between the sections.

---

[218] "Lincoln, Stowe, and the 'Little Woman/Great War' Story," quod.lib.umich.edu/j/jala/2629860.0030.104/--lincoln-stowe-and-the-little-womangreat-war-stor...

- ## The Election of Abraham Lincoln

Many former Whig party members joined with the American Party (Know-Nothings) and others who opposed slavery to form a new Republican party in 1850. The Republican, Abraham Lincoln, won the 1860 presidential election. Southern states feared that the Republicans would abolish slavery cause Lincoln was an opponent to the expansion of slavery.

Southern Secession

The South Carolina state convention voted to secede from the United States and become a separate entity. They had threatened this earlier, in 1835, over a tax that benefited Northern manufacturers but increased the cost of goods in the South. President Jackson threatened to send troops to make the state to stay in the Union, and Congress gave him authority to raise such an army. All the Southern senators walked out in protest before the vote. A compromise prevented the confrontation from occurring at that time, and no troops were sent.

Learning from this experience that going it alone was very dangerous, South Carolina sent representatives to other Southern states urging Southern leaders to follow South Carolina and form a new Southern Confederacy. Six states did just that. Mississippi, Florida, Alabama, Georgia, Louisiana, and Texas voted for secession. Other states in the region voted down secession, at least temporarily.

On April 10, 1861, provisional Confederate forces in Charleston demanded the surrender of the federal garrison at Fort Sumter. The fort's commander, Major Robert Anderson, refused. On April 12, the Confederates opened cannon fire, and by the afternoon of following day, the fort lowered the stars and stripes and surrendered.

Now that war had started. President Lincoln called for volunteers to fil the army. The remainder of the southern states refused to fight against their southern neighbors. They felt Lincoln had exceeded his authority. They changed their thinking and voted in favor of the session. The western part of Virginia did not want session and formed a new state, West Virginia, which remained in the Union..

In 1850, because of all the reasons stated above, war was inevitable. There was deeply felt animosity between the Northern and Southern states. The cause of this animosity was so complex that it is difficult to characterize it. It is probably the case, however, that the original cause of the Civil War occurred when a Dutch ship offloaded a cargo of African slaves at Jamestown, Virginia, in 1619. It took nearly 250 years for this to eventually turn into a war, but that boatload of slaves was the start of it.

In 1860, Henry Clay Young was only nine years old. He attended school and lived at home in what is today the Irish Channel. Also living at home, according to the 1860 US Census were his father, Christian J. Young, age forty; his mother, Mary Young, age thirty-three; his older brother, George W Young, age eleven; and his younger sister, Mary Elizabeth Young, age five. His younger brother, who was born in 1853, had already died. His other brother, William Frederick Young, was not yet born; he would arrive later in 1860.

Henry Clay Young met his future wife, Anna Martzloff, in 1877 and married her on August 24, 1878. He was twenty-seven years old.[219] Anna was born in September of 1856 in the 11th Ward of New Orleans. She would die in New Orleans on November 3, 1927. We don't know anything about her ancestors at this time.

Scientific Achievements

During the second half of the nineteenth century, there was much activity in science. In astronomy and environmental science, Johann Gottfried Galle and Heinrich Louis d'Arrest: discovered the planet Neptune in 1846. In 1871, Lord Rayleigh published his "Diffuse sky radiation (Rayleigh scattering)" theory, which explained why the sky appears blue. In 1861, John Tyndall conducted experiments in radiant energy and published them to reinforce the atmospheric greenhouse effect. In 1896, Svante Arrhenius derived and published the basic principles of the greenhouse effect.

In chemistry and physics, Lord Kelvin published his theory of absolute zero in 1848. The scientist James Clerk Maxwell, proved and published his theory of electromagnetism in 1864. In 1865, Rudolf Clausius published the definition of entropy, and in 1877, Ludwig Boltzmann published his own statistical definition. In 1873, Johannes Diderik van der Waals published his theory of intermolecular forces, which we know today as "van der Waals force." Frederick Guthrie published his discovery of thermionic emission, and Willoughby Smith published his discovery of photoconductivity. In 1869, Dmitri Mendeleev published his theory of periodicity and the periodic table. In 1875, William Crookes invented the

---

[219.] 1900 Census, roll T623 574, page 11A, enumeration district 110.

Crookes tube and published his studies of cathode rays. A year later, Josiah Willard Gibbs published his findings of chemical thermodynamics and the phase rule. In 1880, Pierre Curie and Jacques Curie published their theory of piezoelectricity.

In 1887, Albert A. Michelson and Edward W. Morley published what might be the most famous failed experiment in history, which is generally considered to be the first strong evidence against the existence of the luminiferous ether. The luminiferous either theory hypothesized that Earth moves through a medium of either that carries light. In the late nineteenth century, luminiferous ether (*luminiferous* meaning "light-bearing") was the postulated medium for the propagation of light. Albert A. Michelson, later in 1907, received the Nobel Prize in physics, becoming the first American to win the Nobel Prize in science.

In 1895, Wilhelm Conrad Röntgen discovered x-rays, and a year later, Henri Becquerel discovered radioactivity. In 1897, J. J. Thomson discovered electrons present in cathode rays, and two years later he proposed his model of an atom.

In biology and life science, Rudolf Virchow theorized that cells could only arise from preexisting cells in 1858. Charles Darwin and Alfred Wallace published their theory of evolution by natural selection in 1859. In 1861, Louis Pasteur published his paper on germ theory. Gregor Mendel postulated his laws of inheritance, which is the basis for all genetics, in 1865. In 1884, Jacobus Henricus van Hoff published his discovery of the laws of chemical dynamics and osmotic pressure in solutions (in his work "Etudes de Dynamique chimique"). In 1888, Friedrich Reinitzer discovered liquid crystals. In 1892, Dmitri Ivanovsky identified a virus for the first time. In 1898, Martinus Beijerinck published his conclusions about virus infections replicating in the host; thus, they were not a mere toxin. He contributed the name *virus*.

Death of Henry Clay Young

Henry Clay Young died on July 20, 1898. He and Anna had been married for one month short of twenty years. The US Census of 1900 shows that Anna was living with her six children at 2424 Laurel Street in the Irish Channel. Oliver Joseph is listed as Joseph Oliver, and a twenty-year-old baker. William F. is listed as an eighteen-year-old baker. The other four children were either at school or too young for school.

By the 1910 US Census, Oliver, William, and Eva Marie had moved out, but Anna remained at 2424 Laurel Street with the three other children. Oliver got married on October 2, 1907, and moved down the street to 2418 Laurel Street. William had moved around the corner to 738 Fourth Street. Eva had married Robert Lockwood on November 5, 1907, and moved out to live with her husband.

Anna Martzloff Young passed away on November 3,1927. She was seventy-one years old and was buried in the Metairie Cemetery tomb of her husband.

Generation 2: Oliver Joseph Young

Oliver Joseph Young, Jim Bourg Jr.'s maternal grandfather, was born on November 20, 1878, in New Orleans and died there on February 20, 1928. He married Anna Mary Frances Rappold. She was born on March 16, 1884, in New Orleans and died at 927 Third St. on January 23, 1954. When Oliver was born, Henry, his father, was twenty-seven, and his mother, Anna (Anne), was twenty-one. They were living at 562 Constance Street (downtown on Constance between Howard Avenue and Poeyfarre Street). They lived just three blocks from Julia Street and nine blocks from Canal Street.

When Oliver married into the Rappold family, he married into a family of German bakers. Oliver's father was in the retail business, and the union of the families developed the idea of a retail bakery business. Young's Bakery was the name of the company he opened in the 2400 block of Laurel Street. Oliver was the retail businessman, and his father-in-law, Lewis L. Rappold, was the master baker from Germany. Lewis was a member of the Bakers Union #23. Lewis and Oliver started Young's Bakery, and it was successful enough to make Oliver a somewhat wealthy man.

Historical Events

During the year 1878, many historical events happened in New Orleans. Another major outbreak of yellow fever started this year. The epidemic was reported to start when the *Emily B. Souder*, a steamer from the tropics, docked in New Orleans. More than 27,000 people contracted yellow fever, and four thousand four hundred and forty-six people died. A quarantine of New Orleans was enforced, and the city became known as *the wet grave*.

Not knowing that mosquitos spread the fever, authorities attempted many things to deter the spread of the disease in the Crescent City. They burned carbolic acid and sulfur in an attempt to keep away the fever. They gave Charity Hospital patients saltshakers filled with calomel and urged them to take a pinch whenever they felt like it. Still, every day, as many as forty-seven people died from the fever. Carriages of the dead piled with coffins traveled to the cemeteries. This outbreak had a particular impact on children in the New Orleans area.

During Reconstruction, efforts at integration were started in the South. However, Jim Crow laws were also passed by state legislatures in the Southwest and Midwest. Jim Crow segregated blacks and whites in all aspects of public life, including attendance of public schools.[220]

On a social season forefront, the New Orleans premier of Bizet's *Carmen* opened in the French Opera House, reopening after a several-year closure. The Krew of Comus did not parade in 1879; they saved the money to spend on running a soup kitchen for stricken citizens all through September. Edgar Degas remained in the city of his mother's birth to continue painting. During this time, he painted the oil on canvas work "A Cotton Office in New Orleans."

While Oliver Joseph Young was growing up in the Irish Channel of New Orleans, many changes were taking place in the city. Some 76 million people lived in the United States in 1900, and 287,104 of them lived in New Orleans. New York City, by comparison, had 3.4 million people in 1900, twelve times the population of New Orleans. The New Orleans population had increased by 33 percent from the 216,090 people who lived there in 1880. Population growth at the beginning of the twentieth century was tied to land availability. The low-lying nature of the city away from the river prohibited the construction of safe housing that would not flood.

New Orleans grew because of pump technology. These pumps led to the draining of the low-lying swampland located between the city's crescent ridge and Lake Pontchartrain. These new levees meant that people could live in what was previously marshland. Four hurricanes damaged the city a lot in 1909, 1915, 1947, and 1965. But they did not have the catastrophic effect that Hurricane Katrina had in 2005.

The New Orleans/Metairie/Kenner area is unusual in that water surrounds it. Drainage in New Orleans was a significant concern. The city was founded on land that is essentially below sea level. Gravity alone cannot be used to remove surface water. As such, virtually all rainfall occurring within the city must be

---

[220] "Jim Crow Laws," National Park Service, retrieved November 1, 2013.

removed through either evaporation or pumping. Artificial levees built to keep out rising river and lake waters had the negative effect of keeping in precipitation.[221]

In 1871, the city built some thirty-six miles of canals for both improved drainage and small-vessel shipping within the city. However, in the 1890s, it was still common for water to cover the streets from curb to curb after a rainstorms in neighborhoods away from the river.[222] In 1893, New Orleans formed the Drainage Advisory Board to come up with better solutions to the city's drainage problems. The board constructed extensive topographical maps and consulted some of the nation's top engineers.

In 1899, the city floated a bond issue, which funded the new Sewerage & Water Board of New Orleans. It was responsible for draining the city along with constructing a modern sewage and drinking water system for the city. This was different from the Orleans Levee Board, which was responsible for the city's levee and flood protection. A. Baldwin Wood, a young engineer for the S&WB, not only supervised the plans for improved drainage and pumping but also invented several improvements in the pumps themselves. These improvements were used in New Orleans and adopted all over the world.

As the twentieth century progressed, the city drained a lot of the land that was swamp and unfit for use. This allowed expansion from the natural higher ground close to the river, and the natural bayou formed oak ridges. This system would work pretty effectively until Hurricane Katrina in 2005 exposed its weaknesses.[223]

By 1900, the city's streetcars were electrified and no longer pulled by horses or mules. New Orleans jazz was born in its clubs and dance halls.

The Children of Oliver Joseph Young

Oliver Joseph Young and Anna Mary Frances Rappold bought a large house at 1138 St. Andrew Street, which has a side-address at 2011 Camp Street. This allowed their house on Laurel St. to become commercial bakery. This also allowed them to have a large family. Oliver and Anna had eight children: Anna Mary (1908–1952), Mary Agnes (1910–1978), Agnes Louise (1912–1984), Oliver Joseph

---

[221] "Drainage in New Orleans," *Wikipedia*, https://en.wikipedia.org/wiki/Drainage_in_New_Orleans.

[222] "Drainage in New Orleans."

[223] Craig E. Colten, *An Unnatural Metropolis: Wresting New Orleans from Nature* (Baton Rouge: Louisiana State University Press, 2005)

(1915–1993), Claire Camille (1917–1975), Dorothy Frances (1919–2001), Louis Joseph (1922–1971), and Audrey Louise (1925–). Their lives are discussed in more detail in the following sections.

Anna Mary Young

Anna Mary Young was born in New Orleans on August 30, 1908, when her father, Oliver, was twenty-nine years old and her mother, Anna, was twenty-four years old. She grew up in the house on the corner of St. Andrew Street and Camp Street. She completed four years of high school at Redemptorist High in 1926.

When Anna Mary's father died in 1928, she and her mother became the heads of the household. Anna was twenty, Mary was eighteen, Agnes was sixteen, Oliver was thirteen, Claire was eleven, Dot was nine, Lewis was six, and Audrey was only three. They lived at the family home at 1138 St. Andrew Street.

Anna Mary married Lawrence Harry Huber on June 18, 1930. Lawrence was born on February 11, 1905, in New Orleans. He was the son of Jacob F. Huber and Anna Bode. Jacob was born on October 15, 1876, in Louisiana and died in December of 1945 in New Orleans. Anna Bode Huber was born in December of 1886 and died on February 28, 1963. Lawrence and Anna Mary had three children together;

- Elaine Huber was born in 1933 in New Orleans. She attended Redemptorist High. When Elaine's mother, Anna Mary Frances Rappold, died in 1952, Elaine was only twenty-one years old. She and her siblings moved in with their Aunt Agnes Young Bourg and Agnes's husband, Jim Bourg, who lived at 927 Third Street. Elaine worked as a bookkeeper in a downtown office.

In July of 1956, when she was twenty-three, Elaine married Jules Hugh Tracey in St. Alphonsus Church. Her uncle, Jim Bourg, gave her away. She moved with her husband, Jules, to Jackson, Mississippi, and died there in 1964. The cause of her death is not known to this family history.

- Lawrence Harry Huber Jr. (called "Hubba" all his life) was born on January 15, 1934, in New Orleans. When Hubba was born, his father was twenty-eight and his mother was twenty-five. He attended Redemptorist High School and also studied bookkeeping.

When his mother died in 1952, he was eighteen years old and decided to enlist in the army. He studied electronics in the army and became a radar technician. When he was released in 1958, Elaine had already married and moved out, so Lawrence moved in with his aunt and uncle at 927 Third Street. He went to work as a payroll bookkeeper at Strachan Shipping Co.

He lived with Jim and Agnes until he met and married his wife, Mary Lu. He never produced any children of his own but adopted Mary Lu's five girls, all of whom considered Larry their father. Larry was always overweight and had diabetes as a result. Before he was married Mary Lu, he stopped overeating and lost a lot of weight. He died on March 17, 1997.

- Shirley Ann Huber was born in 1937. When Shirley was born, her father was thirty-one and her mother was twenty-nine. She attended Redemptorist High and studied secretarial skills. When her mother died in 1952, Shirley was only fifteen years old. She moved in with her aunt and uncle at 927 Third Street and went to work at the same company as her sister.

She married John Charles Dunn in September of 1957 at St. Alphonsus Church. Her husband John (J. C.) had joined the military, and right after the wedding, they moved to Oklahoma for his duty. While he was away in the army, their first child, Karen Marie Dunn, was born.

When they returned to New Orleans from the service in 1962, they moved to an upstairs apartment at 924 Third Street, New Orleans, across the street from her Aunt Agnes and Uncle Jim. It was there that they had their second daughter, Elizabeth Dunn, who later married a Gandolini. Shirley and J. C. then had two more children, John Charles Dunn Jr. and Mary Lynn Dunn (who later married an Adams man.).

J. C. and Shirley were later divorced. J. C. died in Metairie in 2000 at the age of sixty-six. Shirley died on July 19, 2014 at the age of seventy-seven years.

Anna Mary Young Huber died on May 13, 1952, at the age of forty-three. The cause of death is not known at this time.

Mary Agnes Rita Young

Mary Agnes Rita Young was born on August 15, 1910, in New Orleans. When she was born, her father was thirty-one years of age and her mother was twenty-six. She was raised in the family home on St. Andrew Street at Camp Street. She graduated from Redemptorist High School.

In 1919, when Mary was ten years old, World War I came to an end. The Red Summer Riots of 1919 took place. Race riots happened in more than thirty cities throughout the United States, with bloodiest events were in Chicago and Washington, DC. The cause of the riots were as follows:

- Labor shortages in the North and Midwest because white men were enlisting in World War I and the US government had halted immigration from Europe.
- The Great Black Migration of African-Americans moving from the South to Northern and Midwestern cities for work and to escape Jim Crow.
- Racial strife due to working-class white workers in Northern and Midwestern cities resenting the presence of African Americans, who were now competing for employment.[224]

The end of the war brought significant change in the United States. As soldiers returned home, higher unemployment gave rise to increased competition for work. Racial tensions led whites in cities across the country to take out their frustrations on innocent African Americans. All through the summer of 1919, many black neighborhoods across the country were attacked and destroyed. The people in these neighborhoods were beaten and sometimes killed.

Mary met Clifford James Marks (1910 – 1980) and started to date him. They were married on October 2, 1929. Clifford was born on January 14, 1909, in New Orleans. He would die there on January 1, 1980. Clifford was the son of George Parenton (1888–1973), who was born on July 10, 1888, in Louisiana, and Julia Bourg (1885–1955), who was born in May of 1885, also in Louisiana. Julia was the sixth child and fourth daughter of Oscar P. Bourg and Amanda Marie Melvina Juneau (the great-grandparents of the author on the Bourg side, already discussed in chapter 3. I do not understand the difference in surnames between Clifford Marks and his father, George Parenton. There is no indication that George's wife, Julia Bourg, was previously married. Perhaps it was an adoption.

Clifford married Mary a year and a half after her father died. In the 1940

[224.] Femi Lewis, "The Red Summer of 1919 in U.S. Cities," ThoughtCo., https://www.thoughtco.com/red-summer-of-1919-45394.

US Census, they were living at 2111 Laurel Street (between Jackson Avenue and Josephine Street). By 1954, they had moved into a house at 2505 Annunciation Street in New Orleans, across from Clay Playground. Clifford was a mortgage examiner for the FHA.[225] Clifford and Mary had the following children together:

- Geraldine Marks was born on July 21, 1930, in New Orleans. Her father and mother were both twenty-one years of age at her birth. She married Calvin Matthews Albro, who was born on September 21, 1929, in Louisiana (probably New Orleans). He would die on November 9, 2008, in Gretna. Calvin's father was Samuel Francis Albro (1892–?). His mother was Madagelena Estrade (1897–?). Calvin's siblings were Eleanor Madeline Albro, born in 1926 and died on October 22, 1962, in New Orleans; Audrey Katherine Albro, born December 13,1930, in Louisiana, died on December 30, 1989, in Kenner, Louisiana; Malroy Raymond Albro, born November 29, 1932, in New Orleans, died in 2010; Addis Leonard Albro, born in 1933, died on September 30, 1934; and Martha Patricia Albro, born February 9, 1938, in Louisiana, died January 23, 2007, in Houston, Texas, after evacuating for Hurricane Katrina. Although Calvin got Geraldine pregnant numerous times, the vast majority of these pregnancies ended in miscarriage. This history study has found no children for Calvin and Geraldine. Geraldine died in February of 1981 when she was fifty years old. Calvin died on November 9, 2008. Both died and were buried in Gretna, Louisiana.
- Clifford Joseph Marks Jr. was born on September 9, 1931, in New Orleans. He met Helen Mary Martin and married her on June 7, 1953, in New Orleans. Their daughter, Cynthia Ann Marks (Verdin) was born on September 25, 1962, in Marrero, Louisiana. She died on December 1, 2006, in Isabel, Louisiana. Clifford Jr. died on February 12, 1983, in Harvey, Louisiana. He was fifty-one years old.
- Elvye Marie Marks was born in 1939 when her parents were twenty-nine years old. She attended St. Alphonsus Grammar School. Elvie graduated in 1957 from Redemptorist High School. She met and married her husband, Michael William Mason, in July of 1961 in New Orleans when she was twenty-two years old. She currently lives in Marrero, Louisiana.

---

[225] "US City Directories, 1822-1995," New Orleans, Louisiana, City Directory, 1954.

- Timothy Marks was the fourth and youngest child of Clifford and Mary Marks. He was born on January 26, 1956. His mother was forty-five years old when he was born. His niece was seven years older than her uncle when he was born.

Mary Agnes Rita Young died on March 30, 1978. She was sixty-seven years old. Clifford Marks, her husband, died in February of 1983 in Harvey, Louisiana.

Agnes Louise Young

Agnes Louise Young (the mother of the author) was born on December 28, 1912, in New Orleans and died there on September 22,1984, in New Orleans. Her story begins in this chapter in Generation 1.

Oliver Joseph Young

Oliver Joseph Young was born on March 10, 1915. He is the fourth child and first son of Oliver and Anna. He graduated from Redemptorist High School in 1934. After Pearl Harbor, Oliver enlisted in the Marines. During the war, he participated in the US invasion and battle for Saipan. On June 15, 1944, the US Marines stormed the beaches of the Japanese island of Saipan. The island was significant because it contained a crucial airbase from which the U.S. could launch its new long-range B-29 bombers directly at Japan's home islands.[226]

There was fierce fighting by Marines against more than 25,000 soldiers of the Japanese army on the island. US generals saw how difficult it was to take the island and the mass civilian suicides on Saipan. This difficulty left these military leaders with a firm understanding that Japan would not fall easily.

The next island in the Marianas was Tinian. Tinian Island was strategic because it provided airfields from which the US forces could bomb Japan. It was the place where bombers took off to drop the atomic bombs on Hiroshima and Nagasaki. Tinian is one of three islands in the Marianas that is small in size and only 1,500 miles south of Tokyo. The round-trip flight to Tokyo by B-29 is only twelve hours. This closeness to Japan is one reason Tinian was the headquarters for the 509th Air Group. Tinian was easy to supply by water and the perfect for launching point for air attacks against Japan. The US forces referred to Tinian by the codename Destination.

Tinian was invaded on July 24, 1944. The battle August 1. Three hundred American and six thousand Japanese soldiers lost their lives in this battle. Navy

---

[226] "Battle of Saipan," History.com, https://www.history.com/topics/world-war-ii/battle-of-saipan.

construction battalions known as Seabees began bulldozing just days after the island was secured. They completed six runways within two months, and Tinian soon became the biggest airbase in the world. The airfield consisted of four smaller airfields and supported 269 B-29s.[227]

Oliver was part of the taking of Saipan and Tinian and was stationed there during the construction. Technicians on Tinian started to assemble Fat Man, the first atomic bomb to be dropped on Hiroshima. The Seabees also built docks to accommodate the USS *Indianapolis*, which was steaming to Tinian to deliver atomic bomb components for Little Boy, the second atomic bomb. Completing that mission, the USS *Indianapolis* sailed for the Philippines. On July 30, 1945, the Indianapolis was torpedoed by a Japanese submarine and sank quickly. Nearly 800 of her 1200 crew members lost their lives, many allegedly to sharks.

Oliver was told of the bomb of great destruction while it was being assembled. He and his fellow Marines were in constant fear that the Japanese would detonate the bomb with their aircraft.

Tinian served as the forward operational base from which bombers flew to Japan. The XXI Bomber Command launched relentless attacks on the Philippines, Okinawa, and mainland Japan. The ground shook as planes took off every minute of every day. The XXI BC was created when the Mariana Islands were captured. On August 5, 1945, a B-29 named the *Enola Gay* piloted by Lt. Col. Paul Tibbets took off. On August 6, at 8:15 a.m., it dropped the Little Boy atomic bomb on Hiroshima. On August 9, a B-29 took off and dropped the atomic bomb Fat Man on the city of Nagasaki at 11:02 a.m.

After the war, when Oliver returned home to the United States, for the longest time, he experienced symptoms of post-traumatic stress disorder (PTSD). These symptoms included difficulty sleeping or falling asleep, decreased concentration, hypervigilance (an over-awareness to, searching for, possible dangers), and outbursts of irritable mood and exaggerated startle response (overly responsive when startled). He eventually got over his PTSD symptoms. He was a New Orleans firefighter all his life until his retirement.

Oliver married Claire Meagher on June 1, 1936. Claire was born on November 6, 1912, in New Orleans. She was the daughter of Mathew James Meagher (1880–1961) and Mathew's wife, Elizabeth (Lilly) Augusta Siebrant (1882–1954). Both

[227]"Tinian Island," Atomic Heritage Foundation, https://www.atomicheritage.org/location/tinian-island.

were thirty years old when Claire was born. Oliver and Claire had no children. Oliver died on December 21, 1993, in New Orleans.

Claire Camille Young

Claire Camille Young was the fifth child and fourth daughter of Oliver Young and Anna Rappold. She was born on March 30, 1917, in New Orleans. Her father was thirty-eight and her mother was thirty-three when she was born. The great influenza epidemic of 1918–1919 swept the city of New Orleans that year. The Spanish flu pandemic occurred between January 1918 and December 1920. It was a very deadly influenza pandemic involving the H1N1 influenza virus. Some 500 million people were infected. The epidemic peaked in New Orleans from mid-September to mid-November of 1918. Only Pittsburgh and Philadelphia had higher death rates than New Orleans in the United States. Over 50 million people died worldwide from this flu. The Young family survived the epidemic.

Claire grew up in the home on St. Andrew Street and Camp Street. She graduated from Redemptorist High School. She met Octave B. Stiles and married him on August 16, 1946. The marriage came eight years after the death of her father. Octave was born on August 21, 1914, in New Orleans. He died in October 1977. Claire and Octave had two children, Audry Stiles (1949–) and Keneth Stiles. Claire died on April 30, 1975, in New Orleans, at the age of fifty-eight.

Dorothy Frances Young

Dorothy Frances Young was born on October 10, 1919, in New Orleans. She is the sixth child and fifth daughter of Oliver Young and Anna Rappold. On the previous June 28, World War I, "The Great War," ended when the Treaty of Versailles was signed in Paris, bringing the fighting to an end between Germany and the Allies. It was called "the war to end all wars." More than 70 million military personnel were involved. It was one of the largest and deadliest wars in history. Nine million combatants and seven million civilians died during the war.

Dorothy (Dot) graduated from Redemptorist High in 1937. She met Edward Bernard McGinnis Jr. (1913–1966) and started to date him. They were married on April 22, 1944, in New Orleans. Edward was the son of Edward Mcginnis (born 1883) and his wife, Barbara (maiden name unknown). Edward was their fourth child and first son. His siblings were Thelma (born 1908), Clare (born 1910), Adele (born 1912), and Edward B. Jr. (1913–1966).

Dorothy and Edward were married on April 22, 1944, when she was twenty-five and he was thirty-one. Their first child, Edward Bernard McGinnis III (1946–1991), was born in 1946 in New Orleans, when his father was thirty-three and his mother was twenty-seven. He grew up on Constance Street in the Irish Channel and went to St. Alphonsus Grammar School and Redemptorist High School. He was a good athlete in both football and baseball. He was the starting quarterback on the high school junior varsity football team until he broke his arm in practice, and that was that. He was the centerfielder on the 1962 Redemptorist Baseball varsity baseball team and a terrific hitter (although his friends and teammates called him Mr. Magoo because he wore such thick glasses).

After Eddie graduated from Redemptorist, he worked for a couple of years and then joined the army as the Vietnam War was heating up. He was sent to Vietnam in early 1966 and returned and was discharged in 1967. He and his cousin Jim Bourg Jr. spent the afternoon in Tracy's Bar shooting pool and drinking beer on the day Jim met his future wife, Jeanne Favret.

After the war, Eddie took a job with a barge company, working with his cousin Clifford Marks Jr. He met a lovely lady who had children and married her. In 1989, he developed leukemia (probably from cleaning barges with benzene products), and he died on August 15, 1991.

Louis Young

Louis Young was born on May 22, 1922, and died in July of 1971 in New Orleans at forty-nine years of age. Louis lost his hand as a boy while working in his grandpa's bakery. He got his hand caught in a dough kneading machine, and it was damaged so much it had to be amputated. Even with this disability, Louis was a pretty good baseball player. He would bat with one hand, and he would catch the ball, transfer the glove beneath his arm, take the ball out, and throw it. He could do this at high speed.

Louis worked at a New Orleans coffee and peanut roasting company (name not known). He would always visit his sisters for dinner with a large bag of peanuts for the kids. Some believed that Louis was a sports bookie. There is no hard evidence for this. However, it was discussed around the family table of the author.

Audrey Louise Young

Audrey Louise Young was born on June 2, 1925. She married Claude Paul Sartin on January 23, 1946. Paul was born in Lawrenceburg, Indiana, and was on leave from the navy in New Orleans when he met Audrey. As of this publishing, Audrey still lives in Indiana.

Audry and Paul had two children together: Paula Ann, born about 1948 in the Lawrenceburg, Indiana, area, and Timothy Ray, born on October 25, 1949, in the Lawrenceburg Indiana area. Both are still living at this time.

Death of Anna Mary Frances Rappold Young

Anna Mary Frances Rappold Young died on January 23, 1954. She was sixty-nine years old. Her daughter, Anna, had died just twenty months before on May 13, 1952. Her grandson, the author of this book, recounts the circumstances around her death.

Anna Mary Frances must have had some medical issues, such as a stroke. She was confined to a hospital-type bed and was being circulated monthly between the homes of her daughters for hospice-type care. The author remembers visiting her at her daughter Mary's house on Annunciation Street. She passed away at the home of her daughter Agnes (also the home of the author). The doctors told the family she would pass away soon, so many of her children and their families came to 932 Third Street to say the rosary for her. She died late in the evening around 10 p.m. on January 23, 1954.

The Rappold Family

Another ancestral family of Agnes Louise Young was the Rappold family. The Rappolds were a German family from the Bavarian region. Bavaria is a landlocked state of Germany, occupying its southeastern corner. It is the largest of German territories as far as land area. It makes up a fifth of the total area of Germany. It has 13 million inhabitants and is Germany's second most populous state after North Rhine-Westphalia. Bavaria's main cities are Munich (the capital and the largest city of Bavaria), Nuremberg, and Augsburg.

Bavaria was once inhabited by Iron Age Celtic tribes. It was a conquests of the Roman Empire in the 1st century BC and became a duchy after the collapse of the Western Roman Empire. It was later incorporated into the Holy Roman Empire, became an independent kingdom, joined the Prussian-led German Empire while retaining its title of the kingdom, and finally became a state of the Federal Republic of Germany.

Bavaria has a unique culture, mainly because of the state's Catholic majority and conservative traditions. Bavarians have traditionally been proud of their lifestyle, which includes a language, cuisine, architecture, festivals such as Oktoberfest, and elements of Alpine symbolism. The state also has the second-largest economy among the Germans, giving it a status as a rather wealthy German region.[228]

The Rappolds and the Youngs were two German families who came together in New Orleans to produce the family of Agnes Louise Young. The rest of this chapter traces the history of the Rappold family ancestors, starting with Agnes' grandfather Lewis Rappold.

Generation 3: Lewis L. Rappold

Lewis L. Rappold was the father of Anna Mary Frances Rappold. He was the son of Jacob Rappold and Rosalie Welsch and was born in October of 1861 in Bayern (English word *Bavaria*), Germany. His German name was *Lewis*, but sometimes, when dealing with American customs, they refer to him with the French spelling of *Louis*. He arrived in New Orleans with his father, Jacob, on December 1, 1871, on the USS *New York*. The ship embarked from Bremerhaven. The names of Lewis Rappold, Jacob Rappold (his father), and Rodalie Welsch Rappold (his mother) were all on the passenger manifest. He traveled in steerage (third class) in compartment 360.

In the 1880 US Census, Lewis (Louis) was living with his mother, Rosalie Welsch Rappold (born in France), and his father, Jacob Rappold (born in Bavaria), at 452 N. Liberty Street. Both Lewis and his father were bakers according to the manifest. Jacob and Rosalie had to be only about fifteen years old when they had baby Lewis.

The Children of Lewis L. Rappold

Lewis married Amelia Louise Lentz on December 29, 1881, in New Orleans. She was the daughter of John Lentz (born in May of 1836 in Baden-Wuerttemberg, Germany, and died on July 24, 1900, in New Orleans). Amelia was born in April of 1860 in Louisiana. In 1900, according to the US Census, Louis Rappold was living at 2307 Dryades Street with his wife, Louisa; his father-in-law, John Lentz; and his seven children:

1. Anna Mary Frances Rappold, whose life is discussed in Generation 2 of the Young family above
2. Caroline P. Rappold, born June 8, 1884

---

[228]"Bavaria," *Wikipedia*, https://en.wikipedia.org/wiki/Bavaria.

3. John Rappold, born June 15, 1886
4. William Rappold, born January 24, 1889 (Uncle Willie)
5. Jacob Louis Rappold, born December 22, 1892
6. Louise Rappold, born September 9, 1896
7. Rosalie Rappold, born June 5, 1899

Although Lewis was a foreign-born German national, his wife and therefore his children were all US citizens because they were born in the United States. In 1899, Lewis went through the naturalization process of the time. After passing the English and civics exam during the interview, he participated in the oath ceremony on the very day he was interviewed. He was granted citizenship and given a certificate of naturalized citizenship on August 1, 1899, taking the oath of United States citizenship in Las Vegas.[229]

Lewis was listed as a baker. There is also a border in the house, twenty-year-old Frederick Hosch, who was also a baker. Frederick was born in Louisiana but was also of German parents. This information comes from the 1900 US Census.

Lewis died on June 9, 1925, in New Orleans. Amelia Louise died on May 6, 1944, in New Orleans. Lewis's obituary appeared in the *Times-Picayune* as follows:

On Tuesday, June 9th, at 10:30 A.M. Louis Rappold, beloved husband of Louise Lentz, age 62, a native of Germany and a resident of the city for many years. Members of Bakers union #23 and Monroe Benevolent association are invited to the ceremony. The funeral will take place from the home of his daughter, Mrs. O. J. Young, 2414 Laurel St. At 4 P.M. Internment will take place in Metairie Cemetery.

Generation 4: Jacob Rappold

Jacob Rappold, the father of Lewis Rappold, was the son of Steven Rappold (no date information available) and Anna M. Hoffman (no date information available). Both Steven and Anna were born in Bavaria, Germany, around 1825. Jacob was born on September 12, 1847. Jacob married Rosalie Welsch in Bavaria in about 1860, and soon after, on October 23, 1861, they had a son, Lewis.

There were many factors that contributed to Germans leaving their homeland, including heavy taxation, the seizure of property, continual warfare caused by a

---

[229] "What Are 'Naturalization Texts & Cermonies' in Nevada?" Las Vegas Defense Group, https://www.shouselaw.com/nevada/immigration/naturalization-tests-ceremonies.

conflict with France (Napoleon), and the unification of the German kingships into one nation under the "Iron Chancellor" Otto von Bismarck (1815-1898). However, religious persecution was the primary cause of Jacob moving his family to the United States. For Jacob, prospects were much better in the United States than in Germany. Given that none of the German states had overseas colonies, the United States became the preferred destination for most Germans who wanted to emigrate.

Bismark annexed two Protestant states in West Germany because they opposed him in the recent conflicts: Hanover and Hesse-Kassel. They were a particularly welcome acquisition because they bridged the previous gap between the central Prussian kingdom and Prussian land on the Rhine. All other German territories north of the river Main were now merged under Prussian leadership in a new North German Federation. This federation produced a more coherent Protestant bloc.

The three Catholic states south of the Main River (Baden, Württemberg, Bavaria) were now a separate group, recognized as having "an internationally independent existence"—a condition agreed to by Bismarck with the Catholic emperors to the west and east, in France and Austria. However, these Catholic regions retain a strong economic link with North Germany. A continuation of the old Prussian alliance was agreed to in 1867, again incorporating all the German-speaking areas except Austria. With Austria reduced to impotence by its defeat in the Seven Weeks' War, the only neighbor inclined to challenge Prussia's inexorable growth was France. The clash between the new unified Germany and France came sooner than France might wish. But Bismarck was ready.

Franco-Prussian War: 1870-71

Ever since Prussia's rapid success in the Seven Weeks' War of 1866, with the resulting consolidation of Prussian territory on the Rhine, there was alarm and resentment in France at the growth of this ambitious German neighbor. The German Empire was unified in 1871 into a country with a Protestant majority and sizeable Catholic minority, speaking German or Polish. Anti-Catholicism was common.

The mighty German Chancellor Otto von Bismarck, a devout Lutheran, joined with secular liberals in 1871 through 1878 to launch a "culture struggle." It was most felt in Prussia, the largest state in the new German Empire. Its aim was to remove the Catholic Church's political power and the influence of the Pope. There were many Catholics in Bavaria and the Rhineland, and they fought back. Bismarck wanted to end the Catholics' loyalty to the Pope (ultramontanism) and bring all Germans under his power.

Priests and bishops who came out against the "culture struggle" were put in jail or removed from their parish responsibilities. At the height of this anti-Catholic push, half of the Prussian bishops were in prison or in exile. A quarter of the churches had no priest. About half of the monks and nuns left Prussia, while a third of the convents and monasteries were closed. As many as 1,800 parish priests were imprisoned or exiled, and thousands of their parishioners or laypeople were imprisoned for helping the priests.[230] There were anti-Polish elements in Greater Poland, Silesia.[231] The Catholics refused to comply; they strengthened their Centre Party.

In the midst of all this, Jacob and his family boarded the steamship US *New York* in Bremerhaven in November of 1871 on his way to New Orleans, according to passenger manifests. Arriving in New Orleans in the winter of 1871–72, they lived in a house at 452 N. Liberty Street. Jacob was naturalized as a citizen on April 25, 1899. His US naturalization papers are on file at the author's residence.

In 1900, Jacob and his wife were living at 2137 South Liberty, according to the US Census of 1900. John Shafer, a twenty-one-year-old baker, was listed as living with them as their adopted son.

Jacob's wife, Rosalie Welsch Rappold, passed away on October 16, 1903, in New Orleans. She was fifty-seven years old. Jacob remarried on November 3, 1908, to Louisa Seeger. They had no children together, as she was fifty-three years old when they were married. They lived at 2613 Fourth Street, according to the 1910 US Census. Jacob passed away on May 16, 1921. Agnes Louise Young, the mother of the author and the grandmother of Jason, Jonathan, and Jameson Bourg, was the granddaughter of Jacob Rappold.

---

[230] "Anti-Catholicism," *Wikipedia*, https://en.wikipedia.org/wiki/Anti-Catholic.

[231] Michael B. Gross, *The War against Catholicism: Liberalism and the Anti-Catholic Imagination in Nineteenth-Century Germany* (University of Michigan Press, 2004).

Jim Bourg Sr. Military

James (Jim) Bourg

Figure 7 - Jim Bourg through the years

Joseph Charles Bourg and his
dog "Bloutch taken in 1909.
He is 29 years old.

The Harness Shop - 1930

Joseph Charles Bourg and his wife Lucy in
the front year of their Napoleonville home

Figure 8 - Joseph Charles Bourg Through the Years

Agnes First Communion

Agnes at 35 years of age

Oliver Joseph Young

Figure 9 – The Young Family through the years

Top Row (Left to right) - Anatole Talbot, George C. 'Cook' Talbot, Lucy Talbot, AUBER TALBOT, Middle Row - Nycee Augustine Boudreaux , Mirtyl Leandre Talbot (Lucy's Uncle), ARTHUR CHARLES TALBOT, Bottom Row - Josephine Aline Talbot, Samual Joseph Talbot, Eword Joseph Talbot,

Lucy Talbot at 18 years

Figure 10 - Lucy Talbot through the years

Lloyd in the Army   **Lloyd and Jeanne**   **Lloyd's Wedding**

Figure 11 – Lloyd Favret Through the Years

George Pratt Landry Sr. – through the years
Figure 12

From left to right - Mary "Eliska" Victoria Landry, Alma Marie Landry, Marie "Juanita" Philomene Landry, Marie Natica Landry and Regina (Reggie) Eva "Marie" Landry

Jerome Emanuel Landry M.D (left), George Pratt Landry (center) and John "Juan" Gustave Landry (right)

Figure 13 – The Landry Siblings

Jeanne Louise Rose Develle

Jeanne Develle on her wedding day

Four generations from Left – Yvonne Landry, Jeanne Louise Rose Develle, Elizabeth Ambrozine Jung, Marie Azelie le Dusso d' Hebecourt

Figure 14 – Jeanne Louise Rose Develle

CHAPTER 6

THE FAVRET FAMILY

Ancestors of Lloyd Francis Favret

My dad takes most of the pictures in our family, and he makes scrapbooks. This means he gets to figure out what's important for us to remember. I guess my mom could make a scrapbook, but she doesn't. And I could do it and so could my brothers, but then we would need extra pictures. Plus we're just kids and we don't have time for that. I know the scrapbooks we'd make would be different from Dad's. But the person who does the work gets to write the history.
—Holly Goldberg Sloan

The sacrifice our ancestors gave yesterday gave us today and our tomorrow.
—Stephen Robert Kuta

It's time to turn my family history back toward the French side of the family, particularly those who lived in the River Parishes below New Orleans: the Favrets and the Petersons. This chapter was particularly hard to write for several reasons. From a genealogy standpoint, I could not find a lot about these two families, and my research soon became bogged down. Because this was the family of my wife's surname, I had not met many of her aunts and uncles. I did not get a lot of stories about this side of the family. Because Point à la Hache and Plaquemines Parish, Louisiana, is close to New Orleans and not a very populated community, there is not a lot of history written about this town and its people.

Writing a history of this part of our family required me to stop writing for a couple of months and go back into my research to find out more about these ancestors. The genealogy of this family does not go back as far in history as other factions of our family, so the skeleton is rather meager, and there is not a lot of information to put flesh on its bones.

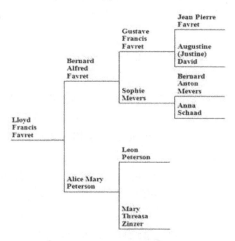

Figure 15– Favret Family Tree

Gustave Francis Favret

We begin our story with Gustave Francis Favret. He was born in Courbenon, France, on January 28, 1853. We know little about his parents except for their names and dates. Gustave's father was Jean Pierre Favret. Jean Pierre was born in France on January 18, 1814. He died in France on May 26, 1888, at the age of seventy-four. Gustave's mother was Augustine "Justine" David, who was born April 4, 1819, in Granges le Bourg, Crevans, France, near Lyon and Grenoble. Justine was the daughter of Joseph David. Justine died in the after 1868 after emigrating to Louisiana.

The Siblings of Gustave Francis Favret

Jean Pierre and Justine David Favret had the following eight children:

- Ermence "Fanny" Favret was born September 30,1847, in Courbenans, France, and died there on August 1, 1861.
- Victorine Elise Favret was born February 27, 1849, in Courbenans and died in New Orleans. She emigrated to Louisiana with her brother Gustave.
- Pierre Joseph Favret was born December 22, 1852, in Courbenans.
- Gustave Francis Favret was born in January of 1853 in Courbenans and died on September 15, 1923, in New Orleans.
- Philomene Adele Favret was born January 7, 1855, in Courbenans; her date and place of death are unknown.
- Abel Favret was born about 1856 in France and died September 13, 1903, in New Orleans.
- Marie Hortense Favret was born May 18, 1860, in Courbenans; her date and place of death are unknown.
- Hortense Eleonore Favret was born May 25, 1862, in Courbenans and died there February 19, 1895.

Gustave came to the United States in 1868 when he was sixteen years old with his sister Victorine Elise (Eliza) Favret. He settled in the New Orleans area and eventually in Pointe à la Hache, Louisiana. The 1870 US Census has Gustave and his sister "Eliza" living in New Orleans at the home of his uncle (his mother's brother), Joseph David, and Joseph's family. He was listed as a clerk in Joseph's grocery store.

According to this US Census, Joseph David was forty-four, having been born on September 17, 1826, in Gelucourt, France. His occupation was listed as grocer. His wife was listed in the census as Therese David (probably Therese P. Saugier). Joseph was listed as having six children: Hortense (age sixteen), George (age twelve), Leon (age eight), Louise (age seven), Josephine (age seven), and Blanche (age two).

Sometime about 1870, Gustave married his first wife. As of this printing, we do not know the name of this wife, but Gustave has two children with her:

Able Favret (born 1874) and Blanche Favret (born 1876). This wife divorced him sometime before 1880.

The 1880 US census lists Gustave Favret at age twenty-seven living in 3rd Ward, Plaquemines, Louisiana. His marital status was divorced, and his occupation was listed as a grocer.

In 1881, Gustave married Sophie B. Mevers, the daughter of Bernard Anton Mevers (who worked as a tailor) and Anna Schaad. Bernard Mevers was born in Westphalia, Germany, on April 5, 1827. He was the son of Clement Mevers (born in Bavaria about 1792) and Dorothea Schmidt (born in Bavaria in 1913). Anna Schaad was born on October 31, 1833, in Oberhallau, Schaffhausen, Switzerland. She was the daughter of Johann Hans Conrad Schaad (born March 29, 1810, in Switzerland and died November 10, 1887, in New Orleans). Anna's mother, Catharina, was born in Switzerland on November 10, 1802, and died on June 21, 1869, at sixty-six years of age.

The Favret family and the Mevers family were both immigrants to Louisiana. Bernard Anton Mevers arrived from Germany on November 20, 1837. We talked in a previous chapter of the pressures causing German citizens to come to the United States. But Jean Pierre Favret, Gustave's father, came to the United States from France.

Why did Gustave Favret's Family Come to the US from France?

Between 1795 and 1866, metropolitan France (without colonial possessions) was the second most populated country in Europe. At that time, it was the fourth most populated country in the world (behind China, India, and Russia).[232] The French population in 1789 was roughly 28 million, and by 1850, sixty-one years later, it was 36 million (only a 28 percent increase in more than half a century). By contrast, the population of England and Wales from 1780 to 1850 grew from 7.5 million to 18.5 million, a growth of 147 percent. This population growth allowed the Industrial Revolution to take place. The population of the United States during that same period grew 334 percent. In 1790, there were 3,929,214 citizens. By 1840, that number had grown to 17,069,453.

Slow growth in France was a major political issue, as the archrival Germany continued to outgain the French in population and industry. Ways to reverse the

---

[232] Claude Diebolt and Perrin Faustine, *Understanding Demographic Transitions: An Overview of French Historical Statistics* (Springer, 2016), 176.

trend became a major political issue.[233] In 1850, people slowly began to move into cities away from the rural areas where they had mostly lived until that time. Unlike in England, industrialization was a late phenomenon in France. The French economy in the early nineteenth century had a limited dependence on iron. The majority of commerce depended on local farming. Change in the latter half of the century was fueled by primary education, especially schools of engineering.

In the 1830s, the French railroad began and continued to escalate. Imported British engineers help fuel this industry. By the revolution of 1848, a growing industrial workforce had started to impact French politics, but the second empire paid little attention to their needs and hopes. When France lost Alsace and Lorraine to Germany after the Franco-Prussian War, they also lost important coal, steel, and glass production from that region. The industrial worker population increased from 23 percent in 1870 to 39 percent in 1914.

Nevertheless, France remained somewhat rural even at the beginning of the twentieth century. Over 40 percent of the people were still farmers in 1914. While exhibiting a similar urbanization rate as the United States (50 percent of the people in the United States were engaged in agriculture in the early 1900s), the urbanization rate of France was still well behind that of the United Kingdom (80 percent urbanization rate in the early 1900s).[234]

In the nineteenth century, France experienced the immigration of political refugees from Germany, Poland, Hungary, and Russia. Many were Ashkenazi Jews. Refugees came from Mediterranean countries as well. France was the first country in Europe to emancipate its Jewish population during the French Revolution. By 1872, an estimated 86,000 Jews were living in France.

French immigration to the United States has generally paralleled religious, political, and economic upheavals in the country. It began during the seventeenth century in Louisiana. It intensified as France expelled Protestants for religious reasons during the eighteenth century. Migration from Acadia in 1755 originated with the forced removal of the Acadians by Great Britain. The voluntary movement of French Canadians to New England to work on the assembly lines of shoe and textile factories began in 1900.

Between 1819 and 1870, approximately 250,000 immigrants of French ancestry arrived in the United States. Their numbers continued to rise from 8,868 during the 1820s to 45,575 during the 1830s. In the 1840s, 77,262 French

---

[233.] Joseph J. Spengler, *France Faces Depopulation* (1938), 103.

[234.] Francois Caron, *An Economic History of Modern France* (1979).

immigrants came, and another 76,358 arrived in the 1850s. Political turmoil in France was the cause of this increasing the number of French immigrants.

The following were some of the reasons for French emigration to the United States:

- *Freedom*

    Early French immigrants came to the United States in the late 1700s because of the US atmosphere of freedom and its potential prosperity. Roughly 10,000 French immigrants from the same period moved to the United States to flee the French Revolution.

- *Religion*

    The French Revolution brought a wave of Roman Catholic refugees to the United States. There were wealthy aristocrats and working-class people, such as chefs and hairdressers, who depended upon the aristocrats for their livelihood. Another critical group of refugees to arrive at this time included a hundred French Catholic priests. Since there were only twenty-five Catholic priests in the American colonies before this, these priests greatly influenced the growth of the Catholic Church in America. This influx of Roman Catholic clergy was for missionary work. Approximately ten thousand political refugees left France during the period of the French Revolution.[235]

- *Security*

    Napoleon's defeat in 1815 caused much French migration, which lasted until the American Civil War. Napoleon's brother Jérome came to the United States with several hundred former French soldiers and tried unsuccessfully to establish settlements in the South.[236]

- *Gold*

    The California Gold Rush convinced a considerable number of French immigrants to make their way to the United States. About 30,000 arrived between 1849 and 1851, with an all-time high of 20,000 coming in 1851 alone. Unfortunately, few of these immigrants ever found gold.

- *Instability in France*

[235.] Laurie Collier Hillstrom, "French Americans," Countries and Their Culture, http://www.everyculture.com/multi/Du-Ha/French-Americans.html.

[236.] "French Immigrants," Immigration to the United States, https://immigrationtounitedstates.org/510-french-immigrants.html.

During the 1860s, the decade of the US Civil War, the number of new French immigrants declined to less than forty thousand. The US Census counted 115,260 US residents born in France in 1870. A significant number of them were in Louisiana. When France lost the province of Alsace-Lorraine to Germany in 1871, number of French Alsatians came to the US, including a large number of French Jews.[237] The number of US French-born residents declined in 1880 to 104,143. The 1900 census showed a further decrease in the size of the French-born population, whose numbers had dropped to 102,535. Stability in France slowed emigration. Between 1875 and 1914, France's economy was a little more stable.

We don't know the exact reason Gustave Francis Favret came to the New Orleans area and settled in Pointe à la Hache between 1868 and 1875. It was probably a combination of the reasons above.

The Mevers

We continue the story with Sophie B. Mevers Favret, the wife of Gustave Francis Favret. Sophie was born in Point à la Hache, Louisiana, on January 23, 1855. Her father was Bernard Anton Mevers. He was born April 5, 1827, in Westphalia, Germany. He died in the New Orleans area on March 7, 1895, at sixty-seven years of age.

Bernard arrived in the United States on November 20, 1837, at just twenty years of age. His father was Clement Mevers, who was born in Bavaria, Germany, in 1792. He died in New Orleans, La, about 1877. His mother was Dorothea Schmidt, who was born in Bavaria, Germany, in 1813. She died on August 12, 1883, in New Orleans, Louisiana.

Bernard had two siblings, both were younger than him. His sister, Marie Emily Mevers, was born in Mississippi in 1845. She died on February 11, 1882, in New Orleans. His brother, Antony Joseph Mevers, was born in Louisiana in 1847. Antony died in 1937 in New Orleans.

Bernard married Anna Maria Schaad, the daughter of Johann Hans Conrad Schaad and Anna Baumann, both of Switzerland. Johann was born on March 29, 1810, in Oberhallau, Schaffhausen, Switzerland. He died in New Orleans on

---

[237] "French Immigrants."

November 10, 1887. Anna was born in Oberhallau as well, on April 10, 1809. She died in Gulfport, Mississippi, on July 6, 1913.

Sophie was the first of seven children born to Bernard and Anna Shaad Mevers, all in Pointe à la Hache, Louisiana. Her siblings were as follows:

1. Eudora "Dora" Mevers was born on February 12, 1857.
2. Francis Clement "Frank" Mevers was born on January 10, 1859. He would later become sheriff of Plaquemines Parish, Louisiana.
3. August Mevers was born in 1860.
4. Clementine Mevers was born in 1861. She would pass away on December 19, 1899, in New Orleans.
5. Bernard Mevers II was born in 1867. We don't know the exact time of his death, but it must have been before 1880, because he is not with the family in the 1880 US Census.
6. William Adam Mevers was born in 1871. He died on September 8, 1959, in New Orleans.

The 1870 US Census shows Sophie's father, Bernard, as forty-four years old, with her mother, Anna (listed in the census as Hannah), as thirty-three. It lists Sophie as being fifteen (this confirms her 1855 birth). It includes her siblings Eudora, thirteen (this confirms her 1857 birth); Frank, eleven (this confirms Francis Clement "Frank" Mevers' 1859 birth); Clementine, nine (this confirms her 1861 delivery); and Bernard Jr., three (this confirms his 1867 birth); and her

The 1880 census lists William Mevers as nine years old, confirming his 1871 birth. Bernard Jr. is not listed, which probably means he had passed away by this time. Eudora is also not living with the family, because she is married to Alfred Andignac, a twenty-seven-year-old baker).

Sophie and Gustave

Gustave Francis Favret and Sophie Mevers met in Pointe à la Hache, Louisiana, sometime between 1875 and 1880. He was a relatively recent French immigrant to Louisiana, but she was a daughter of German immigrants born in Louisiana. They were married in 1881 when she was twenty-six and he was twenty-eight. Sophie gave birth to her first child and son, Bernard Alfred Favret, on July 7, 1884. Their second child and son, Lionel Favret, was born in January of 1886. Jean Pierre Favret, Gustave's father, died on May 26, 1888, in Courbenans, Haut-Saône, France.

Sophie gave birth to a third son, Raoul C. Favret, in January of 1890. She had a fourth son, James Favret, in April of 1894. Things were going great for the Favret family in 1895. However, Bernard Anton Mevers, Sophie's father, died on March 7, 1895, at the age of sixty-seven. Sophie bore a fifth son, Clarence Favret, on Christmas Eve, December 24, 1896. So that Sophie's mother would not have to live alone at age sixty-five, Anna moved in with her daughter's family after her husband's death.

The US Census of 1900, because she was the oldest in residence and because it was a multi-family household, lists Anna as the head of the family. Eudora "Dora" Andignac, Anna's daughter and Sophie's sister, had lost her husband by this time and was also living with the family, along with her son, Walter Andignac. Gustave, Sophie, Lionel, Raoul, James, and Clarence were all living in the household as well. Bernard Alfred Favret, who was sixteen years old, had already moved out of the house to another residence.

By 1910, Gustave and Sophie are the head and wife in their household in Point à la Hache. The 1910 US Census shows Bernard Alfred, who was already out of the house in the 1900 US Census, had married his wife, Alice Mary Peterson, on June 7, 1906. Their son James L. Favret passed away (we don't know how or why) on June 22, 1906, at the age of twelve. Lionel Favret married Marie Erath on November 10, 1908, and of course, moved out of the house. Raoul C. Favret moved out of the house at this time and is believed to have been living and working in New Orleans.

In 1910, Frank Mevers, Gustave's brother, was living next door to Gustave's home and family. Frank C. Mevers was the sheriff of Plaquemine Parish from 1896 to 1916.[238] The *Lower Coast Gazette* was published by Frank C. Mevers, the Plaquemines Parish sheriff, and edited by John Dymond (1836–1922). The newspaper was founded in 1909.

Dymond, who was born in Canada, had a brokerage business for sugar and cotton. He owned sugar plantations in Plaquemines Parish and was active in state politics. He entered the newspaper business after one of his plantations burned down in 1907. Dymond moved to New Orleans and served as president of the Louisiana Press Association. He published several journals, one of which was the *Louisiana Planter and Sugar Manufacturer*. For several years, Dymond headed the National Editorial Association. He started this organization in New

[238]Plaquemines Parish, http://www.ppso.net/page.php?p=history.

Orleans in 1885 to serve the interests of small-town newspapers throughout the United States.[239]

The Lower Coast Gazette was the official newspaper of the Plaquemines Parish school board. It was a four-page weekly paper. It focused heavily on agriculture and concentrated on growing figs in Plaquemines. It also tried to encourage the growing of rice. News briefs from around the state plus local personals from all towns in the parish. Although the Gazette was an English-language paper, in the beginning, it carried a French novel about life in antebellum Louisiana in French. In August 1925, the Plaquemines Protector absorbed the Lower Coast Gazette.[240]

In 1920, Gustave and Sophie were living alone at 4959 St. Claude Avenue. Gustave was sixty-seven years old. This census was the last US Census for Gustave, as he died just a little over three years later on September 15, 1923. Sophie spent the last years of her life living with her youngest son, Clarence, and his family on 1719 Upperline Street in New Orleans. During this period, Clarence's family included his wife, Lydia Leonor Ehrhard Favret, and his daughter, Doris, who was two years old. Lydia Leonor Ehrhard's mother, Josephine (sixty-one years old), lived with them. Sophie died on December 1, 1934.

The Point à la Hache Story

Pointe à la Hache is the southernmost town on the east bank of the Mississippi River and is located fifty miles south of New Orleans. It is the parish seat of Plaquemines Parish. An outpost was established there by the French in the early 1700s. Most of the population was still of French ancestry in the nineteenth century. Many English and German descendants moved into the parish in the early 1900s. The majority of the landmass of the parish was either swamp or of salt-marsh. One-third was located on a natural or man-made levee along the Mississippi River.

The local economy was agricultural, and the principal crops were sugarcane, rice, and citrus fruits. Fishing and oyster canning were also essential industries and enjoyed an international market. Pointe à la Hache was an unincorporated

---

[239] "Lower Coast Gazette," LSU Libraries, https://www.lib.lsu.edu/collections/digital/dlnp/newspaper-histories/LowerCoast-Gazette.

[240] "Lower Coast Gazette," LSU Libraries, https://www.lib.lsu.edu/collections/digital/dlnp/newspaper-histories/LowerCoast-Gazette

community in Plaquemines. It was a Native American settlement in the area south of New Orleans that went back thousands of years. The European settlement there was by the French in about 1700. The name *Pointe à la Hache* translates to "ax point or cape."

In the Mitchell Map of 1755, the name was listed as "Hatchet Point." John Mitchell (1711–1768), produced the map, and it was used as a primary geographical source during the Treaty of Paris for defining the boundaries of the newly independent United States. The map remained essential for settling border issues between Canada and the United States. It was used as recently as the 1980s to settle a dispute over the Gulf of Maine fisheries. The Mitchell Map, made during the colonial era, is the most comprehensive map of eastern North America that exists today.

Bernard Alfred Favret

Bernard Alfred Favret, the twenty-two-year-old son of Gustave and Sophie Favret, married Alice Mary Peterson, on June 7, 1906. Alice, also twenty-two (almost twenty-three), was the daughter of Leon Peterson and Mary Theresa Zinser. She was born on August 31, 1883, in New Orleans. We don't know much about her father, Leon. We think he was of German heritage. He was born in 1858. His father, we believe, was Adolph Peterson. Leon married his wife, Mary Zinser, on August 10, 1882, when he was twenty-four years old. He died on May 6, 1888, after being married less than six years. We don't know the cause of Leon's death at age thirty.

The Zinsers

Leon's wife, Mary Theresa Zinser, was born on February 19, 1859, in New Orleans. She was only twenty-nine years old when Leon's death made her a young widow with two young children: five-year-old Alice and three-year-old Leon Peter. Mary Theresa was the daughter of Soloman Zinser (August 3, 1823–May 29, 1863) and Genovefa Guth (December 1829–December 19, 1914). Both were born in Gartringen, Böblingen, Baden-Württemberg, Germany. They emigrated to the United States sometime around 1845 and were naturalized on October 31, 1853. They both eventually died in Louisiana.

Soloman Zinser was the son of Gottlob Zinser (June 10, 1786–December 17,

1853) and Anna Maria Riehm, both born and raised in Gartringen, Böblingen, Baden-Württemberg, Germany. Gottlob was the son of George Martin Zinser (April 8, 1749–1819) and Friederika Wolfiz (1755–?). They lived in Gartringen all their lives. George Martin was the son of Johann Michael Zinsser (August 21, 1702–February 17, 1779) and Sara Lutz (July 16, 1725–May 4, 1802). He was from Gartingen, Herrenberg, Württemberg, Germany, and she was from Aidlingen, Herrenberg, Württemberg, Germany. They both lived in small villages on the east side of the Black Forrest in southeastern Germany. She moved a short distance to another town to be with him.

Bernard and Alice were living in New Orleans at 1527 N. Claiborne in 1930, according to the US Census. They were both twenty-six years old at this time. They had been married for four years and already had two children: Bernard Alphonse (May 11, 1907–March 1971), age three, and Sophie Marie (October 22, 1908–November 9, 1993), age two. Sophie's nickname, all of her life, was Pip. Bernard's brother Raul, age twenty-one, was also living with the family. Bernard was listed as a being in the dry-goods business.

Over the next several years, Bernard and Alice produced three more children. First, there was Gustave (1915–April 3, 1921), who died when he was five and a half years old as a result of being hit by a car. Gustave's nickname was Mookie. Next was Stanley J. (October 4, 1918–May 22, 1995. Stanley never married and lived with his mom or his sister Sophie most of his life. Finally there was Lloyd Francis, who was born on December 22, 1920, in Point à la Hache, Plaquemines Parish, Louisiana.

Lloyd Francis Favret

Lloyd was a very handsome boy and a man with a great personality. He was always the life of every party. His brother, Gustave (Mookie), was killed by a vehicle in front of the family house on April 3, 1921. His brother's death left a lasting impression on Lloyd, and he talked about it all of his life.

The Point à la Hache area has always experienced seasonal hurricane damage, some years worse than others. The hurricane of 1915 was an intense Category 4 hurricane that made landfall near Grand Isle, Louisiana. The storm reached a peaked intensity of 145 miles per hour. It weakened slightly by the time of landfall on September 29, 1915. Recorded winds were 126 miles per hour, making it a Category 3 hurricane that killed 275 people and caused more than $10 million in damage. The storm ravaged the area, breaking levees and flooding the land. Thirty-one persons died in Pointe à la Hache.[241]

Sometimes in the 1920s, the Favret family moved to New Orleans. In 1930, Bernard's family, including Lloyd, were living at 2107 Elysian Fields Avenue, New Orleans. Lloyd grew up in the Gentilly part of town. In the 1930 US Census, Lloyd's father Bernard was manager of a grocery store. Lloyd (age seven) lived with his mom (forty-seven) and dad (forty-eight), his brother Stanley (eleven), and his older sister Sophie (twenty-one) and her husband, Clifford Toepfer (twenty-three).

By 1940, Bernard A. Favret was a clerk and living at 557 N. Dorgenois Street. Lloyd was still living with his mother and father at that time.[242] He lived around the corner from the home of George Pratt Landry at 1516 Gentilly Boulevard. At that home lived Pratt's daughter, Jeanne Claire Landry. Lloyd began to visit the Landry home and eventually started to date Jeanne. By September of 1942, Jeanne and Lloyd were engaged.

The 1939 Nazi invasion of Poland sparked World War II. The war dragged on for six bloody years until the Allies defeated Nazi Germany and Japan in 1945. On December 7, 1941, Japan attacked British and American holdings in Asia and the Central Pacific. These attacks included one on the American fleets at Pearl Harbor and the Philippines, landings in Thailand and Malaya, and the Battle of Hong Kong.

The Selective Service Act was passed by Congress on September 16, 1940, establishing the first peacetime conscription in US history. The draft was in preparation for the United States being pulled into the war. All men between the ages of eighteen and sixty-four had to register. The initial ages were twenty-one and thirty-five to serve for twelve months, but in 1941, the service period was lengthened to eighteen months, and the age limit was raised to thirty-seven.[243]

The Japanese carried out a sneak air attack on Pearl Harbor on Sunday, December 7, 1941. Subsequently, the United States declared war against the

---

[241.] "1915 New Orleans Hurricane," *Wikipedia*, https://en.wikipedia.org/wiki/Louisiana_Hurricane_of_1915; "American FactFinder," United States Census Bureau, retrieved May 14, 2011.

[242.] "US City Directories, 1822-1995," Ancestry.com online database (Provo, UT: Ancestry.com Operations, Inc., 2011); New Orleans, Louisiana, City Directory, 1940.

[243.] "Selective Service System," *Wikipedia*, https://en.wikipedia.org/wiki/Class_1-A.

Empire of Japan, and a few days later, against Nazi Germany. The military service period was then lengthened in early 1942 for the length of the war.

Soon after Pearl Harbor, in early 1942, Lloyd registered for the draft. His family had moved to 2436 Laharpe Street in New Orleans. Lloyd was working for his uncle Lionel F. Favret in the construction business. Although Lloyd and Jeanne were engaged, their wedding was postponed until his return from the war.

Lloyd entered the army on October 7, 1942. He joined the 30th Infantry Division, Artillery Corps, Communications Company. This was a unit of the Army National Guard beginning in World War I. It was still active in preparation for World War II. It bore the name in honor of President Andrew Jackson of the "Old Hickory" division. The Germans nicknamed this division "Roosevelt's SS"[244] S. L. A. Marshall regarded the 30th Infantry Division as the best infantry division in the European Theater. It was involved in 282 days of intense combat over a period from June 1944 through April 1945.[245]

The president called reserve divisions into federal service on September 16, 1940. They were assigned to Camp Atterbury, Indiana, from November 10, 1943, to January 26, 1944.[246] They trained for two years in the United States. The 30th Infantry Division was under the leadership of Major General Leland Hobbs. They arrived in England on February 22, 1944, and trained for the Allied invasion of Normandy until June.[247]

Lloyd and the division landed at Omaha Beach, Normandy, on June 11, 1944, five days after the initial D-Day landings of June 6, 1944. They secured the Vire-et-Taute Canal and crossed the Vire River on July 7.[248] Beginning on July 25, the 30th division was involved in and spearheaded the Saint-Lô activity of Operation Cobra, which was intended to break out of the Normandy beachhead, thus ending the stalemate that had occurred. During the Battle of Mortain, US typhoons devastated German tank and mechanized columns attempting to reach the French coast. This battle concluded on August 7, 1944.

During the operation, on July 24–25, 1944, the 30th division had a devastating

---

[244] "Fact Sheet: The 30th Infantry Division Veterans of WWII."

[245] "30th Infantry Division (United States)," *Wikipedia*, https://en.wikipedia.org/wiki/30th_ Infantry_Division_(United_States).

[246] IndianaMilitary.org.

[247] Alwyn Featherston, *Battle for Mortain: the 30th Infantry Division Saves the Breakout August 7-12, 1944* (Novato, CA: Presidio, 1998), 16.

[248] Alwyn Featherston, *Battle for Mortain: the 30th Infantry Division Saves the Breakout August 7-12, 1944* (Novato, CA: Presidio, 1998), 16–17.

friendly fire incident. As part of the effort to break out of the Normandy hedgerows, US Army Air Force (USAAF) bombers from England were sent to carpet bomb a one-by-three-mile corridor of the German defenses opposite the American line. However, USAAF planners, in complete disregard or lack of understanding of their role in supporting the ground attack, loaded the heavy B-24 Liberator and B-17 Flying Fortress bombers with 500-pound bombs, destroying roads and bridges and complicating movement through the corridor. They used these bombs instead of lighter hundred-pound bombs intended as antipersonnel devices against German defenders.

Air planners also switched the approach of attack by 90 degrees without informing ground commanders. Thus, a landmark road to guide the bombers to the bombing zone was miscommunicated as the point to begin the bombing run. Start point confusion was further compounded by red smoke signals that suddenly blew in the wrong direction, and bombs began falling on the heads of the American soldiers. There were over 100 friendly fire casualties over the two days, including Lieutenant General Lesley J. McNair, commander of army ground forces.

It was during this Battle of Mortain that Lloyd Francis Favret was decorated with the Bronze Star for Valor. The 30th relieved the veteran 1st Infantry Division near Mortain on August 6, 1944.[249] The German drive to the town of Avranches started shortly after the deployment. The 30th division met with the elite 1st SS Panzer Division, and fierce fighting broke out. The division frustrated enemy plans and broke the spearhead of the enemy assault in a violent struggle from August 7–12.

The Battle of Mortain was critical to the more extensive campaign in Normandy. Although easily overshadowed by the D-Day landings and the Battle of the Bulge, Mortain was a very crucial operation, as it marked a failure of the Germans to counter the American breakout from Normandy. The Germans under General der Panzertruppen Leo Geyr von Schweppenburg's defensive strategy was a counterattack inland after the allies took the beach. Geyr conceived a Panzer counterattack with air support committed to this mobile battle.

After establishing a beachhead, the Allies planned to advance in Normandy and break out from the hedgerows. This plan would offer movement in the more open ground of France. In the more open field was where the Germans planned to counterattack. The German had the advantage at the town of Mortain. They

---

[249.] Antony Beevor, *Battle for Normandy* (Penguin, 2010), 402.

had a more massive army, with SS forces and a better position with regard to the Panzer tanks. Mortain is the battle where the Americans showed that they could fight on terms chosen by the enemy; they could sustain losses and still have the resilience and skill to win.

The infamous Field Marshall Erwin Rommel was the officer who made the German defensive plans. He insisted that the panzer reserves in the west be positioned near the invasion beaches. From there, they could counterattack the Allied troop landings as quickly as possible. Rommel believed that in the face of Allied airpower, their reserves should be just far enough back from the beaches to avoid the pre-invasion bombardment. They should be close enough, however, to enter combat within twenty-four hours of the landing. However, Rommel's superior in the West, Field Marshall Gerd von Rundstedt, convinced Adolf Hitler to disapprove of Rommel's proposal. Hitler reasoned that no officer should control all the mechanized reserves, so he formed a centralized reserve but with three separate panzer divisions.[250]

Field Marshal Rundstedt initially agreed with Rommel's counterattacks near the coast. However, in time, Rundstedt changed his view because one could not dependably project where the Allies would land. Rather than gamble on which beaches the Allies would invade, keeping the panzers away from the beaches would allow for a better response. The coastal defenses would slow the invasion and soften them for a strong counterattack. General Rundstedt is quoted as saying, "No dispersion, no piecemeal commitment, no thin soup!"[251]

In November, the central panzer reserve was positioned and concentrated under Geyr's command in November 1943, as Panzer Group West.[252]There was a dispute over the deployment of the panzers between Rommel on one side and Rundstedt and Geyr on the other. In March of 1944, Rommel wanted a broadening of his authority. That would make both of the other generals irrelevant.

Although Hitler wanted to support Rommel, he did not want to abandon Rundstedt. He finally decided to satisfy no one. Rommel maintained control of three panzer divisions in the reserves. Geyr kept three panzer and one panzergrenadier divisions in the west. Geyr was in charge of his Panzer Group

---

[250]Thomas E. Griess, ed., *The Second World War: Europe and the Mediterranean* (Wayne, NJ: Avery Publishing Group, 1989), 270–271.

[251]Gordon A. Harrison, *Cross-Channel Attack* (Washington: Office of Military History, 1993), 153–155.

[252]Harrison, 247-248.

West but could not commit his divisions without the approval of Adolf Hitler himself.

On June 29, Rundstedt was relieved of command and replaced by Günther von Kluge.[253] However, on July 15, Rommel was severely wounded by an air attack on his car. He was required to return to Germany to recover.[254] Kluge took over the leadership of the German Army Group B in place of Rommel.[255]

The Germans were not able to do anything close to the concentrated armored counterstroke based on his command structure and battle plan. The Allied breakout was part of a plan called Operation Cobra. It was launched on July 25. By the end of July, the American 1st Army had punched a hole in the overstretched enemy lines on their western flank. The newly activated Third Army exploited the overstretched enemy lines under George S. Patton.[256] Patton's troops drove to the east. This movement threatened Paris and the rear of the Germans, facing the British and Canadians in the neighborhood of Caen. To deal with the Allied position, the Germans decided upon a multi-divisional mechanized counteroffensive.

The German counterattack at Mortain was labeled Unternehmen Lüttich or Operation Liége.[257] At this point in the war, the only US Army divisions with combat experience were the 1st and 9th Infantry Divisions, the 82nd Airborne, and the 2nd Armored Division. The rest had to learn combat the hard way. This lack of experience resulted in increased casualties. However, in the process, American units developed their skills at integrated tanks and infantry in combined operations.[258]

The Ultra intelligence program also helped the Allies through the decryption service at Bletchley Park. The information helped Omar Bradley, 12th Army Group Commander, better understand the offensive. This allowed him to realign

[253]C. Peter Chen, "Günther von Kluge," World War II Database, http://ww2db.com/person_bio. php?person_id=124, accessed 18 April 2012.

[254] C. Peter Chen, "Erwin Rommel," World War II Database, http://ww2db.com/person_bio. php?person_id=A4, accessed 18 April 2012.

[255] Mark J. Reardon, *Victory at Mortain: Stopping Hitler's Panzer Counteroffensive* (Lawrence: University of Kansas Press, 2002), 48.

[256]Martin Blumenson, *Breakout and Pursuit* (Washington: Office of Military History, 1989), 247–281.

[257]Mark J. Reardon, *Victory at Mortain: Stopping Hitler's Panzer Counteroffensive* (Lawrence: University of Kansas Press, 2002), 51.

[258]Reardon, 10–11.

his forces to meet the offensive. As the Germans started "Operation Lüttich" on the night of August 6, Bletchley Park forwarded more information to Bradley, clarifying the German timetable and initial objectives.[259] Most of this "Ultra intelligence" was late in coming, however, and not shared with lower levels of command. Thus, on a tactical level, it had little or no effect.[260]

The Germans tried to counter the Allied advances with two panzer divisions, the 2nd and 116th. The 2nd SS Panzer Division, called "Das Reich," was under the command of General Hans von Funck. He was a competent general with Eastern Front experience. He had performed well against the Canadians at Caen, but he was highly disliked by his subordinates and enlisted men, because he hounded them relentlessly yet never visited the front line. [261]

Kluge compiled more panzer units for Operation Lüttich. They were frustrated, however, by the advance of the British, Canadian, and Polish forces from Caen toward Falaise. The panzers would have to be moved from that end of the front and sent to face the Americans. This move would require giving up territory to shorten the line and substituting less capable infantry and paratrooper units for mechanized forces to assemble for the offensive. All the while, the Germans faced not just the American breakout, but also English and Canadian pressure. This pressure slowed the move of the 1st SS Panzer Division so that it departed the front in a piecemeal fashion, and arrived to participate in Operation Lüttich late and in pieces.[262]

By August 6, the panzer divisions assigned to Lüttich were assembled east of Mortain, ready to move west under cover of darkness. The counteroffensive started before dawn on August 7. In the north, the German 116th Panzer Division moved along the north bank of the Sée River, without prior assembly, and took up positions to the right rear. This was done to protect the north flank. The primary push in the center was with the 2nd Panzer Division. It was reinforced by one panzer and several battalions. Its primary path of advancement was along the Sée River's south bank and the St.-Barthélemy-Reffuveille road. This would mean attacking through Mortain and covering the southern flank of the advance. This was done by the 2nd SS Panzer Division, supported by the 17th SS Panzer Division.

---

[259]John Keegan, *Six Armies in Normandy* (New York: Penguin, 1994), 245–246
[260]Reardon, 94.
[261]Reardon.
[262] Reardon, 50–53.

The 17th was reduced because of combat to only the strength of a regiment. The 1st SS Panzer Division was ready to exploit success and capture Avranches.[263]

The Germans expected good conditions, with morning fog to assist the attack. Should the fog clear later that day, the air cover promised would protect the attack with three hundred fighter planes. The Germans knew there were just two enemy divisions in Mortain: the 30th Infantry and 3rd Armored.[264]

The first day's action was not successful for the Germans. The southern columns did have some surprise and overran the 30th Infantry Division's roadblocks en route to Mortain. Particularly hard hit was the American 1st Battalion of the 120th Infantry Regiment, 30th Infantry Division. The regiment's 2nd Battalion found a defensive position on the nearby Hill 317. They were isolated and cut off.[265] The Germans pressed their advance but did not achieve anything close to a decisive breakthrough. Kluge made an error in committing the Liebstandarte to the north of Mortain instead of to the south of St.-Hilaire, where American resistance was virtually nonexistent.

It seemed to Hitler that the entire attack was hasty and executed carelessly. Kluge should have waited for three more panzer divisions to assemble and aid the attack. Another failure was the Luftwaffe. Despite its promises, it did not supply air support in the fighting of August 7. Instead, Allied airpower dominated the battlefield. Allied activities around Paris kept their German counterparts occupied and away from Mortain. American medium bombers strafed the roads used in the advance, with British Hawker Typhoon fighter bombers armed with rockets flying 294 sorties between noon and dusk, mainly against the 2nd Panzer Division north of Mortain.[266]

The American 9th Air Force did not have many rocket-armed planes ideally suited for anti-tank strikes. American fighter bombers were only able to drop bombs, which was not as effective against the moving tanks. Thus the Americans asked the British to send as many of their rocket-armed Typhoons to the St.-Barthélemy area as possible.[267] Operation Lüttich was effectively over by the afternoon of its first day. The advantage passed to the Americans, who went on the

---

[263] Blumenson, 461.
[264] Keegan, 246.
[265] Reardon, 99-101.
[266] Keegan, 245-246.
[267] Reardon; 137.

attack themselves. Not only were the Germans critically hurt by Allied airpower but allied artillery played a vital role in the battle.

Control of Hill 317 was essential to the success of the allies at this battle, as the Germans moved troops in an attempt to destroy the American positions.[268] German success proved impossible because of the efforts of Lieutenant Robert L. Weiss. He was an observer for B Battery, 230th Field Artillery Battalion. He was positioned on the hill before Operation Lüttich began.[269] Weiss's problem was not so much accessing and directing the massive firepower of American artillery. He could easily maintain his position on a hill that became the object of the Germans' lethal attentions. His problem was keeping his radio operating with just two sets of depleted batteries.[270]

With a few hundred soldiers, Robert Weiss defended Hill 317 against intense German counterattacks. For the six days and nights of fighting around August 6, these Americans were cut off from their supply lines. They were fighting for survival without adequate food, water, medical supplies, or ammunition. They had a portable radio powered by batteries, but they only had one set of batteries left and no spares. Weiss and his men directed a barrage of heavy artillery fire that continuously turned back the German offensive. However, their radio batteries soon ran down. Division headquarters needed to run communication lines to the surrounded and cut-off soldiers on the hill. Lloyd Favret volunteered to take a new radio and communication lines to those troops. Lloyd carried the wire and the radio over the shelled fields and to the hill.

Once he reached the hill, Lloyd realized he was part of a group that was cut off and surrounded. When German mortar fire cut the communication wires, Lloyd volunteered to carry another line back to headquarters. While laying the wire back down from the hill, Lloyd had to tie it to something sturdy every fifty yards. He was running so fast, and he was so scared. He came to a stretch where there was nothing substantial except a dead German soldier with a pipe in his mouth. Lloyd tied a clove hitch around the pipe and kept running. When he looked back, he saw the smoking pipe dangling on the line. He ran back, and with the heel of his boot, jammed the pipe down the throat of the dead soldier.

He continued his mission to headquarters, and communication with Hill 317

---

[268]Keegan, 294.

[269]Keegan, 83.

[270]Robert Weiss, *Fire Mission! The Siege at Mortain, Normandy, August 1944* (Shippensburg, PA: Burd Street Press, 1998), 119-120.

was restored. The decisive artillery bombardment, much of which was launched by intel from the forward observer Robert Weiss, made the difference in this pivotal battle of the Normandy breakout. Lloyd was given the Bronze Star for his bravery during this military action. The division frustrated enemy plans and broke the counterattack of the enemy assault in a violent struggle from August 7 through August 12.

By this time, the German army was much more concerned with its survival than an offensive. The killing ground that would be known as the Falaise Pocket was beginning. It was not closed completely due to a deliberate decision by General Bradley. He doubted that the four available Allied divisions could hold its eastern end closed in the face of nineteen desperate German divisions bent on escape.

The killing within the pocket was still very large. By the end of August 17, it contained about 100,000 German troops, confined in an area of 200 square miles. The Germans tried to retreat down one road that was finally closed on August 20. The confusion caused traffic congestion. In the end, 10,000 Germans were killed and 50,000 were taken prisoner. About 40,000 Germans did managed to escape, though many were non-combat troops and ordered out early.

Operation Lüttrich had a big impact on the German armies in the Falaise Pocket. Mechanized units that should be used to defend against the British and Canadians were used against the Americans in a rushed, long-shot offensive. As the Germans attempted to gain strength around Mortain, they had to concede strength around Caen and Falaise. That strength proved inadequate. The German forces used in Operation Lüttich failed and were out of place to defend the Falaise Pocket. The German offensive was poorly planned in its basic concept.

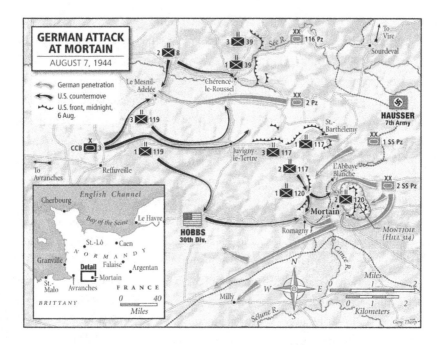

Map by Gene Thorp Printed with permission by Rick Atkinson

The Battle of Mortain also proved some significant misconceptions about the Allied capabilities to fight. By August of 1944, German officers should have had a better understanding of the impact of American artillery. Also, the impact of American and British tactical airpower should not have been a secret and thus no surprise on August 7. Ultra intelligence intercepts were kept a secret and continued to be kept for three decades after the war. So the Germans would not change their communications methods. Ultra intelligence was given credit for winning the war, but it had little direct effect Operation Lüttich.

The credit for victory at Mortain goes to the differences in fighting between the Americans and the Germans. The Americans were less experienced but had learned enough since June 6 to perform better than expected. By contrast, the vaunted German Army and SS did not perform to their usual reputation. Schwerin's failure on the first day of the offensive was just the start. Officers of the 30th Infantry Division believed that many Germans seemed more concerned with escape and survival than pressing the attack.

Just as the offensive was a military failure, it was a political failure as well. Kluge, Rommel, and Schwerin were involved in the officers' plot to kill Hitler. Their activity was influenced by the failure of the assassination attempt. Hitler replaced Kluge with Field Marshal Walter Model, who was loyal to Hitler. Kluge was called back to Germany two days later, and he killed himself with a cyanide capsule. Model too would kill himself in the last days of the war.

In the end, Operation Lüttich was an excellent concept that was poorly executed. Its viability might have been increased had it not been for Patton's operations to the south. The Battle of Mortain was not unusually large compared to D-Day. Nonetheless, it was an essential operation in the battles in Normandy in 1944, and especially as a transition between the American breakout and later Allied victories. It also was an important, and perhaps underrated, episode in which the American army showed it could fight the Germans and win.

After the liberation of Paris, the 30th division drove east through Belgium, crossing the Meuse River at Visé and Liège on September 10th. Parts of the 30th division were sent to the Netherlands on September 12, and the town of Maastricht fell the next day. Moving into Germany and taking up positions along the Wurm River, the 30th division launched its attack on the heavily defended city of Aachen on October 2, 1944. It succeeded in contacting the 1st division on October 16, resulting in the encirclement and takeover of Aachen.

The 30th Infantry Division moved on to capture the town of St. Vith at the close of the Battle of the Bulge in January 1945. After a rest period, the 30th division eliminated the enemy northeast of Aachen on November 16th, pushed through Alsdorf to the Inde River on November 28, and then moved to rest areas. On December 17, the division did a forced march south to the Malmedy-Stavelot area to help block the powerful enemy drive in the Battle of the Bulge. This Battle of the Bulge was a last-ditch offensive by the Germans to win a decisive victory. Again the 30th fought against the 1st SS Division and broke the spearhead of its assault. The 30th division launched a counterattack on January 13, 1945. It reached a point two miles south of St. Vith, Belgium on January 26. It crossed the Roer on February 23, 1945, near Jülich.

The 30th moved back for R&R on March 3, and on March 24 made an assault crossing of the Rhine. It pursued the enemy across Germany, mopping up enemy pockets of resistance. It took Hamelin on April 7 and Braunschweig on April 12, and it helped to reduce Magdeburg on April 17. The division joined the Russians at the town of Grunewald on the Elbe River. The end of World War II in Europe came soon afterward. After a short occupation period, the 30th division began its return to the United States, arriving on August 19, 1945.[271] Japan surrendered shortly afterward, bringing the war to an end.

The 30th Division sustained the following casualties:

- Total battle casualties: 18,446–3,003
- Killed in action: 13,376
- Wounded in action: 903
- Missing in action: 1,164
- Prisoners of war: 237

Shortly after the end of its occupation duties, the 30th Infantry Division returned to the United States early in August of 1945. They came back on the *Queen Mary*. General Black quickly deactivated the group at Fort Jackson, South Carolina, on November 25, 1945.[272]

Lloyd's Postwar Activities

Lloyd had several jobs after his return from the war. He worked at a gas station where Gentilly intersected with Broad Street. He went into the hardware store business with his father-in-law, George Pratt Landry, which was not successful. He went to work for Alumaglass installing windows. He went into business for himself building and installing kitchen and bathroom Formica countertops. In the last stages of his working life, he worked for a barge company on the river working for the Taffer family, his cousins.

Lloyd smoked all his life and eventually contracted lung cancer in 1973. He survived cancer for a while but finally died from the illness on April 19, 1982, in Metairie, Louisiana.

[271.] "30th Infantry Division," U.S. Army Center of Military History, https://history.army.mil/html/forcestruc/cbtchron/cc/030id.htm.

[272.] History of he 30th Infantry Division Veterans of WWII. http://www.30thinfantry.org/history.shtml

CHAPTER 7

THE LANDRY FAMILY

The Ancestors of George Pratt Landry Sr.
History is the essence of innumerable biographies.
—Thomas Carlyle

Just like our ancestors, we too will fall out of living memory and be forgotten.
It will take a future genealogist to find us again. Make it a good find.
—Stephen Robert Kuta

Tradition is the glue that binds past with present, and eventually
with the future. As traditions are passed down, we get a chance
to reach back and touch one small part of our history.
—Ann Christine Tabaka

This chapter will investigate nine generations of Landrys moving backward in time.

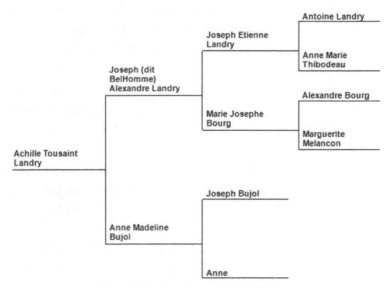

Figure 16 – The Landry Family Tree

Generation 1: George Pratt Landry

George Pratt Landry Sr. was the great-grandfather of Jason, Jonathan, and Jameson Bourg (their mother's grandfather). Pratt, as he was called all his life, was born on Monday, January 28, 1901. He was born at 1001 First Street in New Orleans at the corner of First and Constance Street. His parents Jerome Joseph Emanuel Landry (1856–1926) and Marie Conception Parra (1854–1924) were forty-five and forty-six years respectively when he was born. He was the baby of the family. He was baptized twenty days later on Sunday, February 17, 1901, at the Notre Dame Catholic Church in the Irish Channel by the Redemptorist Priest Father le Gregarré CSSR.

The Siblings of George Pratt Landry

The eight other children of Jerome Joseph Emmanuel Landry and Marie Conception Parra were as follows:

1. Alfred Joseph Landry was born on June 10, 1878, in New Orleans and died on January 16, 1884, at the age of five. When Alfred was born, the Landry family was living in the home on 485 Annunciation Street.

2. Mary Eliska Victoria Landry was born on October 7, 1879, while her father was living on 485 Annunciation Street in New Orleans. When she was twenty-five, she fell in love with and married Trudeau Bartholomew Livaudais (1869–1942) on September 27, 1905. After their marriage, they moved to and lived at 3241 Chestnut Street in New Orleans. Trudeau was born on March 4, 1869, in New Orleans, the son of Barthelemy Jules Enoul Dugue Livaudais (1826–1902), who was born on July 13, 1826, in New Orleans. Barthelemy died on May 15, 1902, in New Orleans. Trudeau's mother was Marie Zima Trudeau (1832–1898), who was born in 1832 in New Orleans. Marie Zima died on September 15, 1898, in New Orleans. Trudeau and Mary Eliska had the following children together, all born in New Orleans:
    *   Marie Beatrice Livaudais (1908–1983), born September 15, 1908
    *   Lloyd Joseph Livaudais (1910–2007), born March 11, 1910
    *   Alys Marie Livaudais (1912–1960), born June 1, 1912
    *   Trudeau Bartholomew Livaudais Jr (1914–1966), born January 7, 1914
    *   Eliska Clare Livaudais (1918–1998), born August 12, 1918

Trudeau died on October 20, 1942, in New Orleans. Mary Eliska passed away on December 24, 1963, in New Orleans.

3. Jerome Emanuel Landry MD ("Doc") was born on August 6, 1881, in New Orleans. His older brother, Alfred, would die just two-and-a-half years later. Doc attended Tulane University for his undergraduate degree and Tulane School of Medicine for his MD. He was a doctor on the staff of Tulane Hospital most of his life. He married Llewellyn Benoit in on January 4, 1911 in New Orleans.[273] Llewellyn was born in February 1885 in Mississippi. She was the daughter of Augustine Williams Benoit, who was born in January of 1857 in Mississippi and died in 1922, and Ida H. Blanton, who was born September 16, 1859, in Washington County,

---

[273] New Orleans, Louisiana, Marriage Records Index, 1831–1964.

Mississippi, and died February 19, 1902, in Memphis, Tennessee. Llewellyn had five siblings:

- Ruth B. Benoit (born October 1879)
- N. Blanton Benoit (born March 1882)
- Celest Benoit (born after Llewellyn in February 1888)
- Idele Benoit (born January 1890)
- U. W. Benoit (born January 1899)

They all were born in Mississippi but lived for a while in Memphis (Shelby County, ward 11), Tennessee.

In 1910, the Landry family was living on 1001 First Street. After the wedding, Doc and Llewellyn moved to 2336 Milan Street. In 1920, they were living there with their daughter, Miriam, and Llewellyn's father, Augustine, who was old and would die in 1922. Doc and Llewellyn had a daughter together, Miriam Loretta Landry (1915–1982), born on December 20, 1915, in New Orleans. Llewellyn died on February 22, 1929, in New Orleans.

After Llewellyn died, Doc Jerome married his nurse, Gwendolen Rosetta Laubenthal (1908-2000), in April of 1930. He was forty-nine years old and Gwen was just twenty-seven. They had twenty-one great years together until Doc Jerome died on July 14, 1951, in New Orleans. Gwen would not die until June 11, 2000, in Gulf Breeze, Florida. We will learn in the chapter on the Develles that Gwen married Bob Develle, brother-in-law of Doc's brother Pratt.

4. Alma Marie Landry was born on January 26, 1883, in New Orleans. In 1900, the Landry family was living at 2319 Constance Street. At the age of twenty, Alma married Franklin Bovard Chapman (1879–1917) on July 8, 1903. After the wedding, they moved to 719 Philip Street, between Annunciation Street and Laurel Street. They had two children together: Yvonne Mary Chapman, born June 26, 1904, in New Orleans, and Alma Marie Chapman, born on September 19, 1906, in New Orleans.

After Franklin's death in March of 1917, Alma and her two girls moved back in with her sixty-four-year-old father and mother on Coliseum Street. Alma later married George Danner (1868–1937). George's father was John Gottlieb Danner, who was born in 1821in Leipzig, Germany, and died on December 19, 1894.

George's mother was Fredrica Giessler, who was born in June of 1840, also in Leipzig. Fredrica died on February 10, 1926, in New Orleans.

George was Alma's second husband, and Alma was George's second wife. Alma died on August 28, 1968.

5.   Marie Juanita Philomene Landry was born on February 25, 1885, in New Orleans. In 1900, the family was living at 2319 Constance Street. She married William L. Parra in 1907. He was born on October 9, 1881. William was the son of Francois Paul Parra, who was born on January 23, 1844, in Louisiana. Francois died on March 30, 1906, in Larose, Lafourche Parish, Louisiana. William's mother was Josephine Parret, who was born in May of 1849 in Louisiana. After the wedding, Marie Juanita and William moved to 1519 Burdette Street in New Orleans. They had the following six children together, all born in New Orleans:
   - Edwina Marie Parra was born on August 26, 1908 and died in 2002
   - Ruth Marie Parra Aultman Grote was born on January 3, 1912, and died on September 27, 2004. She married Orrin Roy Aultman in July of 1931. He died on January 24, 1935. She married her second husband, William Grote, in June of 1940. William was born on February 23, 1913. He died in June 1969.
   - James Parra was born in 1912.
   - Llewellyn Parra was born in 1914.
   - Rita Carmelite Parra was born on December 17, 1919, and died in 2008.
   - William L. Parra Jr. was born on January 9, 1924, and died in 1929.

William died on August 24, 1943, in New Orleans. Marie Juanita died on February 14, 1956.

6.   Marie Natica Landry was born on September 8, 1886, in New Orleans. In 1900, she was still living with the Landry family at 2319 Constance Street. She married Arthur Jay Chapman, who was born on July 8, 1887, in New Orleans. His father, William Wesley Chapman (1852–1912),

and his mother, Mary Elizabeth McLin, were married on May 14, 1873. Arthur had the following siblings:

- Rachel Brown Chapman (1855–1861)
- George Francis Brown Chapman (1858–1899)
- George Francis Brown Chapman (1858–1899)
- Clara Bell Chapman (Meyer) (Ladner) (1863–1942)

Arthur's father, William, married a second wife, Lily Lee McChesney (1868–1937), on April 8, 1902. They had no children together. Arthur and Marie Natica had the following children together:

- William James Chapman, born May 24, 1874, died 1879
- Herbert Wesley Chapman, born June 28, 1878, died 1943
- Franklin Bovard Chapman, born November 30, 1879, died 1917
- Warren Wynton Chapman, born May 26, 1883, died 1884
- Arthur Jay Chapman, born July 8, 1887, died 1957
- Camilla Creevy Chapman (Tribble) (Phillips), born October 26, 1890, died 1977

Arthur Sr. died in 1957 and Marie Natica in February of 1956, both in New Orleans.

7. John "Juan" Gustave Landry was born on December 17, 1892, in New Orleans. He studied architecture and was an apprentice in 1910. He was seventeen and still living at home with his parents and three of his siblings; Dr. Jerome E Landry (then age twenty-eight), Marie Landry (fourteen), and George P. Landry (nine). Not too much is known within my data about his wife and children.

8. Regina Eva "Marie" Landry was born on August 8, 1895, in New Orleans. She met and married James Andrew Swayne on January 18, 1916. He was born in Tennessee on January 12, 1880, but was living in Georgia, and not much is known about his family. In 1930, James Andrew (thirty-eight) and Virginia Swayne (twenty-four) were living in Hattiesburg, Mississippi, according to the 1920 US Census. The 1930 US Census has them still residing in Hattiesburg (he was fifty-nine and she was forty-four). There is no information regarding children in either

census. James Andrew died on October 18, 1954. We don't know the date of Regina's death at this time.

George Platt Landry married Jeanne Louise Rose Develle, daughter of Ernest Jules Develle and Elizabeth Ambrozine Jung, on December 28, 1921, in St. Rose de Lima Church in New Orleans. Jeanne was born on August 25, 1903, in New Orleans, and died on April 22, 2001, in a Slidell, Louisiana, nursing home at the age of ninety-seven. More about Jeanne in chapter 8 on the Decelles. George died on August 4, 1971, in New Orleans.

When Pratt was born in January of 1901, William McKinley Jr. (1843–1901) was the 25th president of the United States. He served from March 4, 1897, until his assassination six months into his second term on September 14, 1901. During his presidency, the United States won the Spanish–American War. He instituted several economic measures to protect American business; they were tariffs to protect American industry and rules to keep the nation on the gold standard in a rejection of the free silver expansionary monetary policy. McKinley was the last president to have served in the American Civil War. He started the war as an enlisted soldier. Theodore Roosevelt was McKinley's vice president and, upon the assassination, became the twenty-sixth US president.

Queen Victoria was the Queen of Great Britain for sixty-three years. She died at the age of eighty-one on January 22, 1901. She conducted official business until two weeks before her death. Her son, Albert, Prince of Wales, followed her as King Edward VII.[274]

The twelfth US Census, conducted in 1900, determined the resident population of the United States to be 76 million people, an increase of 21 percent over the 63 million persons counted during the 1890 Census. The world population was 1.6 billion people. New Orleans had a population of 287,000 people.

New Orleans still much its French nature in 1902. A quarter of the people spoke French in daily gossip, and almost three quarters could understand what they were saying.[275]

New Orleans suffered repeated epidemics of yellow fever throughout its history. In 1905, yellow fever was reported again in the city. Since people

---

[274] "Queen Victoria," *Wikipedia*, https://en.wikipedia.org/wiki/January_1901#/media/File:Queen_Victoria_by_Bassano.jpg.

[275] Scott S. Ellis, *Madame Vieux Carré: the French Quarter in the Twentieth Century* (University of Mississippi: 2010), 8.

understood by that time that mosquitoes spread the disease, the city started a massive campaign to drain, screen, or oil all standing water. They also started a campaign to educate citizens on their vital role in preventing mosquitoes. These efforts were a success. They stopped the disease before it could become an epidemic. President Theodore Roosevelt came to the city to show how safe it was. The city has been free of yellow fever since. The city's levee system was maintained pretty well in the early part of the twentieth century, and it narrowly escaped being topped in the Great Mississippi Flood of 1927.

Pratt spent most of his life in the Irish Channel and Garden District areas of the city of New Orleans. He was born in the home on 1001 First Street at the corner of First Street and Constance Street. In 1918, he lived at 2225 Constance Street, between Phillip Street and Jackson Avenue. By 1922, he was listed as a salesman living at 2325 Coliseum, between First Street and Phillip Street.

In the census of 1920, Pratt was eighteen years old and living with his parents at 2325 Coliseum Street in the Garden District. According to the census, the group living in the house besides George Pratt were as follows:

- James J. Landry, Pratt's sixty-four-year-old father
- Marie Conception Parra Landry, Pratt's mother, who was also sixty-four.
- Alma Landry Chapman, Pratt's sister, who was thirty-four years old; Alma's husband, Frank Chapman, had died in March of 1917.
- Yvonne Marie Chapman, age fifteen, Alma's daughter and Pratt's niece
- Alma Yvonne Chapman, age fifteen, Alma's daughter and Pratt's niece

Pratt's work was listed as a salaried "Mill Supply" clerk—probably a hardware store clerk. In 1918, he was working as a clerk at Joseph Chalona Co. on 423 S. Front Street.

Pratt attended a party in the Gentilly neighborhood of New Orleans, and at this party, he met Jeanne Rose Develle. We will learn more about Jeanne and the Develles in chapter 8. Jeanne was living with her father, Ernest Develle, and mother, Azine Develle, at their home on 2927 Grand Route St. John (between N. Dupre Street and N. White Street). The house was a block and a half from Gentilly Boulevard and Stallings Playground. Pratt started to court Jeanne, and soon they were engaged. Jeanne and Pratt were married on December 28, 1921, in St. Rose de Lima Church, located at 2545 Bayou Road in New Orleans.

After they were married, they lived at 2325 Coliseum in the Garden District of New Orleans. By 1924, Pratt was a salesman for the Beacon Supply Co. in New Orleans and was residing with Jeanne at 1516 Gentilly Ave. In the 1950s, Pratt worked as a traveling salesman for Stratton Baldwin Hardware Supply Co, selling wholesale supplies to retail hardware stores around the state. He was doing well financially. Pratt was a man who loved boats. His first boat was the *Daisy*, and his last boat was the *Mickey*, named after his oldest grandson, Michael Gamotis.

The Descendants of George Pratt Landry

We will spend most of this chapter going backward and documenting the ancestors of George Pratt Landry. In this section, however, we will look forward to Pratt's descendants. George Pratt Landry Sr. and Jeanne Louise Rose Develle had the following children and grandchildren.

Marie Yvonne Landry

Marie Yvonne Landry was born on February 27, 1923, in New Orleans. She grew up in the Landry family home at 1516 Gentilly Avenue. Marie Yvonne attended St. Rose de Lima Grammar School and St. Joseph Academy High School. She was a very devout Catholic, and she developed a vocation to serve God as a nun.

In 1941, at the age of eighteen and after high school, Marie Yvonne entered the convent as a novice. By 1942, she had realized the religious life was not for her, and she left the convent. She met Lawrence Oswald Gamotis Jr., who was born on June 7, 1920. Lawrence was the son of Lawrence O Gamotis Sr., who was thirty-two when Lawrence Jr. was born. Lawrence Jr.'s mother was Eloise L Pritchard Gamotis, who was twenty-five when Lawrence Jr. was born.

Lawrence Jr. was born on Millville Court Avenue in Tucson, Arizona. His mother, Eloise, according to the 1920 US Census, was born in Mexico or possibly New Mexico. He lived around the corner from Yvonne at 2625 Laharpe Street in New Orleans with his three aunts who raised him. Lawrence's father had left his mom, and his three kids lived with his sisters). In 1930, Lawrence was nine years old, attending school, and living at 2625 LaHarpe Street with Henry F. Castarede (age fifty-three), Lawrence's step-uncle; Henry's wife Ida Gamotis Castarede (age fifty-two) Lawrence's aunt; his aunt Hattie Gamotis (age forty); his aunt Wenona

Gamotis (age thirty-six); his sister Gladys Gamotis (age fourteen); and his brother Roland Gamotis (age eleven).

In 1940, according to the US Census, Lawrence was at the same location living with the same people. He worked as a clerk at the Diamond Match Co., located in the Whitney Bank Building at 228 St. Charles Avenue, Office 323. This building was located downtown at the corner of Camp Street and Gravier.

Lawrence and Marie Yvonne had the following children:

- Michael Henry Gamotis was born on June 24, 1945. He married Diedra Donald on November 29, 1969, in Mobile, Alabama.
- Jerome Edward Gamotis was born on January 10, 1948. He married Paula Baker on March 15, 1975.
- Delane Marie Gamotis was born on January 10, 1950. She married Phillip R. Tretter on April 7, 1969.
- Mary Carol Gamotis was born on February 14, 1952. She married Jeffrey I. LeBlanc on October 26, 1974 in Mobile Alabama. The marriage ended in divorce.
- Vivian Marie Gamotis was born on July 26, 1954. She married Joseph Duley. The marriage ended in divorce.
- Lynette Marie Gamotis was born on April 11, 1961.
- John Thomas Gamotis was born on March 8, 1962. He passed away in June of 2019.

Jeanne Claire Landry

Jeanne Claire Landry was born on July 5, 1925, in New Orleans. She grew up in the family home at 1516 Gentilly Avenue. Jeanne attended St. Rose de Lima Grammar School and St. Joseph Academy High School. She married Lloyd Francis Favret, son of Bernard A. Favret and Alice Peterson, in St. Rose de Lima Church in New Orleans. He was born on December 22, 1920, in Pointe à la Hache, Louisiana. He died on April 19, 1982, in Metairie, Louisiana. His story is told in detail in chapter 6.

Lloyd Francis Favret and Jeanne Claire Landry had the following children:

1. Jeanne Marie Favret was born on August 20, 1947, in New Orleans when her mother was twenty-two years old. She married James Anatole Bourg

Jr., son of James Anatole Bourg Sr. and Agnes Louise Young, on May 17, 1969, in Metairie, Louisiana, at St. Lawrence the Martyr Church. Jim was born on December 21, 1946, in New Orleans. They had three children together:

- Jason Pratt Bourg, born October 30, 1973
- Jonathan Ryan Bourg, born February 2, 1980
- Jameson Lloyd Bourg, born December 5, 1984

2. Mary Lisa Favret was born on August 8, 1957, when her mother was thirty-two years old. She married John Joseph Roche Jr., who was born on October 3, 1956, in Dallas, Texas. His father was John Joseph Roche, and his mother was Barbara Jean Brian. Mary and John had two children together: Christopher Brian Roche and Katelyn Jeannelle Roche.

Jeanne Claire Landry died on July 5, 2017.

George Pratt Landry Jr.

George Pratt Landry Jr. was the third child and first son of George Pratt Landry and Jeanne Rose Develle. He was born on April 21, 1933 at home in New Orleans. The doctor who helped deliver Pratt Jr. at home was his uncle, Jerome Emanuel Landry MD. He was a big baby (over ten pounds) with a large head. As the first son of his father, he was Pratt Sr.'s pride and joy. His second child and youngest daughter, Jeanne Clair Landry, complained that she had been replaced as her father's pride and joy by her "big head brother" (as she called him). Pratt Sr. taught his son how to hunt, fish, and take care of a boat. But most importantly, he showed his son how to be an excellent salesman.

Pratt Jr. attended St. Aloysius High School, where he was in the Crusader Band. He married Jeanne Higginbotham on June 12, 1953. She was born on July 17, 1934, and died on June 17, 1998. Pratt and Jeanne had five children together: George Pratt Landry III, John David Landry, Collette Landry (Wiever), Timothy James Landry, and Amy Lynn Landry (Bode).

Generation 2: Jerome Joseph Emanuel Landry

Jerome Joseph Emanuel Landry was the son of Joseph Gustave Landry and Rose Eliska Mire. He was born on Thursday, November 6, 1856, in Louisiana.[276] When Jerome was born, the Great Storm of 1856 had just occurred three months before. It was one of the deadliest hurricanes in Louisiana history.

The storm was observed first as a minimal hurricane in the Gulf of Mexico on August 9. At least 183 people drowned as boats sank in seas turned up by the storm. "Last Island" (it's official name was Isle Dernière, often misspelled as Îsle Dernière, Isle Dernier, L'Îsle Dernière, and Île Dernière) was a barrier island and a pleasure resort off the coast southwest of New Orleans. A storm surge of twelve feet completely submerged "Last Island." It destroyed every structure, including the hotels and casinos on the island. It ruined all of the crops. The storm split "Last Island" itself into two parts.

Heavy rainfall caused the Mermentau River to overflow. The flood ruined crops and almost every home in Abbeville. The storm produced thirteen inches of rain in New Orleans. In Plaquemines Parish, fields were covered by several feet of water, while the orange trees lost all their fruit. The storm killed two hundred people.

The US Census of 1850 determined that the resident population of the United States was 23.1 million, an increase of 35.9 percent over the 17 million counted in the 1840 census. Of course, the country was more divided than it is in 2020. The start of the Civil War was just five years away, and at this point in history, that war was virtually inevitable.

Jerome met and married Marie Conception Parra on February 7, 1877, in New Orleans. After they were married, they lived in 1880 at 485 Annunciation Street. In 1900, they had moved and were living at 2319 Constance Street. Marie Conception Parra was the daughter of Juan Jose Parra and Carmelite Sanchez. Marie Conception was born on July 27, 1854, in New Orleans. Her father was born in Valez, Malaga, Spain. He arrived in the United States from Spain via Havana, Cuba, on December 2, 1845. He died on December 7, 1874. Carmelite Sanchez, his wife and Marie Conception's mother, was born in July of 1824 in New Orleans and passed away on April 28, 1910.

Marie Conception Parra had the following siblings:

---

[276] DOB from gravestone.

- Carmelite Marie Parra, born about 1856, died 1901
- Rosa Eugenie Parra, born about 1858, died 1896
- Adele Parra, born in March of 1861, died 1940
- Juanita Parra, born in February of 1867, died 1939
- John Lino Parra, born in January of 1868, died 1928
- Edward Peynallo Parra, born on February 5, 1873, died 1932

Jerome Joseph Emanuel Landry and Marie Conception Parra had nine children together. Only eight survived to adulthood. They are listed above as the siblings of George Pratt Landry. The US city directories listed Jerome as an accountant/bookkeeper. In 1901, his occupation was listed as a manager of the fancy goods department of a store.

Jerome died on November 9, 1926, in New Orleans. Marie Conception expired on May 12, 1924, in their home on 2325 Coliseum Street in New Orleans. Marie's obituary in the Times-Picayune on May 13, 1924, page 2, column 8, read as follows:

On Monday, May 12th, 1924 at 7:50 P.M., Marie C. Parra, beloved wife of Jerome J. Landry, a life-long resident of the city, survived by her children Dr. Jerome E., Juan G., George Pratt, Mrs. W. L. Parra, Mrs. A. J. Chapmen of Donaldsonville, La., Mrs. James A. Swayne of Hattiesburg, two brothers, J. L. and E. P. Parra, and two sisters, Juanita and Adel Parra, age 69 years. Relatives and Friends of the family also K of C council #714 invited to the funeral from her late residence at 2325 Coliseum St. on Wed. May 14, 1924.

Generation 3: Joseph Gustave Landry

Joseph Gustave Landry was the son of Achille Toussaint Landry and Modeste Braud. He was born on December 24, 1818, in Donaldsonville, Louisiana. Joseph Gustave was the seventh child and fifth son of the nine children of Achille and Modeste. His father and mother were thirty-five years old when Joseph was born.

The Siblings of Joseph Gustave Landry

In addition to Joseph Gustave, Achille and Modeste had the following children:

- Joseph Landry was born July 5, 1807, and died in 1844 at age thirty-seven.
- Achille Landry was born on February 13, 1809, in St. Gabriel, Iberville, Louisiana, and died in 1870.
- Franc Amadeo Landry was born on November 30, 1809, on Homeplace Plantation in Ascension, Louisiana, and died in 1863.
- Marie Lise Landry was born on February 14, 1814, in Louisiana and died in 1828.
- Pierre Theodule Landry was born on December 10, 1814, in Louisiana and died in 1872.
- Anne Algae Landry was born on December 29, 1816, in Louisiana and died in 1932.
- Marie Arthemise Landry was born January 1, 1821 in Plattenville, Assumption, Louisiana, and died in 1845.
- Marie Josephe Irma Landry was born October 30, 1822 in Louisiana and died in 1845.

Joseph Gustave's father, Achille, died in 1823 when Joseph was only about five years old. After Achille's death, Modeste Braud, his wife, married Achille's brother, Tresimond Landry. Tresimond later served as the lieutenant governor of Louisiana.

Joseph Gustave met and married Rose Eliska Mire, the daughter of Jean Baptiste Evariste Mire. Jean Baptiste was born on August 13, 1800, in St. James Parish, Louisiana, and died there on May 22, 1874. Rose Eliska's mother was Anne Clemence Gaudet, who was born on January 13, 1802, in St James Parish. We do not know the date of her death in this study.

The Children of Joseph Gustave Landry

Joseph married Eliska Mire on April 16, 1844, in St. James Parish. At this wedding, there were about twenty witnesses, including Joseph's uncle and stepfather, Tresimond, and Ed Nicholls, ex-mayor of Donaldsonville.[277] Rose Eliska Mire was born on October 4, 1825, in St. James Parish, Louisiana. She and Joseph lived in Donaldsonville originally, but by 1848, they had moved to New Orleans. The couple had the following children together:

[277.] Baton Rouge Dioese (1844), 375.

- Augustin Gustave Achille Landry was born on October 15, 1846, in Donaldsonville, Ascension, Louisiana, and died in 1852 at the age of five.
- Anne Graziella Landry was born in June of 1851 in St James Parish, Louisiana, and died in December of 1873 in West Baton Rouge Parish, Louisiana.
- Mary Alice (Celeste) Landry was born in 1853 in New Orleans and died on August 3, 1879, in Ascension Parish, Louisiana.
- Joseph Jerome Landry was born on November 6, 1856 in New Orleans and died in 1926.
- John Baptiste Mire Landry was born December 27, 1858, in New Orleans and died in 1929.
- Marie Louise Artemise Landry was born in 1861 in New Orleans and died in 1926.
- Andre Gustave Rosario Landry was born on October 2, 1863, in New Orleans. Andre died at the age of three years, nine months, on July 10, 1867. This death information comes from his death certificate.
- Jean Marie Thelisade "Taff" Landry was born on September 7, 1866, in New Orleans and died on May 7, 1924, in Baptist, Tangi, Louisiana.

Joseph Gustave got permission to take his deceased son, Andre Gustave Rosario Landry, to his uncle Franc Amadeo (Ferimond) Landry (1809–1863), who was born November 30, 1809 on Homeplace Plantation in Ascension, Louisiana. The permission certificate read as follows:

Permission is granted Mr. J. G. Landry to remove the body of his infant child from the city to the Plantation of Ferimond Landry in the Parish of Ascension for internment. Permission is further granted to the Captain of the Steam Boat Margenta to receive the body on board.

I can't make out the signature of the MD, but an official for the board of health signed the certificate.

Joseph Gustave Landry was a man of many talents and business activities. While he was living in Donaldsonville, Ascension Parish, on February 20, 1843, he was appointed by the governor of Louisiana, Alexander Mouton, to be the sheriff of Ascension Parish. The appointment occurred before he met and married Rose. We don't know how long his tenure as sheriff lasted.

We do know that Joseph Gustave moved to New Orleans sometimes in 1848–1849. His tenure as Ascension Parish sheriff must have ended after that move. In the 1850 US Census, Joseph Gustave is thirty years old. He is listed as living at 311 Constance with his wife, Eliska, and his oldest son, Augustin Gustave Achille Landry. His business interests seem to be diversified. His occupation listed as a steamboat captain, and from this time on, he is often called Captain Landry. He became involved in the Bayou Sarah mail service.[278]

In 1860, he was living with his wife and four of his living children born by 1860: Anne Graziella Landry, Calista Landry, Joseph Jerome Landry, and John Baptiste Mire Landry. His occupation is listed as "auctioneer."

Joseph Gustave, Steamboats and Mail on Louisiana Bayous

Bayous are a system of secondary waterways that are tributaries to larger bodies of water. Bayous are shallow and slow-moving, but they are navigable using shallow-draft vessels like canoes or dugout boats the Cajuns call *pirogues*.

Joseph started a company called the Bayou Sara Navigation Co. He owned at least five steamboats that were run out of New Orleans. The list of his steamers includes the following;

- The *Eliska* was a steamboat out of Donaldsonville, registered on October 12, 1846. It ran the New Orleans and Upper Bend Route. Its owners were Joseph Gustave Landry and William C. Winchester. The captain or master of the vessel was J. G. Landry. A newspaper account of the time read, "We had the pleasure a day or two ago to make a trip with Capt J G Landry of the Baton Rouge packet Eliska and found her to be a delightful and comfortable boat. The officers are all gentlemen and particularly accommodating."[279] The *Eliska* was abandoned in 1848.
- The *Patrick Henry* was a steamboat enrolled in the Port of New Orleans. It was sold in August 1850 to Joseph G. Landry and ran the New Orleans and Bayou Sara route. Its owner was Joseph G. Landry. It was dismantled and used as a wharf boat in 1854.
- The *Laurel Hill* was a steamboat enrolled on February 20, 1858. It ran the New Orleans and Bayou Sara route. Its owners were Joseph Gustave Landry & John M Hall.

[278.] 1869 New Orleans City Directory.
[279]From the New Orleans *Daily Picayune* (May 16, 1849), 2.

- The *New Latona* was a steamboat enrolled on May 14, 1851. It ran the New Orleans Upper Coast to Donaldsonville twice weekly. Its owner and master were Joseph Gustave Landry. It was sold in February 1853 to Emile Frances Gross.

- The *Emperor* was a steamboat christened on July 28, 1852. It ran the New Orleans to Vicksburg and New Orleans to Bayou Sara route. Its owners were Joseph G. Landry and J. A. Cotton. It was sold in Mobile in 1854.[280]

- The steamboat *Mary Foley* was put into service in the late 1840s when it ran the river between New Orleans and Bayou Sara. This steamboat was sold in November of 1850 to a group including Joseph Gustave Landry. It is believed it was rechristened as the Eliska and was docked in Lockport in Bayou Lafourche. The boat steamed between Lockport and New Orleans in the high-water season and between Donaldsonville and New Orleans during low water season. The steamboat was retired in 1857.

- The steamboat *Caddo No. 2* operated between Shreveport, on the Red River, and New Orleans. It served as a mail contract riverboat. Because it did not carry a US agent aboard, all loose letters were marked "WAY [5¢ postage + 1¢ fee paid to the steamboat captain]" when the captain turned them in to the New Orleans post office.

- The steamboat *Granada* operated the Red River and Mississippi River Route

- The steamboats *R. E.* Clark and *Water* With operated the Grand Bayou–Red River–Mississippi River Route.

- The steamboat *Piota* plied the Red River and its tributary bayous and rivers from 1852 until 1858, when the vessel exploded and burned to the waterline.

- The steamboat *Rockaway No. 2* operated from Shreveport to New Orleans.

- The steamboat *Red Chief* had the Bayou Pierre route and the Red River–Black River–Mississippi River route.

- The steamboat *Carolina* had the Bayou Pierre route and the Red River–Mississippi River route

- The steamboat *Sydonia* traveled the Bayou Lafourche route its whole lifespan.

---

[280]Way's Packet Directory 1846–1983, New Orleans Ship Registers, vol. 4, 5, SLU Library.

F. A. Dentzel, listed as a postal clerk in the 1851 New Orleans' city directory, performed dockside services to enable the expedited handling of mail entering the port.

During the Civil War, Joseph Gustave Landry served with a group called the Confederate Guards. Also called the Home Guard, they were a "regiment of wealthy citizens enrolled in the militia." As New Orleans was being occupied, solders were boarded on top of freight cars while the members of the state troops, such as the Home Guards, traveled inside the cars. The Home Guard was described as "made up of rich and overweight old men, who would rather die than live under Yankee rule." The train took the solders to Camp Moore, where some stayed, but most chose to go home to New Orleans.[281]

Joseph was also an auctioneer. He auctioned land and slaves. He owned an auction house in New Orleans in 1860. McCarren, Landry & Co. was so prosperous that they fitted up Masonic Hall, at the corner of St. Charles and Perdido Streets, as an "auction mart" with "a large commodious and attractive salesroom, with spacious accommodations for slaves." Local editorial items called attention to their Tuesday and Saturday sales of real estate, slaves, and various other kinds of property.

Joseph Gustave Landry died on April 22, 1873. Rose Eliska passed away on August 6, 1873, in New Orleans, just three and a half months after her husband.

Generation 4: Achille Toussaint Landry

Achille Toussaint Landry was born on November 1, 1784, in Donaldsonville, Louisiana. He was the son of Joseph dit BelHomme Alexandre Landry. His father was born in 1752 in Grand Pre, Acadia, which is today in Nova Scotia, Canada. His father had two wives. Joseph's first wife was Isabel LeBlanc (1751–1777). She was born in 1751 in Grand Pre. She married Joseph in Donaldsonville on April 17, 1775. She had one child with Joseph: Achille's half-brother Louis Landry (1776–1831), born on May 12, 1776, on the New Hope Plantation in Ascension, Louisiana. Isabel would die just two years and four months after the marriage on September 1, 1777, in Donaldsonville. Joseph's second wife, and Achille's mother, was Anne Madeline Bujol. She was born in 1757 (during and right after the great expulsion from Acadia) in Oxford, Talbot, Maryland, in the United States. Anne's father was Joseph Bujold (1723–1806), and her mother was Anne Leblanc

---

[281] John D. Winters, *The Civil War in Louisiana.*

(1732–1812). Both were born in Acadia, Nova Scotia, Canada. Anne Madeline Bujol died on November 26, 1816, in Donaldsonville. Joseph Alexander died on November 15, 1823.

The Siblings of Achille Tousaint Landry

In addition to Achille, Joseph and Anne had the following children, all born in Donaldsonville:

- Juana Carmela Landry was born on January 23, 1780, and died on May 5, 1803, at the age of twenty-three years.
- Maria Celeste Landry was born on March 5, 1781, and died as an infant in April of 1781.
- Maria Celeste Landry was born December 25, 1782. This child was given the same name as her infant sister who had died the year before. She died in 1848.
- Joseph Narcisse Landry was born on October 15, 1786, and died in 1835.
- Phillip Ursin Landry was born on May 25, 1788, and died in 1831.
- Isidore Valery Landry was born on April 4, 1790, and died in 1863.
- Marie Melanie Landry was born on November 1, 1791, and died in 1857.
- Jean Trasimon Landry was born on December 16, 1795, and died in 1873.
- Jacques Landry was born on February 15, 1796, and died in 1819.
- Marie Delphine Landry was born on July 3, 1797, and died as an infant in 1798.
- Marie Delphine Landry was born on March 15, 1799.
- Marguerite Jeanne Landry was born on June 3, 1804.

The Children of Achille Tousaint Landry

Achille met and married Marie Modeste Braud (possibly Brand), who was born in 1793 in St. James Parish, Louisiana. They were married on August 25, 1806, at St. Jacques De Cabanoce Church in St. James, Louisiana. They had the following children together;

- Achille Landry Jr. was born on February 13, 1809, in St. Gabriel, Iberville, Louisiana, and died in 1870.
- François Amadeo Landry was born on November 30, 1809, on Homeplace Plantation in Ascension, Louisiana, and died in 1863.
- Marie Lise Landry was born on February 14, 1814, in Ascension Parish, Louisiana, and died in 1828.
- Pierre Theodule Landry was born on December 10, 1814, in Ascension Parish and died in 1872.
- Anne Algae Landry was born on December 29, 1816, in Ascension Parish and died in 1932.
- Joseph Gustave Landry was born on December 24, 1818, in Donaldsonville and died in 1873.
- Marie III Landry was born on January 1, 1821, in Plattenville, Assumption, Louisiana, and died in 1910.
- Marie Arthemise Landry was born on January 1, 1821, in Plattenville, Assumption, Louisiana, and died in 1845.
- Marie Josephe Irma Landry was born on October 30, 1822, in Louisiana and died in 1845.

Historical Events

On January 14, 1784, just ten and a half months before the birth of Achille, the Continental Congress of the United States ratified the Treaty of Paris, officially establishing the United States as an independent and sovereign nation and ending the Revolutionary War. The Continental Congress signed the treaty in Paris on September 3, 1783. It required Congress to return the ratified document to England within six months.

On December 23, 1783, George Washington resigned as commander-in-chief of the Continental Army. He went back to his home at Mount Vernon.[282] Washington's resignation affirmed the new nation's commitment to the principle of civilian control of the military. It prompted King George III of the United Kingdom to call him "the greatest character of the age."[283]

---

[282] Thomas Fleming, "The Most Important Moment in American History," History News Network, Retrieved 2016-05-17.

[283] Richard Brookhiser, *Founding Father: Rediscovering George Washington* (Newark, NJ: Free Press, 1996), 103.

Pre–Civil War Louisiana was a slave state. African American slaves had comprised the majority of the population during the colonial period of the eighteenth century. By the time the United States acquired Louisiana in 1803, the institution of slavery was entrenched. Louisiana became a state in 1812. By 1860, 47 percent of the state's population consisted of slaves. However, the state also had one of the largest free black communities in the United States. Many of the white people, particularly in the cities, supported Southern states' rights and slavery.

Louisiana seceded from the United States on January 26, 1861. New Orleans was the most populous city in the South. It was a large port because of its location on the Mississippi River and its easy access to the Gulf of Mexico. Early on, the US War Department made plans for its capture. US. Army forces took the city on April 25, 1862. For the latter part of the war, both the United States and the Confederacy had their own Louisiana governors.[284]

Louisiana Governor Thomas Overton Moore, in January of 1861, ordered the Louisiana militia to occupy both US forts guarding New Orleans from the south: Fort Jackson, and Fort St. Philip. Moore, a wealthy planter and slaveholder, acted aggressively to engineer the secession of Louisiana from the Union by a convention on January 23. The state's military actions were done before secession had been voted. That order was not supported by the state constitution. The constitution called for a popular vote to call for a convention. Govenor Moore tried to justify his actions by saying, "I do not think it comports with the honor and self-respect of Louisiana as a slave-holding state to live under the government of a Black Republican president."[285]

The convention put forth strategies to defend Louisiana and the other Gulf states of the Confederacy. The first was an unofficial embargo of cotton to Europe; this was an attempt to force Britain to use its navy to protect the new Confederacy. The second was a privateer fleet that would sweep the sea clear of US naval and commercial ships while protecting Louisiana's booming port economy. The third strategy involved the ring of prewar forts. The fourth was a fleet of revolutionary new ironclads to safeguard the mouth of the Mississippi from the US Navy. All of these strategies were failures.[286]

---

[284] Chester G. Hearn, *The Capture of New Orleans in 1862* (Louisiana State University Press, 1995).

[285] "Louisiana in the American Civil War," *Wikipedia*, https://en.wikipedia.org/wiki/Louisiana_in_the_American_Civil_War.

[286] Hearn, 2–31.

In March 1861, George Williamson, the Louisianan state commissioner, addressed the Texas secession convention, where he called upon US slave states to declare secession from the Union to continue practicing slavery.[287] One Louisiana soldier gave as his reasons for fighting for the Confederacy, "I never want to see the day when a negro is put on an equality with a white person. There are too many free n … … s now to suit me, let alone having four million."[288]

In response to Moore's leveraged secession, President Abraham Lincoln realized that the Mississippi River was the "backbone of the Rebellion." He said, "If control of the river were accomplished, the largest city in the Confederacy would be taken back for the Union, and the Confederacy would be split in half."[289] Lincoln rushed to back Admiral David Dixon Porter's idea of a naval advance up the river to capture New Orleans. This naval proposal got Lincoln's political support, and its success would ensure a supply of cotton to Northern textile manufacturers and renewing of trade and exports from the port of New Orleans. The US Navy would become both a formidable invasion force and a means of transporting Union forces along the Mississippi River and its tributaries. This strategic vision would prove victorious in Louisiana.[290]

As a significant slave state, Louisiana seceded from the United States in January 1861 and joined the Confederacy in March of 1861. Between 50,000 and 60,000, Louisianans served in the Confederate army, but more than 5,000 other Louisianans, including immigrants, fought for the Union. The 1st and 3rd Louisiana Native Guard fought for the Union and were among the first African American units to see combat.

The home front, with few Confederate defenders, suffered greatly. Subject to martial law following the Union's 1862 seizure of New Orleans, city residents were robbed and abused, and women who insulted Union troops were arrested for prostitution. Guerilla fighters tried to defend the state, which brought Union reprisals. Some guerillas, known as Jayhawkers, even preyed on fellow residents.

---

[287] E. W. Winkler, *Journal of the Secession Convention of Texas*, 1861, retrieved September 8, 2015.

[288] James M. McPherson, *For Cause and Comrades: Why Men Fought in the Civil War* (New York: Oxford University Press, 1997), 109.

[289] "Louisiana in the American Civil War," *Wikipedia*, https://en.wikipedia.org/wiki/Louisiana_in_the_American_Civil_War.

[290] Chester G. Hearn, *The Capture of New Orleans, 1862* (LSU Press, 1995).

The disruption of trade, wartime inflation, and food scarcity led many to flee Louisiana.

Generation 5: Joseph dit BelHomme Alexandre Landry

The Cajun Component of the Landry Family

Joseph (dit BelHomme) Alexandre Landry was born in Acadia, the French colonized portion of Nova Scotia. Therefore his ancestors (which we will study here) and his descendants whom we have already considered are classified as Cajuns. We will explore that history along with the history of the intertwining of the Landry family with the Bourg family.

Marie Josephe Bourg had the same great-great grandparents (Jean Claud Landry and Marie Sale) as Joseph Etienne Landry's great-grandparents. Although the origins of the families are in France, the majority of these ancestors lived their lives in Acadia. Before deportation, the Landry ancestors in Acadia had lived there for 125 years (1630–1755). The Landry ancestors in the United States had been in this country for some three hundred years. They resided in Acadia approximately 36 percent of the time. Their heritage is truly Acadian.

The Acadian Heritage

The French Acadians are the descendants of the French settlers, and sometimes the indigenous peoples, of parts of Acadia. After the French and Indian War, the British eventually deported all the Acadians from the region. Many were sent back to Saint-Malo on the coast of France. After thirty years, many migrated from there to Louisiana, where they became known as Cajuns, a corruption of the word *Acadiens* or *Acadians*. Henry Wadsworth Longfellow's epic poem "Evangeline" helped define Acadian identity.[291]

The survival of the Acadians depended on successful cooperation with the native peoples of the region. In the early years of Acadian colonization, a small number of recorded marriages between Acadian settlers and indigenous women were recorded. Some documents showing marriages between Acadian immigrants and indigenous women in formal Roman Catholic rites have survived—for

---

[291]"History of the Acadians," *Wikipedia*, https://en.wikipedia.org/wiki/History_of_the_ Acadians.

example, the union of Charles La Tour to a Mi'kmaw woman in 1626.[292] There were also reported cases of Acadian settlers marrying indigenous spouses according to Mi'kmaq rites and subsequently living in Mi'kmaq communities.[293]

There were several sailings from the French Atlantic Coast to Acadia between 1632 and 1636. These sailings were probably when the Landry Family and the Bourg Family immigrated to Acadia. A typical sailing crossing took about thirty-five days, with about seventy-five passengers per ship and a crew of approximately fifteen sailors. With these ships, Acadia began a slow shift from being primarily a matter of explorers and traders to permanent settlers, including women and children.

The presence of European women in Acadia is a signal that settlement was beginning, although the territory was still basically a community of transient Europeans and Native Americans. The migrants were established at Port-Royal.[294] In 1636, Pierre Martin and Catherine Vigneau were the first French couple to birth a child in Acadia. The firstborn child was Mathieu Martin. In part because of this distinction, Mathieu Martin later became the Seigneury of Cobequid in 1699.[295]

Historian Gregory M. W. Kennedy argued that the emigrants from France carried their customs and social structure to Acadia. They were frontier people who constructed settlements based on kinship. They optimized the use of farmland with their dikes and emphasized trading as a means of commerce. They were politically active. The French and the Acadian villages were all similar in terms of prosperity, equality, and independent-mindedness. Kennedy says that a distinct Acadian identity evolved from the gradual adaptation of traditional French methods, institutions, and ideas to the North American environmental and political situations.[296]

In 1654, there was a major war between France and England. A flotilla from Boston, under orders from General Cromwell, arrived in Acadia to chase the French out. The fleet seized La Tour's fort, then Port-Royal. During this English occupation of Acadia, Jean-Baptiste Colbert, Louis XIV's minister, forbade the

---

[292]P. Buckner and J. Reid, eds., *The Atlantic Region to Confederation: A History* (Toronto University Press, 1994).

[293]N. E. S. Griffiths, "1600–1650. Fish, Fur, and Folk," in *The Atlantic Region to Confederation: A History*, ed. Phillip Buckner and John G. Reid (University of Toronto Press, 1994), 56.

[294]Griffiths, 54–55.

[295]Griffiths, 193.

[296] Gregory M. W. Kennedy, *Something of a Peasant Paradise? Comparing Rural Societies in Acadie and the Loudunais, 1604-1755* (MQUP, 2014).

Acadians from returning to France. As a result of the English rule, no new French families settled in Acadia between 1654 and 1670. The Treaty of Breda, signed between the French and British on July 31, 1667, returned Acadia to France. Marillion du Bourg was sent to take possession of the territory for France.

In 1670, the first census of Acadia was taken. Listed in the census were Antoine Bourg (sixty-two); his wife, Antoinette Landry (fifty-three); children François (twenty-seven), Jean (twenty-four), Bernard (twenty-two), Martin (twenty-one), Abraham (nine), and six daughters; twelve cattle; and eight sheep. It also included Rene Landry (fifty-two); his wife, Perrine Bourg (forty-five); children Pierre (thirteen), Claude (eight), and five daughters; ten cattle; and six sheep. The census showed that there were approximately sixty Acadian families, with about three hundred inhabitants in total. These inhabitants were predominantly engaged in farming along the shores of the present-day Bay of Fundy.

In 1671, more than fifty colonists left La Rochelle, France, aboard the ship l'Oranger. During this time, several colonists married Acadian indigenous people. During the latter part of the seventeenth century, Acadians began to migrate northeast from Port-Royal to settlements (villages) like Grand-Pré, Chignecto, Cobequid, and Pisiguit. Although not common, in some years, epidemics ravaged the people of Acadia. From 1732 to 1733, some 150 people died of smallpox in the colonies.[297]

The history of the Acadians before the deportation shows that people had a tough life. For almost every good harvest year, it seemed there was one in which crops failed. In one or two instances, widespread fires destroyed crops, livestock, and farms. Famine and starvation were common and frequently occasioned desperate pleas for supplies from Louisbourg, Québec, and even France itself. In 1756, scarcity on Isle Saint-Jean prompted authorities to relocate some families to Québec.[298]

During the early eighteenth century, the British tried six activities to conquer Acadia and its capital. They finally defeated the French (the Acadians, the Mi'kmaq, and the French soldiers) in the Siege of Port-Royal in 1710. The Acadian and Wabanaki Confederacy resisted the British invasion and occupation of Acadia during the four French and Indian Wars and two local wars before the expulsion of

---

[297] Earle Lockerby, "The Deportation of the Acadians from Ile St.-Jean, 1758," *Acadiensis* XXVII 2 (Spring 1998), 45–94.

[298] Lockerby, 45–94.

the Acadians.[299] The Mi'kmaq and the Acadians were allied through their Catholic religion and numerous intermarriages. The Mi'kmaq had the military strength in Acadia even after the conquest of the territory in 1710.[300] They primarily resisted the British occupation of Acadia and were joined in their efforts on numerous occasions by French Acadians.

Even though many of the Acadians traded with the New England Protestants, Acadians' participation in the wars indicated that many were reluctant to be ruled by the British. When Charles Lawrence took over, he took a stronger stance against the Acadians. He was not only a government official but also a military leader for the region. Lawrence's primary objective in Acadia was to defeat the French fortifications at Beausejour and Louisbourg. The British saw many Acadian colonists as a military threat in their allegiance to the French and Mi'kmaq. The British also wanted to interrupt the Acadian supply lines to the strong fortress at Louisbourg, which, in turn, supplied the Mi'kmaq.[301]

The British finally conquered Acadia in 1710; however, they didn't defeat the alliance. The French monarchy just got tired of the territory and ceded it to the British in a treaty. During the next forty years, the Acadians continually refused to sign an unconditional oath of allegiance to Britain. During this period, Acadians, who were supposed to be neutral, participated in various militia operations against the British. They maintained vital supply lines to the French fortresses of Louisbourg and Fort Beausejour.[302] In the French and Indian War, the British tried to neutralize any military threat posed by the Acadians.[303]

Many Acadians might have signed an oath to the British monarchy had their circumstances been better. In contrast, other Acadians did not sign because they were anti-British. The Acadians who might have signed did not sign because of religious reasons. The king was the head of the Protestant Church of England. Another issue was that an oath might commit male Acadians to fighting against France during wartime. Another concern was that their Mi'kmaq neighbors might

[299] Faragher (2005), 110–112.

[300] Plank (2001), 67–72.

[301] Stephen E. Patterson, "1744–1763: Colonial Wars and Aboriginal Peoples," in *The Atlantic Region to Confederation: A History*, ed. Phillip Buckner and John G. Reid (University of Toronto Press, 1994), 125–155.

[302] Grenier (2008).

[303] Stephen E. Patterson, "Indian–White Relations in Nova Scotia, 1749-61: A Study in Political Interaction," *The Acadiensis Reader: Atlantic Canada Before Confederation*, 3rd edition, ed. P. A. Buckner, Gail G. Campbell, and David Frank (Acadiensis Press, 1998), 105–106.

think they were loyal to the British instead of their allies. As a result, signing an unconditional oath might have put Acadian villages in danger of attack from the Mi'kmaq.[304]

The Grand Dérangement, which occurred in two primary stages, deported more than 12,000 Acadians from the colony in 1755 and 1758. The British destroyed around 6,000 Acadian houses and dispersed the Acadians among the thirteen colonies from Massachusetts to Georgia as well as back to France. The single event that involved the most deaths of Acadians was the sinking of the *Duke William* after the deportation. Although there were no purposeful attempts to separate families, this did occur in the chaos of the eviction. With the expulsion of the Acadians during the French and Indian War, the Mi'kmaq and Acadian resistance intensified. After the expulsion began, much of the opposition was led by Charles Deschamps de Boishébert et de Raffetot.[305]

In April of 1757, a group of Acadians and Mi'kmaq raided a warehouse near Fort Edward, killing thirteen British soldiers and, after taking what provisions they could carry, setting fire to the building. A few days later, the same partisans also raided Fort Cumberland.[306]

Some of the Acadians who were moved to British colonies became indentured servants. Massachusetts passed a law in November 1755 placing the Acadians under the custody of "justices of the peace and overseers of the poor." Pennsylvania, Maryland, and Connecticut adopted similar laws. The Province of Virginia under Robert Dinwiddie initially agreed to resettle about one thousand Acadians who arrived in the colony but later ordered most deported to England, writing that the "French people" were "intestine enemies" that were "murdering and scalping our frontier Settlers.[307] During this period, in about 1755, Joseph dit BelHomme Alexandre Landry was deported from Acadia to New England. He eventually made his way down to Louisiana and Ascension Parish.

In 1758, over three thousand Acadians, including the Bourg family, were deported to the coast of France. Attempts were made at resettlement.

Queen Elizabeth's apology to the Acadians for the exportation finally came through the back door by way of the Canadian federal cabinet. The proclamation

---

[304] Reid, John G., *Nova Scotia: A Pocket History* (Fernwood, 2009), 49.

[305] Grenier (2008), 199–200.

[306] Faragher (2005), 398.

[307] Gwenda Morgan and Peter Rushton, *Banishment in the Early Atlantic World: Convicts, Rebels, and Slaves* (A&C Black, 2013), 140.

was signed by Governor General Adrienne Clarkson, the queen's representative in Canada.

"This is a royal proclamation, and it involves two critical acknowledgments for Acadians everywhere," Euclide Chiasson, president of Canada's National Society of Acadians, based in Moncton, New Brunswick, said. "This is important because it makes historical records a fact, and the Crown is admitting it caused irreparable damages to the Acadian people."

The Siblings of Joseph dit BelHomme Alexandre Landry

Joseph dit BelHomme Alexandre Landry was born in 1752 in Grand-Pre, Acadia, Nova Scotia, Canada. His birth was just three years before the "great deportation" began. He was the son of Joseph Etienne Landry (1701–1783) and Marie Josephe Bourg (1711–1792).

Joseph Etienne was born in 1701 and was baptized in St. Isidore Catholic Church in Acadie. Marie Josephe Bourg was born on June 16, 1711, in Grand-Pré. They were married on January 11, 1745, in Grand-Pré. They were deported as resident Acadian exiles to Oxford, Maryland, in 1765. Joseph and Marie had the following children:

- Marie Madeleine (Magdalena) Landry was born in 1747 in Grand-Pré and died in 1800.
- Marie Landry was born in 1748 in Grand-Pré and died in 1788.
- Marguerite Landry was born in 1752 in Grand-Pré and died in 1840.
- Joseph Alexandre Landry (1752–1814) was born in 1752 in Grand-Pré and died in 1814.
- Osite Landry was born in 1753 in Port-Royal and died in 1813.
- Gertrude Anne Landry was born in 1754 in Riviere Aux Canards, Grand-Pré, Acadia, and died in 1790.

The Landry family was deported to Maryland in 1755. A large number of the Acadians came to Louisiana from Maryland. Charles Carroll was a wealthy Maryland landowner who, in later years, became the only Catholic signer of the Declaration of Independence. Carroll went to France in 1752 when France still claimed the Louisiana Territory to ask for land on the Arkansas River, where the oppressed Catholics of Maryland might settle and be free to practice their religion.

Double taxes and other oppressions, both economic and religious, were the method used by the intolerant Protestant government to persecute Catholic Acadians. By 1767, when the Acadians began to flock to Louisiana, life became much better for all the Maryland Catholics. Joseph Etienne died on September 2, 1783, in Donaldsonville, Louisiana. Marie Josephe Bourg died on September 5, 1792, in Donaldsonville.

Marriage and Family

Joseph (dit BelHomme) Alexandre Landry married Anne Madeline Bujol on November 22, 1779, in Donaldsonville. Anne Madeline was born in 1757 in Oxford, Maryland, after her family was deported from Acadia. She died on November 26, 1816, in Donaldsonville. Her father was Joseph Bujold (1723–1806) and her mother was Anne Leblanc (1732–1812). Both parents were Acadians born in Nova Scotia. Joseph had previously married Isabel LeBlanc (1751–1777) on April 17, 1775, in Donaldsonville. Isabel died in 1777 in Donaldsonville, and they had only one child together: Louis Landry, born May 12, 1776 on New Hope Plantation, Ascension, Louisiana. He died in 1831.

Joseph and his second wife, Anne Madeline Bujol, had thirteen children together. They are listed in Generation 4 as the siblings of Achille Toussaint Landry.

Joseph (dit BelHomme) Alexandre Landry died on November 15, 1823. The Landry Tomb in Ascension Church Cemetery in Donaldsonville, Louisiana, is on the National Register of Historic Places. It contains the remains of Joseph Landry; his wife, Anne Bujol, who died on November 11, 1829, in Plattenville; and other members of the Landry and Duffel families. It was built in 1845 by Joseph's family, and his body was move there and placed in the tomb at that time.

Generation 6: Joseph Etienne Landry

Joseph Etienne Landry was born in 1701 in Grand-Pré, Acadia. His father was Antoine Landry, and his mother was Anne Marie Thibodeau. Antoine, his father, was born in 1660 in St. Charles des Mines, New Brunswick, Canada. His mother, Anne Marie, was born in 1665 in Port-Royal, Acadia, Nova Scotia, Canada. Anne Marie's father was Pierre Thibodeau dit Rameau, who was born in

1631 in Annapolis, Nova Scotia, Canada. Her mother was Jeanne Theriau Theriot, who was born in 1644, also in Nova Scotia.

The first Acadian Census took place in Port-Royal in 1671. It was one of the first in Canada. The total count was 392 people, 482 cattle, and 524 sheep. The 1701 Acadian Census included the following Landry family members (and other relatives):

- "Claude LANDRY, 35; Marguerite Theriot [Territo] (wife) 30; Claude 12, Jean 7, Magdeleine 17, Marie 15, Marguerite 10, Anne 5, Jeanne 1; 1 gun, 19 cattle, 14 sheep, 10 hogs, 6 arpents."
- "Pierre Landry 42, Magdeleine ROBICHEAU (wife) 37; Pierre LANDRY 18, Baptiste 12, Rene 9, Francois 5, Joseph 3, Marguerite 15; 2 guns, 15 cattle, 16 sheep, nine hogs, ten arpents."
- "Bernard BOURG 54, Francoise BRUN (wife) 50; Abraham 15, Jeanne 23, Francoise 18, Renee 13, Marie 10, Claire 6."

Census of the Colony of Mines—La Riviere Ste Croix
- "Jean LANDRY, his wife, four boys, one girl, 12 arpents, 20 cattle, 15 sheep, 15 hogs, two guns."
- "Alexandre Bourg, his wife, four girls, eight arpents, 15 cattle, seven sheep, ten hogs, two guns."

Rivière De L'acension
- "Germain Landry, his wife, three boys, six arpents, ten cattle, 13 sheep."

Rivière St-Antoine
- "Antoine Landry, his wife, six boys, five girls, eight arpents, 25 cattle, 25 sheep, 16 hogs, one gun."
- "Claude Budrot, his wife, three boys, five girls, 16 arpents, 15 cattle, 16 sheep, eight hogs, one gun."

Rivière Des Canards
- "Rene Landry, his wife, one boy, two girls, 13 arpents, 12 cattle, 13 sheep, six hogs, one gun."

The 1686 Acadian Census included the following Landry members (and other relatives):

- "Antoine Landry 26, Marie Thibodeau 25; children: Marie 4, Antoine 2, Isabelle 1–2 guns, nine arpents of land, eight cattle, six sheep, ten hogs."
- "Pierre Landry 28, Magdelaine Robichaud 21; child: Pierre 3; 1 gun, two arpents of land, six cattle, six sheep, five hogs."
- "Antoine Bourc/Bourg 95, Antoinette Landry 80; child: Marguerite 18."
- "Perine Bourc/Bourg, mother, 74; Claude Landry 24, Marguerite Terriot his wife 20; child: Marguerite 18 months; 1 gun. three arpents, seven cattle, eight sheep, six hogs"
- "Martin Bourc/Bourg 36, Marie Potet 29; children: Marie 10, Abraham 7, Pierre 5, Jeanne 2; 1 gun, three arpents, four cattle, five sheep, six hogs."
- "Marie Bourc/Bourg (widow of Vincent Brot/Breau) 41; children: Antoine 20, Marguerite 18, Pierre 16, Anne 17, Francoise 11, Jeanne 9, Marie 7, Jeanne 5, Rene 3, Isabelle 5 months; 4 arpents, ten cattle, five sheep, five hogs."
- "Claude Landry 23, Marie Thibaudeau 18; a child one year old; 12 cattle."

Summary of the 1701 census of Port Royal: 592 persons; 95 families,197 men and women, 218 boys, 177 girls, 75 guns, 643 cattle, 627 sheep, 351 hogs, and 377 arpents of cultivated land.

Life in Acadia before the Deportation: Farming

Farming was a significant part of the livelihood of the Acadians. But they were not farmers in the conventional sense of the word. They made use of a system of levees to create their fertile farmland. They used knowledge and skills that were familiar to them from France. The high tides and vast tidal lands of Port-Royal made the area ideal to apply these techniques. It is likely the reason the site was chosen in the first place. Upon arrival, the Acadians knew precisely what to do and began the process right away.

The Acadians settled on the rivers, which emptied into the Bay of Fundy. The Bay of Fundy, because of its funnel shape, has very high tides. This affects the rivers draining into it. At high tide, these rivers overflow their banks, covering a large area of marshland. When the tide went out, these marshlands were still wet with leftover salt tidewater. The marshy terrain built up acres of fine fertile soil due to the twice-a-day tidal flow.

The Acadians built dikes or long walls around the perimeter of these tidal grounds. The dams were so tight that they stopped the river water from flooding these lands. The Acadians then hand-dug ditches on this land, each draining towards an aboiteau or gate. The one-way gate led back out to the river. Rain and snow washed the salt off the land, into the ditches, and out to the rivers and the sea through the aboiteau.

The drainage happened at low tide when there was no saltwater on the seaside of the one-way gate. The salt water in the river could not come back in when the tide was high, because the doors only opened one way. As the tide came in, the salt water would push on the one-way gate, causing it to close. This sealed tighter as the tide came up. After two years, the salty soil on the marshes became desalted and dry. These marshes thus made excellent fertile soil for farming.

It was clear that the Acadians used ground that would not flood above the marsh for their houses and buildings. This guaranteed a dry location. They were not lazy but simply good readers of their landscape. They were in harmony with the land. They knew how to use the natural resources around them. Considering the agricultural methods and tools of that period, the marshlands were more efficient and more productive than clearing uplands of farming purposes.

Coarse salt hay (spartina) on the seaside of the dikes, which grew in the marshes in the saltwater ebbing of the tides, was another natural resource that the Acadians quickly harvested. During low tide, the spartina marsh grass was exposed. The Acadians used this marsh grass for hay and piled it on platforms, which they built to keep it dry. They later baled the salt marsh hay and stored it in barns to feed their animals all winter. They did not have to slaughter their cattle in winter because of lack of hay, as was the practice in most of the New England settlements. They did not depend on replenishing their cattle each year.

This method of feeding provided the Acadian colony at Port Royal with stability and self-sufficiency. The Acadians soon had more delicate grasses growing on the dry-land side of the dikes. However, they continued to harvest it on the seaward side of the levees.

Before 1755, the Acadians were self-sufficient on their marshland farms. They farmed the soil and grew abundant crops of wheat corn and other grains. They also grew hemp, which they used for rope and clothes. In their gardens, they grew vegetables for cooking. Cabbages and turnips were particularly important in their diet.

The Acadians raised cattle, sheep, and pigs—as seen from the census documents. Their pigs were kept in pens and also roamed freely in the forest.

The pigs fed on kitchen scraps and, in the winter, on waste from the cabbages and turnips. The Acadians eat a lot of pork but little beef. They preferred to keep their cattle for milk, as working animals (oxen), and for trade.

The Acadian life was hard, but it was good in many ways. They understood their environment and made it meet their needs. They could supplement their needs by hunting and fishing, as well as by picking berries and making various liquids. They brewed their beer from the branches of fir trees. They ate dried fruit and berries as well.

Those Acadians were very busy, depending on the season. Their days consisted of dike building, making hay, mending fences, and building houses. They also cut firewood, cleared wooded land, gardened, hunted, and looked after domestic animals. They made candles, soap, butter, and clothing. They also preserved food and made furniture, tools, and toys in their leisure time, depending on weather and crops.

Family Life

Acadians had large and extended families. When a son married, he would start another little village. In the census of 1671, there were 361 Acadian people. By 1686, that had almost doubled. This included thirty soldiers. By 1733, there were small Acadian villages as far away as Paradise. Acadian communities formed little family hamlets. This was sort of clan concept very common in France.

Brenda Dunn says, "The extended family, gathered at the same hearth and under the same roof, a large social group, based on several generations, with the old parents, the married children and their spouses, the youngsters of the different couples."[308] The family followed a patriarchal concept, as it was dominated by the male head of the family. The patriarch decided the destiny of each family member, directed the management of the farm, allotted the tasks, and chose his successor. These solidly established family communities that were generally linked to the possession of a domain were also found in many communities of France.

---

[308] Brenda Dunn, "Looking into Acadia."

Women's Role

The early settlements in Acadie (Champlain's expedition and others) were almost exclusively male, and it was assumed that men in these frontier establishments would intermarry with the native population. From 1632 onward, settlements became more permanent, however, and the land was brought under cultivation by entire families who were recruited to come to the new colony.

French law ensured that women were respected in their own right. Legally, men and women were both considered minors until the age of twenty-five or marriage, whichever came first.[309] Even after marriage, though, women continued to be known by their original family surname. However, the name of the married couple was that of the husband. Proof of this can be seen in the Acadian census information. The custom of Paris provided for a marriage contract to be drawn up before a couple wedded. That marriage established a community of goods between the couple. Neither husband nor wife could conduct property transactions without the other's written consent.

French law required, and marriage contracts usually stipulated, that on the death of one spouse, one half of the couple's property was to be inherited by the survivor and the other half divided among the children, male and female. This method of French inheritance meant that widows and widowers had legal autonomy. This right continued until remarriage, which in Acadia was almost inevitable. There appears to have been very few single women in Acadie, as the pressures of survival in the new land demanded partnership.

Women played important roles in a society based on family and kinship interconnections.[310] They were involved in almost every aspect of Acadian life. There was very little variety in Acadian Christian names. The majority of Acadian women were named Marie, Anne, Madeleine, Cécile, Jeanne, or Françoise. One of the reason for the repetition, was that the children often took their godparents' names.[311] Wives kept their maiden names all their lives; widows in seigneurial families were the exceptions. They were known as "Madame" rather than widow.[312]

Joseph Etienne Landry met and married Marie Josephe Bourg on January 11,

---

[309] Dunn.

[310]Dunn.

[311]"Life in Acadia Before Deportation," Acadian.org, https://www.acadian.org/history/life-acadia-deportation/.

[312]"Life in Acadia Before Deportation."

1745, in Grand-Pré/Port-Royal, Acadia. Grand-Pré is a rural community today, but in Acadia, it was a significant community. Its French name translates to "great or large meadow," and the village lies at the eastern edge of the Annapolis Valley on a peninsula jutting into the Minas Basin surrounded by vast diked farm fields. The Gaspereau and Cornwallis Rivers frame it. The community was made famous by Henry Wadsworth Longfellow's poem "Evangeline."

Port Royal is located in western Acadia and is the oldest permanent European settlement in Canada. It was founded in 1605 by the Sieur de Monts and Samuel de Champlain.[313]

Joseph Etienne and Marie Josephe had six children together; they are listed in Generation 5 as the siblings of Joseph (dit BonHomme) Alexandre Landry. The family was forcefully deported by the British in 1755 to Maryland. Joseph Etienne died on September 2, 1783, in Donaldsonville, Louisiana. Marie Josephe passed away on September 5, 1792, also in Donaldsonville.

Generation 7: Antoine Landry

Antoine Landry was born in 1660 in St. Charles des Mines, Acadia. Antoine was the only Landry who was born and died in Acadia. His son, Joseph Etienne Landry, was born in Acadia but died in Louisiana. His father, Rene Landry, was born in France and died in Acadia. Antoine married Anne Marie Thibodeau on January 11, 1745.

Anne Marie's father was Pierre Thibodeau, who was born in 1631 in France at Marans, Departement de la Charente-Maritime, Poitou-Charentes, France. Pierre died on December 26, 1704, in Port-Royal, Acadia. Anne Marie's mother was Marie Goubeilla, who was born in 1631 in France and died in 1672.

The Children of Antoine Landry

Antoine and Anne Marie had the following twelve children together;

---

[313] "Port Royal: Oldest Permanent European Settlement Canada," United States History, https://u-s-history.com/pages/h842.html.

- Marie Cecile Landry dit LeJeune was born on September 4, 1682 in Canard, Acadia, and died in 1776.
- Antoine Landry (dit LeJeune—"the lesser") was born December 4, 1683, in Grand-Pré, Acadia, and died in 1756.
- Jeanne Isabelle Elisabeth was born on June 23, 1685, in Grand-Prè and died in 1710.
- Anne (Ann) Landry was born in 1688 in Grand-Pré and died in 1767.
- François (Francis) Landry was born in 1692 in Grand-Pré and died in 1767.
- Marie Francoise (Mary Frances) Landry was born 1693 in Grand-Pré and died in 1767.
- Joseph Landry was born in 1697 in Pisiquit, Acadia and died in 1741.
- Germain Landry was born in 1697 in Acadia and died in 1770.
- Jean Baptiste Landry was born 1698 in Grand-Pré and died in 1789.
- Joseph Etienne was born 1701 in Grand-Pré and died in 1783.
- Pierre Godin Landry born 1704 in Grand-Pré and died in 1736.
- Angelique Landry was born about 1704 in Grand-Pré and died in 1773.

Antoine died on February 16, 1711 in Grand-Pré. Anne Marie Thibodeau died on February 16, 1711.

Generation 8 and 9: Rene Landry and Jean Claude Landry

A Very Confusing Part of the Landry History

There is some controversy involving the identity of Rene and Jean Claude Landry. I will attempt to write and discuss this controversy logically. Antoine Landry is often referred to in the genealogy records as *Antoine dit LeJeune Mi'kmaq*. From where does this title come? Antoine's father is always listed as Rene Landry. However, there are multiple origins for Rene Landry. These origins present a very contested issue.

Most historians (although not all) agree that Rene Landry is Rene Landry le Jeune ("the younger") and the son of the European Frenchman Jean Claude Landry, and his French wife, Marie Sale. Jean Claude Landry, the European Frenchman, was born in 1618 in La Chausse, Loudun, Vienne, France. It has been assumed that because Rene and his siblings use the family name "Landry," their father must have been Jean Claude Landry.

That is not necessarily the case, and herein lies the controversy. The Métis are a distinct group of Canadian people who developed a unique culture that grew out of Canada's fur-trading heritage. The Métis are descendants of French Canadians involved in the fur trade, and First Nations people. Métis genealogists believe that Jean Claude's omission from any census of French citizens in Acadia, and the use of only Jean Claude in the local register, is evidence that he, Jean Claude (Rene's father), was a Mi'qmak Indian and part of the Métis people rather than a white French European. His daughter, Antoinette Landry, and Rene's sister, who married Antoine Bourg (see chapter 3), were listed as such in the *Dictionnaire Genealogique des Familles Acadiennes* (part 1, published in 1999 by Stephen A. White of the Centre d'Etudes Acadiennes, Univertite de Moncton). If this is true, and the truth is not known for sure, Antoine may not have been the first Landry ancestor to be born in Acadia, and it is a mystery how Jean Claude's Métis children came to adopt the family name of Landry.

Rene Landry was one of the patronymics of the Landrys in Acadia. Rene Landry le'jeune ("the younger"), who is of Mi'qmak Indian heritage, shared that honor with another Landry of the same first name, Rene l'aine Landry of French European heritage. It is not known when both arrived in Acadia, and there is no correct information that exists as to who the parents of Rene Landry le'jeune were and from what part of France he came. Without verifiable data or evidence one way or the other, I will assume that Rene Landry is Rene l'aine Landry of French European heritage, and the rest of this chapter will proceed on that assumption.

Records show that Rene Landry was born in 1618 in La Chausse, Loudun, Vienne, France. He died in 1686 in Port-Royal, Acadia. He married Marie Bernard in 1659 in Port-Royal. Although Rene and Marie were not enumerated in the 1671 census of Acadia, we are sure that they were in Acadia, probably established in an outlying area within some distance of Port Royal. But in 1686, Rene and Marie were established at Port-Royal as enumerated by the 1686 census. The census list Rene at the age of fifty-two years, which places his birth in 1634, and Marie at age forty-one years. They had ten arpents of land in cultivation, sixteen cattle, twenty sheep, and two guns. Rene and Marie had fifteen children—eight sons and seven daughters, born between 1660 and 1693. Their female children married into other Acadian families, creating daughters-in-law with extended family names of Babin, Bellemeres, Blanchards, Brossard, Dupuis, Guilbauts, Leblanc, Melansons, Prejean, Racois, Richards, Theriault, and Thibodeaux.

The Children of Rene Landry

After Rene and Marie's sons married and started their own families, seven of their eight sons left Port-Royal to establish their families in the Minas Basin at Grand-Pré and Pigiguit. The youngest son, Charles, stayed in Port-Royal, and it is possible that he inherited his father's original Landry family site at Port-Royal. The fifteen children of Rene and Marie were married as follows:

- Abraham Landry married Marie Guilbault, probably in Port-Royal, in 1701.
- Anne Landry married René Blanchard about 1700.
- Antoine Landry married Marie Thibodeau about 1681.
- Catherine Landry married Jacques Leblanc about 1700.
- Cécile Landry married Pierre Thériault about 1685 in Grand-Pré. She married her second husband, Étienne Racois dit Derosier, on August 8, 1725.
- Charles Landry married Catherine Broussard in Port-Royal on October 29, 1708.
- Claude Landry married Marie Catherine Thibodeau about 1684. He married his second wife, Marie Babin, in 1725. His third marriage was to Jeanne Célestin dit Bellemère in Grand-Pré on May 15, 1741.
- Germain Landry married Marie Melançon about 1694.
- Jean Landry married Cécile Melançon about 1687.
- Jeanne Landry married Jean Thériault about 1692.
- Marguerite Landry married Pierre Richard about 1686.
- Marie Landry married Martin Dupuis about 1686.
- Pierre Landry married Madeleine Broussard in Port-Royal on January 7, 1704.
- René Landry married Anne Thériault about 1691.
- Charles Landry—little is known about him.

In 1755, up to the great expulsion, there was a large number of Landry ancestors in Acadia related to Rene. After they were expelled, Rene's descendants were scattered throughout the world. They were in Canada, France, New England, and Louisiana. Most of the Landrys in southwest Louisiana today can trace their lineage back to Rene.

Mi'kmaq History

Before European exploration, the Mi'kmaq people flourished in Acadia. Like their neighbors, the Maliseet, the Mi'kmaq remained allies of the French during all their activities in Acadia. The Mi'kmaq and the Maliseet subsisted on a wide variety of riverine resources, including salmon, striped bass, eel, and gaspergeau. They also used the resources along the seacoast. They participated in seal hunting and shellfish gathering. During the winter months, they hunted moose, caribou, and porcupine for subsistence.

The name *Mi'kmaq* comes from the word *ni mak*, or "my close relatives." The use of Mi'kmaq or Micmac became prevalent over the centuries. The Mi'kmaq were called various other names, depending on the European language spoken. Many believe the Mi'kmaq migrated from Northern Canada because their language has common characteristics with Cree.[314]

The Mi'kmaq were hunter-gatherers. They wore clothes made out of mammal skins, bird feathers, and fish scales to protect them against the winter cold. Tools were made from bones, tendons, and animal teeth, as well as stones and clay. Men were in charge of tool-making, whereas women were in charge of making clothes as well as baskets.

Jean Claude Landry

Jean Claude Landry was born in 1593 in La Ventrouze, Mortagne, France. He died in 1671 in Montague, Perche, France. He married Marie Salle. She was born in 1600 in Cougnes, Larochelle, Annis, France. She died in 1686 in Port-Royal, Acadia. Jean Claude Landry had the following children that we know of: Antoinette Landry, born in 1618, died in 1686 in Port-Royal, and Rene Landry, born in 1618, died in 1686 in Port-Royal.

---

[314] "Mi'kmaq History," Acadian and French Canadian Ancestral Home, http://www.acadian-home.org/Mikmaq-history.html.

CHAPTER 8

THE DEVELLE FAMILY

Plus the Jung and the d'Hebecourt Families

The Ancestors of Jeanne Louise Rose Develle
If you don't know history, you don't know anything. You
are a leaf that doesn't know it is part of a tree.

—Michael Crichton

You live as long as you are remembered.

—Russian proverb

All progress occurs because people dare to be different.

—Chinese fortune cookie quote

Process note: This chapter focuses on the Develle family—Jeanne Louise Rose Develle and her ancestors. It does not focus on her marriage to George Pratt Landry and their descendants. The previous chapter tells of that history. This chapter focuses only on Develle ancestors.

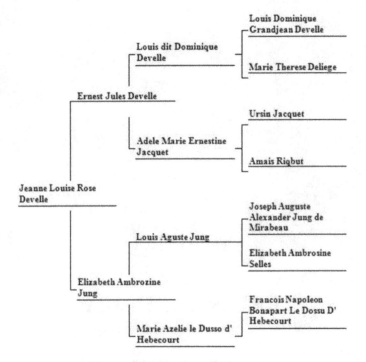

Figure 17 – The Develle Ancestors

Jeanne Louise Rose Develle

Jeanne Louise Rose Develle was born on August 25, 1903, in New Orleans. She was the daughter of Ernest Jules Develle (1852–1923) and Elizabeth Ambrozine Jung (1866–1943). Jeanne Develle is the mother of Jeanne Claire Landry Favret, who is the mother of the author's wife, Jeanne Marie Favret. Jeanne Louise was the fourth child and first daughter of her father's second marriage to Elizabeth.

The Siblings of Jeanne Louise Rose Develle

From her father's first marriage to Amelia V. Hopkins (1859–1891), who died on July 9, 1891. Jeanne had the following half-siblings:

- Louis Ernest Develle was born on January 10, 1881, in New Orleans and died on May 16, 1881, when he was just four months and six days old. The cause of death is not known. However, there were several cases of measles in the city in 1881, and two or three deaths came from the viral disease.

- James Mortimer Develle (possibly Mortimer James) was born on June 2, 1882, in New Orleans. When he was eighteen, in 1900, he was living with his family at 2604 Barracks Street in New Orleans. In 1912, he married Mary Agnes Cusack. Mary Agnes's father was James Cusack, and her mother was Ellen Matthews. In 1918, James Mortimer and Mary Agnes were living on 418 South Alexander Street in New Orleans. They had two children together: Ernest (1913–?) and Mathilde (1916–1991). Mortimer died on March 29, 1969, in New Orleans at the age of 86. Mary Agnes died on May 24, 1965.

- Marie Lucille Develle was born September 9, 1884, in New Orleans. She married Jules Albert Font on November 22, 1906. She died on December 28, 1961, at the age of 77. She and Jules had three children together: Elton William, born September 6, 1906, in New Orleans, died in 1976; Harry Simon, born August 7, 1908 in New Orleans, died in 1973; and Henrietta E'Louise Font, born March 18th, 1911, in New Orleans, died in 1981.

- Lucie Anita Develle (1886–1888) was born on October 28, 1886, in New Orleans and died on November 27, 1888, just after her second birthday.

- Cecile Ernestine Develle was born on October 21, 1888, in New Orleans and died on April 1, 1909. She married Edward Joseph Font, who was born on September 21, 1881, in New Orleans. They were married on September 16, 1908, in New Orleans. I could not find a lot about Edward Joseph. Cecile died on April 1, 1909.

Amelia died on July 9, 1891. Ernest married a second wife, Elizabeth Ambrozine Jung, who was the mother of Jeanne Louise Rose Develle, on June 3, 1893. Ernest and Elizabeth had the following children.

Albert Louis Develle Sr.

Albert Louis Develle Sr. was born on October 25, 1894, in New Orleans. He was the first male grandchild of Louis A. Jung, father of Albert's mother, Elizabeth Ambrozine. Albert inherited the artistic abilities of his Develle ancestors. He created many paintings and drawings, some of which will be displayed at the end of this chapter.

In April of 1921, when he was twenty-seven years old, he met and married Marie Noemie Bonnet. She was born on October 13, 1901. Her father was Charles A. Bonnet (1868–1917), and her mother was Mathilde Valadie (1869–1907).[315] In 1930, they were living on 1550 N. Broad Street. Living with them was Marie Noemie's sister, Elenore M Bonnet (1894). They had the following children together: Marie-Salonge (1926–), Albert L. (1927–), Charles A. (1929–), and Elizabeth (1942–2011).

Elizabeth (Betty) Develle was born on February 26, 1942, and died of pancreatic cancer on September 19, 2011, in Houston, Texas. After a brief period as a novice nun, she married Lloyd Guerin on August 16, 1969, in New Orleans. They moved to Houston for his job as a computer programmer and analyst for a major oil company. Betty and Lloyd had four children together: Marcel, Justin, Andre, and Noemie (Mimi).

There is much to know about Albert Develle. On September 15, 1978, the author, James A. Bourg Jr., sat down with Albert at his home and tape-recorded an interview. The recording was made on a Motorola cassette tape recorder (inferior quality by 2020 standards). Albert revealed much information about his life to be written in this book. This interview is available on CD. Contact the author at (504) 799-9146 if you would like a copy.

Albert was very nervous about the recording process, because he didn't want to make a mistake. In the recording, he discussed his life and his adventures as a young man, as well as his wife and children. His father, Ernest Develle, was a very tall and good man. Ernest's occupation was a cotton sampler on the cotton exchange.

Albert started school at John McDonogh School on 2426 Esplanade Avenue but finished at Isidore Newman School. He would play at the house on the corner of Esplanade Avenue and White Street with Josie Arlington's daughter. Josie (1864–February 14, 1914) was a brothel madam in the Storyville district of New Orleans. Albert started working at Woodward, Wight, and Co. (wholesale hardware) but quit.

The above is the type of information that is in the recording. Albert died in May 1979 in New Orleans at the age of eighty-five. Marie Noemie passed away on October 10, 1972.

---

[315]New Orleans, Louisiana, Birth Records Index, 1790-1915 - Marie Noemie Bonnet - Birth Date: October 13th, 1901Gravestone of the Bonnet family - shared on Ancestry - February 9th, 2017

Louis Joseph Develle

Louis Joseph Develle was born November 3, 1896, in New Orleans. While single, in 1920, he lived with his family on 2927 Grand Route St. John in New Orleans. He married Beatrice Magdalen Burg on August 18, 1920. Beatrice was born on August 14, 1898. She was the daughter of Louis J. Burg and Bertha Bagur.

Louis Joseph and Beatrice had two children together: Louis Joseph Jr. (L. J.) (1924–) and Edna (Eda) M. (1927–). Louis Joseph died on June 17, 1983, in Houston, Texas, at the age of eighty-seven. Beatrice Magdalen passed away on October 10, 1971, in Houston at the age of seventy-three.

Alexandre Develle

Alexandre Develle was born in January 1899 in New Orleans, and died on August 18, 1900, when he was nineteen months old. The reason for his death is not known, but yellow fever epidemics occurred in Louisiana until 1905. Due to the frequency and severity of these epidemics, it was often referred to as the "saffron scourge." Saffron is the material that makes the banana yellow.

Yellow fever is a disease caused by a virus, and it is transmitted by the common mosquito. When a mosquito bites a human who is infected with the virus, the mosquito becomes a carrier. It then infects the next human it bites. The name of the disease comes from the description of a patient's skin, which often becomes jaundiced. This jaundice occurs when the virus attacks the liver.[316]

Joseph Roger Develle Sr.

Joseph Roger Develle Sr. was born on March 18, 1901, in New Orleans. He met and married Mary Yvonne Chapman in October 1923. Yvonne, as she was called, was born on June 26, 1904, in New Orleans. She was the daughter of Alma M. Landry (1883–1968) and Franklin Bovard Chapman (1879–1917), born November 30, 1879, in New Orleans. Frank and Alma are the same couple discussed in chapter 7 as the brother-in-law and the much older sister of George

---

[316] George Augustin, *History of Yellow Fever* (New Orleans, LA: Searcy & Pfaff, 1909); Jo-Ann Carrigan, "Impact of Epidemic Yellow Fever on Life in Louisiana," *Louisiana History* 5:2 (Spring 1964), 5–34.

Pratt Landry (Joseph Roger's sister Jeanne's husband). Roger and Yvonne had the following children together:

- Mary Frances Develle was born December 19, 1925, in New Orleans. In April of 1943, Mary Francis married John "Johnny" Joseph Robert. Johnny Robert was the son of James Lewis Robert (1887–1961) and Mercedes Louise Cressy (1893–1961). Mary Francis died in 2013.
- Joseph Robert "Brother" Deville (1928–1988) was born March 31, 1928. He was living with his parents at 1520 Bayou Road. He met and married Helen Elizabeth Villarrubia in February of 1953. I could not find any children of Brother and Helen. They did adopt children.
- Frank C. Develle (1934–)

Roger died on November 5, 1993, in New Orleans at the age of ninety-two. Yvonne died on June 12, 1969, while on vacation with her daughter in Broward, Duval, Florida.

Jeanne Louise Rose Develle

Jeanne Louise Rose Develle was born on August 25, 1903, in New Orleans. She died on April 22, 2001, at Heritage Manor of Mandeville, (on the West Causeway approach to the Causeway Bridge) in Mandeville, Louisiana. She was buried in Metairie, Louisiana. She was ninety-seven.[317]

Jeanne married George Pratt Landry Sr. on December 28, 1921, in St. Rose de Lima Church in New Orleans. Jeanne and Pratt Sr. had three children together. These children are listed in chapter 7 as the descendants of George Pratt Landry, Generation 1.

Robert Edward (Edouard) Develle

Robert Edward (Edouard) Develle was born November 27, 1906, in New Orleans. He met Zoe Jane Carey in 1935. Zoe was born about 1909 in Lafayette, Louisiana. She was the daughter of Michael Carey and Blanche Carey, both of Lafayette. In 1930, Zoe was living in New Orleans with her family at 2919 Bruxelles Street. They were married in New Orleans in November of 1935. Robert

---

[317] "Social Security Death Index: U.S.," Brøderbund Family Archive #110, vol. 1, ed. 4.

and Zoe had the following children: Michael (Carey), born on February 22, 1939, in New Orleans, died in October 2014 in Skagit, Washington; and Robert Edward, about whom information is not known.

Robert's second wife, Gwendolen (Gwen) Rosetta Laubenthal, was the nurse and wife of his brother-in-law, Dr. Jerome Emanual Landry. Robert died on January 1, 1994, in New Orleans at the age of eighty-seven.

Ernest Jules Develle

Ernest Jules Develle was born on Friday, April 16, 1852 in New Orleans. He was the son of Louis Dominique dit Develle (1820–1885), who was born in Paris, Île-de-France, and Adele Marie Ernestine Jacquet (1826-1909), who was born on December 14, 1826, in New Orleans. Marie Ernestine's father was Ursin Bruno Jacquet, who was born in New Orleans on October 6, 1797, and died on September 4, 1830. Adele Marie Ernestine's mother was Marie Caroline Rigaud, who was born about 1799 in Santiago, Cuba.

The Siblings of Ernest Jules Develle

Louis Dominique arrived in the United States in 1829, and his naturalization was not until 1868. He married Adele Marie Ernestine Jacquet on June 20, 1849. After their first son, Ernest Jules Develle, Louis and Adele Marie Ernestine had the following children together:

- Ernestine Louise Develle was born on March 28, 1856. She met and married Henry W. Hanemann (1851–1913), who was born on August 31,1851, in New York City. Henry was involved with the cotton exchange and came to New Orleans for the cotton business. Since Louis Dominique was in the cotton business, Henry W. met Ernestine through that business association.

Henry's father was John T. Hanemann. His January 29, 1887, obituary in the *American Register* newspaper read as follows: "John T. Hanemann, who for forty years was prominent in the New York cotton trade, and a member of the Cotton Exchange, of which he was one of the founders, died January 8th, at the age of sixty-seven years. He went to New York from New Orleans in 1865. Since his retirement, in 1874, he had devoted his time to charitable work, and at his heath was President of the German Hospital in New York, and a large hospital in Hamburg, Germany."

Henry and Ernestine were married on May 15, 1879 (during post–Civil War reconstruction) and almost immediately moved back to Manhattan. They had the following children together: John Theodore Hanemann Sr., born June 14,1880 in New York, died in1960; Edward Louis Hanemann (1883–1940), born July 6, 1883 in New York, died in 1940; and Henry William Hanemann (1895–1968), born August 8, 1895, in New York, died in 1968.

Henry W. died on September 15, 1913, in New York City. Ernestine Louise passed away on January 6, 1922, in New York City. She was buried in Green-Wood Cemetery, lot 33943, section 123, Brooklyn, New York, on January 9, 1922, with her husband.

- Louise Marie Develle (1858–1924) was born on May 15, 1858, in New Orleans. She married Victor Joseph Gueringer (1851–1880) on October 6, 1877, in New Orleans. He died on April 2, 1880, at the age of twenty-nine. His 1925 passport application describes his age at twenty-two years old; his height at 5 feet 8 inches; his eyes as greenish-blue; his mouth as small; his chin as rounded; his face as long; and his hair and complexion as dark. His father was Ernest J. Gueringer, born in Louisiana, and his mother was Aurora (surname unknown), born in Cuba. As best as can be determined, Louise and Victor had no children.
- Marie Therese Mathilde Develle was born on December 16, 1860. She died on January 28, 1931, in West Carroll Parish, Louisiana.
- Marie Hermine Develle was born on January 2, 1862, in New Orleans. She married Joseph Louis Lambert Bercier (1840–1895) on February 11, 1882, in New Orleans at the age of twenty. Joseph Louis, born September 25, 1840, in New Orleans, was forty-two years old. There is much confusion regarding the history of Joseph Louis.

Marie died on December 19, 1883, in New Orleans, just twenty-two months after their marriage, when she was twenty-one years old. The two had no children. Joseph Louis went on to marry Elene Eugenie Elizabeth Jouet, who was born on October 2, 1859, in New Orleans. The wedding was on July 20, 1889, in New Orleans. Joseph Louis and Elene Eugenie Elizabeth had three children together, including Philippe Herwig Lambert Bercier, born September 25, 1890, in New Orleans. Phillipe died on May 15, 1891, just eight months later.

After Elene's death, Joseph Louis married Alice Morlot (1854–1887). Joseph Louis died on March 19, 1895, in New Orleans.

- Marie Blanche Develle was born on January 2, 1864, in New Orleans. She died on November 28, 1959, in Covington, Louisiana. She married Martin Paul Julian Jr. (1860–1936) on September 18, 1886, in New Orleans. They had the following children together:
  - o Henry Edward Joseph Julian was born on June 29, 1887, in New Orleans, and died in 1972.
  - o Marie Blanche Julian was born on February 3, 1889, in New Orleans. She died on February 15, 1892, when only three years old.
  - o Martin Paul Julian III was born on October 11, 1890 in New Orleans and died in 1985.
  - o Edward William Julian was born on February 8, 1894, in New Orleans and died in 1976.

Martin Paul died on November 21, 1936, in New Orleans. Marie Blanche passed on November 28, 1959, in Covington. She is buried in New Orleans.

- Jeanne Develle was born on February 7, 1867, in New Orleans. She married William B. Smith (1870–1937) on October 9, 1907, in Seattle, Washington. They may have had a daughter together, but the child's last name was not Smith, so this source is very dubious. The child was Jean Develle Foster (1912–1985), born January 23, 1912, in Port Townsend, Jefferson County, Washington.

William B. Smith died on July 20, 1937, in Port Townsend, Jefferson, Washington. Jeanne Develle died on April 1, 1946, in Sequim, Clallam, Washington.

- Henri Louis Develle was born on October 4, 1870, in New Orleans. He met and married Aimee Gazave (1879–1966) on June 6, 1906, in New Orleans. They had the following children together: Melba Louise, born March 11, 1907, in New Orleans, died in 1993; Aimee Marie, born June

19, 1910, in New Orleans, died in 1986; and Henri Louis, born October 11, 1915, in New Orleans, died in 1974.

Henri Louis Develle died on June 18, 1952, at the age of eighty-one in New Orleans. Aimee passed away on November 12, 1966, in New Orleans.

Life in New Orleans Before and During the Civil War (1850–1870)

During the period when the family of Louis Dominique Develle was growing and developing in New Orleans, there was a sizeable civic issue that had a significant effect on their life: the US Civil War and its aftermath. Ernest Jules was born in 1852, and by 1850, conflict between the North and the South was inevitable. Neither side—Northern pro-Union slavery-free states or Southern states-rights pro-slavery states—was willing to compromise over the social, economic, and political issues that had been building up over many decades and ultimately contributed to the war's outbreak.

The city of New Orleans, on the bend at the mouth of the Mississippi, was founded by Jean Baptiste Le Moyne, Sieur de Bienville, in 1718. It was named for the regent of France, Philippe II, Duc d'Orleans. It was a French colony from its founding until 1763, when it was ceded to Spain after the French and Indian War. Although governed by Spain, the city remained a stronghold of French language and culture.

New Orleans has an extensive and very diverse history. People from all parts of the world came together to share their cultures: Africans, Indians, and European settlers. Encouraged by its French ancestry, this strategy for producing an influential culture in a problematic place marked New Orleans as different and unique. It evolved as a distinctive cultural gateway to North America. People from Europe and Africa melded their lives and customs with those of the New World. This melding resulted in a way of life that was very different from the culture created in the English colonies of North America.

New Orleans' Creole population (those with ancestry rooted in the city's colonial era) ensured many differences from the rest of the country. English as a language was shared with the French; Catholicism was pervasive as Protestantism was scorned; and Catholic schools were the norm as opposed to public education. New Orleans remained far removed geographically and culturally from the way of life of the English colonies of Virginia and Massachusetts.

Although river and ocean transportation connected French Louisiana to the rest of the country, New Orleans was steeped in its particular way of living. Although a real hub of American commerce, it remained a strange place in the Southern history of America. Until the 1850s, a more significant number of migrants arrived in the city from Northern states than from the other states of the South.

The city's culture became even more complicated as more foreign immigrants than Americans came to take up residence there almost throughout the nineteenth century. Although French culture dominated, the largest waves of immigrants were Irish and German. In some neighborhoods, because of immigrants, the language dialects were more like that of Brooklyn or Chicago.

In the mid-nineteenth century, Irish and Germans made New Orleans one of the leading immigration ports in the country, second only to New York. New Orleans was the first city in America to have a significant population of Italians, Greeks, Croatians, and Filipinos. African Americans comprise about half of the population, even to the present.

Most Africans came to the city as slaves directly from the West African coast and not through Latin America. They developed complicated relations with both the Native American and European populations. Their descendants born in Louisiana were called Creoles. The Spanish governors reached out to the black community for support with the French settlers. They allowed many slaves to buy their freedom. These free blacks, along with Creole slaves, created the earliest black urban community in the country.

Immigrants thought the Creoles were quite exotic and different, as the black Creoles were Catholic, they spoke French or a version of it, and they lived a different lifestyle. Different kinds of people resolved their differences by living in different areas of the city. Eventually, the European immigrants concentrated in new uptown neighborhoods.

New Orleans, until the Civil War, was a city of dramatic growth. In the 1850 census, it was the sixth largest city in the United States, with a population of 168,675. It was the only city in the South that had a population of 100,000 people. By 1840, New Orleans had the largest slave market in the country. This market accounted for a significant portion of its wealth. Before the Civil War, 670,000 slaves moved from other slave states to the Deep South. It is estimated that slave trading made up 13.5 percent of the city's GDP, generating tens of billions of dollars through the years.[318]

New Orleans, before the Civil War, was the economic heart of the South. Cotton contributed half of the estimated $156 million (in 1857 dollars). Cotton was followed by sugar and tobacco exports. Some 50 percent of all the cotton grown in the US for export came through the port of New Orleans (1.4 million bales). This volume was three times more than at the second-leading port of Mobile. The city also had many federal government buildings, including the New Orleans Mint and the US Customs House.[319]

New Orleans became another place where the river, the bayous, and the sea intersected as an open transportation roadway. The people turned swamplands into a refuge for the diverse, the independent, the defiant, and the creative "unimportant" people. They tore down all the barriers of language and culture among peoples throughout the world and continued to sing to them of the joy and triumph of the human spirit. People in New Orleans lived in peace and, to a certain extent, harmony.

The tensions that led to the Civil War had been building for years. But the months following the election of Abraham Lincoln solidified the conflict. It started with the Confederate capture of Fort Sumter in April 1861. Tensions and divisions built between citizens of the slave states of the Southern United States and citizens of the free states of the Northern United States over the topic of slavery. In the many decades between the Revolutionary War and the Civil War, such divisions had become increasingly irreconcilable and contentious.[320]

On January 26, 1861, the Louisiana Secession Convention was called to order. Judge James G. Taliaferro of Catahoula Parish was the most outspoken opponent of secession. He warned that withdrawal threatened the interests and destiny of Louisiana, as he predicted war and ruin for the State. In spite of his warning, the convention adopted the ordinance of secession with a vote of 113 to 17 votes (or 87 percent in favor).

The Develle family must have been conflicted regarding secession, just like the rest of the city. The people had not been so much in favor of secession. When delegates to the Louisiana convention were elected statewide, the vote had been 54 percent for delegates in favor of leaving the Union and 46 percent for those

---

[318]Walter Johnson, *Soul by Soul: Life Inside the Antebellum Slave Market*, 2–6.

[319]*Harper's Weekly: A Journal of Civilization*, February 16, 1861.

[320]James M. McPherson, *Battle Cry of Freedom: The Civil War Era* (1988), chapters 1–8.

against. In the New Orleans vote of the people, the majority in favor of secession had been only about four hundred votes.[321] In 1860, the population of the city of New Orleans was 168,675, so 400/168675 means that only 0.2 percent of the population favored secession over those who did not support leaving the Union.

The Louisiana governor, who had not voted for secession at the convention, signed the ordinance out of duty to his native state. Many patriotic men who did not believe in it supported secession after the ordinance was signed on January 26, 1861. On February 18, 1861, President Jefferson Davis delivered his inaugural address. He explained the position taken by the seceding states. He denied that their act was revolutionary and declared that they had merely asserted the rights which the Declaration of Independence of July 4, 1776, defined to be inalienable.[322]

On March 4, 1861, Lincoln was inaugurated as president. In his address, he asserted his belief in the perpetuity of the Union. Once formed, the United States had no end. Three Confederate commissioners—John Forsyth, of Alabama, Martin J. Crawford of Georgia, and Andre Bienvenu Roman of Louisiana—had been sent to Washington to try to negotiate a peaceable resolution. After some delay, on April 8, Lincoln refused to recognize them.

On April 12,1861, General G. T. Beauregard opened fire on Fort Sumter, and the terrible Civil War began.[323] Although the shooting started in 1861, the Civil War really started when the founding fathers failed to deal with the issue of slavery when they wrote the Constitution. The fighting had only been delayed eighty-five years.

On April 21, Louisiana Governor Moore called for five thousand troops, plus three thousand called for by the president of the Confederate States. On that occasion, the governor addressed the people of Louisiana, saying the following:

Rise, then, people of Louisiana, in your might in defense of your dearest rights, and drive back this insolent barbaric foe. Like your brave ancestry, resolve to conquer or perish in the effort, and the flag of usurpation will never fly over Southern soil. Rally, then, to the proclamation which I now make on the requisition of the Confederate Government.[324]

---

[321]Alcee Fortier, *A History of Louisiana, Volume IV: The American Domination* (Gouple & Co of Paris, 1904).

[322]Fortier.

[323]Fortier.

[324]"A History of Louisiana," Internet Archive, https://archive.org/stream/historyoflouisia04fortuoft/historyoflouisia04fortuoft_djvu.txt.

On April 29, Governor Moore viewed the troops in New Orleans. Five thousand men were in arms. On May 21, four batteries of artillery left for Virginia. This organization was represented in the army of Northern Virginia by four gun batteries, and in the army of Tennessee by the fifth battery.

On June 25, Bishop Leonidas Polk of Louisiana, was commissioned a major general in the army of the Confederate States.[325] The military enthusiasm continued to grow in Louisiana, and the state had recruited 60,726 troops in and out of the state. Louisiana also had a naval force, and on October 12, 1861, Commodore George H. Hollins led an attack on the federal fleet at Southwest Pass with a ram, fire-rafts, and steamers, and inflicted considerable damage. The people of New Orleans were pleased by Hollins's success. They felt sure the federal fleet would never be able to sail up the river. A few months later, however, Union Admiral David G. Farragut did just that, in what then seemed to be an impossible feat.

The Capture of New Orleans

The Confederates generated a naval fleet of rams and ironclads. Fort Jackson was on the west bank of the river below the city; Fort St. Philip was on the east bank below the city. Both were significantly strengthened to defend New Orleans. Across the river, near Fort Jackson, a log and chain protection had been put across the river to stop any ships. Each of the forts had a garrison of 700 men, and the Confederates had 126 canons in the forts and 26 guns in their naval fleet, which consisted of 12 vessels. They also had the ram *Manassas* and the ironclad *Louisiana*, which was not completed at that time. The ironclad *Louisiana* had to be secured to the riverbank during the battle with the federal fleet. The guns on the Union side numbered 302, including those on their mortar-flotilla.

The Union fleet crossed the bar at the mouth of the river with great difficulty. On April 16, Union Commander Porter started bombarding the forts from the mortar-flotilla. The Confederates replied with heavy fire. The bombardment lasted five days.

Then Farragut decided on a bold move: he was going to "run the gantlet" of the forts. On April 24, before daybreak, he began his attack. His fleet used three divisions: the first was under the command of Captain Theodorus Bailey, the second under Flag-Officer Farragut, and the third under Captain Henry H. Bell.

---

[325]"A History of Louisiana."

The wood and chain cable in the river had been separated on April 20, and the obstructions presented little difficulty.

Captain Bailey's division succeeded in passing the forts and met with resistance from the Confederate fleet. Especially heroic was the conduct of Captain Beverley Kennon, commander of the Confederate gunboat. He attacked the Union ship, *Varuna*, and fired at her through the bow of his boat. The ram *Stonewall Jackson* then struck the *Varuna*, and she sank. The disabled *Governor Moore*, surrounded by five US ships, was burned by her commander at the riverbank, her colors still flying. Captain Kennon was taken prisoner and later kept in solitary confinement on board the Colorado, in close imprisonment on board the Rhode Island, and at Fort Warren for three months, on account of specific false reports.

Farragut silenced the Chalmette batteries quickly on both sides of the river and reached New Orleans on April 25. He had accomplished one of the most seemingly impossible feats that history can record: passing two strong forts and immediately afterward destroying a hostile fleet. The British, during the War of 1812, had not been able to pass a single fort on the Mississippi. By his capture of New Orleans, Farragut acquired renown that has placed him on a level with the most celebrated naval commanders. He was presented as a conqueror of the city where he had spent time as a child.

On Thursday, April 24, the commander of the Confederate army in New Orleans gave orders to destroy cargo on the banks of the city. News of Farragut's success had reached the city, and the work of destruction had to be done quickly before the arrival of the Union fleet. Everything that could be used by the Union Army was destroyed by burning. Containers of sugar and barrels of molasses were broken and destroyed. They burned all boats in the harbor and allowed them to float down the river till they sank.

Farragut reached the city on April 25. The scene was grand and weird. The river was ablaze with burning boats. Vast columns of smoke arose from the shore, the rain fell in torrents, and an immense crowd of people had gathered on the levee, hurling insults at the Union soldiers. Farragut's boats anchored in front of the city mid-afternoon on April 25, 1862, and immediately, he sent Captain Bailey to demand the mayor surrender New Orleans. Lieutenant George H. Perkins accompanied Captain Bailey. It was a dangerous journey from the fleet to City Hall, as they were surrounded by a multitude of angry men. But they arrived safely at their destination, and the captain told the mayor he had been sent to demand the city's surrender.

Mayor Monroe replied that he had no authority to comply. That required the military commander of the city. So they sent for General Lovell, who said that he would not surrender. He would withdraw his troops to avoid the shelling of New Orleans, and he would let the city authorities act as they thought proper. The matter was submitted to the City Council, and the two Union officers left. The city soon surrendered.

New Orleans was captured without a bombardment of the city itself. It was not destroyed as many other confederate towns of the American South were in the war. It kept its historical flavor, with a wealth of structures built beyond the boundaries of the French Quarter. After the surrender, the city was restored to the Union. It had been in Confederate hands for 455 days.

As the people feared, the Civil War changed the world to which they were accustomed. Union forces, led by General Benjamin F. Butler, occupied the city. Later, the residents called him "Beast" Butler because of his actions and orders. After Southern women harassed Union troops, he warned that if it happened again, his men would treat such "ladies" as those "plying their avocation in the streets," implying that they would handle the women as prostitutes. His reputation as the "beast" was solidified. He also was called "Spoons" Butler because of his troops looting the silverware in the city.

Butler stopped the teaching of the French language in city schools. After the war, in 1868, federal representatives further strengthened the English-only policy. With a large number of English speakers, that language had become dominant in business and government in the city. French usage had begun to fade by the end of the nineteenth century. French was also fading in its dominance because of Irish, Italian, and German immigrants.[326] As late as 1902, "one-fourth of the city's population still spoke French in ordinary daily intercourse. Another three-fourths could still understand the language. And as late as 1945, just outside the city, many elderly Creole women spoke no English."[327] The last major French-language newspaper, *L'Abeille de la Nouvelle-Orléans* (New Orleans Bee), ceased publication on December 27, 1923, after ninety-six years.[328]

---

[326] Jay Gitlin, *The Bourgeois Frontier: French Towns, French Traders, and American Expansion* (Yale University Press, 2009), 159.

[327] Robert Tallant and Lyle Saxon, *Gumbo Ya-Ya: Folk Tales of Louisiana* (Louisiana Library Commission: 1945), 178.

[328] Carl A. Brasseaux, *French, Cajun, Creole, Houma: A Primer on Francophone Louisiana* (LSU Press, 2005), 32.

New Orleans is the largest city in the United States ever occupied by enemy forces for an extended period. The city was threatened with possible Confederate recapture even as late as 1864. Gerald M. Capers finds that the occupation orders of General Benjamin F. Butler were successful. Butler's policies were by no means as vicious as legend would have it. Banks at first reversed Butler's strict rules but eventually became less lenient. Banks established a civil government under Lincoln's orders, but Congress refused to recognize the civilian government. A Reconstruction government was imposed at the end of the war.[329]

Capers states life for the average resident of New Orleans was better during the occupation than it was in other cities still in Confederate control. The relative economic decline in the city had begun in the 1850s. New Orleans, however, enjoyed a war boom during the last two years of the war.

Ernest Develle Continued

Ernest Develle was born in New Orleans into a family with Parisian French ancestry. He was the son of Louis dit Dominique Develle and Adele Marie Ernestine Jacquet. He was born on April 16, 1852, and he died on June 19, 1923, in New Orleans. He married Elizabeth Ambrozine Jung on June 3, 1893, in New Orleans.

Ernest spent his entire life in the Crescent City surrounded by the events leading up to the Civil War and the events during and following that war. New Orleans, in the years preceding the Civil War, was a city of considerable growth. The 1850 census showed that New Orleans was the sixth largest city in the United States, with a population reported as 168,675.

Ernest's father, Louis dit Dominique Develle of Parisian nobility, was born in Paris, France, in 1820. Ernest's mother, Adele Marie Ernestine Jacquet, was born in New Orleans but also came from rich French ancestry. She was the daughter of Ursin Jacquet and Amaris Riqbut.

Louisiana rejoined the Union in 1868. Its 1868 Constitution granted suffrage to all men. Both races were elected to local and state offices. In 1872, Lieutenant Governor P. B. S. Pinchback followed Henry Clay Warmouth as governor of Louisiana. He was the first black governor of a US state. He was the last African

---

[329] Gerald M. Capers, Tulane University, *Occupied City: New Orleans Under the Federals 1862–1865* (University Press of Kentucky).

American to lead a US state until Douglas Wilder's election in Virginia 117 years later.

During Reconstruction, New Orleans has a race riot in 1866 called the Mechanics Institute riot. The city operated a successful racially integrated public-school system. Trade for the port city was negatively affected due to damage to levees along the Mississippi River. The government tried to correct problems with the levees, but it took a lot of effort and money. White descendants of French immigrants remained an intact and vibrant community. They were maintaining instruction in French in two of the city's four school districts.[330]

On September 14, 1874, a mob led by the White League defeated the integrated Republican metropolitan police and their allies in a downtown battle. The White League forced a temporary flight of the William P. Kellogg government, installing John McEnery as governor of Louisiana. After United States troops restored order, Kellogg and the Republican administration were reinstated to power. Segregationists celebrated the short-lived triumph of the White League. They called it a victory for "white supremacy." They called the conflict the Battle of Liberty Place. A monument to memorialize the event was placed near the foot of Canal Street. This monument was taken down on April 24, 2017. Unfortunately, the removal occurred at the same time that three southern states—Alabama, Mississippi, and Georgia—observed Confederate Memorial Day.

Not until President Hayes withdrew the troops in 1877 and the Packard government fell did the Democrats hold control of the state and city. The city had significant flooding in 1882. The city hosted the 1884 World's Fair. It was called the "World Cotton Centennial." The fair was a financial failure, but the festival is generally considered the beginning of the city's tourist business. An electric lighting system was introduced to the city in 1886. Limited use of electric lights in a few areas of town had preceded this by a few years.

Ernest married his first wife, Amelia Victoria Hopkins, on a cold Thursday, January 3, 1880. Amelia was born in 1859 in New Orleans. She was twenty-one years old at the time of the marriage. Amelia was the daughter of James A. Hopkins and Adalise LeBreton. Not much is known about James Hopkins except that he was probably of Irish ancestry. Adalise, was born on July 23, 1829, in Louisiana. She grew up on the west bank of the river in Jefferson with her father, François Joseph Lebreton, who was born in 1800 in New Orleans and died there

---

[330] Jay Gitlin, *The Bourgeois Frontier: French Towns, French Traders, and American Expansion* (Yale University Press), 166.

on June 20, 1869; her mother, Victoire Aimee Amanda de la Barre, who was born on May 2, 1807, in Louisiana and died in 1853; and her five siblings: Charlotte, Eliska, Cecilia, Alcie, and Leonie. Joseph and Victoire were married on April 19, 1827, in New Orleans.

The children of Ernest and Amelia are described in more detail earlier in this chapter in the section on Jeanne Rose Develle. Amelia died on July 9, 1891, in New Orleans. I have no information regarding the cause of her death. It is not because of childbirth, as her last child was born years earlier in 1888. However, New Orleans was constantly struggling with disease breakouts such as yellow fever, typhus, smallpox, and cholera.

Epidemics of the nineteenth century were more lethal because they had fewer of the medical advances that made twentieth-century epidemics much rarer. Viruses and bacteria were known in the eighteenth century, but it was not until the late nineteenth century that the knowledge was applied to health. Experiments by Spallanzani and Pasteur disproved spontaneous generation, allowing germ theory to take hold. Robert Koch discovered that microbes cause the transmission of disease. Throughout the nineteenth century, there was only the most basic, common-sense understanding of the causes, prevention, and treatment of epidemic diseases . The late nineteenth century saw the beginning of widespread use of vaccines.[331]

In 1891, Ernest was living at 2604 Barracks Street. He had three living children out of the five born from his first wife, Amelia; all were under ten years of age. Ernest was working as a cotton sampler at the cotton exchange. He was a tall man with a mustache. He worked for a friend of his named Lehmann. Ernest went on strike, so he was fired.

He needed to find a job and a mother for his children. He lived just one and a half blocks from the home of Louis Aguste Jung, a wealthy energy baron. Louis Jung lived in a vast mansion at 2623 Esplanade Avenue. He was the head of his own company, Jung and Sons Coal Co. Jung would soon sell his company to the Texas Oil Company (Texaco). He would become the first vice president of Texaco in Louisiana. Louis A. Jung's wife was Marie Azelie le Dusso d'Hebecourt. The

---

[331] A. M. Stern, H. Markel, "The History of Vaccines and Immunization: Familiar Patterns, New Challenges," *Health Aff.* (Millwood, 2005), 24:3, 611–21. doi:10.1377/hlthaff.24.3.611, PMID 15886151; Derrick Baxby, "Edward Jenner's Inquiry: A Bicentenary Analysis," *Vaccine* 17:4 (1999), 301–07.

history of the Jung family and the d'Hebecourt family is fascinating, and both will be explored later in this chapter.

Louis's oldest daughter, Elizabeth Ambrozine Jung, was twenty-seven when she met Ernest. Ambrozine, or "Azine," as she was called, was getting a bit old for the age that women usually married at that time in history. The reason for this, we do not know. Ernest was forty-one years old in 1893 and a bit desperate to be married. Possibly, so was Ambrozine. Ernest was not nearly as affluent as Louis Aguste Jung, but Louis allowed Ernest to court his oldest daughter, and Ernest eventually married Ambrozine on June 3, 1893.

The children of Ernest and Ambrozine are listed in detail earlier in this chapter in the section on Jeanne Rose Develle. Ernest Jules Develle died on June 19, 1923, in New Orleans. He was living at 2531 Columbus Street, but in 1920, he was living at 2927 Grand Route St. John. He died at seventy-one years of age. Ernest's obituary in the *Times-Picayune* on Wednesday, June 20, 1923, read as follows:

On Thursday, June 19, 1923, at 6:10 P.M. age 71 years two months, Ernest J. Develle, beloved husband of Ambrosine Jung a native of this city, Relatives, and friends of the family and acquaintances are respectfully invited to attend the funeral, which will take place this Wednesday afternoon at 4 o'clock from his home at 2927 Grand Route St. John between White and Dupree Sts. Internment in St. Louis Cemetery #3, Esplanade Ave.

His wife, Ambrozine, died on June 28, 1943, at the home of her daughter, Jeanne Rose Develle Landry at 1516 Bayou Rd. (Gently Boulevard). She was seventy-six years of age when she died.

Louis dit Dominique Develle

Louis dit Dominique Develle was born in Paris, France, in 1820. He was the son of Louis Dominique Grandjean Develle (1799–1868). His mother was Marie Therese Deliege (1797–1867). Marie Therese was the daughter of Ursin Jacquet from the town of Spa, located in Belgium, in the province of Liège. The city is situated in a valley in the Ardennes Mountains, thirty-five kilometers southeast of Liège, and forty-five kilometers southwest of Aachen. The Ardennes forest is where the Battle of the Bulge took place in December of 1944. Marie Therese's mother was Marie Caroline Ragusa, who was born in San Diego, Cuba. Louis dit Dominique came to New Orleans with his parents in 1829 because the Theatre d'Orleans hired his father as a set designer for the French Opera. Besides painting, he worked as a cotton broker in the cotton exchange.

Cotton investors created the New Orleans Cotton Exchange. At a point in history, one-third of all cotton in the United States came through the port of New Orleans for export. The Exchange sought to end highly speculative cotton pricing by creating a trading office where information about market conditions and prices could be obtained. The Exchange also established standards for the classification of cotton and facilitated payments between buyers and sellers.

There was concern in New York that the trading of cotton in New York was not advantageous for sellers. Traders were eager to modernize their operations.[332] New Orleans merchants agreed to form their own exchange. The formal New Orleans Cotton Exchange opened for business on February 20, 1871 at the corner of Gravier and Carondelet Streets. This was an area that had already had a lot of activity for cotton merchants for some time.[333]

The Exchange was a landmark in developing advanced techniques for gathering information about various aspects of the cotton market.[334] Colonel Henry G. Hester led the exchange for many years as its secretary. The Exchange compiled reports and then transmitted them by telegraph to New York. This report transmission was a novel method at the time. Hester also introduced the practice trading in futures to the Cotton Exchange. These advanced methods of doing business were a great benefit to the local cotton market. Because of these practices, New Orleans again became the primary cotton market of the world and one of the leading futures market, outranked only by Liverpool and New York.[335]

Louis dit Dominique married Adele Marie Ernestine Jacquet (Ernestine) on June 20, 1849, it St. Louis Cathedral in New Orleans. Adele was born in December of 1827 in New Orleans. She was the daughter of Ursin Jacquet and Amais Riqbut. Louis dit Dominique and Ernestine's children are listed in detail earlier in this chapter in the section on Ernest Jules Develle. Ernestine was pregnant when this

---

[332] "Commercial and Financial Review," the *Daily Picayune*, New Orleans (November 29, 1870).

[333] "Commercial and Financial Review," the *Daily Picayune*, New Orleans (February 21, 1871).

[334] Richard Campanella, *Time and Place in New Orleans: Past Geographies in the Present Day* (Gretna: Pelican, 2002), 128–31.

[335] Ellis L. Tuffly, "The New Orleans Cotton Exchange: The Formative Years, 1871–1880," *The Journal of Southern History*, 39:4 (November 1973), 545–64, doi:10.2307/2205967.

summer of 1870 census was taken as her ninth child, Henri (Henry) Louis Develle, was born on October 4, 1870.

Louis dit Dominique died on May 9, 1885, in New Orleans. The following obituary for Louis Dominique Develle ran in the *Daily Picayune* on May 10, 1885, page 8, column 3:

On Saturday, May 9, 1885, at 9:15 AM Louis Dominique Develle age 65 a native of Paris France and a resident of New Orleans for 55 years, Relatives and friends are respectfully invited to attend his funeral, corner of Marais and Columbus Streets on Sunday morning at 10 o'clock.

Marie Therese Deliege died on January 17, 1909, in New Orleans. The following obituary ran in the *Daily Picayune* on January 18, 1909:

Develle - On Sunday, January 17, 1909, at 5:30 PM, Ernestine M. Jacquet, widow of the late Louis D. Develle, age 81 years a native and life-long resident of the city. The funeral will take place from her late residence # 2539 Ursuline Ave. at 4 PM today. Internment St. Louis #3.[336]

Louis was a soldier in the Confederate Army during the Civil War (1861–1865). In 1880, he was sixty years old and still working on the cotton exchange. He was living on 2226 Ursuline Avenue at that time.

Louis Dominique Grandjean Develle

Louis Dominique Grandjean Develle was born in 1799 in Paris, France. He was an artist who was actively painting in New Orleans from his arrival in 1829 until his death in 1868. Louis was known for many things, but he is best known for his set designs at the Theatre d'Orleans. The theater was formally located on Orleans Street between Royal Street and Bourbon Street in the French Quarter. Sophisticated French Creoles widely attended the theater. The North American premieres of many French operas were often performed in the Theatre d'Orleans, with top European performers and sets designed by Develle.[337]

Louis was named after his father, also a Louis. For reasons that are not known at this time, his dad changed the family name from Filbert to Develle. Louis Dominique was a student of Pierre-Luc-Charles Ciceri, a famous Parisian designer of opera sets. One of Develle's projects was the decoration of the Rheims Cathedral for the 1824 consecration of French King Charles X. He then worked

---

[336.] Dominique Develle's Obituary, *Daily Picayune*, May 10, 1885, page 8, column 3.

[337.] "Louis Develle," 64 Parishes, https://64parishes.org/entry/louis-develle.

as a set designer in Le Havre for three years. In 1829, Develle arrived in New Orleans, having accepted a position as a set designer at the Theatre d'Orleans where they performed French opera.

At the height of operatic performance in New Orleans, operas were performed in French. This height was between the 1830s and 1840s. Both French dramas and operas were shown primarily at the Theatre d'Orleans, while the St. Charles Opera House staged Italian opera. The strong repertoire of the Theatre d'Orleans included Halevy's *La Juive*, Meyerbeer's *Les Huguenots*, a French version of Verdi's *Jerusalem*, and others like Robert le Diable's *Les Trios Mousquetaires* and *Les Martyrs* were all performed in front of Develle's set designs. They were described as "splendid" and "magnificent" in the local press, with draftsmanship compared to that of French artist Jacques-Louis David. They were noted for their precise portrayal of perspective.

In the nineteen seasons between 1840 and 1860, the theater produced 109 operas by thirty-five different major and minor composers, comprising 1,550 performances. Within this rich musical milieu, Louis Dominique Grandjean Develle's sets, like the performers, consistently received top billing, and in 1846 they prompted two curtain calls.

Develle was very famous, but he was also very modest. Louis was frequently honored at benefits, customary during this period, which allowed him to return to France during the off-season, as did many wealthy New Orleanians. The New Orleans opera troupe and the sets they used were occasionally transported to New York and Philadelphia in the summer. This introduced French opera to the people in those cities.

Develle also worked as an artistic painter and a painting teacher. His best-known pupil was Leon Pomarede. In 1842, Louis Dominique decorated the inside of the St. Louis Cathedral in New Orleans with his art. This art was done for the memorial Mass in honor of Fernand, the eldest son of Louis Philippe, king of France. Also, he collaborated with Parisian artist Auguste de Chatillon to depict the battle of Resaca de la Palma during the Mexican-American War. The two artists reportedly set their easels at the battle front, capturing the ferocity of combat. This painting was then completed at Destrehan Plantation. It was unveiled at the St. Louis Hotel ballroom in New Orleans in 1847 and was reportedly sold to a patron in Washington, DC. In 1850, Louis' panorama of *Jerusalem* was shown for a year at the Theatre d'Orleans.

Louis Dominique died in 1868. Today, at the Historic New Orleans Collection,

Develle's painting *The Red Store* hints at the vibrant scenery that graced the Theatre d'Orleans during the golden age of opera in the city.[338]

Louis Dominique Grandjean Develle married Marie Therese Deliege Jacquet. Her father was Ursin Jacquet, and her mother was Marie Caroline Ragusa. She was born in 1797 in Spa, Belgium. Louis and Marie Therese had the following children together: Louis dit Dominique Develle, born 1920 in Paris, died 1885; Denise Marie Louise Develle, born 1825 in Paris, died 1895; and Louise Hypolite Develle, born 1830 in New Orleans, died June 6, 1885.

Louis Dominique Grandjean Develle died on June 22, 1868, in New Orleans when he was sixteen years old. His obituary was in the *New Orleans Bee* newspaper on June 24, 1868, page 1, column 6, and page1, column 2. His wife, Marie Therese Deliege, died on October 18, 1867, in Mandeville, Louisiana.

Dominique Louis (Armand) Greadjean Filbert dit Develle.

Dominique Louis (Armand) Greadjean Filbert dit Develle was born in 1769 in Paris. He is the son of Louis Filbert dit Develle and Anne Lecronier. He lived in Paris from his birth until he came to Louisiana as part of his son's getting a commission to paint for the French opera in New Orleans in 1827. He lived through the time before and during the French Revolution.

The French Revolution was a period of vast upheaval in France and its colonies, both socially and politically. It began in 1789 and continued for ten years until 1799. The Revolution was the cause of many changes in France. The French monarchy was overthrown, and a republic was established. There was a period of violent political turmoil, culminating in a dictatorship under Napoleon

Liberal and radical ideas inspired the revolution. It profoundly altered the course of modern history by starting a global decline of absolute monarchies. Liberal republics and democracies replaced these monarchies.[339] Louis Dominique lived through this period of great turmoil.

The causes of the French Revolution are complex. It resulted from two crises in government during the 1750s–80s—one constitutional and one financial. The financial crisis provided the tipping point in 1789. During this economic crisis, desperate action by government ministers backfired and unleashed a revolution

---

[338.] Maclyc Le Bourgeois, *The Historic New Orleans Collection*, December 10, 2013, last updated February 25, 2014.

[339]"French Revolution," *Wikipedia*, https://en.wikipedia.org/wiki/French_Revolution.

against the wealthy, detached aristocrats who enjoyed wealth and privilege while divorced from the suffering of the French people who had to pay for it.

The idea of a government and king operating with constitutional checks and balances had grown to be vitally important in France. Parliament considered itself the vital check on the king's power. In 1771, the Paris parliament refused to work with Chancellor Maupeou. The chancellor responded by exiling the entire parliament. He also changed the system by creating a new group that conformed to his wishes. When this new parliament responded in the same way as the first one, he abolished them as well. The people, who had wanted more checks on the king, suddenly found that those needed checks were disappearing. The political situation was going backward.

The financial crisis that led to revolution began during the American Revolution. France spent over a billion livres (French livres had the value of one pound of silver), about the state's entire income for a year. The livre (French for "pound") was the currency of the Kingdom of France from 781 to 1794.[340] Almost all the money was obtained by loans. In an attempt to cover the debt, a package of tax reforms was put in place. These taxes were the most sweeping reforms in the French crown's history. The changes included a land tax to be paid by everyone, including the previously exempt nobles.

Many were against paying new taxes, many had reasons to dislike the government, and many genuinely believed no further tax should be imposed without the king first consulting the nation and the people. But the king and his government began forcing laws by using the practice of *lit de justice*' (the method of the Parlement of Paris, under the presidency of the king, for passing royal edicts.) The king said, essentially, "It's legal because I wish it."[341]

The financial crises reached its peak in 1788 when the government couldn't bring in the required tax revenues. This shortage was caused by bad weather that devastated the harvest. The French treasury was bankrupt, and no one was willing to accept more loans or changes. The bottom line is that financial troubles created citizens who, awakened by the Enlightenment, demanded more say in government. They refused to help solve the economic problem until they had more of a say. No one realized how far this demand would go.

The storming of the Bastille in July of 1789 is widely regarded as the most iconic event of the Revolution. Many Parisians saw Louis's actions as an insult to

---

[340.] "French Livre," *Wikipedia*, https://en.wikipedia.org/wiki/French_livre.
[341.] Doyle, *The Oxford History of the French Revolution* (2002), 80.

the people and began an open rebellion. They were afraid that arriving soldiers, mostly foreign mercenaries, had been summoned to shut down the people and their assembly. Riots, chaos, and widespread looting started all over Paris. The French Guard soon supported the mobs.[342]

On July 14, the mob focused on the large weapons and ammunition stockpile inside the Bastille fortress. After several hours of fighting, the Bastille fell. Governor Marquis Bernard-René de Launay was killed and decapitated. The governor's head was placed on a pole and displayed. The Bastille served as a symbol of everything hated under the regime of the king and his nobles. The mob accused the mayor, Jacques de Flesselles, of betrayal and butchered him as well.[343]

The king, alarmed by the violence, used the Marquis de Lafayette to take up command of the National Guard in Paris.[344] But authority rapidly deteriorated with random acts of violence and theft breaking out across the country. Many members of the nobility, fearing for their safety, fled the country.

By late July, the revolutionary beliefs spread throughout France. In rural areas, many citizens began to form militias and arm themselves against a foreign invasion. Wild rumors and paranoia caused widespread unrest and civil disturbances that contributed to the collapse of law and order.[345] The French Revolution had started.[346]

On August 4, 1789, the Constituent Assembly abolished the entire feudal system. It abolished both the Second Estate and the taxes gathered by the First Estate. Tithes were one-tenth of the annual earnings taken as a tax for the support of the church. Thus, the peasants got their property free and also no longer paid the tithe to the church.

On August 26, 1789, the assembly published a charter of human liberties called the Declaration of the Rights of Man and the Citizen. This declaration stated the principles that inspired the revolution. The basic principle of this declaration was "men are born free and equal in rights." It served as the preamble to the French Constitution.[347]

---

[342] Schama (2004), 331.

[343] Schama (2004), 344.

[344] Schama (2004), 357.

[345] Hibbert, 93.

[346] Anirudh, "10 Major Events of the French Revolution and Their Dates," Learnodo Newtonic, December 5, 2018, https://learnodo-newtonic.com/french-revolution-events-dates

[347] "Declaration of the Rights of Man and of the Citizen," *Encyclopaedia Britannica*, https://www.britannica.com/topic/Declaration-of-the-Rights-of-Man-and-of-the-Citizen.

The long-awaited constitution was put into law on September 30, 1791. France was, at that point, a constitutional monarchy. The National Assembly was dissolved. It was replaced by a new government body, the Legislative Assembly. King Louis XVI became now a figurehead, forced to swear an oath to the constitution.

Bad harvests in France had resulted in a dramatic increase in the price of flour, which in turn raised the price of bread. Bread was the staple food of most French people. Many people in Paris were hungry. After getting unsatisfactory responses from city officials, on October 5, 1789, a large crowd of protesters, mostly women, assembled at the markets. The women marched to the king's Palace of Versailles. They were convinced that the royal family was oblivious to their problems.

The women stormed the palace and demanded the king to live as the people lived. Louis XVI ultimately conceded and agreed to go to Paris. The royal family was placed under the "protection" of the National Guard, thus legitimizing the National Assembly.

King Louis XVI became afraid of the direction the revolution was heading, and he feared for the safety of his family. Unable to deal with his circumstances, he decided to leave France and seek refuge in Austria. He hoped he could be reinstated on the throne eventually.

On the night of June 20, 1791, the royal family fled France dressed as servants. However, the king was recognized, arrested along with his family, and returned to Paris. He was then suspended by the assembly and put under guard. The king's trying to flee had a significant influence on the public. They turned even more against the royalty. The king was considered a traitor who was willing to go into exile and try to get another government's assistance to return to power.

In 1792, France was attacked by the Germans. Because he'd attempted to flee the country secretly, the people viewed the king as a traitor. On August 10, 1792, twenty thousand Parisians laid siege on the official home of King Louis XVI. The king and queen were placed under arrest. On September 21, 1792, France was declared a republic and no longer a monarchy. The king, Louis XVI, was charged with treason and found guilty on January 15, 1793. On January 21, he was paraded through the streets of Paris to the guillotine and lost his head. The queen, Marie Antoinette, was found guilty of numerous crimes on October 16 and guillotined that same day.

Before the execution of Louis XVI, the legislative assembly had disbanded and was replaced by a new political body named the National Convention. In March of 1793, the Committee of Public Safety was created. Its role was to protect the newly established republic. It consisted of twelve members, the most influential of which Maximilien Robespierre. This committee became the de facto executive government in France from September 5, 1793 to July 28, 1794.

In an attempt to eliminate the enemies of the Revolution, an estimated 500,000 people were arrested. During this "Reign of Terror," 17,000 people were officially executed, and 25,000 more died in executions without having a trial.

By mid-1794, Robespierre and the National Assembly had become a target of the people. Robespierre was arrested and executed on July 28, 1794, bringing an end to the Reign of Terror. After the death of Robespierre, the National Convention chartered a new constitution on August 22, 1795.

The new constitution created the Directory, and the executive power of the government was given to the five members of the Directory, each with a five-year term limit. The Directory, however, became involved in corruption and financial problems. A coup d'état, on November 9, 1799. was led by Napoleon Bonaparte. This coup is regarded by many as the end of the French Revolution.

Revolutionary France was now dangerous in the eyes of the other European monarchies. They viewed it with both fear and anger. This fear led to the French Revolutionary Wars, a series of military conflicts lasting from 1792 until 1802. These wars caused the French to battle against Great Britain and Austria. The wars began when France declared war on Prussia and Austria in the spring of 1792.

Initially, France suffered some losses, but under the leadership of Napoleon Bonaparte, France was able to defeat a large number of territories by 1802, including the Louisiana Territory in North America. Success in the French Revolutionary Wars allowed the spread of revolutionary principles over much of Europe.

Dominique Louis (Armand) Greadjean Filbert dit Develle, having been born before the revolution, experienced many of its causes and effects. It may be that his name was changed from Filbert to Develle because of the Reign of Terror. Being considered noble was a potential threat, and Filbert was probably a noble name.

Dominique Louis married Louise Clemence Savigny; the date of their marriage is not known. However, since their son Louis Dominique was born in 1799, the wedding had to be before 1798. Louise Clemence was born in 1775 in Paris and was the daughter of Duplex Savigny (mother not known). Louise died on September 30, 1835, in New Orleans. Dominique passed away on November 11, 1836, in New Orleans, just a year after his wife, at the age of sixty-seven.

The Jung Family

Elizabeth Ambrozine Jung

Elizabeth Ambrozine Jung (1866–1943) was the mother of Jeanne Louise Rose Develle. She was born in New Orleans on July 26, 1866, as the eldest daughter of Louis Aguste Jung (1845–1918) and Marie Azelie le Dusso d' Hebecourt (1846–1936). For her family story, we will trace the Jung family ancestry as far as we can go and then the d'Hebecourt ancestry.

We have understood already that Elizabeth Ambrozine married Ernest Jules Develle on June 3, 1893. They had six children together, all of which are documented above in the section on Jeanne Rose Develle. Elizabeth's father, Louis Aguste, was born in Martinique in 1845. He came to the United States and New Orleans sometimes around 1848, because one of his sisters, Marie Jung De Mirabeau, was born in Martinique in 1847, and his next sister, Rose Louise Euphrasie Jung De Mirabeau, was born in New Orleans in 1849. Elizabeth Ambrozine was born in New Orleans in 1866 when her father was twenty-one years old.

She grew up at a house on 354 Hospital Street, which is in the sixth ward running parallel to Barrack Street south of Broad Street and North of Claiborne Avenue. She was fourteen years old in 1880. She married Ernest Develle on June 3, 1893, thirteen years later, when she was twenty-seven years old. Elizabeth Ambrozine died on May 28, 1943, in New Orleans at the home of her only daughter, Jeanne, at 1516 Gentilly Boulevard. She was seventy-six years old when she passed.

Louis Aguste Jung

Louis Aguste Jung was born in January of 1845 in Plateau Jung, Saint Pierre, Martinique. He was the son of Joseph Auguste Alexander Jung de Mirabeau (1817–1897). His mother was Elizabeth Ambrosine Selles (1821–1865). Elizabeth was the daughter of Peter Louis Selles and Mary Ann Arillette Lallemand.

Saint-Pierre is a town and commune of France's Caribbean overseas department of Martinique, founded in 1635 by Pierre Belain d'Esnambuc. Saint-Pierre was destroyed in 1902 by the volcanic eruption of Mount Pelée. It was the most important city of Martinique, both culturally and economically. It was known as "the Paris of the Caribbean." While Fort-de-France was the official administrative capital, Saint-Pierre was the cultural capital of the country. After the disaster, Fort-de-France grew in economic importance.

The Jung plantation in Martinique grew coffee. Coffee plantations were numerous in Martinique, with some 18 million coffee trees planted.[348] Until the earthquake of November 7, 1727, the island produced, by itself, more coffee than was consumed by all of France. Substantial agricultural development did not occur on the island until the French colonized it in 1635. After the French settled on the island, sugarcane became a widely harvested resource that made Martinique one of France's prime overseas territories. The island was even more lucrative to France after the introduction of Coffea (coffee) in 1723, and the productivity of the isle became important to other foreign powers.

The Dutch tried to take the island in 1674 but did not succeed. The British attacked it twice unsuccessfully, in 1693 and 1759. The British did finally conquer the island in 1762 but returned it to the French after the Treaty of Paris of 1763. [349] Slaves from Africa provided most agricultural labor on the island. Many slave uprisings took place during the early nineteenth century. These ultimately led to the abolition of slavery in 1848. Workers from India and China were used after that to keep labor costs down.[350]

Louis Aguste moved from Martinique to New Orleans sometime between 1848 and 1850, probably because of financial reasons and also because of slave revolts. It's a good thing he did, because Mount Pelée (the name is French for "bald mountain" or "peeled mountain") erupted in 1902.[351] The eruption destroyed the town of Saint-Pierre and killed 28,000 people in the space of a few minutes. It was

---

[348.] "The History of Coffee," National Coffee Association, retrieved June 9, 2019.

[349.] "Martinique," *Encyclopædia Britannica*, retrieved October 17, 2019.

[350.] "Martinique," *Encyclopædia Britannica*, retrieved October 17, 2009.

[351.] Alwyn Scarth, *La Catastrophe: Mount Pelee, the Worst Volcanic Eruption of the Twentieth Century* (Oxford: Oxford University Press, 2002), 2.

the worst volcanic disaster of the twentieth century.[352] The primary eruption, on May 8, 1902, left only two survivors in the direct path of the blast's flow.

It was sweltering and humid in New Orleans most of the year. To help keep the people cool and comfortable, architects designed houses that had very high ceilings so that the heat would rise and long windows that opened top and bottom to allow for the thermal circulation of the air. This design made the houses very hard to heat for the small number of months when the weather outside was cold. To heat the house, each room was designed with a tiny fireplace. Count Rumford developed a fireplace to keep as much heat as possible in the room. The back of the fireplace was only about one-third of the width of the opening in the front, and the two sides were angled toward the front opening at an angle of about 135 degrees. The small firebox efficiently burned coal while it reflected as much heat as possible out into the room.

Most fireplaces in nineteenth century New Orleans were built for coal, not wood. Once upon a time, coal vendors drove their carts down the streets, calling out to hawk their products. Following the Civil War, the expansion of the coal trade accelerated. Louis A. Jung made his fortune in coal. He organized Jung and Sons Coal Co. In 1878, he shipped three million tons of coal from mines in Maryland and West Virginia.

Railroads opened up massive coal reserves west of the Mississippi River. Coal mines in Missouri and Illinois existed at this time but were limited to the steamboat trade down the Mississippi River. Jung and Sons got into the business of shipping this abundance of coal down the river by steamboat to Louisiana. The company was very lucrative and profitable. Coal had indeed become a national endeavor in the United States.

Louis A. Jung began as a clerk in a wholesale flour store. He worked with Cambon and Avec for twelve years. In 1888, at the age of thirty-six, he went into the coal business for himself. In 1895, he took his sons into the business, and it became a corporation named Jung and Sons.

At the time of the founding of Texas Oil Company (Texaco), oil was used

---

[352]Pierson Wright, USGS Circular 1073 (1992), 39; Tilling, *Volcanoes* (USGS, 1985), 16–17; "USGS document of the 1902 eruption of Mount Pelee," USGS, archived from the original on September 4, 2013; retrieved March 29, 2017; R. J. Blong, *Volcanic Hazards: A Sourcebook on the Effects of Eruptions* (Orlando, FL: Academic Press, 1984); Angelo Heilprin, *Mont Pelee and the Tragedy of Martinique*, (Philadelphia: J. B. Lippincott Company, 1903), retrieved 2009-08-15.

primarily for lighting and as fuel for factories and locomotives. Texaco met this need with its first consumer product, Familylite Illuminating Oil. The product was introduced in 1907. After 1910, however, the advent of the automobile industry revolutionized the oil industry. Louis A. Jung got into business with Texaco. I'm not sure if he sold his company to Texaco or merged with it. Because Louis had a family history of managing a business in Martinique, he became a high-ranking manager, vice president, in Texaco. He became a rich man because of this merger. He purchased a beautiful mansion at 2623 Esplanade Avenue and raised his family there.

Louis Aguste married Marie Azelie le Dusso d'Hebecourt in New Orleans in 1865. Marie Azelie was the daughter of François Napoleon Bonaparte le Dossu d'Hebecourt (1801–1868) and Marie Mercelite "Caroline" Boucher (1811-1891). More about the d'Hebecourt ancestral history will be presented later in this chapter, beginning in the section on Francois Napoleon Bonapart le Dossu d'Hebecourt.

The Children of Louis Auguste Jung

Louis Auguste and Marie Azelie had the following seven children:

- Elizabeth Ambrozine Jung was born July 26, 1866, in New Orleans, and died in 1943. Read more about her in the beginning of this section on the Jung Family.
- Francois Louis Jung was born on May 24, 1868, and died on January 6, 1869, at the age of six months.
- Charles Joseph d'Hebecourt Jung (Joseph Charles) was born on October 8, 1869, in New Orleans. He married Marie Louise Rita Buisson (1870–?) on August 3, 1893, in New Orleans. They had the following children together;
    - o Inez Marie Jung was born on September 14, 1894, in New Orleans. She married Maurice Joseph Rivet. She died on September 18, 1954, in New Orleans.
    - o Mildred Jung was born on February 18, 1903, in New Orleans.
    - o Odette Jung was born on May 26, 1904, in New Orleans.
    - o Joseph Charles Jung Jr was born in 1908.
    - o Solange Jung was born in 1909 in New Orleans.

- Theodore Auguste Jung Sr. was born on December 10, 1870, in New Orleans and died there on March 20, 1940. He married Eva Marie Seghers, who was born about 1877 in New Orleans. They had two children together:
  - o Dr. Theodore Auguste Jung Jr. was born June 25, 1896, in New Orleans. He married Louise Marie Colomb in November 1921. He died on October 6, 1964, in New Orleans.
  - o Althea Marie Jung was born November 18, 1898, in New Orleans. She married Frederick Robert Duplantier (1888–1962) in October of 1932 in New Orleans. She died on June 13, 1990.
- James Albert Jung was born August 29, 1875, and died on September 27, 1883, in New Orleans. He was eight years old when he died. It was this child after which the couple's grandson, Albert Develle, was named.
- Henry Louis Jung was born about 1877 in New Orleans. He married Mary Jane Holton Davis (1877–1947) on December 3, 1901, in New Orleans. They had the following children together: Margaret Azelie Jung, born October 26, 1902, in New Orleans, died in 1983; and Louis Emmanuel Jung, born January 30, 1904, in New Orleans, died in 1962. Henry died on September 19, 1909, in New Orleans at the age of thirty-two.
- Rita Louise Jung (1882–1959) born in May of 1882 in New Orleans. She married Samuel Barton Stewart on June 5, 1902, in New Orleans. They had two children together: Dorothy L. Stewart (1903–1989) born July 13, 1903, in New Orleans, and died there on February 9, 1989; and Samuel B. Stewart Jr., born in 1910.

This one picture below taken on the fiftieth wedding anniversary of Louis Aguste Jung and his wife, Marie Azelie le Dusso d'Hebecourt Jung, shows the confluence of three families, the histories of which will continue to be discussed in the remainder of this chapter: the Develle family (already discussed), the Jung family, and the d'Hebecourt family. Let's continue with the Jung family.

Top row from left – Albert Louis Develle, Louise Marie Coulomb Jung, Dr. Theodore Jung, Althea Jung, Louis Develle, Ernest Jules Develle, Ambrosine Jung, Joseph Charles D'hebecourt Jung , Marie Louise Rita Buisson (Jung), Maurice Rivet, Inez Jung Rivet. Second row from left – Azelie Jung, Rita Stewart Jung, Sam Stewart, Dorothy L Stewart, Samuel B Stewart Jr., Marie Azelie d'Hebecourt Jung, Louis A. Jung, Solange Jung, Marie Vorrice Jung (wife of deceased Henry Jung), Theodore Auguste Jung , Eva Marie Seghers Jung, Robert Develle, Bottom row from left – Roger Develle, Jeanne Louise Develle, Joseph Charles Jung Jr., Odette Jung, Louis Jung (son of Henry), Mildred Jung.

Picture taken at the 50th Wedding Anniversary of Louis A. Jung and Marie Azelie d'Hebecourt

Figure 18 – The Jung Family

Louis Aguste Jung died on July 26, 1918, in New Orleans, not quite three years after the picture was taken. His obituary read as follows:

On Friday, July 26, 1918, at 8:45 PM age 73 years six months, Louis Aguste Jung, beloved husband of Marie Azelie Le Dorso (de Hebecourt) a native of Martinique and a resident of the city for 70 years, the relatives, friends, and acquaintances of the family, those of his sons J.C. & T.A. and the late H.L. Jung and of his sons-in-law E. Develle and S.B. Stewart are respectfully invited to attend the funeral which will take place Saturday, July 27 at 4 PM from the residence of the deceased at 2623 Esplanade Ave. near Broad. Internment at St. Louis Cemetery #3 on Esplanade.[353]

Marie Azelie le Dusso d'Hebecourt Jung died on February 11, 1936, in New Orleans and is buried in St. Louis Cemetery #3 on Esplanade.

Joseph Auguste Alexander Jung de Mirabeau

Joseph Auguste Alexander Jung de Mirabeau was born on December 3, 1816, in Saint-Pierre, Martinique. He was the son of Nicolas August Jung and Catherine

---

[353]"Obituary of Louis Aguste Jung," *Daily Picayune*, July 27, 1918, page 2, column 5.

Rose Billouin. He married Elizabeth Ambroisine de Salles in 1841 in Saint-Pierre, Martinique. Elizabeth was born in Saint Pierre, Martinique, in 1821.

The Children of Joseph Auguste Alexander Jung de Mirabeau

Elizabeth and Joseph Auguste had the following children together:

- Marie Jung De Mirabeau was born in 1847 in Martinique. A year after her birth, the family moved from Martinique to New Orleans because of the slave revolt of 1848.
- Rose Louise Euphrasie Jung de Mirabeau was born on January 3, 1849 in New Orleans. She died in 1891.
- Emilie Jung was born about 1851 in Louisiana.
- Frederita Augustine Laure Jung was born on May 19, 1853 in New Orleans.
- Emmanuel Jung was born about 1857 in New Orleans.
- Elisabeth Augusta Edmie Jung was born about 1859 in New Orleans.
- Ida Jung was born about 1860 in New Orleans.

Joseph Auguste Alexander Jung de Mirabeau died in New Orleans in 1897 at the age of eighty. His wife, Elizabeth Ambroisine de Salles Jung, passed away in New Orleans on May 16, 1865, at only forty-four years of age.

Nicolas Auguste Jung

Not much is known about the history of Nicolas Aguste Jung. It is not known if he was born in Martinique or Paris. Since his oldest son, Joseph Auguste Alexander Jung de Mirabeau, was born on December 3, 1816, in Saint Pierre, it would make sense that he would have been born in the late eighteenth century. The French had been in Martinique since 1635, and coffee was introduced to the fertile volcanic soil of the island in 1723. It makes sense that he was born on the island, as would have been his wife, listed as Catherine R. Billouin. But nothing is known about her family history either.

The d'Hebecourt Family

François Napoleon Bonapart le Dossu d'Hebecourt

François Napoleon Bonapart le Dossu d'Hebecourt is the great-grandfather of Elizabeth Ambrozine Jung and the great-grandfather of Jeanne Louise Rose Develle. He was born on September 30, 1801, in Gallipolis, Ohio. He was the son of Francois Anaclet Le Dossu d'Hebecourt (1768–1832) and Genevieve Magdaleine Felicite Maret (1776-1841), who was born in Brie, Ille-et-Vilaine, Bretagne, France. Genevieve was the daughter of Pedro Marrat and Marla Magdalena Farand.

Gallipolis, Ohio, was known as the French City. Europeans first settled Gallipolis in 1790. "The French 500" were French aristocrats, merchants, and artisans who were fleeing the violence and disruption of the French Revolution.[354],[355] The 500 were led by Count Jean-Joseph de Barth, an Alsatian member of the French National Assembly.[356]

Gallipolis was the second city founded in the Northwest Territory of the United States. Because of its beginning, it is known as the Old French City.[357] The Gallipolis Epileptic Hospital Stone Water Towers, built in 1892, is listed on the National Register of Historic Places. In the mid-eighteenth century, the American territories were controlled by the British on the eastern coast and the French from Louisiana to Canada following along the Mississippi Valley. The Spanish were in Florida. The European powers were competing for dominance in North America. All were trying to claim the most land possible. Due to Spain's minuscule settlement, the primary fight for dominance was between Great Britain and France.

There were no clear lines that separated New France from the British colonies, so constant arguments arose about who could claim that land. The Ohio

---

[354] William Mumford Gregory and William Backus Guitteau, *History and Geography of Ohio* (Ginn (1922), 23.

[355] "The French 500," Gallia County Genealogical Society.

[356] William Henry Smith, "The St. Clair Papers: The Life and Public Services of Arthur St. Clair, Soldier of the Revolutionary War; President of the Continental Congress; and Governor of the North-western Territory; with His Correspondence and Other Papers" (1882), 195, retrieved August 13, 2016.

[357] John Gladden, "Best Hometowns 2012: Gallipolis," *Ohio Magazine* (November 2012), accessed September 6, 2018.

Valley region involved the most significant controversy. France first discovered the Ohio territory and claimed control of it, not only because they had arrived first but because they had established centers of trading there to ensure a lasting dominance. In contrast, the British demanded ownership because of land grants issued by the monarchy. These grants allotted the colonies to the land from the east coast to the west coast.

Since there was no defined border, British colonists expanded their settlements into French territories because of overcrowding in the east. They took over already established French areas for their specific use. The French and many Native American nations became frustrated by these British imperialistic actions.

Things became hot when the French built a fort for trading. Fort Duquesne, as it was known, was near current-day Pittsburgh. The British felt that this was well within their colonial territory. They sent a representative, twenty-one-year-old George Washington, to demand that the French relinquish their fort. France refused to accommodate. This refusal provoked Washington and the small number of soldiers accompanying him to attack. The attack precipitated the French and Indian War in 1756.

The first fight occurred at Fort Duquesne, where the French were pitted against Washington and the newly arrived General Edward Braddock. The British outnumbered the French. However, the British fought in the typical European style of the open battlefield. In contrast, the French opted for a more guerilla warfare style of concealing themselves from the British while surprise attacking them. Many Native Americans who were angered by the expansion of British colonies into their lands aligned with the French during the war. The Iroquois sided with the British due to their frustration with France's settlers.

Most of the fighting occurred in the Lake George and Lake Champlain areas. Great Britain began the conflict with unsuccessful attempts to capture French forts. The advantage shifted to the British when their military seized Fort Carillon, later named Fort Ticonderoga. They went on to take Quebec.

With Canada taken by the British, India lost, and no success in Europe, France realized that victory was unattainable. In response, France organized a peace agreement with Great Britain. But the British demands were simply too great to accept. So King Charles III of Spain came to the aid of his cousin, King Louis XV of France. Spain would not get involved if the British agreed to the treaty's terms by May 1st, 1762. This deal was known as the Family Compact. The alliance provided an incentive for the British to end the war.

Overall, this was not strategically beneficial to the British. The Spanish Navy completely overpowered their navy, and any battle would involve the Caribbean Islands and the Philippines. With this loss of territory and the failed invasion of England, the French diplomats sought peace.

In 1763, Great Britain, France, Spain, and Portugal collectively signed the Treaty of Paris, thus ending seven years of war. Great Britain received the primary advantages from the agreement. France and Spain both gave up territories they held in North America. Great Britain, however, paid a high price to fight the costly multi-front war and had massive debts. To pay these debts, the British government began to issue higher taxes upon the citizens of their colonies and on the products they bought.

Also, to keep harmonious relations with American Indians in the region, the king proclaimed in 1763 a reduction in the westward expansion of British settlers. With higher living expenses and reduced capabilities to expand, English colonists became angry with the British government. That would eventually lead to the American Revolution.

By 1789, the French Revolution was well on its way. Many of the French nobles emigrated from France to the United States to avoid persecution. The French and Indian War had ended with the Treaty of Paris twenty-five years earlier. This postwar era was a time of great land speculation in the Northwest Territory, which was again opened following the Indian Wars. The French had worked with the Scioto Company, a purported land development company registered in Paris in 1789, paying its agents for land along the Ohio River. They sailed to the United States on several ships, most to Alexandria, Virginia, outside Washington, DC. From there, they traveled to Gallipolis.

These new arrivals were city people, and they were shocked by the undeveloped frontier they found.[358] The settlers found their deeds worthless when they arrived at Gallipolis. The land was not owned by the Scioto Company. They survived by building cabins in close proximity to each other in what is now the city park. A defensive fortification was constructed, of which François Napoleon's father was a significant part.

In 1795, President George Washington granted the settlers free land in Ohio. The colonists had to live on the property for five years and cultivate it to become owners. Those who chose to stay in Gallipolis had to pay again for their plots,

---

[358] "The French 500," Gallia Genealogy, retrieved April 8, 2018.

this time to the Ohio Company. Most either sold their land in the French Grant or arranged to have tenants farm it.

The name *Gallipolis* is a construct of the Greek or Latin prefix *Galli-* and the Greek suffix *-polis*; together, the name means "city of the French." A US post office called Gallipolis began operating there in 1794.[359] Life was hard for François Bonapart and his father, brother, and mother.

François Anaclet le Dossu d'Hebecourt

Captain Francois Anaclet le Dossu d'Hebecourt was born on July 28, 1768, in Epernal, France (Champagne province) to Joseph Nicolas le Dossue Seigneur d'Hebecourt and Marie Jeanne de la Court. The following is an extract taken from the archives of Epernay, a city in the province of Champagne, France. The archive reads as follows:

In the year of our Lord, 1768, on the 28th day of July, I the undersigned vicar of this parish have baptized a son born this day of legitimate marriage between Joseph Nicolas le Dossue, Seigneur d'Hebecourt, squire captain in the Queen's regiment of infantry, and Marie Boyer le al court, mother and said child residing in this parish.[360]

To this child have been given the names of Francois Anaclet. The godfather has been the high and powerful Lord, Jean Anaclet, Knight, Count of Bassompierre, Captain of Carabineers. The godmother, Dame Marie Francois de Silly, Countess of Coucy. Anuter, Vicar, Epemay province of Champagne.[361]

The Count of Bassompierre was of a powerful and wealthy family, renowned in the wars of France, and the Godmother, the Dame de Silly, was of one of the oldest and noblest houses of France, whose proud boast was "Neither Lord nor King am I, I am the sire of Coucy." The high rank of the infant's sponsors at the baptismal font spoke for the high esteem in which the Lord of Hebecourt was held. With such powerful friends, it would seem that the future of the boy was to be one of unmixed brilliancy and prosperity.

The name of Francois Anaclet d'Hebecourt holds an important place among

---

[359] "Post Offices," Jim Forte Postal History, archived from the original on October 13, 2015, retrieved June 11, 2016.

[360] "François Anaclet le Dossu D'Hébécourt Boyot," Geneanet. https://gw.geneanet. org/turandot1?lang=en&n=le+dossu+d+hebecourt+boyot+de+la+court&oc=0&p= francois+anaclet

[361] "François Anaclet le Dossu D'Hébécourt Boyot."

the early New Orleans colonists. His father, Joseph Nicolas leDossue, Seigneur d'Hebecourt, was at the time of Francois' birth, squire captain in the regiment infantry of Marie Antoinette. Joseph Nicolas was a Musketeer.

Nothing is said of the early life of d'Hebecourt, but when he was old enough, he was placed at military school at Brienne sur l'Aude to prepare him for a career in the Army. That was the only career, save that of the church, which was at that time deemed worthy that a member of the high nobility could pursue. While in the Ecole Militaire (French for "military school"), he formed the acquaintance of a remarkable man; this acquaintance quickly ripened into an intimate friendship. His friend was Napoleon Bonaparte, who was a fellow student. So close was this friendship that when both had graduated with honor and received their grades, Bonaparte as Sub-Lieutenant of Artillery and d'Hebecourt as Sub-Lieutenant of Infantry, they both resolved to go to America, and there in the depths of the forest, on the banks of Ohio, to lead a colony, of which they would be the chiefs. Steps were taken to this end. Lands were bought from Joel Barlow, an agent of the Scioto Co., in Paris, and the two young men were ready to go when the family of Bonaparte persuaded him to remain in Paris. By doing so, he changed the destinies of many in Europe.

The narrative of Anaclet d'Hebecourt states: "My grandfather never ceased to cherish the remembrance of his friendship with Bonaparte fondly, in their younger days, and before the war bulletins had declared to the world Napoleon a great genius, he, my grandfather, had given to one of his sons, (who was my father), the name of Bonaparte." D'Hebecourt, accompanied with many servants and fellow noblemen, landed at Gallipolis Oct. 21, 1790, and for several years after, his life was one of constant hardship, and often of great danger. He was appointed Captain on May 6, 1791, at the outbreak of Indian hostilities in that year.[362]

About a year before the French Revolution (1789), at a time when many men of noble background emigrated from France to the United States to avoid persecution. François Anaclet d'Hebecourt, then twenty-one years old and fresh out of military school, was granted a leave of two years from the French court guards to come to America. He hoped that during that lapse of time, the difficulties caused by the Revolution would be settled.

In 1790, d'Hebecourt, with many others, arrived at a small place on the Ohio River, which was after that known as Gallipolis, the French City. So depressed

---

[362.] "Life History of Francois Anaclet Ledusso d'Hebecourt," Gallia County Genealogical Society, http://galliagenealogy.org/French500/d'hebecourt.htm.

was the king of France, Louis XVI, about his nobles leaving that he is credited with having said to his barber while getting a shave and a haircut, "They are all going to Gallipolis, would that myself, I be going there with them."

The following year, d'Hebecourt was commissioned as captain of the second regiment of militia to the county of Washington by the honorable Winthrop Sargent. Sargent was appointed as the first secretary of the Northwest Territory. He took up his post in 1788. Sargent served as both a civil and a military leader. He was wounded twice at the Battle of the Wabash on November 4, 1791.[363] He also served in the French and Indian Wars of 1794–95 and became adjutant general.[364]

Sargent gave a passing mention of the early days of this remarkable man, d'Hebecourt: "As a boy, d'Hebecourt was sent to a military school at Brienne sur l'Aude to prepare him for a career in the Army. While at school, he met Napoleon Bonapart, and the two became fast friends. Bonapart was graduated at the same time d'Hebecourt entered the infantry as a sub-lieutenant."[365]

Another person whose close friendship was linked to that of Bonapart was Pierre Napoleon Morel. "Morel's father was at that time an intimate friend of the Bonapart. Bonapart held the Morels in high esteem, and it is said that he often took advice from Morel's father. As all three matured, they learned to love and respect one another. It was during those days of mutual comradeship, while Morel and Bonapart had been engaged in some real work, that Bonepart gave Morel a pair of tongs, which has been kept in the Morel family for four generations. It is now in possession of his great, great-grandson, Ernest L. Morel of 2714 Canal Street. It is interesting to note how the names of d'Hebecourt and Morel were associated with that of Bonepart's."

The names of d'Hebecourt and Morel were to be united in the future. Later, Christoval Morel, Pierre's son, married one of d'Hebecourt's daughters. Bonapart and d'Hebecourt were very ambitious and adventurous. They planned to leave France and come to America in a quest for adventure. But destiny said otherwise for Bonapart. His relatives convinced him to change his mind, and he stayed in France to fulfill his destiny, which cemented his name in French history.

---

[363] "Biography of Winthrop Sargent," Ohio History Central, retrieved February 24, 2009.

[364] J. G. Wilson and J. Fiske, eds., "Sargent, Paul Dudley," *Appletons' Cyclopædia of American Biography* (New York: D. Appleton, 1900).

[365] "François Anaclet Le Dossu D'Hébécourt Boyot," Geneanet, https://gw.geneanet. org/turandot1?lang=en&n=le+dossu+d+hebecourt+boyot+de+la+court&oc=0&p= francois+anaclet.

D'Hebecourt followed his original plan, however. He went to Gallipolis and found great hardship. He was unable to provide for the people who came with him. They soon left Ohio. D'Hebecourt experienced great difficulty and almost starved. He wrote to his family, asking them funds. During these hard times, he also wrote to a friend, Mr. Vaudun, in New Orleans. He wondered if it were possible for him to come to New Orleans to earn a living. To his request, Mr. Vaudun encouraged him, stating that he had just finished the home of a wealthy planter, the Marquis de Marigny, and he was sure du Marigny would be pleased to have him instruct his two sons, Bernard and Gustave, in fencing.

D'Hebecourt made up his mind to travel to New Orleans. He received financial help from his family and was appointed to the job of postmaster-general of Gallipolis. This job gave the income he needed. After struggling for a long time in Gallipolis, he finally left the place in 1790 for Marietta, Ohio. A short while after, he married a popular lady in that city. They bought a log house for the sum of three hundred dollars. He and his family lived on the first and second stories. They rented the third story.

Mr. and Mrs. d'Hebecourt had the rare privilege of entertaining the French refugee Louis Phillip, Duc d'Orleans, who had stopped in the community before going to New Orleans. Mr. d'Hebecourt, through a mere chance of luck, happened to pass by and recognize his friends while they were buying bread at a bakery. Having invited them to breakfast, Mr. d'Hebecourt hurried to tell his wife of their guests that morning. Mme d'Hebecourt was in the habit of preparing the meals herself, and she made no exception that day. The American ambassador, who was traveling with them, accompanied these noblemen.

As Mr. d'Hebecourt was not familiar with the English language, he requested Mr. Green to be at breakfast so that the latter would be the company for the ambassador. The breakfast consisted of eggs, sugared cakes, and coffee. The Duc d'Orleans, after having coffee, asked Mme d'Hebecourt for more, saying that he had never tasted better coffee, "even in Paris." The topic of the conversation fell on the different ways of making coffee, to which Mme d'Hebecourt explained that hers consisted of adding the entire egg along with the powered shell.

Thereupon, the Duc d'Charters remarked that he knew of a better way of making coffee. It was to drip it through a piece of flannel; the coffee made according to this process was called "Cafe a la Grecque," or Greek coffee. During the meal, Mme d'Hebecourt referred to a wound she noticed on the Duc d'Orleans forehead. Her allegation influenced him to relate his experience at the battle for Cherbourg and how he contracted the injury.

During the conversation, Ferdinand, the young child of Mme d'Hebecourt, came running in with a large book in which he looked at the pictures from time to time while playing with it on the floor. The Duc d'Orleans, noticing the book, saw that it was the *History of the Revolution of Portugal* and remarked to Mme d'Hebecourt, "Is it thus, Madame, that you treat the kings?"—never supposing that he one day would be in that category.

After having stayed a few years at Mariette, Mr. d'Hebecourt asked the permission of the Spanish governor of Louisiana, Don Juan Manual de Salcedo, to come to New Orleans. The consent having been granted, d'Hebecourt, with his wife and his two sons, Ferdinand and Francois Napoleon—the latter having been named after Bonaparte—moved to New Orleans. The trip was made aboard a barge, and they took three months to make the journey, landing at la Point Coupee from whence they came here.

Burthe's home stood on the corner of Bourbon and Esplanade. He met with crowning success, as many prominent families sent their boys to his school to be educated. So successful was his endeavor that he had to move into larger quarters. He, therefore, rented a spacious mansion on Burgundy St., between Orleans and St. Ann, where for seventeen years, he educated the elite of the city. Having reached the goal of his ambition as an instructor, he moved his school to Bayou St. John. For twenty-five years, he diligently imparted his knowledge to many distinguished Louisianians from all over the state. His home stood near the City Park Avenue, but it has long since been destroyed by fire.

After a few years spent on the Bayou St. John, Mr. d'Hebecourt bought that tract of land adjoining the old Magnolia Gardens (Lakeview) and left it in the name of his children.

The following account was printed in the *Times-Picayune* newspaper of July 27, 1927, about Francois Anaclet d'Hebecour and the First Fencing Club in New Orleans. The article is reprinted here with the permission of the *New Orleans Advocate*, which owns the copyright.

How New Orleans Got Its First Fencing Club Old Fencing Matches Recalled Between Bayou St. John and Orleans Fencing Clubs; The Story of the Morels and the D'Hebecourts, and Some Illustrious Fencing Masters

By Claire Agnes Carriere

There are so many illustrious names in Louisiana, many of which bear marks of recognition with France in those days of our most ruling passion that one oops baffled in the obliteration of some of them. Of those that have disappeared we know practically nothing save for some scattered instances and documentary pieces of evidence from which a writer has gathered fragments which will serve as a text for this narrative. True to tradition, Francois Anaclet d'Hebecour Seigneur d'Hebecourt being at the time of his birth squire captain in the regiment of infantry of Marie Antoinette. It was about a year before the French Revolution at which time most of the nobles emigrated from their country to the United States to avoid persecution that Francois Anaclet d'Hebecour, then twenty-two years old was granted a furlough of two years from the court to come to this country in hopes that during that lapse of time the hostilities caused by the revolution would be settled. In 1790, d'Hebecourt with many followers landed at a small place on the Ohio River, which was after that known as "Gallipolis," the French City. So depressed was the king of France, Louis Seize, about the departure of the nobles that he is credited as having said to his barber while lingering at the fancy bathe latter, "They are all going to Gallipolis, would that myself, I be going there with them." The following year, d'Hebecour was captain of the second regiment of militia to the county of Washington by the honorable Winthorp Sargent, who at the time was governor and commander and chief of the territory of Ohio. It is necessary to give a passing mention of the early days of this remarkable man at this juncture, and the following is an extract from the archives of Epernal, in the province of Champagne, France. "in the year of our Lord 1768, on the 28th day of July, I under the signed vicar of this parish have baptized a son born this day of legitimate marriage between Joseph Nicolas LeDossaue, Seigneur d'Hebecourt, a Captain in the Queen's order of infantry and Rennie de la Cour, father and mother of said child residing in Paris. To the child has been given the name of Francois Anaclet. The godfather has been Francois Ancelet, Knight, and Count of Bassompierre, Captain of Carabineer and the godmother, Dame Marie Francoise de Lilly, Countesse de Coucy. As a boy, d'Hebecourt was sent to military school at Brienne sur d'Aube (Brienne-le-Château), to prepare him for a career in the army; while at school he met Napoleon Bonaparte and the two became fast friends. Bonaparte was graduated at the same time as d'Hebecourt, and the two became fast friends. Bonaparte was graduated at the same time as d'Hebecourt entered the infantry as a sub-lieutenant. Brienne-le-Château Another figure whose close friendship with linked to that of Bonaparte was Pierre Napoleon Morel; the latter is a few years younger having been named for "le petit Caporal." Morel's father being at the time a close friend of the Bonaparte's. Bonaparte held the Morels in high esteem, for it is said he often took advice from Morel's father. As all three grew up into manhood, they learned to love and respect one another. It is interesting to note that the names of d'Hebecourt and Morel were associated with that of Bonaparte's. But the names of d'Hebecourt and Morel were destined to be united; for in after years, Cristoval Morel, Pierre's son, married one of the d'Hebecourt daughters. Bonaparte and d'Hebecourt were both full of ambition and adventure: and they planned to leave their country to come to the American quest of daring feats. But destiny had spread her wings under Bonaparte. At the last moment, his relatives persuaded him to change his mind, and he remained to fulfill the military career that has made his name great in the history of France. However, d'Hebecourt followed his original plan. His earliest days at Gallipolis were measured with hardship. He was unable to provide for the men who had come with him, and they being discouraged, disbanded, and left the place. D'Hebecourt, at the time, was almost reduced to starvation. He wrote to his family in France asking them for money. It was while he was so afflicted that he wrote to a friend, Mr. Vaudun, of this city (New Orleans), inquiring if it were possible for him to come here to earn a living. To this request, Mr. Verdun encouraged him, stating that he had just finished the home of a rich planter, the Marquis de Marigny. That the latter, he was sure would be pleased to have him as an instructor for his two sons, Bernard and Gustave. He had made up his mind to come to New Orleans, when he received some financial help from his family: and also at this special time appointed post general of Gallipolis. This promotion in business gave him an income of ten thousand a year. He then opened a small country store, but the community not being very large at the time, he lost most of his money. Having struggled long and hard at Gallipolis, he finally left the place in 1790 for Marietta, Ohio. He had too much spirit, however, to become a burden to his friends, and immediately determined to qualify for some office which would enable him to earn a livelihood and be independent. A short while after he married one of the most popular belles of the locality. Property in those days was not worth our present day's prices; the old document from which the life of this most interesting man was taken mentions a home which he bought for the mere sum of $300. The name of the home was "Log House," a three-story house. They occupied the first and second stories and rented the third story to a family named Green. It was during their stay at Log House that Mr. and Mrs. D'Hebecourt had the rare privilege of entertaining as their guests the French refugees, Louis Philip, Duc d'Orleans, afterwards king of France; the Duc de Chartes; Duc de Beaujolais and their lead Mr. de Montjole, who had stopped at Mariette before coming to New Orleans. Those noblemen had suffered much from hunger, and it was when they were buying bread at Therry bakery that Mr. d'Hebecourt, through a mere chance of luck, happened to pass by and recognize his friends. Having invited then at breakfast, Mr. d'Hebecourt hastened to notify his wife of the guests she was to receive that morning. Mme d'Hebecourt was in the habit of preparing the meals herself and made no exception that day. The American ambassador accompanied the nobleman "au duen … ; as Mr. d'Hebecourt was not familiar with the English language, he requested Mr. Green to be of the party so that the latter would be the company for the ambassador. The breakfast consisted of eggs, sugared pastrie3s, and coffee. The Duc d'Orleans, after having taken the cup of coffee, asked Mme d'Hebecourt for more saying that he had never tasted better coffee. "Even in Paris," he commented, "it cannot be excelled." The topic of the conversation fell on the different ways of making coffee: to which Mme d'Hebecourt explained that hers consisted of adding the yoke of an egg with the powdered shell. Thereupon the Duc de Charters remarked that he knew of a better way of making coffee. It was to drip it through a piece of flannel: the coffee made according to this process was called "Café a la Grecque" - Greek coffee. During the meal, Mme d'Hebecourt alleged to a wound on the Duc de Orleans forehead. Her allegation brought him to relate his experience at the battle of Cherbourg and how he contracted the wound.

While the conversation was being carried on, Ferdinand, the young child of Mme d'Hebecourt came running in with a large volume in which he looked at the pictures from time to time while playing with it on the floor. The Duc de Orleans noticing the book saw that it was the "History of the Revolution of Portugal," remarked to Mme d'Hebecourt. "Is it thus Madame that you treat the kings?" never supposing that he himself one day would be in that category. The noblemen after having enjoyed a good smoke inquired of Mr. d'Hebecourt if there were some places of interest they could see before returning to their boat: upon which Mr. d'Hebecourt suggested a visit to a hillock near his home. Back from the hillock they took leave of their host and hostess who had accompanied them to their boat. Leaving Mariette, they set sail for New Orleans. It was on this visit which he paid to the city in 1799, that Louis Philip, Duc de Orleand, and his followers were so courteously entertained by many of our most aristocratic families. After having stayed a few years at Mariette, Mr. d'Hebecourt asked the permission of the Spanish governor of Louisiana, Don Juan Manuel de Salcedo, to come to New Orleans. The permission having been granted. The permission having been granted, d'Hebecourt with his wife and his two sons, Ferdinand and Francois Napoleon, the latter having been named after Bonaparte moved to New Orleans. The trip was made upon a barge and they took three months to make the journey, landing a la Pointe Coupe from whence they came here. He opened his fencing school in the Burthe's home, which stood on the corner of Bourbon and Esplanade. He met with crowning success, many prominent families sending their boys to his school to be educated. So successful was this endeavor that he had to move into larger quarters and therefore rented a spacious mansion in Burgundy Street between Orleans and St. Ann. Where for seventeen years he educated the elite of the city. Having reached the goal of his ambition as an instructor, he moved his school onto Bayou St. John, and for twenty-one years he diligently imparted his knowledge to many distinguished Louisianans from all over the state. His home stood near the City Park Avenue but it has long since been destroyed by fire. After a few years spent on Bayou St. John, Mr. d'Hebecourt bought that tract of land adjoining the old Magnolia Gar … in Lakeview and left it in … for his children. He died on the 22nd of November, 1832. After his death, the sum of money was raised to erect a monument to his memory: but owing to the defalcation of one of those in charge of the fund, it was never erected. Thus ended the career of one who not only did honor to the name he bore but whose heart was as royal as his name. The document from which this was gathered was written by his son-in-law, Christoval Morel under the dictation of his widow between the early hours of three and five while Mme d'Hebecourt was dripping her morning coffee as was the custom in the Antibellem days: that the chatelaine of the home would drip the coffee for the whole household. It is written in long-hand and in French. It is in possession of Mrs. Stephen Escoffier, grand-daughter of Mr. d'Hebecourt, who, with Mrs. L Jung, are the only surviving relatives. Mr. d'Hebecourt's sons are deceased, and with their death, the name was extinguished."[366]

Francois Anaclet le Dossul d'Hebecourt died on November 22, 1832, in New Orleans, at the age of sixty-four. Genevieve Magdaleine Felicite Maret, died on February 9, 1841, in New Orleans at the age of sixty-four.

---

[366]How New Orleans Got Its First Fencing Club Old Fencing Matches Recalled Between Bayou St. John and Orleans Fencing Clubs; The Story of the Morels and the D'Hebecourts, and Some Illustrious Fencing Masters By Claire Agnes Carriere

CHAPTER 9

A SUMMARY OF THE PEOPLE AND
CULTURE OF NEW ORLEANS

A people without the knowledge of their past history,
origin and culture is like a tree without roots.
—Marcus Garvey

My father used to say that stories are part of the
most precious heritage of mankind.
—Tahir Shah in *Arabian Nights*

The Culture of New Orleans

What is it that defines a people or a community of people? It is their customs, the art they produce, and their institutions. The word we use to encompass these characteristics is *culture*. Our societies cannot exist without their customs. It is the social behaviors and norms found in human societies that unite us. It is cultures that both springs from and determines our beliefs, our attitudes, and our civic personalities.

In this chapter, we will discuss the national origins and the associated customs that came together to make an extended family. Culture is an overarching name that describes the way we live and how others understand us. If I were to summarize the heritage of my ancestors, I would use the countries from which they came. The history of those countries was infused into the culture of those people.

As a people, my ancestors are a mixture of different cultures (all described in the previous chapters). There can be multiple cultures within a country or city because of immigration. However, over time, one way to describe a culture is by the mores, traditions, and customs that dominate the lives of most of the people of a community.

I have attempted to describe the mores, traditions, and customs of my ancestral heritage in the previous chapters. I will use the nations from which these ancestors descended as a descriptor of their culture. These cultures are what they brought to New Orleans when they emigrated here. Based on this descriptive measure, my family is 37.5 percent of French European heritage (3.1 percent through a generation passing through the island of Martinique), 25 percent of German heritage, 25 percent of French Acadian heritage, and 12.5 percent of Scandinavian heritage.

My ancestors genuinely are multicultural—but our family, the Bourg family, is not unique in its multicultural heritage. Most of the families of New Orleans are of multicultural legacy, especially those who have lived in this city for over a hundred years. New Orleans is a melting pot. It is a neighborhood city.

In the 1980s, the New Orleans City Planning Commission divided the city into seventy-two distinct neighborhoods. Most of these assigned boundaries match traditional local designations. For the most part, these neighborhoods are not culturally pure. They survive their distinction mainly because of the social characteristics, or culture, of the neighborhood, the schools, the places of worship, and the social activities associated with the community.

Because of its cultural history, New Orleans is like few other cities. There are many things unique to it: the easygoing and carefree nature of the people, the music, the food, the tropical climate, and the patterns of speech used by its citizens. The families and the culture of their nationalities are part and parcel of the history of New Orleans. This book is a collection of stories of the history of the merging of many families, nationalities, and cultures. This last chapter is just a summary of these peoples, their nationalities, and the cultural uniqueness they bring to the Crescent City.[367]

Culturally, New Orleans is an eclectic hybrid of French, African American, Cajun, and Spanish influences. Both the French and the Spanish ruled the city before the United States bought it, along with the rest of Louisiana, for $15 million in the Louisiana Purchases of 1803. The forced settlement of slaves from Africa and the West Indies introduced those cultures to the Creole residents.

In the eighteenth century, Creoles were defined as French or Spanish descendants born in the colony of New Orleans. The Cajuns of South Louisiana were originally French colonists who, more than 350 years ago, settled in Acadia (Nova Scotia). The British exiled them, resulting in a wave of Cajuns moving into the swamps and bayous of Louisiana.

The names *Cajun* and *Creole* are sometimes interchanged or used in the same context. But they are not the same and should not be confused. Cajuns are descendants from French Acadia (today, Nova Scotia). Creoles (French: *Créoles de Louisiane*, Spanish: *Criollos de Louisiana*) are descended from the ancestors of New Orleans who were ruled by both the French and Spanish. Creoles share the cultural ties of the French and Louisiana Creole languages and the predominant practice of Catholicism. Creole and Cajun are two distinct ethnic groups with their unique histories, traditions, and cultures. We have seen this in the previous chapters.

Although very different in their backgrounds, Cajuns and Creoles both contributed much to the city of New Orleans. The people and their culture have made the Crescent City unique. New Orleans, because of its buildings and its food, has often been described as a Caribbean city. It is located in a bend of the Mississippi River that was initially occupied by Houmas, Choctaw, and other Native Americans.[368] The prominent cultural influences date to the French and Spanish colonial periods, which dominate the culture of the entire Caribbean. The Africans brought to the city as slaves also give it a Caribbean feel.

Today, English, with New Orleans variations, is the dominant language in the city. French was the prominent language used in the European colonization of the city because of the city's French colonial history. The French language is rarely used in the daily life of the city today; however, French was still in significant use

---

[367] "Culture of New Orleans," *Wikipedia*, https://en.wikipedia.org/wiki/Culture_of_New_Orleans.

[368] "Indian Women," French Creoles, retrieved May 30, 2006.

at the start of the twentieth century. French expressions and pronunciations have influenced the methods of communicating and the dialects of New Orleans today. There are still French immersion schools in the Greater New Orleans community. Schools following the French curriculum are Ecole Audubon Charter School, Ecole Bilingue de La Nouvelle-Orléans and Lycée Français de La Nouvelle-Orléans. Elite social groups in the city still use French.

The city also has a long tradition of Spanish-speaking immigrants dating back to the eighteenth century. Before becoming a US city, it was ruled by Spain from 1762–1803. The governing of Spain came through Cuban lords. These historical links to Latin America have created the influx of people and cultures over the period of four hundred years. The proof of the Hispanic influence is in the cultural aspects of the city, including its music and its architecture.[369]

French, Spanish, and Vietnamese languages are also heard in the city. Cajun French speakers from southwest Louisiana entered the city during the oil boom from 1950 through the turn of the century. A sizable Vietnamese community established itself in New Orleans in the last third of the twentieth century after the end of the Vietnam War.[370]

New Orleans English is American English that is native to New Orleans. New Orleanians speak several varieties of dialect, including the variety used by African Americans, by Cajun Americans, by the more affluent white residents of the Uptown and Garden District areas, by the white people in the South or Southern US English, and by the lower-middle and working-class white residents of Eastern New Orleans, particularly the Ninth Ward, known as Yat since at least the 1980s.[371],[372]

New Orleans natives speak in a dialect unique to New Orleans. The patterns of speech developed more than a hundred years ago are similar to those heard in New York, another port and melting-pot city. When a New Orleanian says, "Let

---

[369] "A Glance at New Orleans' Contemporary Hispanic and Latino Communities," American Association of Geographers, news.aag.org/2017/10/a-glance-at-new-orleans-contemporary-hispanic-and-latino-communities/.

[370] Bernstein & 1997, 2014:220.

[371] Bernstein & 1997, 2014:219.

[372] *Yeah You Rite!* documentary short, dir. Louis Alvarez (USA: Center for New American Media, 1985).

the dog out," the word dog sounds like *dawg*. The term *Yat* refers mainly to the New Orleans accents that sound like the working-class New York City accent.[373] [374]

Yat is only one of many accents of New Orleans. The word comes from the everyday use of the local greeting, "Where y'at?" These words are a way of asking, "How are you?" New Orleans has a distinctive accent. It is a Creole/Cajun accent and not the stereotypical Southern accent so often incorrectly portrayed by film and television actors.

Contributions of the French Culture to New Orleans

Founded in 1718, New Orleans was named for the French Duke of Orleans. New Orleans always saw itself as a city different from, and even better than, other settlements in North America. It was always proud of its French heritage. Even after France sold Louisiana to America, New Orleans kept many French-influenced cultural and culinary traditions.

The French were Catholic, not Protestant, unlike most other settlements in North America. There were many differences in the city from its puritanical neighbors. The Protestant view of life was more sober compared to the French Catholics. Although the French Catholics were traditionally religious in their practices, they certainly enjoyed rich food and other sensual pleasures.

Mardi Gras is the most famous of all New Orleans festivals. Although the people overeat and drink to excess, it is a Catholic holiday. In French, Mardi Gras translates to "Fat Tuesday." It is a time of grand celebration that precedes to the church-imposed abstinence of Lent. The tension between the religious and worldliness, the festival, and the mournfulness has long shaped the Crescent City's character. This tension is seen in the contrast of a jazz funeral, where jazz music is played after and during the burying of famous jazz musicians.[375]

An order of Ursuline nuns came to give the city spiritual support, guidance, and training. The nuns converted people of all races, enslaved and free, into Catholicism. Their presence cemented the already Catholic character of New Orleans. The order started Ursuline Academy, a Catholic girl's school, in 1727.

---

[373] Katie Carmichael and Kara Becker, "That Hoboken near the Gulf of Mexico" (2014).

[374] "What (r) Can Tell Us about English in New York City and New Orleans," paper to be presented at New Ways of Analyzing Variation (NWAV) 43, Chicago, IL.

[375] "French. Culture in New Orleans," NewOrleans.com, https://www.neworleans.com/things-to-do/multicultural/cultures/french/.

It is the oldest such school in the United States and is still operating today. This Catholic nature of New Orleans helped to attract others of the same faith. Other Catholic immigrants came, from the Sicilians to the Irish, from the Haitians who also introduced Voodoo to the Vietnamese who came after the Vietnam War.

New Orleans has always been essentially French. During the forty years of Spanish rule (1763 to 1801), it remained a French city in all of its characteristics except its architecture. From lessons in schools to newspaper articles and even the clothes worn in the city, the culture was influenced by the French. After the Louisiana Purchase of 1803, many Americans entered the city because of business and commerce, and the French character of the town began to change. New Orleans was becoming an American city, but its heart will always keep a French beat.

French words such as *lagniappe* (meaning something extra, a bonus) and expressions such as *laissez les bon temps rouler* (let the good times roll) are entrenched in New Orleans speech. Many street names are French—Bienville and Iberville streets, of course, and also Bourbon—and the people live on French bread po'boys. Restaurants such as Galatoire's and Antoine's still thrive with traditional French menus, and the French influence on the city's cuisine is vast. New Orleans people celebrate Mardi Gras like the French, but New Orleans has made it the city's own.

The French Acadian Contribution to New Orleans (The Cajuns)

Cajuns never wanted to live in the city. Their people always were better suited to a much more rural way of life. Even though they did not live in the city very long, their influence is felt throughout Louisiana and even in New Orleans itself. Acadian culture is felt throughout New Orleans; through their customs, their food, and their music.[376]

The word *Cajun* comes from the conversion of the word *Acadian* by French immigrants in early colonial times. The French Acadians were forced to leave their home by the British. Thousands of Acadians ended up in French-speaking New Orleans a few decades later. Preferring rural life, they settled elsewhere in southwest Louisiana, subsisting off the land as fishermen and hunters in the

---

[376.] "Cajun Influence in New Orleans," NewOrleans.com, https://www.neworleans.com/things-to-do/multicultural/cultures/cajuns/.

bayou country and farming when the landscape allowed. Their old traditions and language were transformed by Louisiana, resulting in a new Cajun culture.

While traditional Creole–French cuisine looks to Europe for inspiration, Cajun cuisine is firmly rooted in South Louisiana and made famous by the many Cajun chefs like Emeril Lagasse and the late Chef Paul Prudhomme of K-Paul's. They brought to the rest of the country their highly seasoned meat and seafood— dishes such as jambalaya, gumbo, and étouffée are Cajun dishes. They are often served in restaurants and are regularly found on home dinner tables everywhere in New Orleans. New Orleanians love to have crawfish boils with friends and extended family in the spring, when crawfish are plentiful in the bayous and flooded rice fields around the city.

Cajun music is played everywhere in New Orleans and throughout southern Louisiana. This music uses a unique combination of instruments: a fiddle, a guitar, and an accordion. The music is almost always in waltz time or a two-step. The lyrics are sung in a distinctly Cajun-French dialect. Zydeco is a very close relation to Cajun music. It descended from the blues dance music of Louisiana Creoles, the French-speaking blacks of the countryside of south Louisiana.

Cajun and Zydeco music are frequently played in clubs and festivals of New Orleans. This playing includes the *fais do-do* stage at the New Orleans Jazz Fest. Visitors to Thursday night at Rock 'N' Bowl in the Carrolton area of the city can listen to Zydeco music and learn a Zydeco two-step. One can hear Zydeco almost anywhere coming from clubs and shops, particularly in the French Quarter and the Marigny neighborhood.[377]

Contribution of the German Culture in New Orleans

When Germans came to the city, like my Young and Rappold ancestors, they quickly developed societies of benevolence to provide aid to other German immigrants in New Orleans. These were similar to, but not as well-known as, the "social aid and pleasure clubs" established by African American communities before the turn of the century. In New Orleans, these organizations helped members find employment, paid for their funerals, and supplied funds to the families of their dead and dying members. These associations also served as social clubs. By the turn of the century, there were over twenty such societies.

The Germans also formed many benevolent trade associations. These were

---

[377] "Cajun Influence in New Orleans."

specifically for the trades and some professional groups. These associations also provided financial assistance for members who became sick or had accidents. They provided financial aid to widows and children.[378]

The Deutsches Haus was founded in November of 1928. It became a meeting location for many German organizations. Today it serves as a social club where people can speak German and maintain ties to their culture. Many of the Germans' first cultural endeavors continue today in many forms.

The Germans started the beer-making industry in Louisiana. At the peak of German brewing, the Jax Brewery used a high percentage of German workers in its operation. The brewery was started in 1890 by Joseph and Lawrence Fabacher. Larry Fabacher is quoted as saying, "It was a relatively unusual place to work. It was written into the union contracts that a worker would get 'X' number of beers per shift. Each department had its keg and its kitchen." The building is no longer used for beer-making. The structure that dominated the French Quarter with its smells is used today as a shopping mall.

The Crescent City Home Brewers Association, a sort of club for home brewers, has a large number of Germans in its membership. German immigrant Wolfram Koehler is the owner, founder, and brewmaster of the Crescent City Brewhouse, a microbrewery and restaurant in the French Quarter. He says with pride that they strictly maintain the 1516 German Purity Law known as *Reinheitsgebot*. This law states that only water, barley, yeast, and hops can be used in brewing.

People often ask when they visit a place, "Where can you find good bread?" New Orleans is a city that has always been noted for its bread. New Orleans French bread is widely known as great bread, and it is the cornerstone of the city's po'boy sandwich. However, French bread is misleading, because most of the "French bread" bakers in the city are German. Kleindienst, Leidenheimer, Reising, Binder, and Haydel continue to dominate New Orleans baking. Lifetime baker Alfons Kleindienst, who came from Hamburg, explains it this way "In Germany, when a young man goes to a bakery, he becomes an apprentice, and he works at this place for three years. He learns the whole bakery from the bottom up." This quote shows why German bakers are so successful. This type of apprenticeship required

---

[378.] Laura Westbrook, "Getting to Gemütlichkeit: German History and Culture in Southeast Louisiana, Folklife in Louisiana, http://www.louisianafolklife.org/LT/Articles_Essays/ German.html.

them to learn in a tedious way, but when they've absorbed it, they know how to bake almost anything.[379]

Many Germans ran small corner grocery stores and markets. Some grew into super groceries, such as Schweggmann's supermarkets. The German baking culture is made clear by the display on the side of Leidenheimer's bakery trucks, which talk about the bread and the culture of New Orleans. The sign states in the words of two caricature New Orleanians, Vic and Nat'ly, "Sink ya teeth into a piece a New Orleans cultcha, a Leidenheimer po-boy!"

In his book, *The Joy of Y'at Catholicism*,[380] Earl Higgins describes the city's food culture in this way: After Sunday mass, an elderly lady was buying French bread loaves. She found one from Falkenstein's, a German bakery, and said, "This is the authentic French bread … Mr. Falkenstein brought the recipe with him from Germany." Falkenstein's bread is long gone, but New Orleanians' view of "authenticity" remains the same.[381] The irony is that Germans made the French bread that is New Orleans, not those with French ancestors.

Elmer and Hubig are German names familiar from New Orleans baked goods. Elmer's bakery in the Bywater neighborhood of the city is still going strong despite Hurricane Katrina. Elmer's also makes candies, and their CheeWees are a prominent chip-type snack in the city. Hubig's fried pies are also very popular in New Orleans. Although the Faubourg Marigny bakery survived Katrina, a fire destroyed it in 2012. The Hubig family is committed to rebuilding, and a new bakery making the pies is due to open in 2020.[382]

Some German foods endure in Louisiana with very different names. That happened in the Louisiana sausage business as well. In France, a sausage stuffed with chitterlings is called *andouille*. It is often diplomatically referred to as "an acquired taste." But upriver from New Orleans in the River Parishes, Louisiana's version of andouille is chunky, peppery, intensely smoky, and has become the baseline flavor for many gumbo and jambalaya recipes. Although the German family makes it, the Schnexnayders, it is still called by its French name. German

[379] Westbrook.
[380] Higgins, Earl. *The Joy of Y'at Catholicism* (Gretna, Louisiana: Pelican Press, 2007).
[381] Westbrook.
[382] Simon Hubig's website, http://www.hubigs.com/portal.aspx?tabid=11.

influences are still influential in New Orleans and are an essential contributor to the culture of the city.[383]

The African American Cultural Contribution to New Orleans

The base of New Orleans life, from its jazz music to its great food, is a product of the African American influence on the city. Unfortunately, that heritage is tragic but also very proud. New Orleans would not be the city it is today or have the culture it has without the role of the African American community. Slavery was very harsh for blacks in America, and its application should never be dismissed or forgiven. But slavery was handled differently in Louisiana and New Orleans than it was in the rest of the country.

Under the French, the Code Noir or Black Code restricted the rights of the slaves. But the descendants of enslaved Africans somehow managed to preserve their heritage and culture. Instead of their culture being eradicated or homogenized, many aspects of African culture persisted in New Orleans, influencing everything from religion and music to what New Orleanians eat for dinner.

Congo Square, located in historic Treme, was an essential place for this cultural preservation and development. In Spanish-controlled New Orleans, slaves were afforded the right to time off from work on Sundays. This time off resulted in African slaves and black laborers meeting to play music, dance, and socialize. This connected community of blacks asserted its heritage to make new traditions during the Mardi Gras celebration in the city.

The number of African Americans grew in the city, including black Creoles, who descended from the children of Africans with the French and Spanish. The African Creoles often were labeled as *gens de couleur libres* ("free people of color") who lived in the Treme neighborhood just outside the French Quarter. This neighborhood is the oldest free black neighborhood in the country. Under the French and Spanish Black Code, some slaves could earn their way to freedom.

---

[383] Ian McNulty, "Beyond Bratwurst. Uncovering Some Enduring Links to German Heritage in Louisiana Food," Nola.com, https://www.nola.com/entertainment_life/article_663ce10b-a44b-58e0-b692-ac57a2736929.html.

Voodoo was introduced to the city by blacks from Haiti, who were fleeing a slave revolt in Haiti. They brought along their traditions when they came.[384]

Music is probably the greatest contribution African Americans brought to New Orleans culture. The Crescent City is considered the point of origin for jazz music. Jazz had its roots in the twentieth century. Those roots can be traced back to Congo Square when black people congregated. Black musicians, however, have been at the forefront of all types of New Orleans music, from hip-hop to funk. They have invented music styles from gospel to bounce and rhythm and blues, which was the catalyst for rock 'n' roll. New Orleans' musical legacy is African American at its core.

Many of the beloved New Orleans Mardi Gras traditions are African American as well, most prominently the Mardi Gras Indians and the Zulu parade that rolls behind Rex on Mardi Gras Day. The Krewe of Zulu grew out of social aid and pleasure clubs. Its traditions ridicule the white Mardi Gras krewes' self-importance as well as white stereotypes of African Americans, with the riders dressed in blackface and grass skirts while handing out spears and coconuts and celebrating life in New Orleans.[385]

The Irish Cultural Contribution to New Orleans

New Orleans has a strong Irish influence on its culture. The Irish have called New Orleans home for a long time. Initially, they were drawn by the city's strong Catholic traditions. They could also align with the historically strong anti-British sentiments of the French, the Spanish, and the Cajuns alike. The first waves of Irish immigrants came to the city at the end of the 1700s. They were fleeing British persecution, and they were easily integrated into the economy and social life of the city.

In 1809, New Orleans celebrated its first St. Patrick's Day celebration. Through most of the nineteenth century, Irish social and benevolent groups formed. There was a robust Irish theater in the city. Irish parishioners wanted to attend Catholic services in English, so they built several churches. St. Patrick's Church, which is still in existence, was built in 1833. St. Alphonsus Church was completed in 1857 in the Irish Channel of the city. It was decommissioned as

---

[384] "The History of African American Culture in New Orleans," NewOrleans.com, https://www.neworleans.com/things-to-do/multicultural/cultures/african-american/.

[385] "The History of African American Culture in New Orleans."

a Catholic church in 1996 and declared a National Historic Landmark because of its architectural significance. Today, it is home to the St. Alphonsus Art and Cultural Center.

More Irish immigrants started to arrive between the 1820s and 1840s. They were fleeing the great potato famine. These Irish immigrants often found cheap passage on cotton ships that unloaded in Liverpool. The holds were filled with human ballast for the return trip. Conditions were very uncomfortable.

Living conditions once these Irish immigrants arrived in New Orleans by the thousands were also very dismal. They were poor and lived in slumlike conditions. They were very susceptible, because of where they lived and worked, to the epidemics that infected the city. Many Irish worked on the New Basin Canal. This project was dangerous. It involved digging through mosquito-infested marshland that claimed many Irish lives. They worked for one dollar per day, and they had the benefit of being buried in the spoil from the digging if they died of yellow fever. However, many more Irish immigrants came to seek opportunities in New Orleans.

Irish immigrants also influenced the city's local accent. The city dialect is not a Southern drawl but more like a Brooklyn accent, from another place where many Irish settled. In New Orleans, a crawfish boil is a "crawfish berl."

The Hibernia Bank was a large bank in the city. Hibernia is another term for Ireland. The bank prospered and grew because of its Irish clientele.[386]

The Irish Channel neighborhood along the river is not an Irish neighborhood anymore. However, it retains its original name, architecture, and neighborhood personality, and it is even today the center of St. Patrick's Day celebrations. There is a Magazine Street parade with riders throwing cabbages, carrots, and potatoes (in addition to green beads and Moon Pies) to the crowds.

Another Irish landmark is the statue of Margaret Haughery on the corner of Prytania and Camp Streets. Margaret Haughery was a poor Irish immigrant. She became a prominent businesswoman and philanthropist in the city. When she died in 1882, she was widely mourned. In commemoration of her good works, this statue of her comforting an orphan was erected. The statue is said to be the first American statue honoring a woman.[387]

---

[386] "Irish Culture in New Orleans," NewOrleans.com, https://www.neworleans.com/things-to-do/multicultural/cultures/irish/.
[387] "Irish Culture in New Orleans."

The Italian Cultural Contribution to New Orleans

Italian immigrants have a rich history in the city and have contributed much to the culture of New Orleans. Most of the Italian immigrants in New Orleans were from Sicily. They started to arrive in large numbers in the 1880s. They came to escape a country with corrupt, dangerous, and unlawful practices. They went to a city where Italian immigrants had already established a community.

Italian-born Henri de Tonti was part of a French expedition that explored Louisiana before New Orleans even existed. Later, he became a leader in the new colony. A city street named after Tonti is still here.[388]

Italian social clubs and benevolent groups started as the Italian population grew in the city. Most were formed along with the influx of Sicilian immigrants in the 1890s. These organizations were formed to provide support for new arrivals. Many of them moved to the lower French Quarter. This neighborhood became known as Little Palermo.

These Sicilians, like other poor immigrants, were discriminated against by the locals. Tensions existed primarily between them and the Irish. The Irish had arrived years earlier, and they were more established and considered more mainstream by 1900. In 1890, New Orleanians accused Italian immigrants of the murder of the police chief, David Hennessey. More than a hundred men were arrested. Most were soon released, and others were acquitted. A mob stormed the jail and lynched eleven Italians. This lynching made news across the country, and pressure from Italy led the United States to pay reparations to the families of the murdered.

Over time, Sicilians integrated into New Orleans culture and society completely. They celebrate St. Joseph's Day on March 18 with parades and other festivities. The Sicilians would also build very elaborate St. Joseph's Day altars. These altars are now a New Orleans tradition at many Catholic churches, other public locations, and even private homes. They welcome the public during the holiday to partake of Italian cookies and cakes.

New Orleans has had two Italian American mayors, Robert Maestri and Victor Schiro. A prominent New Orleans Italian sandwich is the muffuletta. It is a round sandwich on Italian bread with salami, provolone cheese, and olive salad.

---

[388] "Italian Culture in New Orleans," https://www.neworleans.com/things-to-do/multicultural/cultures/italians/.

The muffuletta originated at Central Grocery, a store on Decatur Street in Little Palermo. This store and many sandwich shops continue to sell them today.

Nick LaRocca was a famous Italian American jazz musician at the birth of the genre. At the same time, New Orleans-born Louis Prima became a prominent singer and trumpeter during the swing era. A Sicilian shoemaker first established the elegant Hotel Monteleone. It is a landmark in the French Quarter today and is still run by the Monteleone family generations later.[389]

Final Summary

New Orleans and our family, the Bourg Family, share a multicultural heritage. This cultural heritage is not unique in the city of New Orleans, but it is somewhat unique in the world. Most of the families of New Orleans are of multicultural heritage, especially the families who have lived in this city for over a hundred years.

You may not be interested in all the family names, and cultural heritages talked about in this book. You may be interested in only one. That's okay. This book was written so that my descendants, my grandchildren's children, will understand the cultural heritage of their grandfathers and their great-grandfathers. Hopefully, this book will encourage them to realize the importance of understanding their culture. I close with the quote that was first given in the preface of this book by Paul Tsongas: "We are a continuum. Just as we reach back to our ancestors for our fundamental values, so we, as guardians of that legacy, must reach ahead to our children and their children. And we do so with a sense of sacredness in that reaching."[390]

---

[389] Italian Culture in New Orleans."
[390] "Paul Tsongas," BrainyQuote, https://www.brainyquote.com/quotes/paul_tsongas_372106.

CPSIA information can be obtained
at www.ICGtesting.com
Printed in the USA
BVHW071200200820
586901BV00002B/237

9 781728 344614